The Arkansas Gazette Obituaries Index 1819-1879

by
Stephen J. Chism

SOUTHERN HISTORICAL PRESS INC.

Please direct all correspondence and orders to:

www.southernhistoricalpress.com
or
SOUTHERN HISTORICAL PRESS, Inc.
PO BOX 1267
375 West Broad Street
Greenville, SC   29601
southernhistoricalpress@gmail.com

ISBN #0-89308-398-4

Printed in the United States of America

Introduction

The Arkansas Gazette Obituaries Index 1819–1879 is the result of a five-year project to index each unequivocal report of death in which the person(s) is named. The project was begun in 1984 and reflects the work of ten people.

The key to abbreviations provided follows the format used in the *New York Times Index*. However, some abbreviations appearing in the titles column were added, since the abbreviations used in the *New York Times Index* were not as exhaustive as we wished them to be. If a title abbreviation appears in the body of an obituary, we reproduce it as it is found in the newspaper, without reference to the title abbreviations appearing in the front of this book. Our list of abbreviations refers only to titles we have abbreviated.

The *Arkansas Gazette* is the oldest continuously-published newspaper west of the Mississippi. This index was created using the most complete collection of the paper, filmed by the Library of Congress Photoduplication Service. Microfilm of the paper can be requested through the Interlibrary Loan service of most public and academic libraries. Some issues of the paper have been lost: no issues between December 1861 and March 1862 are known to exist. Also, publication of the paper was interrupted between August 1863 and May 1865 during the Civil War.

This publication overlaps in scope with the *Arkansas Gazette Index*, created by Shannon J. Henderson, which indexes a broad range of subjects for the years 1819–1885, 1890, 1891, 1961–present. Researchers are directed to consult that publication under the heading "deaths" and under individuals' names for time periods not covered here. In this index, we have included 14,329 entries for the years 1819–1879, while the *Arkansas Gazette Index* for the same period lists 4,201 names under the heading "deaths." This can be attributed to our inclusive policy of listing every mention of death, whether it appears in an obituary column or in the text of an article on another subject. This policy required us to examine every page of every known issue of the paper for the sixty years covered. It has been an exhaustive effort, but one we believe we have spared any genealogist or historian from making again.

I would like to mention here a few editorial decisions I made in the collection of data. If a person identified in an obituary used an alias, the index bears an entry under both the alias and the name given at birth. If, as was often the case in those times, a child died before being given a name, the death is listed by the last name with "Infant" in place of a first name. A person's name may appear several times in this index. Also, it may be noted that variations exist in the spelling of a name that is listed several times. Both these instances are the result of our policy of listing the obituaries exactly as we find them. If the name appears spelled differently in two references to a death, we list them as we find them spelled. The appearance of a name several times simply reflects the fact that multiple references to the death appeared in the newspaper.

Since language has changed in the 170 years since the *Arkansas Gazette* began, I will include two definitions which may be useful to researchers. The term "instant" refers to the day of the current month. Therefore, if an obituary listing refers to a death on the 16th instant, you may refer to the date on the masthead of a newspaper and determine that death occurred on the 16th day of that month. The term "ultimate," or sometimes "ult," refers to the day of the previous month.

Finally, I feel compelled to warn the most thorough or desperate of researchers that in a massive undertaking of this kind, a few obituaries will have been missed. No matter how much care has been taken, the result will not be perfect.

Acknowledgements

I wish to thank Bruce Baker and Nan Lawler for many hours of technical assistance with the construction of this index. I also wish to express my thanks to Shirley Brendel for suggesting the idea for this index in 1984. In addition, I would like to recognize and thank the following people for their significant contributions to the project: Allen Rankin, Michael Freels, Teresa Hall, Pat Meinert, Kerry Ludwick, Sadie Adams, and Biccy Whitley.

Abbreviations

TITLES

Abp	Archbishop
Adm	Admiral
Aeg	Assistant Engineer
Ald	Alderman
Apc	Apothecary
Apm	Assistant Postmaster
Arm	Armorer
Art	Artist
Atgn	Attorney General
Att	Attorney
Aur	Author
Aut	Aunt
Bar	Baron
Bgn	Brigadier
Bkm	Brakeman
Blm	Boilermaker
Bp	Bishop
Bro	Brother
Bts	Boatswain
Cae	Cadet Engineer
Cag	Captain of Arter Guard
Car	Carpenter
Car	Cardinal
Cbc	Cabin Cook
Cbm	Chief Boatswain's Mate
Cbs	Cabin Steward
Cck	County Clerk
Cdr	Commodore
Cdt	Cadet
Ceg	Chief Engineer
Cgm	Chief Gunner's Mate
Cgn	Consul General
Cho	Conchologist
Chv	Coalheaver
Cj	Chief Justice
Clk	Clerk
Cmc	Commander's Cook
Cmr	City Marshall
Cnt	Count
Cod	Conductor
Coe	Coroner
Col	Colonel
Com	Commander
Con	Congressman
Cop	Chief of Police
Cor	Corporal
Cot	Constable
Cpc	Captain's Clerk
Cph	Captain of the Hold
Cpm	Captain's Mate
Cps	Coppersmith
Cpt	Captain
Css	Countess
Cxs	Coxswain
Dcm	Deputy Commissioner
Dcn	Deacon
Dml	Deputy Marshall
Dpi	Deputy Inspector
Dr	Doctor

Dra	Draughtshian
Dsh	Deputy Sheriff
Dua	Deputy U. S. Attorney
Ecn	Economist
Emp	Emperor
Eng	Engineer
Ens	Ensign
Erl	Earl
Esq	Esquire
Eye	Engineer's Yeoman
Fat	Father
Feg	First Engineer
Fgs	First Sergeant
Frm	Fireman
Gd	Grand Duchess
Gen	General
Gov	Governor
Hon	Honorable
Jot	Jack of the Dust
Jp	Justice of the Peace
Jr	Junior
Jrw	Junior Warden
Jud	Judge
Jus	Justice
Kng	King
Law	Lawyer
Lcj	Lord Chief Justice
Lcl	Lieutenant Colonel
Ld	Lord
Ldm	Landsman
Ldy	Lady
Lt	Lieutenant
Ltg	Lieutenant Governor
Mac	Machinist
Maj	Major
Mar	Marshall
Mas	Master
May	Mayor
Md	Medical Doctor
Mgn	Major General
Mgr	Monsignor
Min	Minister
Mme	Madame
Mon	Monsieur
Mot	Mother
Mrs	Mrs.
Msa	Master at Arms
Mss	Miss
Ofc	Officer
Pap	Past Assistant Paymaster
Pay	Paymaster's Yeoman
Pcl	Postal Clerk
Pit	Pilot
Pm	Postmaster
Poe	Pope
Pol	Policeman

Pri	Prince
Pro	Professor
Prs	President
Prw	President's Wife
Ptr	Painter
Pvd	Private Detective
Pvt	Private
Qug	Quartergunner
Qum	Quartermaster
Qun	Queen
Ram	Rear Admiral
Rep	Representative
Rev	Reverend
Sco	Ship's Corporal
Sea	Seaman
Sec	Secretary
Seg	Second Engineer
Sen	Senator
Ser	Señor
Sgt	Sergeant
Shr	Sheriff
Sir	Sir
Sis	Sister
Smm	Sailmaker's Mate
Smt	Second Mate
Snr	Senior
Son	Son
Spc	Ship's Cook
Sq	Squire
Ssd	Steerage Steward
Stc	Steerage Cook
Sug	Surgeon
Sup	Superintendent
Swt	Shipwaiter
Unc	Uncle
Upr	University President
Vis	Viscount
Vpr	Vice-President
Wdc	Wardroom Cook
Woc	Warrant Officer Cook
Yeo	Yeoman

MONTHS

Ja	January
Fe	February
Mr	March
Ap	April
My	May
Jn	June
Jl	July
Au	August
Se	September
Oc	October
No	November
De	December

Last	First	MI	Ttl	Yr	Mo	Day	Pg	Col	Last	First	MI	Ttl	Yr	Mo	Day	Pg	Col
Alcorn	Pickney	L		1866	Oc	09	03	02	Alvord			Esq	1874	Jl	28	02	03
Alden			Ram	1878	Ja	09	03	02	Alvord	Thomas			1874	Jl	24	01	05
Alden	Enoch		Mr	1833	Jl	10	03	03	Ambrone	P			1878	De	29	04	03
Alden	Enoch		Mrs	1833	Jl	10	03	03	Amcgruder	Charles	B		1874	Ap	08	01	03
Alders	Peter			1878	Jn	28	04	04	Amelia			Emp	1874	Ja	08	01	02
Aldrich			Mr	1866	Oc	23	02	07	Amelieknap	George		Mrs	1879	Jn	20	05	02
Aldrich	Cyrus		Col	1871	Oc	06	01	04	Ames			Mr	1875	Jl	10	01	03
Aleus	Lewis			1878	Au	22	01	04	Ames	J	W		1878	Ap	09	01	06
Alexandar	Boot			1877	De	16	01	07	Ames	John			1878	Ap	07	01	04
Alexander			Mr	1872	Au	13	01	04	Ames	Johnson			1878	Se	24	01	04
Alexander	A			1878	Au	25	01	04	Ames	Oakes			1873	My	10	01	02
Alexander	Alfred			1875	Mr	04	04	03	Ames	Oakes			1873	My	15	01	01
Alexander	Elizabeth		Mrs	1834	No	18	03	05	Ames	Oakes			1873	My	20	01	01
Alexander	Maga			1859	Oc	08	04	02	Ames	Oakes			1874	Ja	08	01	02
Alexander	Maggie		Mrs	1878	Au	30	01	04	Ames	Willie	T		1878	Se	04	01	03
Alexander	W	W	Cpt	1872	Fe	27	01	01	Ammen	Allie			1875	My	02	04	05
Alexander	William			1831	Se	14	03	04	Ammons	A			1876	Se	26	04	02
Alexander	William			1879	Jn	13	01	03	Ammons	Constance		Mrs	1879	Jl	26	01	01
Alexander	William		Cpt	1838	No	28	03	05	Amoneile	J	J		1878	Se	22	04	03
Allen			Cot	1878	Au	14	01	06	Amos	William	R		1877	De	02	04	06
Allen			Pvt	1876	Jl	09	01	05	Amouette	Katie			1878	Se	22	04	03
Allen	Albert		Sea	1877	No	25	01	04	Amrorer	Joseph			1879	My	29	08	03
Allen	C	A	Bro	1859	Ap	09	02	07	Andeerson	Robert		Gen	1871	No	03	02	02
Allen	Duane		Mr	1871	Fe	05	03	01	Anderson				1877	Oc	13	01	06
Allen	Frances	M	Mrs	1858	Oc	16	03	04	Anderson			Gen	1872	Fe	13	01	04
Allen	George	T		1847	My	08	03	04	Anderson			Mr	1872	My	11	01	03
Allen	George	T		1847	My	08	03	04	Anderson			Mrs	1873	Fe	18	04	02
Allen	J	D		1879	Se	28	01	01	Anderson	A	J		1871	Se	21	01	02
Allen	James			1877	Oc	18	03	01	Anderson	Andrew			1872	Au	20	01	06
Allen	James			1878	Se	24	01	04	Anderson	Butler	P		1878	Se	04	01	03
Allen	James		Mr	1842	Fe	02	02	06	Anderson	Carrie			1877	No	14	01	06
Allen	John			1870	Oc	12	03	01	Anderson	Frank			1879	Se	14	01	01
Allen	John	F		1876	Oc	28	01	03	Anderson	Henry			1877	De	16	01	08
Allen	John	R	Dr	1877	De	01	01	07	Anderson	Hugh	A	Col	1848	Jl	13	03	04
Allen	Joseph	R	Dr	1877	De	01	01	07	Anderson	J			1873	Ja	07	02	03
Allen	Joseph			1878	Ja	12	01	07	Anderson	J	A		1878	Se	22	04	03
Allen	Larkin			1872	Ap	26	01	01	Anderson	J	W	Shr	1878	Oc	13	01	03
Allen	Margaret		Mss	1822	Ap	16	03	01	Anderson	James	B	Mr	1834	Oc	21	03	03
Allen	Mary			1878	Se	04	01	03	Anderson	James	F		1859	Ja	08	03	02
Allen	Minnie		Mss	1878	Ja	17	04	05	Anderson	James	H	Mr	1870	Jn	05	01	03
Allen	Phineas			1873	Jl	06	01	03	Anderson	James	W	Shr	1878	Oc	09	01	03
Allen	Robert			1876	Jn	29	04	02	Anderson	John			1876	Oc	13	01	03
Allen	Rowland		Rev	1872	Se	14	01	03	Anderson	John			1878	My	29	04	07
Allen	Stephen			1878	Ap	18	01	06	Anderson	John			1878	Se	22	04	03
Allen	Thomas	H		1872	My	17	01	01	Anderson	Joseph			1876	Oc	13	01	03
Allen	W	D	Bro	1871	De	27	04	04	Anderson	L	B		1878	Se	22	04	03
Allen	William	H	Mr	1857	Mr	21	03	04	Anderson	Larz			1878	Fe	28	01	05
Allen	William	O	Gen	1820	Mr	25	03	01	Anderson	Lover			1879	Jn	10	01	03
Allerson	Moses		Mr	1879	Au	23	01	03	Anderson	Lucy			1879	Oc	05	01	01
Allerton			Col	1879	My	01	03	01	Anderson	Mamie			1878	Mr	24	04	05
Allies	Infant			1878	Se	22	04	03	Anderson	Mat			1879	De	27	08	02
Allis	Martha	L		1851	My	30	03	07	Anderson	Peter			1879	Jl	18	05	01
Allison	John	G	Gen	1874	Se	04	01	07	Anderson	Rachel			1878	Se	22	04	03
Allison	Russell		Mr	1875	De	05	01	06	Anderson	Reese		Frm	1873	Jn	28	01	02
Allpig			Mr	1872	Jn	25	01	02	Anderson	Robert		Mrs	1878	Ap	21	04	05
Alltson	Russell			1878	Fe	03	01	04	Anderson	Robert	B		1873	Jl	29	01	05
Almond	Susan		Mss	1871	My	10	04	04	Anderson	S	H		1878	Oc	09	01	03
Alnslee	Hugh			1878	Mr	15	01	06	Anderson	Samuel			1876	Jn	07	01	06
Alsod	Selt			1879	Mr	13	04	02	Anderson	Sarah	M		1878	Se	22	04	03
Alston	Robert			1879	Mr	13	04	02	Anderson	Sarah	P	Mss	1838	Mr	14	03	02
Alston	Robert	A		1879	Mr	12	04	06	Anderson	Scott			1875	Jn	29	04	03
Alsup	Margaret		Mrs	1855	Oc	26	03	05	Anderson	Van	A		1879	Oc	19	01	01
Altemus	Willie	E		1872	My	04	04	04	Anderson	William			1873	Au	12	01	03
Althrop	August			1878	Fe	22	04	04	Anderson	William			1874	My	20	05	02
Alting	John			1878	Oc	24	01	05	Anderson	Winston			1878	Mr	06	01	03
Alvis	J	W		1878	Se	11	01	06	Andrew	G	M		1873	No	09	03	01

Last	First	MI	Ttl	Yr	Mo	Day	Pg	Col	Last	First	MI	Ttl	Yr	Mo	Day	Pg	Col
Andrew	James	O	Bp	1871	Mr	11	01	03	Armstrong	John	M		1878	Mr	21	01	05
Andrews				1876	Oc	06	01	05	Armstrong	John	M		1878	Ap	11	01	07
Andrews			Mrs	1874	Mr	12	03	01	Armstrong	John	M		1878	Jl	10	01	06
Andrews			Pvt	1876	Jl	09	01	05	Armstrong	John	M		1879	Jl	04	01	01
Andrews	Augusta		Pcl	1878	Au	08	01	05	Armstrong	Josiah			1878	Se	07	01	05
Andrews	Eliza	A	Mrs	1842	Mr	30	03	02	Armstrong	Nancy		Mrs	1836	Oc	11	03	04
Andrews	George			1874	Ap	29	01	02	Armstrong	Samual			1878	Au	23	01	05
Andrews	John		Mrs	1874	Fe	25	03	01	Armstrong	Thomas			1868	Ja	28	03	05
Andrews	W	H	Cpt	1879	Mr	20	01	05	Armstrong	Thos		Sea	1877	No	25	01	04
Andrews	W	S	Dr	1871	Au	22	01	01	Armstrong	Thos		Sea	1877	No	29	04	03
Andrews	W	W		1875	Fe	17	01	02	Armstrong	William			1872	Au	06	04	05
Andrews	William	R	Cpt	1858	Au	07	03	03	Armstrong	William		Cpt	1847	Jn	24	03	03
Andrews	William	W		1875	Fe	14	01	02	Armstrong	William		Dr	1834	Au	26	03	05
Angelo	Joseph			1872	Ap	21	04	01	Arnand	Fredrick		Sen	1878	Jn	02	01	06
Angolm			Mrs	1871	Au	27	01	04	Arneli	James	M		1868	Mr	31	03	04
Anguste				1876	Fe	04	01	05	Arnett	William		Esq	1849	Fe	22	03	05
Anna	Santa		Gen	1876	Jl	07	01	01	Arnold				1878	Se	22	04	03
Annear	Cinder'?	D		1849	Au	09	03	04	Arnold	Bessie			1878	Se	22	04	03
Annear	William		Cpt	1856	Jl	12	03	07	Arnold	Ella			1879	Se	02	01	01
Anson	John		Sir	1873	Au	03	01	05	Arnold	Emma		Mrs	1879	Se	09	01	01
Anson	W			1878	Se	10	01	03	Arnold	Ezra		Mrs	1872	Mr	20	01	02
Anthony			Pro	1878	Ja	09	03	02	Arnold	Valentine			1870	Oc	12	01	02
Anthony	D	R	Col	1875	My	14	01	01	Arnold	Washy			1879	Se	24	01	02
Anthony	Harriet	A	Mrs	1840	Oc	21	03	06	Arnot	William			1873	My	25	04	03
Anthony	James	M		1878	Jl	09	01	06	Arnott	Kate			1878	Se	22	04	03
Antonacci	Frandson			1877	No	28	03	01	Arrata	John			1872	De	27	01	04
Antonelli				1876	No	08	01	01	Arrata	Louis			1872	De	27	01	04
Antonelli				1876	No	14	02	03	Arrington	Alfred	W	Jud	1870	Au	18	02	03
App	Kate			1878	Se	22	04	03	Artless	Frank			1872	Jl	14	01	05
Appelman	Hiran		Col	1873	Se	05	01	04	Arustren	John	A		1878	Se	22	04	03
Applegate	Charles	G		1858	Se	04	03	04	Ascher			Mr	1877	Ja	10	01	03
Applegate	Johnanna	A		1851	De	05	03	07	Ash	E			1878	Se	22	04	03
Applegate	Josiah			1861	Ap	13	03	02	Ashbrook	James		Mrs	1879	Jl	29	01	01
Appleton	Frank			1874	Fe	12	01	05	Ashbury	George		Lt	1871	Jl	18	01	05
Appleton	George	S		1878	Jl	09	01	06	Ashby	James			1869	Oc	08	02	03
Aquereum	Sebastian			1879	De	25	01	01	Asheley	Henry	C		1852	Jl	30	03	06
Arata	Angelo			1879	Au	09	01	01	Ashford	Ben			1878	Se	10	01	03
Arata	R		Mrs	1878	Oc	19	01	03	Ashley	Chester	G		1876	Oc	08	04	06
Arbuckle			Mr	1873	Fe	19	01	03	Ashley	Francis	F		1853	Se	30	03	07
Arbuckle	J	D		1872	De	14	02	03	Ashley	Henry	C	Cpt	1873	Ja	24	01	01
Arbuckle	John	D	Col	1872	De	17	02	04	Ashley	Mary	V		1834	Oc	07	03	03
Arbuckle	Thomas		Mr	1835	Jl	07	03	04	Ashley	Mary	W	Mrs	1865	Jn	03	03	02
Arbuckle	William		Mr	1836	Jl	19	03	05	Ashley	Saray		Mrs	1858	Se	11	03	04
Archer	Samuel	E	Col	1826	Ja	24	03	03	Ashley	Susan	G	Mrs	1852	Jn	04	03	07
Archibald			Mr	1871	Jl	13	01	05	Ashley	William	E		1868	Au	18	02	02
Archy	Harriet			1879	Se	28	01	01	Ashley	William	E		1868	Au	25	02	08
Aregno	Bernard			1872	Au	13	01	05	Ashluter	George			1878	Au	04	01	05
Arighi	John			1879	Se	18	01	01	Ashluter	John			1878	Au	04	01	05
Arlington	Harriet		Mrs	1867	My	14	03	04	Ashmore	John	D	Col	1871	De	07	01	04
Armitage			Bts	1874	Ap	01	03	04	Ashmore	Samuel		Mrs	1872	No	10	01	06
Armitage			Bts	1874	Ja	08	01	02	Ashmun	J		Mr	1828	Oc	07	02	05
Armont	Henry			1873	Oc	09	01	02	Ashton				1873	Se	28	01	05
Armstrong			Maj	1868	Mr	03	03	05	Ashton			Mr	1874	Oc	01	01	04
Armstrong			Mr	1878	Ja	15	01	04	Ashton	J	S		1873	Se	28	01	05
Armstrong			Mrs	1871	Se	27	01	03	Ashton	Maria		Mrs	1855	Mr	16	03	06
Armstrong			Pvt	1876	Jl	09	01	05	Ashworth	Eda	B		1874	Ja	28	04	04
Armstrong	A	A		1878	Se	12	01	06	Askew	John	M		1873	Se	27	01	02
Armstrong	Armstead		Mr	1836	Se	27	03	05	Assdenna			Pvt	1876	Jl	09	01	05
Armstrong	Davis			1879	De	13	05	01	Assington	Viscount			1874	Ja	08	01	02
Armstrong	Frank	W	Dr	1868	My	19	02	07	Aston	James			1873	No	18	05	03
Armstrong	Henry	A		1872	Oc	19	01	02	Astor	John	J		1875	No	30	03	01
Armstrong	J	A		1878	Se	22	04	03	Astor	William	B		1875	No	30	03	01
Armstrong	J	S		1878	Se	01	01	03	Astor	William	B	Mrs	1872	Fe	17	01	04
Armstrong	James			1877	Oc	13	03	02	Atchinson	Gus			1879	Au	17	01	01
Armstrong	John			1879	Jl	03	01	01	Atchinson	J	H		1878	Se	22	04	03
Armstrong	John		Mr	1842	Ja	19	03	03	Atchison	Ann	E		1832	Ja	04	03	05

Last	First	MI	Ttl	Yr	Mo	Day	Pg	Col
Athy	Eudora	J		1879	Au	03	01	01
Athy	Michael			1879	Au	01	01	01
Atkins	George	R	Dr	1873	Mr	25	01	03
Atkins	Harry			1878	Se	22	04	03
Atkins	Henry			1878	Jl	31	01	04
Atkins	John	C	Mr	1870	Oc	01	04	03
Atkinson				1877	De	19	01	06
Atkinson				1878	Ja	05	01	06
Atkinson				1878	Fe	03	01	07
Atkinson	Charles			1875	No	30	01	03
Atkinson	Elijah			1875	Ap	17	01	03
Atkinson	Henry			1872	Fe	06	01	03
Atkinson	M	J	Mss	1878	Oc	02	01	04
Atkinson	R			1874	Jl	19	01	05
Atkinson	Wash			1877	De	09	04	01
Atkinson	Wash			1877	De	16	02	03
Atlee	S	J	Dml	1873	Oc	15	01	02
Atsman	C	T		1878	Au	30	01	04
Attrick	William			1877	Se	16	01	04
Attwood	William			1879	Au	27	01	01
Atwell	Josie			1878	Mr	02	01	03
Atwood	Albert			1879	Se	20	01	01
Atwood	Cordelia			1879	Au	26	01	01
Atwood	John		Rev	1874	Ja	08	01	02
Atwood	Lulu			1879	Se	09	01	01
Audrain	Ann	M		1836	Se	06	03	05
Audrain	Francis		Esq	1837	De	12	03	03
Audubon	Lucy		Mrs	1874	Jn	24	03	01
Auerbach	Adolphus	K		1870	Oc	01	04	04
Auerback	A	K		1870	Se	20	04	02
Auerback	A	K		1870	Oc	28	04	03
Auffray	Francois		Mr	1874	Oc	20	01	06
Auffray	Francois		Mss	1874	Oc	20	01	06
Augusta	Caroline			1874	Ja	08	01	02
Auguste	Dowager	A	Qun	1877	De	13	04	05
Austin				1873	Au	13	01	03
Austin	Avery	D		1872	Mr	13	01	04
Austin	Benjamin			1820	Jl	08	03	04
Austin	Ellen			1877	Ja	06	01	03
Austin	Grace			1878	Se	22	04	03
Austin	J	E	Maj	1878	Au	22	01	04
Austin	James	E	Mr	1829	Se	30	03	01
Austin	John			1874	Se	03	04	05
Austin	Mary			1877	Ja	06	01	03
Austin	Moses		Mr	1821	Jl	14	03	01
Austin	Samuel	C		1876	Ap	12	04	06
Austin	William			1867	Se	03	03	03
Anthony	Phillip		Mrs	1836	Au	09	03	03
Avant	Benjamin			1879	Au	09	01	01
Avent	B	W	Dr	1878	Se	22	04	03
Avent	D	B	Dr	1878	Se	13	01	04
Avent	James	H	Mr	1875	Fe	20	04	02
Avery	Allen	G		1878	Se	22	04	03
Avery	Benjamin		Hon	1875	De	02	01	03
Avonmore	Viscount			1870	Oc	27	01	01
Aycklin	James	F		1875	Ap	14	01	03
Aycock	Hartly	L		1879	No	01	01	03
Aydelett	James	M		1862	Mr	15	02	06
Aylett	Patrick	H		1870	My	04	03	01
Ayres	Will			1878	Se	07	01	04

B

Last	First	MI	Ttl	Yr	Mo	Day	Pg	Col
Babcock			Pvt	1876	Jl	09	01	05
Babcock	O	S		1878	Se	10	01	03
Baccigalupe	Mary	A		1878	Se	26	01	04
Bache	H	W		1878	No	09	01	03
Bachman	William			1872	Au	03	01	05
Bacigalupo	Vincent		Mme	1878	Se	24	01	04
Bacigulupo	Vincent			1878	Se	18	01	07
Backus	Jay	S	Rev	1879	Jl	04	05	01
Bacon			Mr	1871	Au	29	01	03
Bacon	David			1879	Se	20	01	01
Bacon	F	W		1873	Jn	15	01	04
Bacon	Josiah			1879	Ap	18	01	01
Bacon	Mary			1879	Oc	01	01	01
Bader	Elmer			1878	De	28	01	02
Badgent	Thomas	N		1867	Jl	23	01	08
Badget	W	B		1871	Mr	17	04	05
Badgett	Cornelia		Mrs	1875	Ja	16	04	03
Badgett	Cornelia	T	Mrs	1875	Ja	15	04	07
Badgett	John	O		1834	Jl	29	03	03
Badgett	Noah	H		1879	Au	23	08	06
Badgett	Ophelia	A		1845	Fe	17	03	05
Badgett	Ruth	B		1873	Fe	07	04	05
Badgley	Anthony	S	Mr	1832	My	02	03	05
Baer	L			1873	No	18	04	03
Bagehot	Walter		Ecn	1878	Ja	09	03	02
Baggiano	Eugenia			1879	Au	31	01	01
Bagley	Asher		Mr	1841	Ja	20	03	02
Bagley	Joseph		Dr	1872	My	17	04	05
Bagley	Mary			1878	Au	30	01	04
Bagley	Peter			1879	Fe	12	01	02
Bagley	Robert			1878	Se	05	01	03
Bagley	Virginia	I		1874	Mr	04	04	05
Bahr				1873	No	18	04	03
Bahr	Louis		Mr	1875	My	23	04	04
Bailer	George			1878	No	13	01	05
Bailey				1878	Se	05	01	03
Bailey			Abp	1877	Oc	10	01	04
Bailey			Abp	1877	Oc	11	04	04
Bailey			Mr	1873	Mr	11	01	07
Bailey			Ram	1878	Ja	09	03	02
Bailey	C	R		1878	My	04	01	07
Bailey	Eunice		Mrs	1858	Oc	23	03	03
Bailey	G	A		1877	De	28	01	07
Bailey	John			1873	Au	16	01	02
Bailey	John		Mr	1830	Mr	16	03	05
Bailey	John	M		1872	De	04	02	04
Bailey	Kate		Mrs	1878	Oc	19	01	03
Bailey	Laura		Mss	1879	Oc	14	01	01
Bailey	Theodorus	Gen		1828	Oc	14	03	04
Bailey	William			1871	De	06	01	01
Bain	E	C	Mrs	1869	De	31	03	01
Bainbridge	Willsam		Com	1833	Au	21	03	03
Baine	Infant			1879	Ja	04	04	05
Baird	Mary			1878	Jl	23	04	03
Baity	John			1871	Oc	04	01	02
Bakel	Fat			1878	Au	31	01	04
Baker			Mr	1871	Au	12	04	03
Baker			Mr	1875	Jl	07	01	01
Baker	A	G		1871	My	24	01	01
Baker	Charles			1878	Fe	12	01	07
Baker	Charles			1878	Au	30	01	04

Last	First	MI	Ttl	Yr	Mo	Day	Pg	Col	Last	First	MI	Ttl	Yr	Mo	Day	Pg	Col
Baker	Daniel		Col	1836	De	13	03	06	Baracina	George	M		1871	Au	13	01	06
Baker	F			1873	No	18	05	03	Barber	J	B		1878	Se	01	01	03
Baker	Frank			1878	Se	25	01	06	Barber	John	B	Bro	1869	My	02	02	04
Baker	Irene		Mss	1873	My	10	02	03	Barber	Matilda			1878	Se	22	04	03
Baker	J	D		1871	Se	03	01	02	Barber	Mollie			1878	Au	30	01	04
Baker	John			1876	No	22	04	02	Barbour	Conway			1876	Jl	08	02	03
Baker	John			1879	Jl	31	05	02	Barbour	George	W		1858	No	06	03	02
Baker	John		Dr	1851	Jn	20	03	05	Barclay	John			1872	Oc	05	01	05
Baker	John	E		1874	Au	28	01	07	Barcroft	John		Mr	1826	Jl	18	03	02
Baker	Joseph			1872	Ap	07	01	04	Bardard	Louis			1871	Fe	23	01	01
Baker	L	L	Mrs	1878	Oc	10	01	03	Barden	Charlottee		Mrs	1851	Jl	25	03	06
Baker	Melinda		Mrs	1858	De	18	03	04	Barden	J	J	Mr	1874	Se	10	08	02
Baker	P	R	Dr	1873	My	18	01	02	Barderfell	William			1870	Oc	27	01	02
Baker	Rebecca			1878	Ap	14	04	06	Bardin	Gilbert		Mr	1838	Jn	27	03	05
Baker	Rebecca		Mrs	1878	Ap	14	04	02	Bardom	John	W		1852	No	05	03	03
Baker	Rebecca	E		1878	Ap	14	04	06	Baring	Thomas			1873	No	20	01	04
Baker	Thomas		Mr	1837	Jn	27	03	03	Barkeloo	Frances	A	Mrs	1837	Au	29	03	04
Baker	William		Hon	1872	My	25	01	03	Barkeloo	William		Mr	1837	Jn	13	03	04
Balack	Moses			1875	My	20	01	02	Barker	Caroline			1878	Se	28	01	05
Balch	Charles	L		1872	Au	21	01	04	Barker	Carrie			1871	My	16	04	03
Balch	R	M	Col	1872	Ap	13	01	01	Barker	James	G		1837	Jl	25	03	04
Balcom	Wesley			1871	Jl	28	01	04	Barker	K	C		1875	My	21	01	04
Baldell	Levi			1871	Oc	27	01	04	Barker	L		Mrs	1878	Se	22	04	03
Balduin	Alexander	G	Lt	1835	Au	11	03	06	Barkman	Betsy		Mrs	1821	Au	04	03	01
Baldwin	Blanton		Mr	1852	Oc	01	03	05	Barkman	Jacob		Hon	1852	Se	03	03	07
Baldwin	D	A		1877	De	05	01	05	Barkman	Rebecca		Mrs	1837	Ja	17	03	04
Baldwin	David	D	Mr	1850	No	22	03	06	Barlege	John			1877	Se	12	01	05
Baldwin	Oliver	P		1878	Jl	18	01	04	Barlo	William			1873	Au	10	01	02
Baldwin	William		Mrs	1878	Mr	30	03	01	Barlow	William			1873	Au	13	01	04
Bales			Sgt	1876	Jl	09	01	05	Barna	Fannie	L		1870	De	06	01	03
Baley	Arb			1877	Oc	04	01	03	Barnard			Mr	1871	Ap	26	01	02
Balford	James			1878	Se	22	04	03	Barnard	E	H		1878	Se	04	01	03
Ball			Mss	1878	Mr	16	01	06	Barnard	Frederick			1871	Au	20	01	06
Ball	John		Pvt	1873	Au	26	01	03	Barnard	H	B		1877	Ja	12	01	05
Ball	Louis	F		1872	Jn	14	01	05	Barnard	L	J		1877	Ja	03	01	04
Ball	M	F	Mrs	1878	Se	22	04	03	Barne	Silas			1878	Se	04	01	03
Ball	Polly		Mrs	1878	Se	22	04	03	Barnes				1877	De	02	01	07
Ball	Polly		Mrs	1831	Fe	16	03	05	Barnes	A			1878	Se	22	04	03
Ballaran			Mr	1873	Au	26	01	03	Barnes	Ann			1879	Au	26	01	01
Ballard	Bland			1879	Jl	30	01	03	Barnes	Bartholo			1871	De	31	01	02
Ballaway	William	M	Hon	1873	Mr	05	03	02	Barnes	E	W		1878	Se	01	01	04
Ballenger	C			1878	Se	22	04	03	Barnes	E	W		1878	Se	12	01	03
Ballentine	James			1877	De	19	01	05	Barnes	Frank			1877	Se	13	01	06
Ballew	Joseph		Bro	1870	Se	24	04	03	Barnes	Harritt		Mss	1878	Se	11	01	05
Ballyran	Gus			1873	Au	26	01	04	Barnes	Nancy	W	Mrs	1840	Se	30	03	03
Balomoney	M			1878	Se	22	04	03	Barnes	Rebecca		Mrs	1878	Se	05	01	03
Ban	John			1871	Ja	22	03	01	Barnes	Sarah			1878	Se	04	01	03
Bancroft	Cobourn			1872	Fe	20	01	04	Barnett	Azz			1879	Jl	17	08	03
Bandiham	Ellen			1876	Mr	02	04	03	Barnett	C	M		1878	Au	30	01	04
Baneroft	Lizzie			1876	Se	23	01	03	Barnett	Charles			1867	Ap	09	03	04
Banford	William	H	Mr	1835	Ap	28	03	06	Barnett	Hiram			1879	Jl	17	08	03
Bangs	George	S	Hon	1877	No	18	01	05	Barnett	R	G	Mr	1876	Fe	18	02	04
Bangs	S			1877	No	22	01	07	Barnett	Tim		Mr	1873	Au	02	04	02
Bangston			Mrs	1874	Ap	08	01	01	Barnett	William			1879	Jl	17	08	03
Bankhead	Thomas	M	Esq	1851	Au	08	03	07	Barnnett	N	H		1873	Mr	04	04	06
Bankman	Leanah		Mss	1831	Se	28	03	05	Barns	Chauncey			1871	Jn	24	01	02
Banks	David			1878	Au	30	01	04	Barns	Nathan		Esq	1841	My	26	03	02
Banks	Dinah			1871	Au	31	01	01	Barns	Sarah		Mrs	1858	My	29	03	04
Banks	Gardner		Col	1871	Jl	11	01	06	Barnstein	J			1874	Ap	07	01	05
Banks	Hannah			1876	Mr	02	04	03	Barnum	Richard			1874	De	30	01	03
Banks	Richard	T	Mr	1840	Se	16	03	04	Barnum	Richard		Mr	1874	De	30	01	03
Banks	Robert			1874	Au	16	01	07	Barnum	Richard		Mrs	1874	De	30	01	03
Banks	Sallie			1879	Jn	25	08	02	Barnum	Richard		Mrs	1874	De	30	01	03
Bankston			Dr	1878	Se	17	01	04	Barnwell	Charlotte	C	Mrs	1836	Oc	25	03	05
Bankston	J	S	Dr	1878	Se	19	01	04	Baroos	Robert		Mr	1824	No	09	03	01
Bankston	James		Rev	1831	Se	21	03	04	Barrague	Eugene	B		1867	No	05	07	02

Last	First	MI	Ttl	Yr	Mo	Day	Pg	Col	Last	First	MI	Ttl	Yr	Mo	Day	Pg	Col
Barraque	Antoine		Snr	1858	No	27	03	02	Bates	Edward	O		1872	De	28	01	04
Barret	Arthur	B		1875	Ap	25	01	03	Bates	Elizabeth	W		1834	Mr	11	03	05
Barret	Jim			1874	Ja	23	03	01	Bates	Elizabeth	W	Mrs	1848	Ap	20	03	03
Barrett	May			1875	Ap	29	03	02	Bates	Fleming			1831	Mr	02	03	05
Barrett	F	A		1878	Oc	03	01	03	Bates	Franklin		Col	1876	Ap	01	01	02
Barrett	John			1879	Jl	26	05	01	Bates	Frederic		Gov	1825	Au	30	03	01
Barrett	John	R		1874	Fe	08	04	05	Bates	Horatio			1844	Jl	31	03	04
Barrett	Levina	A	Mrs	1874	Ja	07	04	04	Bates	James	W	Jud	1847	Ja	23	03	04
Barrett	Levina	A	Mrs	1874	Ja	07	04	05	Bates	Maria			1848	Mr	30	03	02
Barrett	Starr			1820	Ap	29	04	02	Bates	Moses		Hon	1873	Jn	17	01	04
Barrett	Tamer			1870	Jl	06	04	02	Bates	William		Esq	1822	Se	17	03	02
Barrett	Thomas			1873	Fe	04	04	05	Batson	Felix	I	Hon	1871	Ap	02	03	01
Barrett	Thomas			1873	Fe	05	04	05	Battersby	John			1879	My	20	06	01
Barrett	Thomas	C		1873	Mr	23	04	08	Battle	H			1873	No	18	05	03
Barrett	W	L	Frm	1877	No	25	01	04	Batto	John	V		1878	Oc	31	01	04
Barrett	William			1873	Fe	05	01	07	Batton	James			1875	My	02	01	04
Barrett	William	M		1851	Oc	17	03	06	Batty	Arthur	C		1870	Jn	02	04	04
Barriere				1877	De	16	02	02	Baulch	Charles			1874	Ap	18	01	04
Barrington			Mar	1876	Jn	07	01	06	Baumer	Henry		Bro	1869	De	25	02	03
Barron	Ellen			1878	Se	04	01	03	Baxter			Mr	1821	Jl	07	03	03
Barron	J	W		1878	Fe	24	01	05	Baxter	E	C	Mrs	1879	Se	13	01	01
Barry			Mrs	1871	Jl	12	01	07	Baxter	J	H	Mr	1858	De	11	03	02
Barry	Delia		Mrs	1879	Jl	24	01	02	Baxter	J	W		1874	Ap	10	01	04
Barry	Edward			1877	Se	30	01	04	Baxter	James	F		1872	Fe	23	01	03
Barry	H	W	Gen	1875	Jn	08	01	03	Baxter	James	R	Esq	1850	No	01	03	07
Barry	Patrick			1871	No	19	01	04	Baxter	John	C		1874	Jl	02	01	04
Barry	Richard		Mrs	1878	No	09	01	03	Baxter	Stacey		Pro	1878	Au	16	04	05
Barston	Ella	E		1870	Oc	09	01	02	Bayard	Taylor			1879	Ja	29	01	04
Barten			Mr	1873	Oc	1	04	04	Bayley	Charles			1873	My	03	04	05
Barth	Jean	B	Dr	1877	De	05	01	07	Bayley	Thomas	J	Mr	1840	Ja	08	09	04
Barth	William			1871	No	05	01	04	Baylor	J	W	Dr	1835	Fe	17	05	05
Barthalow	T	J	Gen	1879	My	22	04	01	Baylor	R	E	Jud	1874	Ja	27	02	02
Barthe	Albert		Mrs	1878	Oc	23	01	03	Bayman	W	B	Smm	1877	No	25	01	04
Barthe	Albert		Rev	1878	Oc	23	01	03	Baynard	George			1872	No	08	02	05
Bartholomew	Martha	A		1873	Fe	26	04	04	Bayonna	Vincent		Mr	1871	My	14	01	08
Bartholomew	O	D	Dr	1878	Oc	09	01	03	Bays	Henry		Mr	1871	My	18	01	01
Bartinello	T		Mrs	1878	Se	22	04	03	Baysted	Issac			1878	Se	22	04	03
Bartlett	Daniel		Mr	1831	Fe	23	03	05	Beach	Chauncey			1876	De	12	01	01
Bartlett	Elijah			1828	Oc	21	03	02	Beach	M		Mss	1872	No	30	01	03
Bartlett	J	W		1871	De	27	01	03	Beach	M	M		1877	De	19	01	07
Barton	Isaac	W		1858	No	06	03	02	Beach	M	M		1877	De	27	01	06
Barton	J	W		1878	Se	18	01	07	Beach	Munson			1873	Jn	05	01	01
Barton	Matilda			1878	Se	22	04	03	Beach	Munson	H		1872	Ap	16	01	03
Barton	Wesley		Esq	1826	No	07	03	01	Beach	R		Mrs	1872	No	30	01	03
Baskil	William			1879	De	30	08	05	Beach	W	D		1878	Fe	05	04	03
Baskins	Elizabeth		Mss	1872	De	27	01	02	Beadles	Ed	P		1830	Mr	09	03	03
Basnam	William			1871	Jl	27	01	05	Beaely	Ephraim			1846	Ja	19	03	01
Bass	Fred			1874	Fe	25	01	06	Beagler	David	O	Mr	1839	Oc	09	03	05
Bass	Gilson	E		1874	Oc	27	04	08	Beakham	Henrietta	E	Mss	1866	No	13	03	03
Bass	Mary	A	Mrs	1875	Ap	25	04	05	Beale	R	R		1872	Jl	27	01	05
Bass	Peter	G		1878	Se	22	04	03	Bealey	Pelina	A	Mrs	1849	Fe	08	03	04
Bass	Sam			1878	Jl	23	04	05	Beall	Mary		Mss	1853	No	04	03	06
Bass	William	C		1838	Se	26	03	04	Beall	Milton			1858	Oc	30	03	02
Bassenel	George			1872	Ja	16	01	03	Beall	Sally		Mrs	1840	Jl	15	03	04
Bassett	Harry			1878	No	02	02	01	Beall	Samuel	T	Maj	1840	Au	19	03	05
Bassett	Isaac		Mrs	1833	Jn	12	03	02	Beall	Sarah	A		1852	Oc	08	03	06
Bassett	Temperanc		Mrs	1833	Jn	19	03	05	Beall	Ulysses			1879	Jn	26	08	02
Bassley	A	A	Maj	1878	Se	01	01	04	Bean	Abraham			1873	No	16	01	03
Bastard			Sgt	1876	Jl	09	01	05	Bean	Hetty		Mrs	1833	Jn	19	02	04
Bateman	Beniah		Cpt	1850	Jn	21	03	06	Bean	Mark			1873	Au	10	02	02
Bateman	Infant			1878	Se	07	01	04	Bean	Mark		Mrs	1833	My	15	03	04
Bateman	Infant			1878	Se	10	01	03	Bear	Yellow			1872	My	22	01	03
Bateman	Morgan	M	Cpt	1870	My	01	04	02	Beard	Charles		Cpt	1872	Ja	23	01	03
Batemas	Thos	S		1879	Au	14	01	01	Beard	George		Maj	1843	No	08	03	03
Bates			Mss	1872	No	22	01	03	Bearsley	Joseph			1877	Oc	12	04	05
Bates	Benjamin			1878	Ja	16	01	07	Beasler	Charles			1879	Se	09	01	01

Last	First	MI	Ttl	Yr	Mo	Day	Pg	Col	Last	First	MI	Ttl	Yr	Mo	Day	Pg	Col
Beasley	John	H	Mr	1851	Se	26	03	06	Bell	Edwin	H		1872	De	27	01	03
Beatty	Calvin			1878	Au	08	01	06	Bell	Gustave			1877	De	05	01	04
Beatty	Clarindo		Mrs	1870	Se	18	01	03	Bell	Hosea		Mr	1874	Ap	18	02	03
Beatty	Jim			1878	Jl	31	01	04	Bell	Irvine			1872	Jl	04	01	05
Beatty	Mary	L		1868	Ja	28	03	05	Bell	James	W		1875	Mr	02	04	02
Beaty	Mary	L		1868	Ja	21	03	04	Bell	Janet			1878	No	01	01	06
Beauchamp	John			1874	Au	04	04	04	Bell	John			1869	Se	12	02	02
Beaumont	W	H	Dr	1879	Oc	01	01	02	Bell	John			1877	No	13	04	05
Beaver				1873	De	07	01	01	Bell	John		Mr	1825	Au	15	03	02
Beaver	John		Mrs	1872	Ja	16	01	03	Bell	John		Mrs	1877	Oc	19	02	01
Beavers				1878	Fe	16	01	08	Bell	John	M	Col	1862	Oc	25	02	05
Beavers	Henry			1877	No	28	03	01	Bell	Joshua	F		1870	Au	24	02	03
Beavers	Willie			1874	Se	22	04	05	Bell	Juliet		Mrs	1877	No	22	04	01
Beazley	George	W	Jud	1872	Ja	31	01	02	Bell	M	L	Mrs	1877	No	24	04	04
Becher	Jacob			1878	Ja	25	04	04	Bell	M	M	Mrs	1878	Oc	10	01	03
Bechtel	George			1872	Ja	19	01	03	Bell	Mary	R		1866	No	06	03	01
Beck	Abraham		Esq	1821	Oc	20	03	01	Bell	Mattie	A	Mss	1874	Oc	04	04	07
Beck	Bill			1872	Ap	24	01	01	Bell	Sam	S	Col	1877	Se	26	04	03
Beck	Black	S		1872	Ap	24	01	01	Bell	W	L	Mr	1867	Au	27	03	02
Beck	Black	S		1872	Ap	26	01	02	Bell	William	R	Jud	1836	No	15	03	02
Beck	Chas	E		1878	No	15	01	05	Bell	William	W	Cpt	1863	Fe	07	02	02
Beck	Sam			1872	Ap	24	01	01	Beller	William		Esq	1850	Mr	08	03	06
Beck	Sam			1872	Ap	26	01	02	Bellew	Aaron			1872	Au	06	01	05
Beckley	John			1871	No	03	01	04	Bellew	James			1873	Mr	23	04	05
Beckner	Julia	B		1868	Mr	03	03	05	Bellows	Henry	A	Cj	1873	Mr	12	01	06
Beckwith	Quiros			1878	Fe	10	04	06	Belt	William			1871	Ap	21	03	01
Beckwiz	R	A		1870	My	04	03	01	Belte	Henry			1876	Oc	24	01	02
Beclgaupa	John			1878	Se	22	04	03	Benda	Martin			1871	Jn	01	01	03
Bedan	P		Rev	1859	Oc	29	03	02	Bender	Annie	E	Mrs	1868	My	19	02	07
Bedenger	Mildred	B	Mrs	1871	No	10	04	02	Bender	Charlott		Mrs	1857	De	19	03	02
Bedford			Mr	1871	Jl	22	01	04	Bender	J	W	Esq	1873	Ja	21	02	02
Bedford	C	R	Mr	1834	Au	19	03	03	Bender	Margaret		Mrs	1857	Oc	31	03	03
Bedinger	Arthur	S		1869	No	13	02	03	Bender	Samuel		Mr	1869	Ja	06	03	03
Bedinger	S	S	Mrs	1871	No	10	04	02	Bender	William	D		1859	Oc	08	04	02
Bedlam	Jas	S		1878	Jn	03	04	07	Bendler	L			1878	Oc	29	01	04
Bedlam	Jas	S		1878	Jl	03	04	07	Bene	Henry			1854	Au	25	03	06
Beebe	Anna	M		1851	Ja	10	03	05	Benedict	George		Rev	1868	Ja	07	03	01
Beebe	Clarisse	E	Mrs	1847	Ap	24	03	05	Benedict	Henry			1859	Jl	09	03	01
Beebe	Francuis	G		1840	Se	23	03	06	Benham	Edward			1873	Jn	17	01	04
Beebe	George	G		1852	Ap	23	03	07	Benham	L	D	Mrs	1872	No	19	01	05
Beebe	Mary	F		1840	Au	26	03	05	Benjamin	David			1879	Se	09	05	01
Beebe	Rosewell		Esq	1856	Oc	18	03	06	Benner			Lt	1878	Oc	29	01	04
Beebe	William			1871	Oc	22	01	03	Benner	Thomas	H		1879	Jl	29	05	02
Beecher	C	J	Rev	1878	Se	01	01	03	Bennet	William			1878	Mr	06	04	06
Beecher	Edward	A	Maj	1873	Ja	21	01	05	Bennett			Dr	1870	Se	22	04	02
Beers	Irvine			1878	Ap	07	01	04	Bennett			Mr	1871	No	09	01	03
Beeson	H	S		1875	Jn	06	03	01	Bennett			Son	1876	Se	23	01	03
Beeson	Marcus	T		1874	Jl	11	01	06	Bennett	Charles	F	Jr	1879	Au	02	01	01
Beggs	Nelly		Mrs	1838	My	30	03	03	Bennett	Degray		Mrs	1878	Se	12	01	03
Behn	Charles			1874	Ap	14	01	02	Bennett	G		Dr	1878	Se	22	04	03
Behrens	J			1873	Jn	06	01	02	Bennett	James			1872	Jn	04	02	03
Beidon	Charles			1877	De	18	01	08	Bennett	James	G		1872	Jn	02	01	04
Beiker			Mrs	1875	My	12	01	04	Bennett	James	G		1872	Jn	05	01	04
Beile	August			1878	Au	27	01	04	Bennett	James	G		1872	Jn	11	01	03
Belau			Dr	1879	Mr	02	01	04	Bennett	James	G		1872	Jn	14	01	04
Belch	John			1872	De	25	01	01	Bennett	James	G	Mrs	1874	Ap	01	01	02
Belcher			Ram	1878	Ja	09	03	02	Bennett	John			1873	De	23	01	03
Belcher	Brabtree			1878	Se	26	01	04	Bennett	John	C	Bro	1870	Mr	30	02	03
Belcher	James		Mr	1870	Se	04	04	05	Bennett	Joseph			1872	Fe	14	01	02
Belding	Ludoricu		Cpt	1833	Oc	16	03	05	Bennett	Lewis	H		1873	Jl	31	04	05
Belknap	C	W	Mrs	1874	No	06	04	06	Bennett	Maggie			1867	Ja	29	03	04
Belknap	William	G	Bgn	1851	De	05	03	07	Bennett	Maggie			1879	Se	10	01	01
Bell			Jud	1871	Jl	02	03	01	Bennett	Peter	H	Esq	1830	My	25	03	05
Bell			Mr	1874	Ap	18	02	03	Bennett	R	E		1871	Ja	14	04	02
Bell	Asa		Mr	1851	Au	01	03	06	Bennett	R	E		1871	My	21	02	02
Bell	David		Mr	1871	My	12	04	04	Bennett	Theodori	A		1837	Se	05	03	04

Last	First	MI	Ttl	Yr	Mo	Day	Pg	Col	Last	First	MI	Ttl	Yr	Mo	Day	Pg	Col
Bennett	W	A		1878	Oc	25	04	06	Best	Thomas			1878	Se	22	04	03
Bennett	W	J	Maj	1878	Se	08	01	04	Bester	Whitman	C		1873	No	14	01	03
Benning	Henry	T	Gen	1875	Jl	11	01	04	Bestwick	Amy		Mrs	1867	Ap	02	03	04
Benot			Mr	1873	Ja	23	01	05	Bethel			Mr	1871	Fe	25	04	04
Benson			Mr	1877	No	23	04	04	Bethel	Elmira		Mrs	1868	Mr	17	03	05
Benson			Mrs	1877	No	23	04	04	Bethel	J	F	Hon	1871	Ap	22	04	03
Benson	Andrew		Frm	1877	No	25	01	04	Bethel	James		Mr	1871	Ap	09	03	01
Benson	N	J	Mrs	1871	Se	20	04	04	Bethel	James	M	Hon	1871	Ap	26	01	02
Bentel	George			1876	Ja	11	01	04	Bethel	James	M	Hon	1871	Ap	28	01	02
Bentley	Eli		Mr	1856	Se	13	03	06	Bettis	Elijah		Dr	1836	Oc	04	03	06
Bentley	George			1872	De	12	01	04	Bettis	Ransom	S	Mr	1842	Ap	13	03	05
Bentley	George		Mrs	1822	Jl	09	03	02	Betz	John			1877	Se	30	01	04
Bentley	John		Mr	1822	Jl	09	03	02	Beudinot	Corniela			1868	Ja	07	03	01
Bentley	Joseph		Mr	1825	Fe	22	03	01	Bevens			Mr	1826	Se	26	03	01
Bentley	Nancy		Mss	1822	Oc	08	03	01	Bex	Thomas			1873	No	01	01	02
Bently	George		Mr	1833	My	08	02	03	Benedict			Mar	1871	No	11	01	03
Benton			Mrs	1876	Jn	23	01	06	Bibb	William		Gov	1820	Se	23	03	04
Benton	Ann		Mrs	1838	Ja	31	03	04	Bibbo	Alice			1879	Se	06	01	01
Benton	T	S		1879	Ja	03	04	03	Bicker	Nicholas			1874	De	19	03	01
Benton	Thos		Bkm	1878	No	01	01	06	Bickford	Celia		Mrs	1870	Oc	09	01	02
Benton	W			1879	Jl	18	01	02	Bickus	Auton			1873	Fe	04	01	04
Bentz			Mar	1872	Mr	06	01	03	Biddle	Charles		Col	1837	Ja	24	03	04
Bentzer	Peter	H		1878	Oc	17	01	03	Biefield	Charles			1877	Ja	06	01	04
Berdise	Martin			1873	Au	19	01	03	Bielefield	Charles			1877	Ja	05	01	03
Berg	Torge	L		1852	Fe	13	03	07	Bienecki	Chrysastomus		Rev	1879	Se	11	01	01
Bergin	Martin			1879	Ja	17	04	06	Bigelow	J	P		1872	Jl	06	01	03
Bergins	John			1879	Se	16	01	01	Bigelow	Tyler		Cj	1878	Ap	13	04	05
Bergman	Mary			1878	Au	28	01	03	Biggs	Horace	H		1878	Se	17	01	04
Berirand	Pierrl			1862	Oc	04	02	05	Bigsby	John		Mr	1833	Jl	03	03	03
Berlekamp	Fred			1879	Oc	28	01	03	Bigsby	Robert			1874	Ja	08	01	02
Berlin	Frank			1877	No	27	01	07	Bilby	Theodore	D	Mr	1858	My	08	03	04
Berlin	W	S		1879	Se	09	01	01	Biler	Father		Rev	1873	Se	28	01	05
Bernard	Constance		Mss	1879	Se	06	01	01	Bill	Grey			1872	Ja	20	01	01
Bernard	Louisa			1879	Oc	16	01	01	Billings			Mr	1874	Oc	08	01	04
Bernard	William			1878	Fe	13	01	06	Billy	John			1874	Ap	08	04	04
Beroset	Lula	M		1879	Au	20	08	06	Binckley	John	M	Hon	1878	My	07	04	05
Berron	Elias			1879	Se	10	01	01	Bingham			Mrs	1875	Mr	27	01	04
Berry	Mrs			1820	Au	12	03	01	Bingham			Mrs	1875	Jn	06	03	01
Berry			Mss	1875	Mr	24	01	05	Bingham	Ann	M	Ms	1851	Fe	07	03	06
Berry	Frederick		Mr	1839	Oc	09	03	05	Bingham	Margaret	E	Mrs	1875	Jn	30	01	04
Berry	Jack			1871	Au	16	01	04	Bingley	Infant			1878	Se	22	04	03
Berry	James			1877	Oc	18	01	06	Birch	George		Maj	1837	No	14	03	05
Berry	Jon			1878	Se	01	01	03	Birchfield			Dr	1878	Se	13	01	04
Berry	Louis			1874	No	01	01	04	Bird	George			1872	Mr	31	04	06
Berry	Mariam		Mrs	1878	Ja	10	01	03	Bird	Ira	H	Mr	1872	Fe	17	01	04
Berry	R	A		1878	Mr	14	04	03	Bird	John			1872	De	31	02	02
Berry	Rachael		Mrs	1849	Au	02	03	05	Bird	John			1878	Se	22	04	03
Berry	Richard			1878	De	06	01	01	Bird	Nathan		Mr	1873	Au	14	04	04
Berry	Thomas			1878	Ap	10	01	05	Bird	William			1878	Au	08	01	06
Berry	Thomas		Cpt	1874	My	21	04	05	Birds	C	M	Rev	1879	Ja	28	03	01
Berry	Thomas		Smt	1877	De	23	03	02	Birdsell	J	S		1872	Ja	20	01	03
Berry	William			1820	Jl	08	03	04	Birkle	John	A	Mr	1871	My	10	04	04
Berryman	George		Mr	1855	Fe	09	03	04	Birman	Charles			1879	Se	10	01	01
Berthe	Lewis		Mr	1834	Fe	18	02	05	Birne	J	T	Rev	1874	No	22	01	05
Berthey	H	S		1878	Se	22	04	03	Birnie	George		Mr	1856	No	15	03	04
Bertholff	W	B		1873	Ja	03	01	03	Bischoff	Robert			1875	My	09	04	03
Bertram	Henry			1879	Au	26	01	01	Biscoe	Henry	A		1837	Jl	18	03	03
Bertrand	Ann	E		1839	My	01	03	05	Biscoe	Henry	L	Esq	1840	Oc	14	03	05
Bertrand	Charles	P	Esq	1865	Se	02	01	01	Biscoe	Phebe		Mrs	1828	De	16	03	02
Bertrand	John	M		1846	Au	31	03	05	Bishoffsheim	L	R		1874	Ja	08	01	02
Bertrand	Mary	S	Mrs	1874	Oc	03	04	08	Bishop	Mary			1872	Se	28	01	04
Bertrand	Sarah	L		1852	Oc	08	03	05	Bishop	William			1871	Ja	20	01	01
Berty	Oscar		Dr	1879	Au	15	01	01	Bissel	Maud		Mss	1878	Jl	09	01	05
Besshoff	Robert			1874	Se	20	04	03	Bissell			Mr	1876	Fe	25	01	03
Best	George			1871	My	12	01	02	Bissell			Son	1876	Fe	25	01	03
Best	John		Mr	1837	Ja	10	03	04	Bissell	Daniel		Gen	1834	Ja	08	03	03

Arkansas Gazette Obituary Index
University of Arkansas Libraries, Fayetteville

Last	First	MI	Ttl	Yr	Mo	Day	Pg	Col	Last	First	MI	Ttl	Yr	Mo	Day	Pg	Col
Bissell	Jeremiah	S	Mr	1837	Mr	28	03	05	Blanton	Charles		Mr	1872	Au	27	04	05
Bittle	Levi			1872	Au	03	04	05	Blanton	J	W		1879	Oc	03	01	01
Bittle	Thomas	N		1872	No	30	01	05	Blanton	John			1879	Oc	02	01	01
Biven	William		Mr	1875	Jl	03	04	02	Blanz	Clarence			1878	Se	22	04	03
Bizzell	James		Mr	1861	Mr	09	03	03	Blasdell	Daniel		Esq	1857	Fe	14	03	03
Black	Ann		Mrs	1835	Oc	06	03	05	Blass	August			1875	My	13	01	04
Black	Brick	M	Gen	1845	No	03	03	03	Blassingame	B	G	Hon	1871	Mr	07	04	04
Black	George			1872	Au	06	01	05	Bledsoe	Albett	T	Dr	1877	De	11	01	05
Black	George	W	Mr	1853	Ja	21	03	04	Bledsoe	James			1830	Mr	09	03	03
Black	James			1872	Jn	30	01	02	Blenden	Sarah		Mrs	1858	De	04	03	03
Black	James			1878	Ap	05	02	04	Blevins	E	D	Mr	1836	Se	27	03	05
Black	Jonathan		Mr	1836	Jn	07	03	05	Bliss	Chris			1878	Jl	19	01	04
Black	Marlah	W	Mrs	1867	Au	20	02	08	Bliss	George			1874	Ja	08	01	02
Black	Mary		Mrs	1852	De	03	03	05	Blitz	Signor			1878	Ja	09	03	02
Black	Murray			1879	Se	16	05	01	Blocher			Maj	1879	No	11	08	02
Black	Samuel		Mr	1836	Ap	19	03	05	Blocher	John	D		1874	Oc	10	04	07
Black	Thulta			1867	Oc	01	03	04	Blocher	W	D	Maj	1879	No	11	08	05
Black	V			1879	De	21	01	01	Blocher	William	D	Gen	1879	No	25	08	04
Black	William		Col	1853	Mr	04	03	06	Block	Abraham		Cpt	1857	Ap	04	03	03
Blackard	George			1875	Mr	27	04	02	Block	Rosaline	E	Mss	1867	Oc	15	02	08
Blackard	George	D		1875	Mr	24	04	03	Blockard	George			1875	Mr	27	04	04
Blackburn	Carrie	E		1866	Oc	23	02	07	Blodgett				1874	Mr	29	01	07
Blackburn	Charlie			1878	Ap	14	04	05	Blodgett			Cpt	1871	Jl	20	01	05
Blackburn	Dick			1871	No	30	01	03	Blodgett	Foster			1877	No	13	04	03
Blackburn	Jack			1874	My	10	04	04	Bloodworth	Littleton			1867	Oc	29	02	04
Blackburn	James		Rev	1828	Ap	16	03	01	Bloom	Moses			1867	Au	20	02	08
Blackburn	Jane		Mrs	1840	Oc	07	03	04	Bloss	G			1876	My	31	01	02
Blackburn	R			1878	Se	22	04	03	Blosser	Jacob			1872	My	30	01	04
Blackman				1877	De	02	01	07	Blount	Lidda		Mrs	1836	Jn	21	03	05
Blackman			Dr	1871	Jl	27	01	05	Blount	R	J	Mr	1841	Mr	17	03	05
Blackman	Lyman		Mrs	1877	De	02	01	07	Blount	Willie		Gov	1835	Oc	06	04	02
Blackmore			Mr	1870	Oc	04	01	02	Blow	Harry			1871	Jl	07	01	06
Blackmore			Mrs	1870	Oc	04	01	02	Blue	M	H	Mrs	1846	Jn	01	03	05
Blackmore	Carroll			1873	Au	21	01	04	Blum	John			1878	Au	17	01	06
Blacksheer	Sam			1871	Jn	30	01	04	Blumkenberg	A	M	Gen	1878	Oc	13	01	03
Blackstein	A	H		1878	Au	31	01	07	Blummerstein	Ben			1876	Ap	05	01	05
Blackwell			Mr	1873	Ja	14	01	04	Blunt	Elizabeth		Mrs	1850	Au	30	03	07
Blackwell	Jack			1872	No	09	01	02	Blythe			Mr	1875	Oc	12	01	03
Blackwell	Mary	A	Mss	1852	De	31	03	06	Bnzree	Stephen		Rev	1873	Se	12	04	03
Blackwood	John			1879	No	05	04	01	Bnzree	Stephen		Rev	1873	Se	12	04	03
Blair			Gen	1875	Jl	11	01	04	Boardman	Norman		Mr	1873	Oc	14	04	07
Blair	Catherine		Mrs	1871	My	10	01	04	Boas	Robert			1879	My	18	01	03
Blair	Cealy		Mrs	1836	No	29	03	05	Boaz			Dr	1878	Se	22	01	05
Blair	Francis	P		1876	Oc	24	02	03	Bobo	Burwell	A	Dr	1878	Oc	03	01	03
Blair	Frank	P	Gen	1875	Jl	10	01	03	Bockrelly	Ann			1871	No	15	01	03
Blair	Frank	P	Gen	1875	Jl	11	01	02	Boddeker	Bernard	B		1872	Mr	31	04	06
Blair	Frank	P	Gen	1875	Jl	11	03	01	Boddle	Van			1878	Oc	16	01	03
Blair	Hattle			1878	Se	22	04	03	Bodie	Thomas			1875	Ap	29	01	03
Blair	Hugh		Rev	1877	Ja	09	01	04	Bodinelli	Anotonio			1878	Au	30	01	04
Blair	William	P	Mr	1829	Jl	15	03	01	Boggan	Joe			1878	Oc	03	01	03
Blaire	Solomin		Jud	1879	Fe	18	01	02	Boggess	Timothy			1872	Mr	19	04	03
Blake	David			1874	Jl	19	04	02	Boggs	George		Mr	1854	Mr	12	03	05
Blake	Sarah	B	Mrs	1868	Mr	03	03	05	Boggs	Joe			1867	No	05	07	02
Blake	Thos			1878	Jn	15	01	06	Boggs	Joseph			1879	Fe	21	01	06
Blakeman	Walter			1875	My	14	01	04	Boggs	Margaret	D	Mrs	1876	Jn	14	01	02
Blakemore	George	W	Col	1840	Oc	21	03	06	Bogy			Sen	1878	Ja	09	03	02
Blakesley	William			1874	Au	12	04	03	Bogy	Lewis	V	Sen	1877	Se	21	04	04
Blakesley	William		Mr	1874	Au	08	04	04	Bohr	Joseph			1875	Oc	10	01	02
Blamire	J	A		1870	My	04	03	01	Boilean	James	M		1873	My	25	01	02
Blanchard	Charles			1872	Fe	11	01	03	Boilleau	Baronne	G	Mdm	1874	Ap	04	01	03
Blanchard	Edith	R		1867	Oc	15	02	08	Boiseu	Richard	F		1879	Au	26	05	01
Blanchard	Jeremiah		Mr	1821	Mr	10	03	04	Boisseau	John			1872	Au	15	02	03
Bland	J	W	Sen	1870	My	04	03	01	Boja	Dosie			1878	Se	22	04	03
Blanes	Mary	L	Mrs	1876	Ja	18	04	04	Bola			Dr	1877	De	08	04	03
Blankenship	Thos			1878	Jl	27	01	05	Boles	Julia	E	Mrs	1872	Mr	29	04	05
Blankenship	W	M		1878	Jl	27	01	05	Bolger	James			1878	Se	22	04	03

Last	First	MI	Ttl	Yr	Mo	Day	Pg	Col	Last	First	MI	Ttl	Yr	Mo	Day	Pg	Col
Bolin	Joseph		Mr	1838	Se	12	03	06	Bourland	Dibrelt	F		1852	De	03	03	05
Boll	Herman			1879	Jn	29	01	03	Bourne	Charles	E		1873	Mr	20	04	07
Boller	Carrie		Mrs	1878	Se	05	01	03	Boushier	Jacob			1875	Jn	29	01	03
Bollinger	Adolph			1866	Oc	23	02	07	Bouton	Charlie			1876	Oc	20	04	02
Bolton	E		Com	1849	Ap	12	03	04	Bovill	Walter		Sir	1874	Ja	08	01	02
Bolton	W			1871	My	21	02	02	Bowan	Edward			1878	My	10	01	07
Bolton	W	C		1876	Ja	01	01	03	Bowan	Edward			1878	My	11	01	07
Bonaparte	Madam	P		1879	Ap	08	01	02	Bowdenay			Jud	1875	Jn	23	01	05
Bonaparte	Napoleon			1873	Ja	14	01	07	Bowemaster	Chambers			1878	Jn	26	04	05
Bonaparte	Napoleon		Emp	1873	Ja	10	01	07	Bowen			Pm	1878	Oc	03	01	03
Bonaparte	Napoleon		Emp	1873	Ja	11	01	06	Bowen	John			1873	Au	14	01	04
Bonaparte	Napoleon		Emp	1873	Ja	11	02	02	Bowen	Maggie		Mrs	1878	Ja	18	04	01
Bonaparte	Napoleon		Emp	1873	Ja	12	01	05	Bowen	N	K	Dsh	1872	De	10	01	04
Bonaparte	Napoleon		Emp	1873	Ja	12	01	06	Bowers				1877	Oc	31	01	06
Bonaparte	Napoleon		Emp	1874	Ja	08	01	02	Bowers	Caroline			1878	Se	22	04	03
Bonaparte	Napoleon		Gen	1879	No	07	06	01	Bowers	George			1875	My	27	01	04
Bonaparte	Patterson		Mrs	1879	Ap	29	04	04	Bowers	William	P	Mr	1858	My	01	03	03
Bond	L	W	Col	1879	De	27	01	01	Bowie	John	R		1859	Ja	15	03	02
Bond	Lewis		Hon	1878	Oc	03	01	04	Bowing	John		Sir	1872	No	24	01	04
Bond	Louis	T		1870	Oc	19	01	03	Bowland	Bengamin		Mr	1877	Oc	18	04	01
Bond	T	L		1878	Se	17	01	04	Bowles			Mr	1874	Ap	08	01	01
Bond	Thomas	E	Rev	1872	Au	21	01	04	Bowles			Mss	1872	Oc	08	01	04
Bonds	Robert			1879	Au	28	01	01	Bowles	Andrew		Mr	1859	Jn	04	03	01
Bonham	William		Mr	1876	Se	24	03	01	Bowles	Jennie			1878	Se	05	01	03
Bonnell	George			1872	No	30	01	03	Bowles	Oscar		Mr	1874	Ap	17	02	03
Bonneville	R	J	Gen	1878	Jn	13	04	02	Bowlesby	Alice	A		1871	Se	02	01	03
Bonolia	Joseph			1877	De	25	01	07	Bowlin	William		Col	1871	De	08	01	04
Boofza	Adolph			1878	No	03	01	03	Bowman			Rev	1878	Se	19	01	04
Boog	Cal			1874	Mr	14	01	04	Bowman	D	K		1879	Oc	15	01	01
Booker	Paul	R	Dr	1870	Mr	29	02	01	Bowman	G		Rev	1878	Se	19	01	04
Boon	Daniel		Col	1820	No	04	03	01	Bowman	Ida			1879	Oc	10	01	01
Boone	Aurend			1833	No	06	03	05	Bowman	Infant			1878	Se	22	04	03
Boone	Emma			1859	Oc	08	04	02	Bowman	Maria			1874	Ap	29	01	02
Boone	J	R		1873	No	18	05	03	Bowser			Con	1872	No	05	01	04
Boone	Jonathan	W	Esq	1830	Se	15	03	01	Boyce	Frank			1878	Au	24	04	07
Boone	Thomas			1859	Au	06	03	02	Boyce	Henry		Jud	1873	Mr	23	02	02
Booth			Cpt	1828	Oc	14	03	04	Boyce	William	R		1873	Au	29	01	04
Booth	D	W		1878	Au	28	01	04	Boyd			Mss	1871	Jl	23	01	05
Booth	Evaline		Mrs	1867	Oc	08	03	03	Boyd	A	W		1878	Se	22	04	03
Booth	James			1871	Se	09	01	03	Boyd	Absalom		Mrs	1879	Au	10	01	01
Booth	R	R		1879	Au	01	05	01	Boyd	Alexander			1879	Au	27	01	01
Booth	Sallie		Mrs	1872	Mr	08	04	02	Boyd	Anderson			1874	Jn	06	01	05
Boothe	Joseph	D	Esq	1840	My	06	03	02	Boyd	Ben			1878	Se	18	04	04
Boott	John	W		1879	Jn	01	04	03	Boyd	Coleman			1870	Se	22	01	02
Borden	Jefferson			1875	Jl	11	01	05	Boyd	David		Mr	1833	Au	14	03	03
Borden	John	B	Mr	1851	Se	19	03	03	Boyd	Fred			1878	Se	22	04	03
Boretto	Antonio			1877	No	13	04	05	Boyd	J	B		1878	Se	22	04	03
Bork	Isadore			1878	Se	05	01	03	Boyd	James			1877	De	27	01	05
Borland	Mary	L	Mrs	1862	Oc	25	02	05	Boyd	John	M	Mr	1822	Se	17	03	02
Borland	Thomas			1859	Ja	15	03	02	Boyd	Kingston	J		1873	De	10	01	02
Borsye	Maggie			1878	Se	22	04	03	Boyd	M			1878	Se	22	04	03
Boselman	E			1878	Se	22	04	03	Boyd	Mollie			1879	Se	07	01	01
Bosley	Jacob			1872	Oc	30	01	05	Boyd	Shell			1878	No	12	01	03
Boss	L			1878	Se	22	04	03	Boyd	Thomas	A	Mr	1876	Mr	15	01	01
Bossenece	L	N		1878	Se	01	01	03	Boyer	Edward			1872	Fe	17	01	04
Bostick	Taliaferro			1856	No	08	03	03	Boyle	Edward			1871	Jl	26	01	02
Boswell	Hartwell		Col	1833	Ja	23	03	01	Boyle	Frances	E		1845	Au	18	03	04
Boswell	James	C	Mr	1856	Se	13	03	06	Boyle	Frank			1872	De	08	01	04
Boswell	Rachel	H	Mrs	1823	No	25	03	01	Boyle	J	T	Gen	1871	Jl	29	01	04
Botsie	Peter			1878	Se	22	04	03	Boyle	John		Mrs	1878	Au	10	01	03
Botto	Antonio	E		1879	Au	02	01	01	Boyle	John	N	Col	1848	Au	17	03	04
Botton	T	C		1878	Se	22	04	03	Boyle	Joseph		Cpt	1879	Au	10	04	01
Botts	George			1872	Ja	27	01	03	Boyle	Martha			1879	Au	24	01	01
Bourchstone			Mr	1871	Jl	16	01	05	Boyle	Thomas			1871	Jn	30	01	04
Bourdenay	Justin			1875	Jl	10	01	05	Boyles	J	B		1874	Jl	03	04	03
Bourier	Henri	V		1877	No	24	04	05	Boyton	Thomas	J	Hon	1871	My	04	01	03

Arkansas Gazette Obituary Index
University of Arkansas Libraries, Fayetteville

Last	First	MI	Ttl	Yr	Mo	Day	Pg	Col	Last	First	MI	Ttl	Yr	Mo	Day	Pg	Col
Bracius	Frank			1878	No	19	01	02	Braunthier			Mr	1873	Oc	23	01	02
Brack	Frederic	J		1874	Se	26	04	08	Brayorton	Chas			1879	Ap	09	01	02
Brack	Margaret		Mrs	1879	Au	22	08	06	Brazelton	S	H		1875	Jn	08	01	03
Bracken	H	D		1879	Se	25	01	01	Brealy	David	D		1833	Oc	09	03	05
Bracken	James		Mr	1872	Jl	09	01	01	Brearley	David		Col	1837	Oc	10	03	05
Brackenridge				1877	No	15	03	01	Brearley	Mary	A		1853	Oc	14	03	07
Brackett	J	C		1871	Jl	06	01	04	Brearly	Pearson		Col	1835	Se	22	03	05
Brackett	W	B	Mrs	1878	Oc	03	01	05	Breathill	Ed			1876	Se	29	01	03
Brackin	Eliza	A	Mrs	1839	De	04	03	02	Breathitt	John		Gov	1834	Mr	18	03	05
Bradford			Mr	1874	Se	25	01	05	Breaupe			Mr	1875	Jn	11	04	02
Bradford			Mrs	1878	Se	22	04	03	Breck	Casper			1878	Mr	06	04	06
Bradford	George			1878	Se	22	04	03	Breckinridge				1875	My	21	01	02
Bradford	Henry	C	Dr	1842	No	09	03	04	Breckinridge	John			1874	Ap	11	01	04
Bradford	R	B		1878	Se	22	04	03	Breckinridge	John	C		1875	Jn	05	02	02
Bradford	William		Gen	1826	No	14	03	01	Breckinridge	John	C	Gen	1875	My	18	01	03
Bradley			Mr	1820	No	18	04	03	Breckinridge	John	C	Gen	1875	My	19	01	03
Bradley	Abraham		Esq	1838	My	30	03	03	Breckinridge	John	C	Gen	1875	My	19	02	03
Bradley	Augustus			1874	Ap	30	01	06	Breckinridge	John	C	Gen	1875	My	21	02	02
Bradley	Henry			1878	Jl	06	03	03	Breckinridge	John	C	Gen	1875	My	22	01	01
Bradley	Jane		Mrs	1835	De	01	03	05	Breckinridge	John	C	Gen	1875	Jn	18	01	04
Bradley	L	R	Gov	1879	Mr	22	01	03	Breden			Mr	1875	Mr	28	04	05
Bradley	Robert	L	Cpt	1870	Oc	12	01	02	Breen	Maggie			1878	Oc	06	01	06
Bradley	William		Mr	1875	Jl	07	03	01	Breeze	Don			1873	Au	05	01	03
Bradly	Infant			1876	De	30	01	03	Breite	Elizabeth			1872	Ap	24	04	04
Bradshaw	Martha		Mrs	1873	Mr	14	04	03	Brelinam	Henry			1878	Se	03	04	04
Bradshaw	O	A	Col	1873	Jl	13	01	02	Brenfan	Patrick			1878	Jl	21	01	05
Bradshaw	Oliver	A	Gma	1873	Jl	26	11	05	Brennan	Ed			1879	Se	11	01	01
Bradshaw	Phillip			1879	De	02	01	03	Brennan	Henry			1878	Ap	10	01	05
Brady	J	C		1875	Mr	02	04	03	Brennan	John			1878	Au	25	01	04
Brady	James			1878	Se	22	04	03	Brennon			Css	1874	Mr	15	01	06
Brady	Pat			1871	Au	13	01	04	Brent			Mss	1871	De	06	04	01
Brady	Thomas		Cpt	1879	Ja	04	04	06	Brenton			Jas	1878	Oc	11	01	03
Bragelton	C		Mrs	1876	Se	23	01	03	Bressman	F			1879	Jn	28	05	02
Bragg	Arabella			1858	Jl	10	03	02	Brett	George	C		1855	Oc	12	03	05
Bragg	Braxton		Gen	1876	Se	28	01	03	Brevtlinger			Mr	1871	Ap	08	01	03
Bragg	Braxton		Gen	1876	Oc	03	02	03	Brew	Micheal			1878	Au	28	01	03
Bragg	Charley			1872	Oc	10	01	01	Brewer	Brown			1873	My	03	04	05
Bragg	Ellen	N	Mrs	1854	Jn	16	03	05	Brewster	August			1871	Se	27	01	04
Bragg	George	F		1879	Jl	19	05	01	Brewster	F	T		1878	Au	23	04	06
Bragg	George	W		1854	Se	22	03	07	Brewster	Lizzie			1857	Oc	31	03	03
Braham	John			1872	My	31	01	03	Brewster	William			1878	Jn	28	03	07
Braham	John		Gen	1834	Jl	29	03	04	Brewster	Williams			1878	Jn	28	03	07
Braham	John		Mrs	1872	My	31	01	03	Bribach	Robert			1871	No	08	01	02
Brahson	Ephraim	B	Mr	1838	Oc	03	02	03	Brice				1871	Jn	28	01	04
Brainero	John		Pro	1878	Mr	13	04	04	Brice			Gen	1875	My	06	01	03
Bramanti	Clementi			1879	Au	08	08	06	Bridges	B	F	Dr	1860	Se	08	03	02
Bramlette			Jud	1871	Mr	07	01	01	Bridges	James	M		1876	De	19	02	04
Bramlette			Jud	1871	Mr	08	01	01	Bridges	John	C		1859	Ja	08	03	02
Bramlette	Thomas	E	Gov	1875	Ja	14	01	05	Bridges	Mary	F		1859	Ja	08	03	02
Bran	John			1878	Se	08	04	05	Briggs	Asa		Jud	1878	Mr	08	04	04
Branch			Mrs	1873	De	23	03	01	Briggs	Charles			1874	Ap	04	01	05
Branch			Son	1876	Se	23	02	04	Briggs	Luther			1878	Au	27	01	06
Brand			Dr	1875	Jn	27	03	01	Bright				1876	Oc	03	01	05
Brand	George	W	Mr	1842	Fe	16	03	01	Bright	David			1878	Se	10	01	03
Brand	W	W	Dcn	1868	Jl	21	03	05	Bright	Francis		Mrs	1849	Fe	22	03	05
Brandon				1878	Se	22	04	03	Bright	Jesse	D		1875	My	23	02	02
Brandon	Luke			1874	Jn	28	01	04	Bright	Jesse	D	Hon	1875	My	22	01	06
Brandstein	John			1874	Au	16	01	07	Brightfield			Pvt	1876	Jl	09	01	05
Brannon	Kate		Mrs	1878	Au	30	01	04	Briley	Charitt	D		1848	Se	07	03	04
Bransford	Sam			1879	Ap	17	01	02	Brimnsool				1876	No	15	03	01
Bransford	William	M	Mr	1856	Jn	07	03	05	Brion	Gustave			1877	No	07	01	05
Brantley			Gen	1870	No	09	01	02	Brisben	Harry			1872	No	17	01	02
Brantley	Benjaman		Dcn	1868	Jl	07	02	06	Brisbin	John	M		1874	Fe	04	04	02
Brantley	Johnanna			1879	Oc	25	08	06	Brisbin	John	M		1874	Fe	05	04	05
Brantley	Mary	G		1872	Au	02	04	04	Brisbin	Mary		Mss	1851	Jn	06	03	05
Brashier	R	H	Dr	1878	Ja	03	04	05	Brisbin	Samuel			1854	Au	04	03	07

Last	First	MI	Ttl	Yr	Mo	Day	Pg	Col
Brisbon	Catherine			1876	Se	26	01	04
Briscoe	John	P		1876	De	12	01	05
Brister	J	L		1874	Au	25	03	01
Bristol	Ed			1874	Jl	07	04	02
Brit	Edwin		Mr	1837	My	16	03	03
Britan	Chadwick	B		1876	Oc	26	01	01
Britsch	Joseph			1874	No	05	04	03
Britt	J	S	Mr	1870	Ap	17	02	03
Britt	Jeferson	P		1869	Ja	21	02	06
Britt	Mary			1878	Se	22	04	03
Brittantine	F			1879	Se	19	01	01
Britton	John			1875	Ap	16	01	03
Britton	Roberts			1878	Se	26	01	04
Brizzolari	James			1878	No	03	01	03
Brock	J	B	Dr	1870	Mr	04	03	01
Brock	Jacob			1871	De	10	04	04
Brock	Jacob		Cpt	1877	Se	23	04	04
Brockerman	Hiram			1873	Ja	30	01	05
Brockhaus	Hermann			1878	Ja	09	03	02
Brockogle	William			1878	Oc	16	01	03
Broderick	James			1873	Se	06	01	02
Brodie				1874	Mr	03	04	03
Brodie	Emily			1857	Se	12	03	04
Brodie	Hiram		Cpt	1875	Fe	26	04	02
Brodie	James			1874	Mr	15	04	06
Brodie	Love			1879	Jn	01	08	04
Brodie	Marian	D		1858	Jn	12	03	03
Brodie	Renton			1873	De	20	04	02
Brodie	Robert			1869	Oc	29	04	02
Brodie	Virginia	P		1871	Mr	12	04	05
Brogan	Hugh		Esq	1857	Jl	11	03	03
Brogan	Mary	E	Mrs	1867	Oc	15	02	08
Brook	S	T	Dr	1879	Ja	04	04	04
Brookin	Martha		Mrs	1873	Jn	01	04	05
Brookin	Samuel			1855	Jn	15	03	06
Brookin	Samuel			1862	Au	16	02	05
Brookins	Infant			1879	Jl	27	08	01
Brooks			Mr	1871	Oc	20	01	03
Brooks	Bessie			1878	Oc	27	01	04
Brooks	Charles			1878	Se	25	01	04
Brooks	Charles	D		1879	Oc	25	05	01
Brooks	Don			1873	Oc	10	01	02
Brooks	J	W	Mr	1871	Jn	10	01	01
Brooks	James			1878	Jn	05	01	06
Brooks	James		Hon	1874	Ap	12	02	02
Brooks	James		Hon	1873	My	03	01	05
Brooks	James		Hon	1873	My	04	01	04
Brooks	Jerome			1871	Oc	28	01	04
Brooks	John		Mr	1825	Ja	25	03	01
Brooks	John		Mr	1825	Ap	19	03	04
Brooks	John	B	Bro	1868	Se	29	03	02
Brooks	M	J	Mrs	1878	Se	22	04	03
Brooks	Mary		Mss	1878	Fe	13	04	06
Brooks	Mary	A		1838	De	26	03	05
Brooks	R	E	Mrs	1878	Se	19	01	04
Brooks	W	F		1873	No	18	05	03
Brooks	W	W	Smm	1877	No	25	01	04
Brooks	William	F		1879	Oc	11	01	01
Brookway	Thomas	C		1831	Oc	26	03	05
Brophy				1877	De	02	01	07
Brophy	James			1877	De	27	01	05
Bros	Godfrey		Abp	1878	Mr	01	01	05
Broussard	Fucay			1878	Se	25	01	06
Brower	Emzy	D		1860	Mr	10	03	01
Brower	H	S	Dr	1876	Mr	30	01	05
Brown				1873	Au	26	04	04

Last	First	MI	Ttl	Yr	Mo	Day	Pg	Col
Brown			Dr	1871	My	30	01	01
Brown			Mr	1872	Oc	29	01	03
Brown			Mr	1875	Mr	18	04	04
Brown			Mrs	1878	Fe	24	01	05
Brown			Mss	1877	No	28	03	01
Brown	A			1878	Se	22	04	03
Brown	A	L		1879	Oc	28	01	02
Brown	Aaron		Mr	1839	No	06	03	04
Brown	Alexander			1878	Ap	23	01	06
Brown	Anna	L		1871	Ap	14	01	03
Brown	Annie		Mrs	1879	Jl	06	01	02
Brown	Charles			1870	Jl	15	04	04
Brown	David	P		1872	Jl	16	02	04
Brown	Ed		Frm	1873	Jl	18	01	02
Brown	Edward			1874	Jn	13	01	06
Brown	Elljah			1878	Fe	24	01	05
Brown	Emma			1878	Fe	13	01	06
Brown	Emma			1878	Se	22	04	03
Brown	Esham			1875	Mr	17	01	01
Brown	Fred			1874	De	03	01	05
Brown	George			1820	Ja	22	03	04
Brown	George			1820	Ja	22	03	04
Brown	George		Ptr	1877	No	25	01	04
Brown	George	L		1876	My	12	01	01
Brown	Hardin			1879	Jn	15	01	02
Brown	Henry			1878	Se	22	04	03
Brown	Jacob		Gen	1828	Mr	26	03	02
Brown	James			1875	Mr	21	01	03
Brown	James			1875	Mr	25	01	04
Brown	James			1877	No	04	01	06
Brown	Jesse	V	Mr	1841	Oc	27	03	05
Brown	John			1859	De	17	03	01
Brown	John			1875	No	30	02	02
Brown	John			1876	Mr	28	04	04
Brown	John			1879	Jl	19	01	03
Brown	John			1879	Se	10	01	01
Brown	John			1879	Oc	07	01	01
Brown	John		Hon	1872	My	14	01	02
Brown	John		Mr	1830	Oc	06	02	01
Brown	John	H		1879	Jl	08	08	03
Brown	John	P		1871	My	21	02	02
Brown	Johnnie			1877	No	04	01	06
Brown	Jonathan	R	Mr	1821	Se	22	03	01
Brown	Joseph			1878	Fe	24	01	05
Brown	Joseph		Mr	1852	Fe	13	03	07
Brown	Lane			1873	De	07	01	04
Brown	Laura	P		1877	Ja	30	01	07
Brown	Leeper			1832	No	30	03	05
Brown	Lindsey			1873	De	06	01	03
Brown	Lou		Cpt	1873	Au	08	02	02
Brown	Louisa	C	Mrs	1849	Fe	22	03	05
Brown	Lucy			1878	Se	05	01	03
Brown	M	D		1878	Se	22	04	03
Brown	Mark			1875	Jl	10	01	05
Brown	Mary			1876	Mr	02	04	03
Brown	Mercer			1878	Jl	14	01	05
Brown	Miranda			1874	Ap	04	01	04
Brown	Mitchell		Snr	1878	Oc	08	01	03
Brown	Monkey			1871	Se	29	01	03
Brown	Monkey			1871	Oc	12	01	03
Brown	Nelson			1871	Ja	17	01	01
Brown	Obadiah			1874	Ap	29	01	05
Brown	P	M		1878	Oc	08	01	03
Brown	P	P	Mrs	1878	Se	22	04	03
Brown	Philenn			1840	Oc	28	03	05
Brown	Porter			1878	My	12	01	06

Last	First	MI	Ttl	Yr	Mo	Day	Pg	Col	Last	First	MI	Ttl	Yr	Mo	Day	Pg	Col
Brown	Russell		Mrs	1874	No	28	01	04	Buckley	Infant			1878	Se	12	01	06
Brown	S	F	Col	1868	Mr	03	03	05	Buckley	James		Jud	1872	Oc	11	01	06
Brown	S	W		1878	Se	05	01	03	Buckley	Nathaniel	H	Esq	1833	Se	11	03	05
Brown	Samuel	G		1874	Fe	03	04	02	Bucklin	Charles			1871	Jl	13	01	05
Brown	Smith		Mr	1826	Jn	06	03	01	Buckner	Nancy		Mrs	1851	Ja	10	03	07
Brown	T	M		1877	De	02	01	07	Buckner	S	B	Mrs	1874	Ja	11	03	01
Brown	Theodore		Mrs	1872	De	29	01	06	Buckrell			Pvt	1876	Jl	09	01	05
Brown	Thomas		Mr	1834	Mr	04	03	04	Budd	Charles	D		1858	De	11	03	02
Brown	Thos	M	Frm	1877	No	25	01	04	Budd	Irvine	P		1858	Ja	30	03	03
Brown	Tom			1878	Se	01	01	03	Budd	John	J		1860	Ja	14	03	02
Brown	Virgil	C		1871	Ap	14	01	03	Budd	Martha	J	Mss	1854	Jl	28	03	06
Brown	W	B	Col	1872	My	19	01	05	Buddington	William	I		1879	No	30	01	02
Brown	W	C		1874	Au	08	01	06	Buesley	Gruet		Mr	1874	Oc	14	01	03
Brown	Willa			1878	Se	21	04	07	Buetsch	John		Mr	1871	My	14	01	08
Brown	William			1874	De	17	04	02	Buffinburger	Peter		Mr	1871	Au	02	01	02
Brown	William	D		1857	My	30	03	03	Buford	Sarah	H	Mrs	1852	Ja	02	03	06
Brown	William	H		1873	Au	08	01	04	Bugbee	James	H	Bro	1869	No	14	04	02
Brown	William	H	Cpt	1875	Jn	30	01	02	Bugbee	John		Cxs	1877	No	25	01	04
Brown	William	S	Cpt	1875	Jn	06	03	01	Bugg	Arthur			1873	Au	07	01	03
Browne	J	W	Gen	1873	Mr	13	01	06	Buhl	John			1878	Se	04	01	03
Browne	Samuel	J	Rev	1872	Se	21	02	04	Bulgaris	Demetrius			1878	Ja	12	01	05
Brownfield	Guy	C		1836	Se	13	03	04	Bulger	John			1878	No	23	01	02
Brownfield	John	G		1836	Jn	28	03	04	Bulkley	Oliphant	A		1872	Fe	15	01	03
Browning	John			1844	Jn	19	03	01	Bull	Charley			1870	Ap	14	01	03
Brownlee	Mrs			1874	Fe	20	01	04	Bull	George	W		1879	De	27	05	02
Brownlow			Sen	1878	Ja	09	03	02	Bullard	B	P		1878	Ap	14	04	05
Brownson	O	A		1876	Ap	18	01	04	Bullines	Charles			1878	Se	22	04	03
Brownwell	Howard			1872	No	02	01	03	Bullinger	John			1878	Ap	16	01	05
Brpwn			Mr	1876	Fe	03	01	05	Bullitt	George		Hon	1834	De	16	03	03
Bruce	Robert		Mr	1873	De	16	01	02	Bulloch	Thomas		Mr	1876	Oc	19	02	04
Brumaister	Matthias			1877	No	11	01	04	Bullock	John	H		1874	Fe	03	01	04
Brumand	Louis			1879	Jl	23	01	02	Buloz	Francis			1877	Ja	13	01	05
Brumback	Frances		Mss	1849	Ap	26	03	04	Buloz	Hector			1878	Ja	09	03	02
Brumback	Tobias			1833	Jl	10	03	03	Bulty	Bustin			1878	Se	22	04	03
Brumbaugh	J	S		1878	Mr	05	01	05	Bulwer-Lytton	Edward			1873	Ja	22	02	03
Brumdidge	Laura	E	Mrs	1867	Oc	22	04	08	Bumgarner	W	J		1878	Ja	20	03	02
Brumly	Connelius			1870	Oc	04	01	02	Bump	Abby	A	Mrs	1854	Fe	03	03	06
Bruner	William			1820	Ap	08	03	01	Bumpap	Mary			1848	Fe	10	03	04
Brwon	John		Hon	1872	My	28	01	01	Bunch	R	H	Esq	1858	De	18	03	04
Brwon	John	P	Cpt	1842	My	04	03	06	Bunger	F			1878	Oc	02	04	04
Bryan	Samuel		Mr	1831	Au	17	03	05	Bunger	Ferdinand			1878	Oc	20	04	06
Bryan	Scipo			1875	Ap	17	01	03	Bunger	Ford			1878	Se	17	04	02
Bryant				1872	Ja	09	01	01	Bunn	Henry			1878	Ap	13	01	06
Bryant	Dan			1871	Fe	28	01	01	Bunnell	James	E	Mrs	1877	De	18	01	08
Bryant	John			1877	Oc	07	01	05	Bunyan	Fred			1878	Se	22	04	03
Bryant	Mary	L	Mrs	1871	Oc	19	04	04	Bunyan	M	K	Bro	1869	De	25	02	03
Bryant	Prague			1874	Ap	11	01	04	Buoy	Edward			1871	Mr	12	03	01
Bryant	William	C		1878	Jn	13	04	04	Burbank, Jr	R	P	Mr	1871	Ap	08	01	03
Bryant	William	C		1878	Jn	15	04	05	Burch	Mike			1873	Fe	09	01	07
Bryce			Gen	1875	My	16	01	04	Burchard	Austin			1879	Se	16	05	02
Bryce	Alex		Pm	1879	No	06	04	04	Burdick	Luisa		Mrs	1873	Se	18	04	06
Bryce	John			1874	De	24	01	02	Burgen	Daniel		Sea	1877	No	25	01	04
Bryson	Thomas			1878	Se	22	04	03	Burger			Dr	1878	Au	23	01	03
Buchanan	James			1854	Ja	06	03	06	Burgess	Joe			1873	Oc	11	04	04
Buchanan	James		Prs	1868	Jn	09	01	02	Burgess	John			1873	No	21	01	03
Buchanan	McKean			1872	Ap	23	01	04	Burgess	Nathan			1875	Jn	19	01	03
Buchanan	Ralph	F	Son	1874	Oc	14	04	08	Burgett	Peter			1873	No	21	01	02
Buchignani	Joseph			1879	Se	10	01	01	Burgett	Peter			1873	De	18	03	01
Buchignani	Teresa			1879	Se	11	01	01	Burgett	Peter	N		1873	De	05	04	03
Buck	R	B		1871	Au	19	01	05	Burgevin	Fannie	B	Mrs	1872	No	05	01	05
Buck	Thomas			1878	Oc	04	01	03	Burghardt	Hattie			1872	No	03	01	05
Buck	William			1878	Se	17	01	05	Burgher	John		Cpt	1872	Au	06	01	05
Buckhart			Mr	1872	Fe	17	01	04	Burk	Frank			1873	Oc	10	01	02
Buckle	H	W		1878	Se	22	04	03	Burk	Mary			1873	Oc	10	01	02
Buckley	David			1872	Jl	02	01	05	Burk	Robert		Ofc	1873	Oc	04	01	03
Buckley	E	J	Mrs	1866	Oc	09	03	02	Burk	Robert	H		1876	Oc	12	02	03

Last	First	MI	Ttl	Yr	Mo	Day	Pg	Col	Last	First	MI	Ttl	Yr	Mo	Day	Pg	Col
Burke				1878	Ja	12	01	07	Burrus	Roland			1874	Ap	30	04	06
Burke			Pvt	1876	Jl	09	01	05	Bursey	William			1866	Oc	16	03	08
Burke	George			1878	Se	03	01	05	Burt	C	W	Mrs	1873	Oc	15	01	02
Burke	Honora		Mrs	1878	Oc	29	01	04	Burt	Nellie			1874	Jl	05	04	03
Burke	James	B		1878	Oc	15	01	03	Burton	Alexander		Mr	1838	Mr	07	03	02
Burke	James	E		1879	Au	26	01	01	Burton	Bob	D		1857	Jl	04	03	03
Burke	James	W		1870	No	26	04	05	Burton	Charles	C	Maj	1866	No	13	03	03
Burke	John			1871	Se	03	01	06	Burton	Joe		Mr	1873	Jn	21	01	03
Burke	John			1872	Fe	17	01	04	Burton	Oscar			1874	Au	08	01	06
Burke	John			1876	De	29	01	02	Burton	Oscar			1875	Ap	21	01	02
Burke	Kate			1876	De	23	02	04	Burton	Philip		Mr	1851	Jl	18	03	07
Burke	Patrick	G		1858	No	13	03	02	Burton	Phillip			1878	Au	23	01	03
Burke	Tom			1873	Mr	29	01	02	Burton	S		Rev	1878	Oc	09	01	04
Burkes	George			1871	Jl	09	01	05	Busby	Tom			1873	De	27	04	02
Burkham	Rosa			1878	Oc	03	01	04	Busckus	George			1876	Oc	17	01	02
Burkhobler	B			1878	Se	17	01	06	Bush			Mr	1872	Jl	19	02	04
Burkley	Thomas			1878	Ja	09	01	07	Bush	B	T		1878	Se	22	04	03
Burkley	William	R		1877	De	28	01	05	Bush	Lee			1872	My	29	01	03
Burklow	Harrison			1878	Jl	06	03	03	Bush	Mary	V	Mss	1876	Se	28	04	06
Burks	Bill			1878	Se	01	01	03	Bush	Mary	W	Mrs	1873	Jn	24	04	04
Burksdale	W	P	Con	1878	Ja	09	03	02	Bush	Robert			1879	Au	31	01	01
Burleigh	George			1878	Au	11	01	05	Bush	William			1878	Se	22	04	03
Burleigh	John	H		1877	De	07	01	07	Bush	William	H		1878	No	27	01	04
Burleson	M	J	Mrs	1878	Oc	08	01	03	Bushnell	Nehemiah		Hon	1873	Fe	02	01	04
Burley	Charlie			1879	De	10	08	05	Bushong	Albert			1868	Jn	02	01	02
Burlingame	Min			1870	Fe	24	01	02	Bushton	William			1878	Oc	10	01	03
Burnett	John			1874	Mr	17	02	03	Bussey	Fred			1873	Au	03	04	04
Burnett	John	D		1870	Oc	08	03	01	Bussy	Elliott		Mr	1837	Ja	10	03	04
Burnett	John	D		1870	Oc	12	01	02	Buster	Henry	G	Cpt	1854	Ja	13	03	04
Burnett	Joseph		Mr	1872	Fe	17	01	01	Busw	William	H		1878	No	27	01	03
Burnett	William	C		1878	Oc	03	04	04	Buth	Frederick		Mr	1871	My	13	01	03
Burnham	Robert		Dr	1878	Se	26	01	04	Butler			Pvt	1876	Jl	09	01	05
Burnham	S	E		1870	My	04	03	01	Butler	B		Mrs	1867	Ja	08	03	03
Burnham	Sophie	E	Mss	1875	Mr	31	01	06	Butler	Beulah	O		1871	Oc	18	04	02
Burns				1871	Jl	25	01	03	Butler	Carrie		Mss	1878	Oc	04	01	03
Burns				1878	Fe	17	01	03	Butler	Edward			1867	No	19	03	02
Burns			Mr	1871	Au	18	01	05	Butler	Felician			1858	Ja	30	03	02
Burns			Rev	1870	No	23	01	01	Butler	George			1878	Oc	01	01	04
Burns	Aaron			1874	Mr	24	03	01	Butler	J	V		1878	No	09	04	04
Burns	Frank		Sea	1877	No	25	01	04	Butler	Jeremiah	V		1878	No	09	04	04
Burns	Jane		Mrs	1820	Se	09	03	02	Butler	John			1873	Se	06	01	02
Burns	John	F		1852	Jn	18	01	06	Butler	John	M	Esq	1856	Jl	05	03	06
Burns	John	I		1878	Ap	11	01	07	Butler	John	S		1878	Oc	11	01	04
Burns	Martin			1878	Mr	30	01	06	Butler	Joseph	C		1873	Jn	15	01	03
Burns	Mary			1879	Jl	29	01	01	Butler	Julia	P		1853	Ja	21	03	04
Burns	Mary	E	Sis	1878	Se	24	01	04	Butler	Margret		Mrs	1878	Oc	10	01	03
Burns	Sallie	M		1872	No	05	01	05	Butler	Martha	J	Mss	1846	Fe	02	03	03
Burns	Sarah			1879	Oc	19	01	01	Butler	Rebecca	E	Mrs	1856	Jn	07	03	05
Burns	Thos			1878	Se	05	01	03	Butler	Samuel			1871	Au	23	01	04
Burnshill	Laura			1878	Fe	07	04	04	Butler	Stephen			1874	Au	21	01	07
Burnside	H	M		1874	Au	21	01	07	Butler	Walter	H		1875	My	25	04	04
Burnstein	A			1878	Oc	01	01	04	Butler	William		Dr	1850	Oc	04	03	02
Burr	Ed			1871	Au	20	01	05	Butler	William	L	Mr	1842	Mr	02	03	02
Burr	Ed			1871	De	07	01	03	Butler	Z	V	Mr	1878	No	03	04	04
Burr	Ed			1872	Mr	23	01	04	Butterfield			Col	1875	Mr	31	04	02
Burr	George			1879	Oc	29	05	02	Butterfield			Col	1875	My	28	03	01
Burress	Benjamin		Mr	1832	Mr	21	03	05	Butterfield			Mr	1875	Jn	01	04	02
Burress	George	W		1868	Jn	02	03	05	Butterfield			Mr	1875	Jn	03	04	02
Burris	Thomas		Mr	1829	No	10	03	02	Butterfield	D	A	Col	1875	Mr	30	04	03
Burriss	Horatio		Mr	1831	Mr	21	03	05	Butterfield	D	A	Col	1875	My	04	04	02
Burroughs	R	F		1872	Ja	10	01	03	Butterworth	Edward			1845	Se	08	03	04
Burroughs	Ransom	F		1872	Jn	04	01	03	Butterworth	Mary	A		1845	Se	01	03	03
Burroughs	Ransom	F		1873	Jn	13	01	01	Butterworth	Rebecca			1845	Se	01	03	03
Burrow	Julia			1868	Jl	14	03	07	Butterworth	Thomas		Dr	1853	Au	12	03	07
Burrow	Mark		Mrs	1856	Se	27	03	06	Button	Robert		Mrs	1878	Oc	11	01	03
Burrow	Tinsley	C		1854	Jl	07	03	06	Butts	Isac			1874	No	21	01	03

Arkansas Gazette Obituary Index
University of Arkansas Libraries, Fayetteville

Last	First	MI	Ttl	Yr	Mo	Day	Pg	Col	Last	First	MI	Ttl	Yr	Mo	Day	Pg	Col
Buxton	Elizabeth		Mrs	1839	Oc	16	03	05	Calhoun	John	C		1879	My	08	08	02
Byam	K	B	Mr	1871	Jl	04	01	03	Call				1871	My	31	01	02
Byers	John		Dr	1871	Au	08	01	02	Callahan			Cor	1876	Jl	09	01	05
Byers	Jos			1878	Au	08	01	06	Callahan	Kate		Mrs	1868	Mr	31	03	04
Byers	Lucy	A	Mrs	1846	Jl	13	03	05	Callahan	Lizzie			1878	No	20	01	03
Byford				1876	Oc	28	01	01	Callahan	Mattie		Mss	1877	De	21	01	06
Byington			Mss	1839	Se	18	03	04	Callahan	Michael			1872	Se	10	01	03
Byington	Edward			1840	Se	30	03	05	Callahan	Michael			1872	Se	14	01	03
Byland	Thomas			1873	No	18	04	03	Callahan	Michael			1877	De	27	01	04
Bynum	Marcus	P	Esq	1844	De	23	03	01	Callahan	William			1879	No	04	05	02
Bynum	William			1878	Se	22	04	03	Calloway	E			1878	Se	22	04	03
Byrd	Ann	L	Mrs	1839	No	20	03	03	Calvert	Daniel			1872	Jn	15	01	05
Byrd	Julia		Mrs	1845	My	26	03	05	Calvert	Samuel			1872	Mr	19	01	05
Byrd	Ludelia			1879	Se	26	01	01	Calvet	Sarah	A		1848	Jn	01	03	03
Byrd	Mary			1851	Au	01	03	06	Cam	Thomas			1874	Ap	01	01	05
Byrd	R	C	Esq	1867	Se	10	03	03	Cambell	A			1878	Oc	04	01	03
Byrd	Richard	C	Gov	1854	Jn	23	03	06	Cambell	Anna	M		1879	Se	09	01	01
Byrd	Stephen		Col	1835	Ap	07	03	06	Cambell	R	J		1878	Se	10	01	03
Byrd	William		Mr	1835	Ap	21	03	05	Cambell	William			1879	Au	14	01	03
Byrd	William	J	Mr	1853	Se	16	03	06	Cameron			Mrs	1874	Jn	20	01	06
Byrne	Andrew		Bp	1862	Jn	28	02	04	Cameron	O	G		1872	Mr	12	01	04
Byrne	Henry	H		1872	Mr	02	01	04	Cammers	Amelia			1878	Oc	18	01	03
Byrne	J		Dr	1878	Se	01	01	04	Camp	T	H		1873	No	18	05	03
Byrne	Myles		Mr	1851	Jl	18	03	07	Camp	William			1878	Se	22	04	03
									Campbell				1871	Jl	06	01	04
									Campbell				1874	Ap	09	01	05
			C						Campbell				1877	De	11	03	02
									Campbell			Mr	1872	Ap	11	01	04
									Campbell			Mrs	1872	Jn	30	01	06
Cabbott	Albert			1872	No	15	01	03	Campbell			Mss	1876	De	10	01	04
Cabell	Williams	L		1867	Oc	08	03	03	Campbell	A	C	Dr	1879	Se	18	01	01
Cadoudal				1878	Ja	03	01	04	Campbell	Alexander		Mr	1872	Mr	17	01	04
Cady	Charlotte		Mrs	1871	Ja	20	04	05	Campbell	Charles			1871	Jl	06	01	04
Cady	Ezekiel		Mr	1862	Se	27	02	05	Campbell	Charles		Mrs	1871	Jl	06	01	04
Cady	Mary	L		1873	No	18	05	05	Campbell	Dan			1872	Ja	25	01	03
Cafe			Mr	1875	Jn	02	04	03	Campbell	Duncan		Mrs	1872	De	27	01	02
Caffey	Phillip	S	Bro	1869	De	25	02	03	Campbell	George			1874	Au	23	04	06
Caffry	Mary	A	Mrs	1874	Se	23	04	07	Campbell	Harry			1874	Oc	11	01	05
Cagle	Martha	J		1852	Se	03	03	07	Campbell	Hugh		Esq	1850	My	10	03	06
Cain	Anice	C		1873	Fe	05	04	05	Campbell	Jack			1875	Se	26	03	01
Cain	Patrick			1873	Se	05	01	02	Campbell	John			1876	Mr	02	04	03
Cairnes	Alexander			1873	Fe	02	01	04	Campbell	John		Mrs	1826	Se	19	03	01
Cairnes	Henry			1873	Fe	02	01	04	Campbell	Kate		Mss	1870	Oc	18	04	05
Calahan	John			1878	Se	04	01	03	Campbell	Oliver	P		1859	Ap	16	02	07
Calahoun	Jason			1878	Se	24	01	05	Campbell	Phoebe			1872	Jn	21	01	06
Calame	Charles			1873	No	12	01	03	Campbell	Randolph			1867	De	31	02	06
Caldwell			Cdr	1878	Ja	09	03	02	Campbell	Thomas	P	Shr	1872	Jl	03	01	03
Caldwell			Mr	1832	Au	01	03	03	Campbell	William			1873	Au	30	01	03
Caldwell	Andy		Eng	1879	Ap	05	01	03	Campbell	William			1878	Au	30	01	04
Caldwell	Gertrude		Mss	1872	Fe	29	04	06	Canby			Gen	1874	Ap	17	01	02
Caldwell	Henry	C		1832	Au	29	03	02	Canby			Gen	1874	Ap	26	02	03
Caldwell	J	H	Col	1857	Oc	10	03	04	Canby			Gen	1873	My	20	01	02
Caldwell	James	H	Jr	1858	Oc	09	03	03	Canby			Gen	1873	My	21	01	04
Caldwell	John	H		1879	Ja	01	04	04	Candis				1878	Ja	05	01	06
Caldwell	M	J	Mrs	1878	Ap	25	04	06	Canepo	Mary		Mrs	1878	Au	28	01	03
Caldwell	Mary		Mrs	1836	Oc	04	03	06	Cangmaid	Josie	A		1878	Mr	16	01	06
Caldwell	Samuel	V	Esq	1836	Fe	23	03	06	Cannon	Richards	W	Dr	1870	Oc	25	04	02
Caldwell	Sarah	A		1837	No	28	03	05	Cantlo	Frank			1879	Se	26	08	02
Caldwell	William		Mr	1836	Fe	09	03	06	Canton	J	H	Gen	1871	Se	29	01	04
Calhoun			Lt	1876	Jl	07	01	03	Canton	John			1874	Oc	21	01	05
Calhoun			Mr	1873	No	13	03	01	Cantrell	Robert		Mr	1872	My	22	01	01
Calhoun	Archibald			1872	My	09	01	04	Capes	Virginia			1879	Au	20	01	02
Calhoun	Dan			1873	Au	09	01	02	Caple	James	P	Bro	1873	Mr	20	04	07
Calhoun	Simeon	H		1875	Mr	25	04	06	Capps	Nimrod		Mr	1876	Ap	05	01	05
Calhoun	Willaim	B		1874	Au	25	04	07	Caran	Infant			1876	No	03	01	03
Calhoun	William		Mr	1820	Se	23	03	04	Cardet	August			1872	De	27	01	03

Last	First	MI	Ttl	Yr	Mo	Day	Pg	Col	Last	First	MI	Ttl	Yr	Mo	Day	Pg	Col
Cardill				1878	Se	22	04	03	Carson	Alfred		Stc	1877	No	25	01	04
Cardin	Amos	S	Mr	1873	Jn	26	03	01	Carson	Chas		Ldm	1877	No	29	04	03
Carewell			Mr	1875	Oc	02	01	03	Carson	J	E	Jud	1876	Ap	27	01	04
Carey				1877	De	02	01	07	Carson	Peter			1878	Se	22	04	03
Carey	William	W		1838	Jl	25	03	03	Carswell	Laura		Mss	1869	Jl	16	02	04
Carken			Maj	1878	Oc	27	01	04	Carter			Dr	1878	Oc	16	01	04
Carl	Boyd			1877	Ja	16	04	04	Carter	Alfred	D	Mr	1839	Ja	09	02	03
Carleton	Jariz	H		1862	Se	20	02	05	Carter	Charles			1878	Fe	02	04	06
Carley	Thomas		Ldm	1877	No	25	01	04	Carter	Emily	P	Mrs	1850	My	31	03	06
Carlin	John			1878	My	26	04	07	Carter	George			1878	De	06	01	01
Carlisle	Elizabeth			1878	Se	05	01	03	Carter	Henry			1872	Au	01	01	06
Carlock	W	I		1873	De	16	01	06	Carter	Henry	M	Mr	1872	Au	01	01	06
Carlton	Herman		Maj	1878	Oc	01	04	03	Carter	Jeft			1878	Au	02	04	05
Carlton	Nancy	B		1838	Mr	07	03	02	Carter	John	W		1878	Ja	26	01	07
Carlyle	Thomas			1876	Ap	22	01	04	Carter	L	F	Lt	1837	Fe	07	03	04
Carmen	Bengiman		Mrs	1878	Ja	17	04	05	Carter	Lawrence	F	Lt	1837	Ap	04	03	05
Carmichael	P	M	Mr	1871	Mr	09	01	01	Carter	M	A	Col	1878	Oc	03	01	03
Carmichael	P	M	Mr	1871	My	16	01	02	Carter	Sarah	C	Mss	1847	Jl	15	03	03
Carmicheal	D	L		1879	Se	23	01	01	Carter	Sarah	E	Mrs	1848	Ap	20	03	03
Carnahan	James		Mr	1824	Jl	27	03	02	Carter	Tallis			1874	De	06	04	02
Carnavan	Alice			1878	Se	04	01	03	Carter	Thomas	C		1879	Se	05	08	06
Carnes	Jane			1878	Jn	01	04	06	Carter	William			1878	Mr	29	03	03
Carnes	Mollie		Mss	1878	Ap	20	01	05	Cartritte	Stephen			1878	De	10	04	03
Carnes	R	S	Mr	1879	My	13	08	03	Caruthers	James			1873	Jn	12	01	04
Carney	Dennis		Mrs	1870	Se	27	02	03	Caruthers	Rachel		Mrs	1826	Se	19	03	01
Carney	Peter		Mrs	1873	My	10	02	03	Carver	Chester		Mrs	1872	Ja	19	01	03
Caroll	Johnny			1870	Oc	04	01	02	Carver	Thos	U		1878	Oc	25	01	04
Carpenter			Mrs	1873	My	10	02	03	Carvier	Fred			1873	Se	28	01	05
Carpenter	James			1872	Se	18	01	02	Cary	H	P		1873	Jl	10	01	02
Carpenter	James			1872	Se	19	01	03	Case	Ben			1878	No	24	01	01
Carpenter	Miles		Mrs	1878	Se	21	01	06	Case	H	N	Bro	1871	Ap	30	01	07
Carpenter	Raymond			1875	Jl	13	01	03	Case	H	N	Dr	1871	Ap	25	04	02
Carper			Mr	1877	Oc	13	01	05	Case	Hiram	M		1871	Se	09	01	03
Carr	A	B		1871	Se	08	01	03	Case	John	P	Mr	1852	Jl	23	03	06
Carr	A	W	Ldm	1877	No	25	01	04	Casey	John			1879	My	15	01	03
Carr	James		Mr	1838	Fe	07	03	05	Casey	John		Mr	1875	Jn	19	01	03
Carr	John		Mr	1832	Mr	28	03	05	Casey	John		Mrs	1875	Jn	19	01	03
Carr	Louisa	B		1867	No	05	07	02	Casey	Richard			1879	My	15	01	03
Carr	Martha	J	Mrs	1878	Fe	07	04	05	Casey	Susan	G	Mrs	1871	Au	11	04	03
Carr	Samuel			1868	Mr	17	03	05	Casey	Thos			1879	Fe	12	01	02
Carr	Sylvester			1875	Jl	10	01	05	Casgill	W	H		1879	Au	31	01	01
Carr	T	J		1878	Se	22	04	03	Cash	Annie	D		1879	Oc	14	01	01
Carr	T	J		1878	Oc	02	04	04	Cash	Jack			1878	Mr	31	01	06
Carr	W	M		1878	Se	14	01	04	Cash	John			1878	Oc	20	01	04
Carraway	J	E		1874	De	27	04	02	Cashar			Pvt	1876	Jl	09	01	05
Carray	David			1878	Mr	14	04	04	Cashell	Jas			1878	Oc	03	01	03
Carrick	H	W		1841	Mr	24	03	06	Cashin	John			1878	Au	10	01	03
Carrick	Robecca			1841	Mr	24	03	06	Cashman	James			1871	Jl	04	01	04
Carrigan	Mike			1878	Se	05	01	03	Casic	Charles			1877	Se	16	01	04
Carrington	Robert			1845	Mr	21	04	05	Casine	Charles	S		1877	De	23	01	05
Carrol	John		Maj	1867	Se	03	03	03	Casler	Keeper			1877	No	24	01	07
Carroll	Charles			1832	De	12	02	03	Casselberry	A	Q		1871	Se	17	01	04
Carroll	J	H	Dr	1874	Jl	01	01	01	Casserly	William			1873	Ja	24	01	06
Carroll	John		Dr	1874	Jl	02	04	03	Cassidy	John			1873	Fe	09	01	07
Carroll	John	H	Dr	1874	Jl	01	04	02	Casson	James			1878	Ap	23	04	03
Carroll	John	H	Dr	1874	Jl	01	04	05	Castanedo	Gustave			1871	Fe	05	03	01
Carroll	John	H	Dr	1874	Jl	01	04	07	Castanova	Julia			1879	Se	04	01	01
Carroll	Joseph	S	Mr	1835	Jl	21	03	06	Castelberg	Ida			1872	Mr	23	04	05
Carroll	Lucy		Mrs	1876	Ap	08	04	07	Castelburg	A			1879	Au	03	08	06
Carroll	W	C		1872	My	23	01	04	Castello	William			1879	Au	19	01	01
Carroll	W	H		1873	Fe	05	01	07	Castine	Gustave			1877	De	05	01	04
Carroll	White			1876	My	30	01	02	Castle	H	B	Mr	1871	Jl	13	01	08
Carroll	William			1875	Oc	08	01	02	Castle	K			1877	No	18	01	05
Carroll	William	J	Bro	1871	Ap	30	01	07	Castle	William			1873	Se	28	01	05
Carruth	Sly			1871	Jl	11	01	03	Castle	William	B		1872	Fe	29	01	03
Carsoft	Charles		Ldm	1877	No	25	01	04	Castlept	Taylor			1874	Jl	07	01	08

Last	First	MI	Ttl	Yr	Mo	Day	Pg	Col	Last	First	MI	Ttl	Yr	Mo	Day	Pg	Col
Castley	James	H		1875	Jn	26	01	03	Chandler			Sen	1879	No	06	01	03
Castling	Frances	R	Mrs	1849	Au	16	03	03	Chandler			Sen	1879	No	14	05	01
Castro			Gen	1875	Jl	20	03	01	Chandler	Andrew	J		1876	De	23	04	04
Caswell	Alex		Upr	1878	Ja	09	03	02	Chandler	Benjamin	L	Dr	1857	Jn	06	03	02
Catchings	Eugene			1876	No	04	01	04	Chandler	Elizabeth		Mrs	1836	My	31	03	04
Cates	Isaac	T		1857	Jl	25	03	03	Chandler	George	B	Col	1858	Fe	20	03	03
Cates	Isaac	T	Mr	1853	Ap	22	03	06	Chandler	J	F		1878	Au	30	01	04
Cates	Robert			1874	Ja	08	03	01	Chandler	John			1832	No	07	03	05
Catesby			Cpt	1878	My	25	04	04	Chandler	John	G		1872	Ap	16	01	03
Catharina	Cordelia		Mrs	1871	Ap	25	01	04	Chandler	L	M	Rev	1871	No	06	01	02
Catherine			Sis	1878	Se	22	04	03	Chandler	N			1872	Au	11	01	06
Catlin	Seth			1871	Jl	18	01	02	Chandler	Polly		Mrs	1831	Ap	06	03	04
Cato	M		Mss	1872	No	30	01	03	Chandler	William			1878	Se	11	01	05
Catron	R	R		1878	Se	25	01	04	Chandler	William			1878	Se	22	04	03
Cattaci	Micheal			1877	No	24	01	06	Chandler	William		Dr	1872	Jl	23	01	03
Cattaro	Pete			1879	Au	26	01	01	Chandler	Zach			1879	No	06	01	03
Catterson	Robert	F		1873	Oc	16	04	07	Chandler	Zach			1879	No	22	05	01
Caughler	John			1875	Jl	03	03	01	Chandler	Zachariah			1879	No	14	01	02
Caulk	Mary	E	Mrs	1853	My	06	03	07	Changarnier			Gen	1878	Ja	09	03	02
Causin	Gerard	N	Col	1848	Jl	13	03	04	Chapin	Owen			1871	Ap	22	01	03
Causine	Elenor			1876	Ja	09	04	05	Chapman	Benjamin			1874	Jl	01	01	01
Cavanaugh			Pvt	1876	Jl	09	01	05	Chapman	Chas			1878	Ja	20	01	06
Cavanaugh	George			1878	Fe	09	04	06	Chapman	Chas		Qum	1877	No	25	01	04
Cave	Catherine		Mrs	1836	De	27	03	03	Chapman	Epaphras		Rev	1825	Mr	08	03	01
Cave	Richard	C	Mr	1834	My	20	03	04	Chapman	G	E		1878	Se	18	01	07
Cavenaugh	Pat			1879	Au	20	01	01	Chapman	Granville	P		1837	De	19	03	05
Cavender	Florida		Mss	1878	Mr	29	03	07	Chapman	J	J	Mrs	1873	Mr	09	01	06
Caverrick	Henry			1876	Oc	04	01	01	Chapman	Johnson		Mr	1868	Se	01	01	02
Cawl	Susan			1871	Jn	28	01	04	Chapman	Josephine	F		1879	Se	12	08	06
Caycey	Nick			1871	My	24	01	03	Chapman	Thomas			1878	Oc	01	01	04
Cayschart	J	D		1878	Oc	09	01	03	Chappel	E	D		1872	Au	09	01	07
Celite	J			1878	Se	22	04	03	Chappell	F	A		1875	My	18	03	01
Cellars	Andrew		Mr	1859	No	12	03	03	Chappelle	William			1870	Se	30	01	01
Cellars	Fred	L	Mr	1869	My	02	02	05	Chapple	R	S		1873	Oc	19	04	03
Cespedes			Prs	1874	Mr	05	01	05	Charity	Sister			1878	Oc	18	01	03
Cespedes	Pedro			1873	No	08	01	03	Charles			Kng	1872	Se	20	01	05
Cespedes	Pedro			1873	No	23	01	05	Charlescraft	S	F	Mr	1838	Se	05	03	04
Cespenez	Fidel		Col	1876	Se	21	01	03	Charley	Boston			1873	Oc	04	01	03
Chades	Lizzie			1879	Au	26	01	01	Charley	English			1874	Mr	10	03	01
Chadesky	Albert			1878	Au	31	01	05	Charley	Henry	F		1872	Mr	03	01	04
Chadwick	Bill			1876	Se	26	01	04	Chartiers			Cpt	1870	My	04	03	01
Chadwick	William	H	Mrs	1875	My	07	03	01	Chase			Cj	1873	My	10	01	01
Chadwicks	William		Mac	1877	No	25	01	04	Chase			Cj	1873	My	10	01	02
Chaeyni	Thomas	J	Mr	1836	Au	30	03	01	Chase			Cj	1873	My	11	01	01
Challen	James		Rev	1878	De	10	01	01	Chase			Cj	1873	My	13	01	01
Chamberlain	Caroline	G		1879	De	31	08	04	Chase			Cj	1873	My	15	01	02
Chamberlain	Cora		Mss	1878	Oc	20	01	04	Chase	Arthur		Mr	1838	Oc	10	03	04
Chamberlain	Della			1878	Oc	19	01	03	Chase	C	J		1874	Ja	08	01	02
Chamberlain	Jacob			1878	Oc	06	01	06	Chase	Cornelia			1851	Ap	04	03	06
Chamberlain	Jason		Esq	1820	Au	12	03	01	Chase	Ella			1878	Au	14	01	06
Chamberlain	Staples		Mr	1820	Au	26	03	02	Chase	L	S		1879	Ap	17	04	05
Chamberlain	Stephen			1872	Jn	26	01	03	Chase	Luther			1854	Oc	13	03	05
Chamberlain	T			1873	Se	10	01	04	Chase	Philip	P		1841	Jl	07	03	02
Chamberlin	Chas	N	Mrs	1878	Oc	15	01	03	Chase	Rosina		Mrs	1851	Jn	20	03	05
Chamberlin	Richard	H		1879	Jl	25	05	01	Chase	S	P	Cj	1873	My	17	01	04
Chambers	Arthur			1876	Jn	06	04	01	Chase	S	P	Cj	1873	My	22	01	02
Chambers	Benjamin	S	Col	1833	Oc	16	03	05	Chase	William	G		1853	De	23	03	06
Chambers	Jack			1876	My	26	02	03	Chase	William	H	Lt	1871	Jl	18	01	05
Chambers	James	A	Cpt	1839	Ja	16	03	03	Chatfield	Andrew	J	Hon	1875	Oc	05	01	03
Chambers	Ned			1879	Jl	26	01	01	Chauler	John	W	Con	1877	Oc	21	01	05
Chambers	Samuel			1878	Mr	23	04	04	Chauncey	Isaac		Com	1840	Fe	26	03	05
Champlain	Robert			1879	Se	27	04	04	Chaundey	John	S	Com	1871	Ap	12	01	03
Champlin	Thomas	H	Mr	1851	Au	15	03	07	Chawanga				1876	Jn	11	03	01
Chancellor	William			1879	Jn	03	06	01	Cheatham	John	W		1858	Oc	23	03	03
Chander				1873	No	15	03	01	Cheatham	Thomas	A		1858	Oc	23	03	03
Chandler			Sen	1879	No	02	01	01	Cheatham	William		Mr	1840	My	20	02	05

Last	First	MI	Ttl	Yr	Mo	Day	Pg	Col	Last	First	MI	Ttl	Yr	Mo	Day	Pg	Col
Chedill	John	H	Gen	1875	Jn	22	03	01	Clanton			Gen	1817	No	19	01	02
Cheek	G	A		1878	Se	22	04	03	Clanton	James	H		1871	Se	29	01	04
Cheek	William			1871	Jl	19	01	03	Clanton	Stephen		Esq	1821	Mr	31	03	03
Cheery	W	P	Mrs	1878	Oc	20	01	03	Clapp	Levi			1873	De	06	01	03
Cheever	Langdon	A		1878	Se	28	01	04	Clapton	Nicholas	B	Dr	1833	Jl	24	02	03
Cheeves	J	A		1878	Se	26	01	04	Clardy	Benjamin		Bro	1875	Oc	08	05	04
Cheiars	C	E		1871	Jn	06	01	04	Clare	Harry			1878	Au	27	01	04
Chenault	Fannie		Mrs	1878	Fe	13	04	06	Clare	Samuel			1878	Se	18	04	04
Chenowith	Charles			1878	Se	12	01	06	Clarin	Edward			1874	Ap	05	01	04
Cherna			Pvt	1876	Jl	09	01	05	Clark			Mr	1871	De	08	01	03
Cherot	Leonie			1879	Au	08	01	01	Clark			Mr	1872	Se	01	01	06
Cherry	Anna		Mrs	1867	Oc	08	03	03	Clark			Mr	1874	Jl	24	04	02
Chesebro	Caroline			1874	Ja	08	01	02	Clark			Mrs	1870	No	01	01	02
Chew	Beverly		Esq	1851	Ja	31	03	06	Clark	A		Dr	1879	Jl	08	01	02
Chidester				1874	Jl	31	04	02	Clark	Aaron		Mr	1855	De	21	03	06
Chidester	Arvelia	C		1872	My	25	04	05	Clark	Abraham		Mr	1851	Jn	13	03	06
Child	Alonzo		Mr	1873	Jn	07	04	02	Clark	Ada			1872	Ja	18	04	04
Childers	H	F		1859	Ja	15	03	02	Clark	Andrew			1872	Jl	13	01	04
Childress	Robertson		Gen	1839	Au	21	03	05	Clark	Ann		Mrs	1874	Ja	03	01	03
Childress	Robertson	W	Gen	1839	Au	14	03	05	Clark	Barney			1878	Se	05	01	03
Childress	Samuel		Esq	1828	Se	09	03	02	Clark	Charles		Gov	1877	De	21	01	06
Childs			Cpt	1876	Se	20	01	03	Clark	Charles	J	Mrs	1873	Mr	30	01	03
Childs	Alexandar	M	Pay	1877	No	25	01	04	Clark	Daniel	A	Mr	1839	Se	11	03	02
Childs	Cephas	G	Col	1871	Jl	09	01	06	Clark	David			1879	De	07	08	05
Childs	Cornelius			1878	Au	10	01	03	Clark	Devine			1878	Ap	07	01	04
Childs	Isaac			1878	Mr	24	01	04	Clark	E	B		1878	Au	16	04	05
Childs	Jacob			1878	Mr	24	01	04	Clark	Eddie		Mr	1878	Oc	19	01	03
Childs	Jerry			1878	Mr	24	01	04	Clark	G		Mrs	1873	Mr	30	01	03
Childs	John	V		1872	Ja	19	01	03	Clark	George			1878	Oc	19	01	06
Chiles	N	R		1871	De	24	01	04	Clark	George	A		1873	Fe	15	04	01
Chilton	R	H	Gen	1879	Fe	19	01	03	Clark	Harriet	J	Mrs	1834	De	16	03	03
Chinn	Mary			1877	De	11	04	05	Clark	Horace	F		1874	Ja	08	01	02
Chipman	John			1873	Mr	06	01	06	Clark	Horace	F	Mr	1873	Jn	21	01	02
Chism	Elizabeth	G	Mrs	1856	Ja	26	03	07	Clark	Infant			1879	Au	13	08	04
Chism	James	D		1858	No	20	03	01	Clark	J	D		1872	Fe	03	01	03
Chism	Logan	H		1877	Oc	18	04	05	Clark	J	N	Ldm	1877	No	25	01	04
Chism	Pessica	P		1851	Se	19	03	03	Clark	James			1871	My	24	01	03
Chism	Stephen	H		1852	Ap	30	03	07	Clark	James		Esq	1838	My	23	03	03
Chisson				1876	Fe	18	04	02	Clark	James		Hon	1852	Fe	20	03	07
Chittenoen	Walter			1878	Au	11	01	03	Clark	James		Mr	1877	No	13	04	05
Choate	Lucinda		Mrs	1867	No	19	03	02	Clark	James	A		1871	Jl	18	01	05
Chochechuma				1841	Ja	27	03	04	Clark	James	M		1868	Fe	18	03	04
Chomail				1877	Oc	20	01	05	Clark	Joseph		Mr	1852	Oc	22	03	05
Chotcay	Louis	P	Mr	1831	Jn	22	03	01	Clark	Julia			1820	Se	16	03	03
Choteau	Auguste		Mr	1829	Mr	25	03	03	Clark	Keller			1872	Jl	07	01	06
Chouteau	Auguste	A	Esq	1836	Au	02	03	05	Clark	Lewis	G		1874	Ja	08	01	02
Chow	Chon			1878	No	07	04	04	Clark	M	A	Mrs	1876	Se	22	03	01
Chrisman	Mary	F	Mrs	1870	Ap	26	02	04	Clark	Marean	B		1877	Se	29	04	05
Christi	R	C	Rev	1878	Oc	17	01	04	Clark	Nathan		Maj	1836	My	10	03	06
Christian	Richard			1875	Jn	13	01	03	Clark	S	M	Mrs	1878	Se	17	01	04
Christian	Rosa			1879	Au	06	01	03	Clark	S	R		1878	Se	21	01	04
Christmore	Mat			1879	Ap	10	04	02	Clark	Samuel		Frm	1877	No	25	01	04
Christopher	Cap			1874	My	06	01	07	Clark	Thomas		Mr	1876	Oc	05	02	03
Christy	W	S	Mr	1873	Jn	18	01	03	Clark	Virginia		Mrs	1879	Se	06	05	03
Chuck	William		Mrs	1872	Oc	17	01	03	Clark	W	A		1878	Oc	20	01	04
Church	M	E		1878	Se	10	01	03	Clark	W	B	Eng	1878	Oc	06	01	03
Church	Mary			1878	Mr	22	01	06	Clark	Wayne		Mr	1871	Se	26	01	02
Church	Rodney			1871	My	30	01	04	Clark	William			1872	Jl	26	01	04
Churchhill	Alexander	P	Col	1878	De	13	04	03	Clark	William	H		1871	My	23	01	03
Churchill	Abbie		Mss	1876	Fe	18	04	03	Clark	William	P		1868	Ap	07	03	04
Churchill	Abbie		Mss	1876	Fe	23	04	05	Clark	William	R		1871	Au	23	01	04
Churchill	Abbie		Mss	1876	Mr	04	04	04	Clark	Winane		Mr	1840	Au	19	03	05
Churchill	Ambrose	S		1860	Ja	14	03	02	Clarke			Mr	1873	Jn	24	01	04
Cissna	W	A		1879	Oc	21	06	01	Clarke	Arthur		Esq	1831	Se	07	03	01
Claiborne	George			1876	Fe	13	04	03	Clarke	Charles	C		1878	Ja	09	03	02
Clair	Saint		Gen	1871	Jn	24	01	02	Clarke	E	H	Dr	1878	Ja	09	03	02

Arkansas Gazette Obituary Index
University of Arkansas Libraries, Fayetteville

Last	First	MI	Ttl	Yr	Mo	Day	Pg	Col	Last	First	MI	Ttl	Yr	Mo	Day	Pg	Col
Clarke	George	S		1859	Jn	04	03	01	Cluskem	Mike	W	Col	1873	Ja	16	02	03
Clarke	Harriet	C	Mss	1840	No	04	03	05	Clyburne	Archibald			1872	Au	24	01	05
Clarke	J	L	Mrs	1878	Se	18	01	07	Clyster			Mr	1873	De	18	01	03
Clarke	Jennie	P		1879	Mr	21	01	05	Coate			Mss	1876	De	10	01	04
Clarke	Lorenzo	N	Col	1845	Mr	21	04	05	Coates	Dick			1875	No	27	04	03
Clarke	Mary		Mrs	1845	Fe	03	03	05	Coates	John		Mr	1835	Jn	30	03	05
Clarke	Oliver	S		1878	Se	25	01	05	Coats	John			1871	Se	27	01	04
Clarke	Richard			1839	Se	11	03	02	Cobb	C	L	Con	1879	My	01	01	03
Clarke	Rose			1879	My	04	01	03	Cobb	C		Mr	1872	Mr	26	04	03
Clarke	Susan		Mss	1851	Jn	20	03	05	Cobb	Charles			1879	My	21	05	01
Clarke	T	C	Mr	1870	Au	21	04	03	Cobb	Frank			1872	De	31	02	02
Clarkson	William		Cpt	1833	Oc	09	03	05	Cobb	Samuel	K	Mr	1834	Fe	25	03	03
Clatyon	Glove			1875	Oc	08	05	02	Cobbett	William			1878	Ja	13	01	05
Clay	Henry			1846	Se	07	03	06	Coblewtz	Marion	V		1871	No	19	04	04
Clay	Joseph	W	Col	1853	Mr	18	03	07	Coburn	Frank			1873	De	07	01	04
Clays	William	T		1840	De	16	03	03	Cocheciser	John			1878	Ap	14	04	06
Clayton	David		Frm	1877	No	25	01	04	Cochran			Dr	1870	Oc	12	01	01
Clayton	Glove			1875	Oc	08	05	04	Cochran	D	M	Rev	1873	Mr	11	01	05
Cleaveland	L			1847	Se	02	03	06	Cochran	Dudley	M	Rev	1874	Ap	06	04	06
Cleaves	Ernest			1878	Se	22	04	03	Cochrane	Catherine			1876	Fe	29	04	05
Clemens	Lloyd		Mrs	1878	Ap	06	01	05	Cochrane	D	M	Rev	1873	Mr	04	01	04
Clemens	Naomi		Mrs	1833	My	01	03	04	Cochrane	Daniel			1872	No	15	01	03
Clemens	William			1877	Ja	03	01	04	Cochrane	Richard	E	Dr	1854	Oc	06	03	06
Clements	Emma	V		1858	Oc	09	03	03	Cock	Ellen			1878	Se	04	01	03
Clements	J			1879	Au	12	01	01	Cocke	Elizabeth		Mrs	1835	Jn	02	03	05
Clements	Jacob			1879	Au	15	01	01	Cocke	John	H	Dr	1837	No	07	03	05
Clements	Jimmy		Unc	1878	Ja	24	03	01	Cocke	Mary	E	Mrs	1847	Fe	13	03	05
Clements	Robert			1873	Fe	20	04	02	Cocke	William	A	Mr	1853	Se	23	03	07
Clements	Robert		Bro	1873	Fe	23	04	08	Cockerill	Davis		Col	1872	Fe	08	01	04
Clements	T	F		1878	Se	22	04	03	Cockrane	David	Y	Mr	1827	Ja	16	03	03
Clemons			Mr	1874	Oc	07	01	05	Cockrell	J		Mrs	1878	No	05	01	03
Clenck	Dwight			1875	My	12	01	04	Codke	Mary	F	Mrs	1836	Se	27	03	05
Clendenin	Elizabeth			1852	Au	20	03	07	Cods	Peter			1876	De	12	01	05
Clendenin	John	J	Hon	1876	Jl	06	04	03	Coe	L	A		1878	Se	22	04	03
Clendenin	John	J	Hon	1878	Mr	08	04	02	Coerrer			Mr	1873	Fe	01	01	05
Clendenin	Mary	E		1878	Mr	08	04	02	Coffee				1877	De	02	01	07
Clendenin	Mary	E	Mrs	1878	Mr	08	04	05	Coffee	John		Gen	1833	Jl	24	02	03
Clenendin	John	J	Hon	1876	Jl	06	01	01	Coffey	George	B	Cor	1837	Au	08	03	03
Cleveland	H	W		1878	Se	04	01	03	Coffin	C	F	Pm	1875	Ap	10	01	04
Cleveland	Henry			1868	Mr	17	03	05	Coffin	Robert	S	Mr	1827	Jn	26	03	04
Clifford	Charity		Mrs	1866	Oc	02	03	01	Coffman				1878	Fe	16	01	08
Clifford	Charles			1866	Oc	02	03	01	Coffman	Clayton			1878	Se	17	01	05
Clifford	James			1878	Jl	13	04	05	Coffman	Jacob			1876	Ap	19	02	04
Clifford	James		Jr	1866	Oc	02	03	01	Coffman	Mary	A		1879	No	05	08	02
Clifford	Julia			1879	Se	07	01	01	Coffman	William	A		1874	Ap	09	04	06
Clifford	Philander	P	Mrs	1875	Ap	13	01	03	Coffroth	James			1872	Oc	11	01	06
Clifford	Robbie			1871	Jl	02	01	01	Cofu	Frank			1873	Oc	04	01	03
Clingman	Peter		Mr	1852	Au	13	03	07	Coggeshall	J	B		1871	My	27	01	03
Clinton			Mrs	1877	No	08	03	03	Coggin			Mr	1873	Jn	21	03	01
Clinton	Andy		Mrs	1871	No	21	01	03	Coggswell	Anthony		Mrs	1874	Mr	07	01	03
Clinton	Charles		Mrs	1873	Jn	01	01	03	Coggswell	M	P		1877	Ja	03	01	04
Clinton	Dewitt		Gov	1828	Mr	26	03	02	Coghlan	John	W	Con	1879	Mr	27	01	03
Clinton	Fraklin		Mr	1842	Mr	23	03	02	Cohen	H		Mrs	1878	Oc	20	01	03
Clinton	George		Vpr	1875	De	02	02	02	Cohen	Harris			1878	Oc	11	01	03
Cloatier	Amelia			1879	De	16	01	03	Cohen	Samuel			1878	No	17	01	02
Clok	P	C	Mrs	1878	Jn	09	04	07	Cohn	Louis			1879	Ap	16	04	03
Clopton	Abraham		Mr	1862	Oc	11	02	05	Cohn	Rapuael	F		1858	Oc	30	03	02
Closen	John			1878	Se	03	01	04	Cohuitt	Francis			1877	De	07	01	07
Cloud	H	W	Dr	1875	My	06	01	03	Colbert	Nathan			1871	No	03	01	04
Cloud	Joseph	C		1873	Oc	17	01	03	Colbreth	G	S	Sug	1877	No	25	01	04
Clough	Annas		Mrs	1850	Oc	04	03	02	Colby	C	S		1879	Jl	22	01	02
Cloyd	Louis	S		1878	Au	23	01	03	Colby	Eli		Esq	1844	Mr	20	03	04
Cloyes	Carolind	L		1858	Oc	09	03	03	Colden	Cadwalla	R		1839	Jn	12	03	03
Cloyts	Nathan		Mr	1831	My	18	03	05	Cole			Mr	1870	Oc	16	03	01
Cluck	William		Mr	1873	Ja	01	01	02	Cole	Charles			1872	Se	25	01	04
Cluck	William		Mrs	1873	Ja	01	01	02	Cole	Charles			1872	Se	26	01	04

Last	First	MI	Ttl	Yr	Mo	Day	Pg	Col
Cole	Frank			1876	Ja	01	05	02
Cole	Fred			1878	Se	22	04	03
Cole	George			1872	My	25	01	01
Cole	George		Dsh	1872	No	03	04	07
Cole	George	W		1873	No	18	05	03
Cole	Gertrude			1878	Au	27	01	04
Cole	Ira		Frm	1878	Fe	16	01	08
Cole	Mary		Mrs	1878	Se	01	01	03
Cole	Merriman			1873	Jn	06	01	02
Cole	Racheal		Mrs	1878	Au	23	01	03
Coleman			Dr	1878	Oc	15	01	04
Coleman			Mr	1871	Se	23	01	02
Coleman	Abraham	B		1879	Jl	23	01	03
Coleman	Ben			1878	Se	11	01	05
Coleman	Ben			1878	Se	22	04	03
Coleman	E			1878	Se	22	04	03
Coleman	Frank			1879	De	27	01	03
Coleman	Gus			1878	Se	22	04	03
Coleman	James			1877	De	12	01	04
Coleman	William	B		1866	Au	18	03	04
Coleman	William	H	Dr	1827	Oc	23	03	03
Coligham	Thomas			1871	Oc	03	01	02
Colkin	Thomas			1874	Mr	27	01	03
Coll	Jos	F	May	1878	Se	04	01	04
Collamer	Jerome			1874	Ap	16	01	03
Collen	William	H		1878	Mr	12	01	06
Collier			Mss	1878	Se	04	01	03
Collier	Clarence			1869	Jl	27	02	03
Collier	Thomas			1871	Se	23	01	03
Collier	Tom		Col	1872	Oc	11	01	07
Collin	Gilbert			1872	De	31	01	03
Collins			Dr	1875	Jl	11	04	02
Collins	Charles			1877	Ja	21	01	03
Collins	Clay		Mr	1871	De	19	04	05
Collins	Clay		Mr	1871	De	20	01	03
Collins	E	K		1878	Ja	24	01	05
Collins	George			1878	Mr	23	04	04
Collins	Isaac	C		1879	Jl	31	05	02
Collins	James			1878	Se	26	01	04
Collins	James		Mr	1873	De	14	01	03
Collins	James	C		1871	Jn	10	01	03
Collins	Jeremiah			1878	Au	21	04	07
Collins	Jimmy			1876	No	17	04	04
Collins	Jimmy			1876	No	18	04	03
Collins	John			1878	Au	27	01	04
Collins	John			1878	Oc	13	01	04
Collins	John		Cpm	1877	No	25	01	04
Collins	John	B		1853	Fe	11	03	06
Collins	Lizzie		Mss	1879	Au	13	01	03
Collins	Mary	A		1877	De	15	04	04
Collins	N	D	Col	1874	Ja	27	03	02
Collins	O	T		1873	No	18	04	03
Collins	Patrick		Frm	1877	No	25	01	04
Collins	Patrik		Mr	1833	My	01	03	04
Collins	Peter		Mr	1852	Fe	27	03	06
Collins	Peter		Mr	1852	Mr	05	03	06
Collins	Pleasant	B	Cpt	1853	Ap	08	03	06
Collins	Pratt		Mr	1833	Se	11	03	05
Collins	Richard	D	Cpt	1841	Jl	07	03	02
Collins	Thomas	B		1851	Au	15	03	07
Collins	Thomas	N		1858	Jl	17	03	03
Collins	William	S	Mr	1842	Mr	30	03	02
Collum	Roberta			1876	Mr	02	04	03
Collyer			Mr	1871	No	08	02	04
Colston	Aleck			1875	Ja	03	01	05
Colton	Andy			1878	No	09	01	03

Last	First	MI	Ttl	Yr	Mo	Day	Pg	Col
Colton	J	M		1879	Au	23	05	01
Colvert	Sarah		Mrs	1839	Jl	17	03	04
Colville	Andrew		Mr	1821	Mr	31	03	03
Colville	Joseph		Mr	1821	Mr	31	03	03
Colville	Polina			1820	Fe	26	02	04
Colvocoresse			Cpt	1872	Jn	19	02	02
Colwell	Joseph			1877	De	16	01	07
Colyer	Vincent		Mrs	1872	No	02	01	03
Combrisson	Irma			1879	No	22	03	01
Combs	Mary		Mrs	1844	Jn	26	03	03
Compton	Ezra			1879	Ap	04	01	05
Compton	Susan	F	Mrs	1871	De	14	01	04
Conatser	A	J	Bro	1873	De	19	04	05
Conatti	Cecella			1878	Se	05	01	03
Conaway	Isaac	D		1879	Oc	24	01	01
Concha			Mar	1874	Jn	30	01	06
Condin	Mary		Mrs	1878	Oc	29	01	04
Condit	F	M	Bro	1872	Se	20	01	06
Condon	John			1875	Jn	05	01	04
Conefielly	Frank			1879	Ap	22	01	02
Coners	Peter			1873	My	06	01	02
Coney	James			1878	Au	29	01	04
Coney	John			1876	No	07	04	03
Congohle	Frederic			1871	My	02	03	01
Conian	Maggie			1878	Au	29	01	04
Conkerton	John	D		1879	Au	22	01	03
Conklin	Sarah			1875	De	04	01	05
Conkling			Jud	1874	Fe	06	01	05
Conkling	Barnabus		Lt	1839	My	22	03	03
Conkling	F	G	Mr	1871	Ap	05	01	03
Conkling	Walter			1871	Se	01	01	03
Conlan	James		Rev	1875	Mr	10	01	05
Conley	Patrick			1878	No	03	01	04
Connel	L			1878	Au	01	04	02
Conneley	Anna	G	Mss	1871	Ap	11	03	01
Connell	James			1872	Au	21	01	03
Connelley	Haskell			1859	Au	20	03	02
Connelly	Alex			1872	Ap	13	01	02
Connelly	Dennis			1878	Se	05	01	03
Connelly	John	Q		1878	Se	11	01	05
Connelly	Mary			1878	Se	22	04	03
Connelly	Thos			1878	Au	27	01	04
Connely	William	H		1872	Ap	14	04	07
Conner	J			1879	Ap	22	01	02
Conner	Micheal			1871	Se	03	01	05
Conner	Pat			1878	Se	22	04	03
Conner	Thomas	H		1871	De	07	01	02
Conners			Dml	1878	Jl	04	04	06
Conners			Dml	1878	Jl	12	04	05
Conners	Johanna	C		1872	De	20	01	03
Conners	Martin			1877	De	28	01	07
Connolly	Micheal			1878	Mr	09	01	06
Connor	C		Mrs	1878	Se	22	04	03
Connor	Job			1878	Mr	27	04	04
Connor	Matthew			1870	Oc	07	01	03
Connors			Mrs	1877	Ja	20	01	03
Conrad			Sen	1878	Fe	12	04	05
Conrey	May	J	Mrs	1878	Mr	21	01	05
Constance			Sis	1878	Se	22	04	03
Constance	Sister			1878	Se	10	01	03
Contel	Dennis			1878	Se	05	01	03
Convay	William	P	Mas	1877	No	25	01	04
Convers	Cornelius		Mr	1872	Ja	31	04	03
Conway			Mr	1871	Se	05	01	06
Conway	Alfred		Mr	1871	Oc	10	02	03
Conway	Ann		Mrs	1845	Au	18	03	04

Last	First	MI	Ttl	Yr	Mo	Day	Pg	Col	Last	First	MI	Ttl	Yr	Mo	Day	Pg	Col
Conway	Henry	W		1832	Ap	11	03	05	Cooper	E		Mrs	1872	Oc	23	01	04
Conway	Henry	W	Hon	1827	No	13	03	01	Cooper	James		Cgm	1877	No	25	01	04
Conway	Henry	W	Hon	1827	No	20	03	05	Cooper	Jeft			1877	Se	16	04	02
Conway	Hugh			1871	Se	02	01	04	Cooper	John			1872	Ap	26	01	04
Conway	James	R	Mr	1837	Oc	03	03	03	Cooper	John		Mr	1840	Se	02	03	04
Conway	John	R	Dr	1868	Jl	14	03	07	Cooper	Lizzie		Mrs	1867	Oc	15	02	08
Conway	Laura	A	Mrs	1840	No	11	03	02	Cooper	Margaret		Mrs	1877	Ja	24	04	06
Conway	Louisa		Mrs	1840	Oc	28	03	05	Cooper	Margaret		Mrs	1877	Ja	25	04	06
Conway	Margaret	E		1842	De	14	03	03	Cooper	R	J	Ldm	1877	No	25	01	04
Conway	Marry	J	Mrs	1878	Mr	05	04	07	Cooper	Samuel		Gen	1876	De	14	02	03
Conway	Mary	E		1845	No	03	03	03	Cooper	William			1876	Oc	06	01	05
Conway	Pat			1878	Jl	13	04	02	Cooper	William		Rev	1830	Jl	14	03	02
Conway	Peter			1873	Fe	11	04	03	Cooperwood	William			1879	Jl	26	01	01
Conway	Silas	W		1859	Jl	09	03	01	Cooyer			Mr	1871	No	08	02	04
Conway	Susan		Esq	1834	Jl	29	03	04	Copeland	C	C	Rev	1869	De	28	04	03
Conway	Thomas		Jud	1835	Se	29	03	06	Copeless	John			1872	Ja	21	01	03
Conway	Thomas	A	Mr	1834	Fe	18	02	05	Copenhagen	Tobias			1875	Fe	26	01	04
Conwy	William	B	Esq	1852	De	31	03	06	Coper	Nannie	J	Mrs	1867	Oc	29	05	06
Conyngham	John	B	Cpt	1871	Jl	18	01	05	Copland	Francis	L		1848	Jn	22	03	02
Cook			Col	1876	Jl	07	01	03	Coppell	Bettie			1878	Se	22	04	03
Cook			Dr	1878	Oc	04	01	03	Copper	George		Mr	1836	03	08	03	05
Cook			Mrs	1827	Mr	13	03	01	Coppinger	Kate		Mrs	1879	Jl	24	01	02
Cook	A	T		1878	Se	22	04	03	Coppinger	W	C		1879	Jl	22	01	02
Cook	Annie		Mrs	1878	Se	22	04	03	Corbet	Micheal			1877	Oc	07	01	04
Cook	Charles			1874	Ja	01	01	04	Corbett	Joseph			1872	Jl	18	01	04
Cook	Charles			1874	Jl	25	01	07	Corbin	B	F		1874	Jn	27	01	04
Cook	Daniel	P	Hon	1827	No	13	01	07	Corbly	Emily		Mrs	1874	Jn	25	04	03
Cook	Daniel	P	Hon	1827	No	13	03	05	Corby	Charles			1872	Mr	29	01	04
Cook	E		Mrs	1877	Ja	03	01	04	Corcoran	Jane		Mrs	1862	Jn	14	02	04
Cook	Edward	D		1840	Fe	19	03	04	Corcoran	Joseph	B		1874	Jl	09	01	06
Cook	Elljah			1878	Au	30	01	04	Cord	Moses			1872	Au	14	01	02
Cook	John			1835	Au	04	03	05	Cordell	Sallie		Mrs	1867	My	21	03	03
Cook	John			1842	Se	14	03	05	Cordoba	Brigade			1876	Se	28	01	01
Cook	John			1873	No	18	05	03	Cordva	Joseph	E		1879	Jl	08	01	02
Cook	Joseph		Mr	1820	No	04	03	01	Core	John	W		1837	Ja	17	03	04
Cook	Kate			1871	No	23	01	03	Core	John	W		1851	Oc	31	03	07
Cook	Kate		Mss	1878	Oc	08	01	03	Core	Willie			1878	My	29	04	04
Cook	Louis			1879	Au	17	01	03	Coreoran	Delia			1873	Jl	27	01	04
Cook	Michael			1878	Se	05	01	03	Corker	Almer			1872	De	18	02	05
Cook	Pat			1878	My	31	04	06	Corning	Erastus		Hon	1872	Ap	10	01	04
Cook	R	H	Mr	1840	No	18	03	04	Cornlins	Isaac			1879	Se	24	01	01
Cook	R	S		1878	Se	17	04	07	Cornman	W	H		1877	No	11	01	04
Cook	S			1879	Oc	22	01	01	Cornwall	Barry		Mr	1874	Oc	06	01	07
Cook	W		Mrs	1878	Se	22	04	03	Corralles	Antonillo			1872	Au	11	01	06
Cook	W	A	Col	1876	Jl	09	01	05	Corry	Patrick			1871	No	03	01	04
Cook	William		Mrs	1873	My	10	02	03	Corwin	Thomas			1878	Se	22	04	03
Cook	William	L	Att	1842	Mr	16	03	02	Cosby	Robert			1879	Oc	07	01	01
Cooke	Henry			1871	No	06	01	03	Cosgrove	Micheal			1878	Ja	15	01	07
Cooke	Jay		Mrs	1871	Jl	23	01	05	Coshen	J	S		1871	My	21	02	02
Cooke	Stephen			1878	Se	22	04	03	Coshen	Joe			1878	Au	11	01	06
Coolbaugh	William	F		1877	No	15	01	06	Coshen	Patrick		Mrs	1878	Au	11	01	06
Coolbaugh	William	F	Hon	1877	No	17	01	06	Coste	J	J		1874	Ja	08	01	02
Coolbaugh	William	F	Hon	1877	No	18	04	05	Costello	M	C		1878	Se	22	04	03
Cooley	Charles			1871	Oc	18	01	03	Coster	Phillip		Esq	1851	Ap	18	03	06
Cooley	Judge			1873	Jl	02	01	01	Costerman	H	A		1879	My	01	01	03
Cooley	William	H		1871	Oc	24	01	03	Cotten	Alexander	W	Mr	1828	De	28	03	01
Coolidge	Angelina		Mrs	1850	Oc	11	03	07	Cotton	George			1872	De	25	01	01
Coolidge	R	S	Mrs	1859	Au	20	03	02	Cottrel	S	F	Cpt	1874	De	17	04	05
Cooms	J	M	Rev	1875	Ja	01	01	04	Couch	Jacob	J		1837	Mr	14	03	02
Cooney				1878	Au	30	01	04	Couch	James		Frm	1877	No	25	01	04
Coope	Richard	R	Mr	1839	Jl	31	03	04	Coughlin	Katie			1878	Au	10	01	03
Cooper	Amelia			187	Au	29	01	04	Coulder	J	R		1871	Ja	14	04	02
Cooper	Christoph.C	Jr		1872	Mr	26	01	04	Coultas	Mary	B	Mss	1878	Ap	18	01	05
Cooper	Daniel			1876	Se	24	01	02	Coulter	J	R		1871	My	21	02	02
Cooper	Daniel		Mrs	1876	Se	24	01	02	Coulter	James		Mr	1835	Jl	14	03	02
Cooper	Deasey		Sco	1877	No	25	01	04	Council	Hannah	C	Mrs	1852	Oc	08	03	06

Last	First	MI	Ttl	Yr	Mo	Day	Pg	Col	Last	First	MI	Ttl	Yr	Mo	Day	Pg	Col
Countee	Beckie			1878	Se	22	04	03	Crawford	T	S	Jud	1873	Se	10	01	04
Counts	Irbella	E		1859	Oc	29	03	02	Crawford	William	A	Gen	1874	Jn	23	02	03
Courbet	Gustave		Art	1878	Ja	01	01	04	Crawford	William	A	Gen	1874	Jn	25	04	04
Courtney	Robert	J		1874	Ap	11	04	06	Crawford	William	A	Gen	1874	Jl	21	01	06
Couza	Alexander	J	Pri	1874	Ja	08	01	02	Crawford	William	H	Bro	1873	Ja	26	01	07
Covert	J	J	Dr	1878	Oc	25	01	04	Crawley	George			1879	De	07	01	02
Covey	Lucy		Mrs	1853	Fe	11	03	06	Crawley	Jaems			1871	De	22	01	02
Covey	William			1872	No	30	01	03	Crease	Anthony		Mr	1839	Oc	02	03	01
Covington	Martha		Mrs	1874	Ap	28	01	06	Crease	Jaen		Mrs	1872	Ap	14	04	03
Covode	John		Hon	1871	Ja	12	01	01	Crease	John	H	Hon	1872	No	26	04	03
Cowan	Hexana		Mrs	1867	Ja	29	03	04	Creasy	Willaim			1876	Oc	19	02	04
Cowan	John	C	Bro	1872	Ap	21	01	05	Creed	Thos			1877	No	14	01	06
Cowan	Wallace			1873	Se	23	04	02	Creedere	Daniel			1879	Jl	24	01	02
Cowart	Narcissa		Mrs	1878	My	12	03	01	Creeper	E	T		1878	Se	25	01	05
Cowgell	John	K		1852	Jl	30	03	06	Creighton	Henry			1877	De	19	01	08
Cowgill	Addison	J	Mr	1851	My	16	03	07	Crenan	Mary		Mrs	1872	Au	25	01	04
Cox	Abner			1876	De	13	04	02	Crespel				1878	Fe	19	01	05
Cox	Ezekiel	T	Hon	1873	My	20	01	02	Creswell	Arthur	C		1879	Se	14	01	03
Cox	James			1878	Ja	10	01	04	Cricks	Kiddy			1878	Se	22	04	03
Cox	James			1878	Oc	20	01	04	Crier	Joseph			1874	Mr	18	03	01
Cox	James	H		1872	No	26	01	02	Crimmons	John			1879	Jl	19	01	03
Cox	Joseph			1878	Oc	20	01	04	Crindle			Pvt	1876	Jl	09	01	05
Cox	Lueiada		Mrs	1867	Ap	02	03	04	Crinkshaft	James			1878	Se	08	01	03
Cox	Nellie			1879	Jl	29	05	01	Crippen	Schuyler			1872	Mr	03	01	04
Cox	Robert	M		1851	No	21	03	06	Crisfield			Pvt	1876	Jl	09	01	05
Cox	S	R	Mr	1878	No	16	04	04	Crittenden	A	P		1871	My	07	01	06
Cox	Thomas			1875	Ja	03	01	05	Crittenden	A	P	Col	1871	Jn	11	02	03
Cox	Thomas		Jr	1874	My	12	01	07	Crittenden	Ann	M		1835	Jl	28	03	04
Cox	William			1820	Oc	14	03	02	Crittenden	Henry		Esq	1835	Ja	27	03	05
Coyle	Charles			1871	Oc	03	01	02	Crittenden	John			1824	Au	10	03	01
Cozzens	Theodore			1874	Ap	01	01	02	Crittenden	John		Mrs	1873	Fe	11	01	06
Crabb	Henry		Hon	1828	Ja	15	03	02	Crittenden	Morris		Mr	1826	Oc	17	03	01
Crabb	Robert	F	Mr	1830	Se	01	03	03	Critz	John		Col	1875	Se	26	01	02
Crabbe	H	A		1860	De	01	03	01	Crocker	Alvah			1874	De	30	01	04
Crabtree			Col	1876	Fe	15	04	03	Crocker	James	W		1878	Oc	03	01	03
Craft	James	H		1879	Jl	08	01	03	Crocker	Minnie	OJ		1875	Oc	15	04	05
Craft	William			1878	My	31	04	06	Crocker	Sam			1874	Ap	14	03	01
Craig	Jenius	W		1858	Oc	02	03	03	Crockett	Davy			1874	Jn	12	01	01
Craig	Joel		Cpt	1828	Oc	14	03	02	Crockett	John	B	Mr	1871	Ja	11	04	03
Craig	R			1873	No	18	04	03	Crockett	Martha	T	Mrs	1873	Fe	21	04	06
Craig	Robert	E		1837	Se	12	03	04	Croft	Dan		Mrs	1878	Oc	09	01	04
Craigler	Mr			1872	Se	14	01	03	Croft	George	A	Md	1873	Au	02	04	04
Craigler			Mrs	1872	Se	14	01	03	Crone	Benjamin			1879	Se	19	01	01
Crail	C	H		1876	No	14	01	01	Croney	Chanel		Pri	1874	Ja	08	01	02
Cralle	Richard	K		1870	Ap	28	04	02	Cronin	Daniel	V		1879	Au	19	01	01
Crandall	Deita			1878	Oc	04	01	03	Cronin	J	F		1879	Se	24	01	01
Crane			Cpt	1878	Jn	03	04	06	Cronin	John			1877	De	21	01	06
Crane			Cpt	1878	Jl	03	04	06	Crook	Mr			1872	Jl	19	02	04
Crane	Aaron	T	Cap	1819	No	20	03	01	Crook	F	W	Mr	1841	Mr	03	03	05
Crane	Isaac	A		1876	Ap	11	01	05	Crook	Wylie	D		1853	Au	19	03	05
Crane	Newman		Col	1833	Oc	02	03	04	Crosby	A	B	Pro	1878	Ja	09	03	02
Cranford	Samuel	B		1873	Ja	15	01	04	Crosby	Jerry			1871	No	23	01	03
Cranston	Hiram			1877	Se	18	01	04	Crosby	M			1878	Se	22	04	03
Cratton	Jnos			1878	Se	18	01	07	Crosette	C	C		1878	Se	05	01	03
Craug	Allen			1874	Au	18	01	08	Cross	B	F		1877	De	25	03	02
Crawden	George			1878	No	03	01	03	Cross	Charles	F		1857	No	21	03	02
Crawford	Benjamin			1874	Au	14	03	01	Cross	Laura	E	Mrs	1879	No	11	08	06
Crawford	Benjamin			1874	Se	06	01	02	Cross	Nannie	E		1857	Se	26	03	03
Crawford	Bob		Mr	1878	Ap	05	02	04	Cross	Robert			1872	Jn	26	01	04
Crawford	Charles			1872	Fe	14	04	03	Cross	Sam			1879	Au	23	01	01
Crawford	George	W	Gov	1872	Au	08	02	03	Cross	Uriah		Mr	1850	Au	16	03	07
Crawford	Hays		Col	1838	Oc	10	03	04	Croto	A			1878	Se	22	04	03
Crawford	J	S	Jud	1873	Se	10	01	04	Crouch	Charles			1874	Au	28	01	07
Crawford	James	B	Mr	1870	Jn	05	01	03	Crouch	Spencer		Esq	1832	My	02	03	05
Crawford	Jerome	J		1872	My	17	01	02	Crouch	William			1873	Se	20	01	03
Crawford	Rachael		Mrs	1837	De	12	03	03	Crousen	Morris			1878	Se	08	04	05

Last	First	MI	Ttl	Yr	Mo	Day	Pg	Col
Crow	Asa		Mrs	1871	Se	20	04	04
Crow	C	M	Mrs	1878	Oc	20	01	04
Crow	James			1877	No	14	01	06
Crowder	Eliza	A	Mrs	1875	Mr	07	04	04
Crowders	Infant			1878	Se	22	04	03
Crowley	Jack			1879	Ja	28	01	04
Crowley	William			1871	Se	13	04	04
Crown	John			1874	Se	19	01	05
Crozier	J	M		1878	Jl	13	04	02
Crugblan	Mary			1878	No	10	01	04
Cruger			Mrs	1875	Jl	04	03	01
Cruikshank	George			1878	Fe	03	01	06
Crump			Dr	1876	Se	20	03	01
Crump	William			1878	Se	12	10	03
Crupper	Henry			1879	Oc	23	01	01
Crupper	Henry	W		1879	Oc	24	01	01
Crutcher	R			1878	Se	22	04	03
Crutchfield	Eliza	A		1839	Jn	19	03	03
Crutchfield	Elizabeth			1878	De	12	04	06
Crutchfield	Harriet	F		1841	Oc	13	03	04
Cruttenden	S	W	Dr	1874	Jn	16	04	04
Crwoley	William			1871	Se	14	01	03
Cryer	Morgan		Mr	1833	No	06	03	05
Cucke	John	H	Dr	1828	Se	09	03	02
Cuilley	William			1873	Jn	06	01	02
Culbreth	G	S	Sug	1877	De	02	01	07
Cullen			Mrs	1878	Au	08	01	05
Cullen	William			1871	No	11	01	03
Cullins	Mary		Mrs	1867	De	31	02	06
Cullum	Newt			1878	Ap	05	02	04
Cully	D	A		1878	Se	13	01	04
Cumbaa	David		Mr	1839	Ja	02	03	04
Cummings			Con	1879	Jl	18	05	01
Cummings			Mr	1871	De	16	01	02
Cummings			Mr	1871	De	22	01	02
Cummings	George	D	Rev	1876	Jl	02	01	03
Cummins	Alex			1878	Se	08	01	03
Cummins	Ebenezer		Esq	1857	Mr	14	02	02
Cummins	Francine		Mrs	1835	Jn	23	03	04
Cummins	Henrietta		Mrs	1878	Fe	05	04	03
Cummins	R	A	Dr	1874	Ap	13	01	02
Cummins	William		Esq	1843	Ap	12	03	03
Cumminsky	John	A	Frm	1878	Mr	13	04	03
Cune	Paul			1878	Se	10	01	03
Cune	Paul			1878	Se	22	04	03
Cunningham	Ann			1873	Au	12	01	02
Cunningham	Catherine	M		1823	Oc	23	03	01
Cunningham	Chester	A	Esq	1856	De	27	03	03
Cunningham	Edward		Mr	1851	Ap	04	03	06
Cunningham	Eliza		Mrs	1856	Se	13	03	06
Cunningham	Ellen		Mrs	1879	Au	17	01	01
Cunningham	Frank			1878	Jl	06	03	03
Cunningham	Frank			1879	Au	16	01	01
Cunningham	Isaac		Mr	1822	Jl	09	03	02
Cunningham	J			1878	Se	22	04	03
Cunningham	John			1871	Oc	26	01	04
Cunningham	John	M		1845	Mr	10	03	04
Cunningham	L	B	Esq	1869	De	07	04	01
Cunningham	Leroy	B		1869	De	08	04	01
Cunningham	M		Dr	1835	My	05	03	04
Cunningham	Matthew		Dr	1854	Jn	30	02	04
Cunningham	Matthew		Dr	1856	Se	13	03	06
Cunningham	Mike	J		1878	Au	25	01	04
Cunningham	Reuben			1875	Fe	11	04	02
Cunningham	Robert	E	Esq	1870	My	05	04	02
Cunningham	Sallie		Mrs	1856	Oc	18	03	06
Cunningham	Wiley			1877	De	25	03	02
Cupes	Frank			1876	Oc	13	01	03
Cupples	Samuel		Mr	1828	My	07	03	01
Curant	Jennie			1878	Au	30	01	04
Curnett	Louisa		Mrs	1867	Oc	29	05	06
Curralto	Antonio			1871	My	06	01	03
Curran	James	M		1854	Oc	13	02	06
Curran	Jane		Mrs	1825	Ja	18	03	01
Curran	Katy			1874	Jl	31	01	06
Curran	Thomas		Esq	1826	Ap	18	03	02
Curran	Thomas		Mrs	1824	De	14	03	01
Curran	Woodson			1875	Mr	04	04	03
Currey	John			1878	Au	08	01	05
Currier	Israel	J		1878	No	16	01	04
Currin	James		Mr	1821	Mr	31	03	03
Currin	Lemuel	R	Esq	1821	Mr	17	03	01
Curry			Gov	1878	Jl	31	01	04
Curry	Dan			1878	Se	22	04	03
Curry	Jesse			1872	Se	10	01	02
Curry	John			1872	Oc	27	01	02
Curry	John		Frm	1877	No	25	01	04
Curry	John		Frm	1877	De	02	01	07
Curry	Samuel			1878	Oc	21	01	03
Curtin	E	J		1872	De	27	01	03
Curtis	C	C		1879	Mr	04	04	05
Curtis	Sarah		Mrs	1840	Au	05	03	05
Curvew	W	H		1875	Jn	22	01	04
Cushing	Caleb			1879	Ja	07	01	03
Cushing	H	B	Lt	1871	Jl	18	01	05
Cushman	Charlotte			1876	Fe	19	01	02
Cushman	Charlotte			1876	Fe	22	01	06
Custer			Col	1876	Jl	07	01	03
Custer			Gen	1876	Jl	07	01	03
Custer			Gen	1876	Jl	08	01	01
Custer			Gen	1876	Jl	09	01	05
Custer			Gen	1877	Oc	11	01	06
Custer	T	W	Col	1876	Jl	09	01	05
Cutler	Fred		Jr	1879	Jn	27	05	02
Cutter	Alphens		Mr	1878	Ja	03	04	05
Cutter	C	D		1875	Mr	14	04	07
Cutter	Charles	S		1875	Mr	14	04	07
Cutting	B	D		1878	Se	22	04	03
Cuttle			Pvt	1873	Au	26	01	03

D

Last	First	MI	Ttl	Yr	Mo	Day	Pg	Col
Dabbs	Thomas	A		1879	Se	30	01	01
Dade	F	H	Mr	1872	Fe	08	01	03
Daggett	Frank			1876	Oc	15	01	03
Dago			Mr	1817	Oc	20	01	03
Dahl	Frank	W		1879	Se	09	01	01
Dahra	A			1878	Se	22	04	03
Dailey	Infant			1878	Au	10	01	03
Daishermer	Alexander			1878	Oc	21	01	03
Daken	Thos	H	Gen	1878	My	15	04	06
Dakin	Thomas		Mgn	1878	My	17	01	09
Daley	John			1879	Jn	27	05	02
Daley	Martin			1872	Ap	20	01	03
Daley	Mary			1878	Se	05	01	03
Daley	P			1878	Se	05	01	03
Daley	William			1878	Au	20	03	02
Dallas			Cor	1876	Jl	09	01	05
D'Alliers	Achille		Cnt	1878	Jn	07	04	07
Dallimore	Emily		Mrs	1837	Fe	14	03	06

Last	First	MI	Ttl	Yr	Mo	Day	Pg	Col	Last	First	MI	Ttl	Yr	Mo	Day	Pg	Col
Dallingandbu			Bar	1872	Jn	02	02	05	Davenport	J	L		1878	Jl	04	04	02
Dallmail	John			1878	Se	22	04	03	Davenport	Samuel		Mr	1824	Oc	26	03	01
Dally	Phillip	H	Mr	1831	Jl	06	03	05	Davenport	William	H	Mr	1872	Oc	12	01	04
Dalstrom	Charles			1878	Au	29	01	04	Daverger	Louis			1878	De	01	01	01
Dalstrom	Frank			1878	Au	29	01	04	Davias	Emily	V	Mrs	1839	Au	28	03	05
Dalton	Elizabeth			1878	Se	01	01	03	David	Benjamin			1871	My	20	01	03
Dalton	G	T		1878	Ap	24	04	06	David	Benjamin			1871	My	21	01	05
Dalton	Maggie		Mrs	1878	Se	05	01	03	Davidson	C	B		1874	De	04	01	06
Dalton	Tom			1879	Oc	17	01	01	Davidson	David		Mrs	1829	De	30	03	02
Dameron	James			1878	Mr	14	01	05	Davidson	Elizabeth		Mrs	1875	Fe	28	04	06
Dana	Infant			1873	My	10	02	03	Davidson	Frank			1879	Jl	10	01	01
Dana	Richard	H		1879	Fe	06	02	01	Davidson	Frank			1879	Se	16	01	01
Danborn	Charles	L		1875	Jn	19	03	01	Davidson	G			1872	No	03	01	04
Dandridge	J	W		1879	Au	26	01	01	Davidson	George	W		1871	No	15	04	05
Danford	Peter			1877	Oc	07	01	04	Davidson	John			1872	Ja	05	01	03
Danials	John	W		1878	Mr	02	01	04	Davidson	John	F		1879	Oc	21	01	01
Daniel	Edward	B		1874	Mr	27	01	03	Davidson	Joseph	R		1877	Oc	16	04	04
Daniel	Elisha		Mr	1838	No	28	03	05	Davidson	Samuel	S	Esq	1873	Jl	18	01	02
Daniel	John		Mr	1825	Ja	25	03	01	Davidson	W	E	Hon	1853	Jn	03	03	07
Daniel	Joseph	C	Mr	1852	Fe	13	03	07	Davies	Anthony	H		1863	Au	29	02	03
Daniel	Lucy	A	Mrs	1867	No	05	07	02	Davies	Gerret			1879	Se	16	01	01
Daniel	Robert	B	Hon	1872	Fe	09	02	02	Davies	R	P	Rev	1871	Mr	09	03	01
Daniel	Robert	S		1822	Fe	09	03	03	Davis			Mr	1822	Jl	30	03	02
Daniel	Sadalia	K		1867	Oc	08	03	03	Davis			Mr	1873	Fe	02	04	04
Daniel	Wright		Mrs	1822	De	17	03	01	Davis			Mrs	1827	Mr	13	03	01
Daniels	George		Mrs	1874	Jl	03	01	01	Davis			Ram	1878	Ja	09	03	02
Daniels	M	S		1872	Ja	26	01	02	Davis	A	M	Mss	1878	Se	22	04	03
Daniels	Tom			1874	No	21	01	05	Davis	Alexander			1879	Oc	02	01	01
Daniels	W	A		1868	Ap	07	03	04	Davis	Alexander	W		1849	Jl	12	03	05
Danley	Christopher	C	Cpt	1865	Oc	07	02	02	Davis	Almea		Sco	1877	No	25	01	04
Danley	Eleanor		Mrs	1840	No	18	03	04	Davis	Amelia			1868	Ap	07	03	04
Danley	Eliza	P		1841	Ap	14	03	04	Davis	Aquila		Mr	1839	No	13	03	02
Danley	James		Col	1844	Mr	20	03	04	Davis	Benjaman	M	Mr	1868	Ap	07	03	04
Danley	James	M		1862	Jn	07	02	05	Davis	Byron			1878	Se	22	04	03
Danley	John	F	Mr	1845	Oc	20	03	03	Davis	C	C		1878	Se	22	04	03
Danley	Mary	A	Mrs	1879	Mr	22	04	02	Davis	Catharine	F	Mrs	1856	Oc	04	03	04
Danley	Samuel	W	Mr	1855	No	02	03	06	Davis	Catharine	F	Mrs	1856	Oc	18	03	06
Danley	William			1867	No	05	07	02	Davis	Charity			1878	Se	22	04	03
Dansby	Joshua			1878	Jn	13	03	01	Davis	Clarissa			1878	Se	12	01	06
Danso	H			1878	Se	22	04	03	Davis	Clem		Mr	1873	Jn	03	01	01
Danton	Edwin			1871	Jl	20	01	05	Davis	Dolly			1878	Se	05	01	03
Darboy			Abp	1871	Jn	08	01	05	Davis	Dorothy		Mrs	1869	Au	14	02	03
Darby	Jennie		Mss	1878	Se	05	01	03	Davis	Elizabeth			1835	Jl	28	03	04
Dardeane	Amelia	G		1852	Jl	23	03	06	Davis	Elizabeth		Mss	1840	Oc	28	03	05
Dardenue	Joseph		Mr	1838	Mr	21	03	01	Davis	Elizabeth	C	Mrs	1849	Mr	29	03	04
Darey	Frank			1878	Au	25	01	04	Davis	Emma			1879	My	31	05	02
Dargis	Adolph			1879	Se	12	01	01	Davis	Florence			1878	Au	25	01	04
Dargis	Charles			1879	Oc	01	01	01	Davis	Garret	B		1852	De	24	03	06
Dargis	Joseph			1879	Se	14	01	10	Davis	Garrett			1872	De	11	01	03
Dargis	Mary			1879	Se	11	01	01	Davis	Garrett		Sen	1872	Se	27	02	04
Darlin	Joseph			1877	Se	23	01	04	Davis	Garrett		Sen	1872	De	17	01	04
Darling	James		Mr	1839	Oc	16	03	05	Davis	George	A	Mrs	1878	No	27	06	03
Darmstadler	J		Mrs	1878	Oc	04	01	04	Davis	H	A		1878	Au	23	01	05
Darrow	George	W		1871	Oc	05	01	07	Davis	Infant			1876	Mr	04	04	04
Darwin	Minerva	B	Mrs	1869	Mr	21	03	01	Davis	James	W		1874	Fe	06	01	05
Dashiell	M	H	Mrs	1878	Se	26	01	04	Davis	Jane		Mrs	1878	Jl	16	04	02
Daugherty				1857	Au	08	03	03	Davis	Jeff			1873	Jl	29	01	05
Daugherty				1878	Fe	20	03	01	Davis	Jeff	C	Gen	1879	De	03	05	02
Daugherty	Amanda	B	Mrs	1859	No	12	03	03	Davis	Joe		Mr	1871	Jl	14	04	04
Dauls	Jeff		Jr	1878	Oc	18	01	03	Davis	John			1878	Se	05	01	03
Davage	Jimmie	T		1867	No	19	03	02	Davis	John		Bro	1868	Au	04	03	04
Davbigny	Charles	F	Art	1878	Fe	22	01	05	Davis	John		Mr	1841	Ap	14	03	04
Davenport	Edvard	L	Act	1878	Ja	09	03	02	Davis	Joseph	S		1872	De	18	01	04
Davenport	H	K	Cpt	1872	Au	21	01	04	Davis	Lizzie			1878	Ja	03	01	05
Davenport	J	L		1878	Mr	10	02	04	Davis	M	A	Mrs	1878	No	10	04	06
Davenport	J	L		1878	Jn	04	04	02	Davis	M	E	Dr	1870	Ap	10	02	04

Last	First	MI	Ttl	Yr	Mo	Day	Pg	Col	Last	First	MI	Ttl	Yr	Mo	Day	Pg	Col
Davis	Maria			1879	Oc	14	01	01	Decamp			Mr	1873	Ja	23	01	05
Davis	Marshall			1879	Jn	24	05	02	Decamp	John		Ram	1875	Jn	25	01	02
Davis	Mary			1878	Se	22	04	03	Decan	George			1878	Se	20	01	04
Davis	Mollie			1879	Se	20	01	01	Decane	George			1878	Se	19	01	04
Davis	Motier	L	Mr	1870	Ja	23	04	02	Decartis	Mary			1878	Se	05	01	03
Davis	R			1879	Ap	22	01	02	Decarvallo	Herculano			1877	Se	16	01	04
Davis	R	P	Rev	1871	Mr	01	04	05	Decatur	John	B	Col	1832	No	28	03	04
Davis	Robert			1879	No	12	05	01	Decatur	Stephen		Cdr	1820	My	20	03	03
Davis	Sam			1878	Au	23	01	03	Decavalier			Mr	1875	Fe	19	01	03
Davis	Samuel	B	Maj	1834	De	23	03	04	Decay	Jerry			1874	Ja	01	01	02
Davis	Starr			1873	De	07	01	04	Dechamp	Parson		Rev	1871	Au	17	01	01
Davis	Susan	A		1846	Ap	20	03	05	Dechamp	S	C	Rev	1871	My	04	01	02
Davis	Theo		Jr	1873	No	29	01	02	Dechamp	S	C	Rev	1871	My	05	01	02
Davis	Thomas	F	Rev	1878	De	12	02	02	Decher	Richard			1878	Oc	24	01	04
Davis	William		Dr	1878	Fe	02	01	06	Decker			Pro	1878	Au	15	01	04
Davis	William	A		1846	Ap	27	03	05	Decker	Eliza		Mss	1878	My	15	04	03
Davis	William	H		1870	My	04	03	01	Decourney	Andrew		Mr	1852	Ja	09	03	06
Davis	Woodbury	Hon		1871	Au	15	01	04	Dedrick	Bob			1879	Ja	17	04	03
Davison	Willie			1871	Oc	08	04	04	Deener	Addie		Mrs	1868	Ja	28	03	05
Daviss	Larus			1873	No	29	01	02	Defenner	Adam			1879	Mr	27	01	02
Daviss	Theo			1873	No	29	01	02	DeGoicouria			Gen	1870	My	14	03	01
Davy	Charles	J		1878	Oc	10	01	03	Degran	Annie			1879	My	24	05	01
Dawson			Mrs	1878	Se	22	04	03	Deguersy	Margaret		Mrs	1878	Oc	15	04	02
Dawson	Alice		Mrs	1860	My	05	03	01	Deguersy	Margaret		Mrs	1878	Oc	15	04	06
Dawson	Annie			1878	Se	05	01	03	Degursey	Carrie		Mrs	1870	Se	14	01	04
Dawson	Dick			1878	Jl	06	03	03	Deitrich	Fred			1879	Se	18	01	01
Dawson	Ellen	S		1868	Fe	11	03	04	Dekovan			Dr	1879	Mr	23	01	04
Dawson	G	R	Dr	1878	Se	26	01	04	Dekovan	Jas		Rev	1879	Mr	20	01	04
Dawson	George			1878	My	02	01	06	Del Sol	Jesus			1873	No	23	01	05
Dawson	Henry	F	Mr	1850	No	15	03	07	Delafield			Gen	1874	Ja	08	01	02
Dawson	J	B	Col	1852	No	26	03	06	Delafield	Edward		Dr	1875	Mr	03	03	01
Dawson	James			1877	De	25	04	04	Delafield	Henry		Mr	1875	Mr	03	03	01
Dawson	James		Cap	1874	Mr	27	01	02	Delafield	Joseph		Maj	1875	Mr	03	03	01
Dawson	John			1878	Se	18	01	07	Delaney			Mrs	1878	Se	22	04	03
Dawson	John	W	Col	1872	Ap	30	01	03	Delatere			Gen	1875	My	04	01	04
Dawson	Pascall			1879	My	29	01	02	Delauch	James	C	Mr	1844	No	20	03	06
Dawson	William	H		1877	Se	22	04	03	De la Ware			Erl	1874	Ja	08	01	02
Dawson	William	H	Col	1868	De	22	03	03	Delham	William		Gen	1879	Jn	25	04	02
Dawson	Willie	A	Mss	1860	No	03	03	02	Deloach	Harry			1873	Oc	31	01	01
Day	John	M	Mrs	1878	Mr	26	01	06	Delong	Charles	E	Hon	1876	Oc	27	01	01
Day	Lucy	L	Mrs	1878	Mr	27	07	05	Delony	L	W	Mr	1871	Jn	27	01	03
Day	William	H	Rev	1872	Mr	02	01	04	Delorme			Mr	1873	Jn	21	01	03
Daynor	Mary	J		1874	Jl	21	01	05	Deltour	John			1871	Au	10	01	05
Dayton	York			1878	Se	22	04	03	Demarest	Jacob		Mr	1826	Au	22	05	01
D'Caux	Marquis			1875	Ap	25	01	04	Demarsh	Annie	B		1879	No	02	08	05
De Gasparian	Agenor	E	Mr	1871	Jn	06	01	04	Demby	Joseph		Mrs	1879	Fe	16	04	07
De Lescluse	M			1871	My	30	01	03	Deming	Emily		Mss	1873	My	10	02	03
Dea	M			1878	Se	22	04	03	Demmy	Laura		Mss	1878	Se	17	01	05
Deacon	Junior			1878	Se	22	01	04	Dempewolf	Jules			1872	Ap	13	01	02
Deaderick	Edward	D	Mr	1832	Jn	27	03	05	Denan	Norman			1878	Se	22	04	03
Deal	Robert			1872	Au	28	01	03	Denckla	Johnana		Mrs	1852	Ap	09	03	07
Dean	Harry			1879	Fe	01	01	04	Denford	Charles		Mr	1873	Jn	26	03	01
Dean	Julia			1877	Ja	24	03	01	Denger	Jerry			1878	Ja	06	01	05
Dean	Martha	E	Mss	1868	Fe	04	03	05	Denham	Alfred			1875	No	30	04	02
Dean	Sylvester	E		1878	Se	11	04	06	Denig	H		Aeg	1877	No	25	01	04
Dean	William			1873	Au	05	01	04	Denis	Bill		Col	1873	Ja	25	01	04
Deandres	Felix		Rev	1820	No	18	03	03	Denison	Infant			1879	Jl	08	08	02
Deaton	Cora	A	Mss	1874	Oc	09	04	08	Denison	Leonard		Mr	1879	Mr	23	04	04
Deaton	Cora	A	Mss	1874	Oc	13	04	02	Dennis	Decker		Sco	1877	No	25	01	04
Deavers	George	W	Mr	1839	Fe	06	03	04	Dennis	Fanny			1873	My	25	01	02
Debar	Ben		Act	1878	Ja	09	03	02	Dennis	John			1873	Jl	06	01	03
Debaun	Abraham		Mr	1834	Ap	01	03	04	Dennis	Martha		Mrs	1835	Se	29	03	06
Debaun	Celesta		Mrs	1851	No	28	03	07	Dennison	Gilbert		Mr	1831	Ja	12	03	05
Debaun, Sr	James		Mr	1847	Jl	01	03	03	Denry	Alexander	S	Mr	1878	Mr	02	03	01
Debitt	Owen			1878	Jl	23	04	06	Dent	Frederick			1873	De	17	01	01
Debutts	T	R	Mr	1849	Se	06	03	04	Dent	Frederick			1873	De	21	01	04

Last	First	MI	Ttl	Yr	Mo	Day	Pg	Col	Last	First	MI	Ttl	Yr	Mo	Day	Pg	Col
Dent	J	W		1879	Jn	29	01	03	Dickinson	John	F	Mr	1871	My	10	01	04
Dent	Lewis		Jud	1874	Mr	25	01	01	Dickson			Mr	1875	Ap	04	04	06
Denton	William		Mr	1851	Ja	10	03	06	Dickson	David		Hon	1836	Au	02	03	05
Denton	William	F	Esq	1845	Se	08	03	04	Dickson	J	M		1878	Oc	02	04	04
Denzer	John	S		1875	Ap	06	04	03	Dickson	James	S	Mr	1831	Ja	05	03	05
Deopold	Issac			1878	Se	22	04	03	Dickson	John	P		1867	Oc	08	03	03
Depress	Abraham			1878	Oc	11	01	04	Dickson	Josiah			1871	No	28	01	02
Deranage	Michael			1877	De	27	01	07	Dickson	Lucius		Mrs	1878	Oc	11	01	04
Des Maris	Pamelie			1876	De	27	01	04	Dicloux	Frank			1878	Ja	01	01	02
Desbure	Tillie			1877	Se	13	01	06	Diehl	Henry	P		1874	Fe	04	04	04
Descajzi	Giovanni			1875	Mr	17	01	03	Diehl	Lydia			1879	Ja	16	04	09
Deschamp	Parson			1871	Jn	28	01	03	Dieni	Rebecca		Mrs	1870	Mr	17	01	03
Deschamps			Mr	1871	Ap	27	01	02	Diensman	John			1879	Au	27	01	01
Deschamps			Rev	1871	My	17	01	01	Dietrich			Mr	1871	Jl	28	01	04
Deschamps	L'Olive			1872	Se	20	01	05	Dietrich			Mr	1872	Ja	14	04	02
Desha	Ben		Col	1835	De	01	03	01	Diles	Andrew			1872	De	29	01	05
Desha	Robert	M	Cpt	1822	De	10	03	01	Dill	Gordon			1879	Se	11	01	01
Deshaw	George			1879	My	29	01	02	Dillard	Sarah		Mrs	1878	My	09	04	07
Deshler	Frank			1876	Oc	15	01	02	Dillard	Sarah		Mrs	1878	My	25	02	04
Deshler	John	G		1878	Ja	09	01	05	Dillon	Mike			1878	Se	22	04	03
Deshough	Mary			1851	Au	15	03	07	Dimmick	John	D		1873	My	13	01	02
Desineviller			Mr	1872	Se	20	01	05	Dimmitt			Mrs	1871	My	06	01	01
Desmoine	Maggie	C		1868	No	03	03	06	Dimond	James		Mr	1827	Ap	17	03	01
Desmond	John			1877	Ja	14	04	02	Dineck			Mss	1875	My	14	01	04
Desol	Jesus			1873	No	08	01	03	Dinsmore	G	W	Mrs	1875	Ap	13	01	03
Desoto	Hernando			1870	My	18	02	07	Dion			Ceg	1878	Ap	16	01	06
Dessaure	Florence		Mrs	1878	Au	21	01	04	Dirls	William			1878	Se	07	01	05
Destmarcel	E	B		1878	Ja	22	02	03	Dismokes	Carry	B		1858	Jl	10	03	02
Detcher	W	F		1873	Oc	22	01	02	Dismukes	Addie			1867	Oc	01	03	04
Deusier	Jerry			1879	Jl	31	08	06	Ditter	F	J		1870	Oc	28	04	03
Devaney	George			1877	De	27	01	07	Ditter	F	J	Mr	1870	Ap	29	04	02
Deven			Gen	1878	Ap	07	01	06	Ditter	Francis	J		1870	Se	14	04	04
Devenport	John		Mr	1842	Se	28	03	02	Ditter	Francis	J	Bro	1870	Se	15	04	02
Devens	Thomas		Mr	1824	Se	14	03	01	Ditteringed	Amelia		Mrs	1858	Mr	01	03	03
Deveto	John			1879	Se	19	01	01	Dittman	Charles			1874	Au	08	01	06
Devey	Daniel		Frm	1877	No	25	01	04	Divan	John		Mrs	1875	My	04	01	04
Devillemont	Don	C		1823	Au	19	02	01	Diven	C	P	Dr	1873	Jn	29	01	04
Devillemont	Julius	R	Mr	1834	Se	02	03	03	Divers	John		Mr	1835	Se	01	03	06
Devillemont	Virginia		Mss	1835	Se	29	03	06	Dix			Gen	1879	Ap	23	04	04
Devillemsant	J	H		1879	Ap	13	01	01	Dix	E	T	Cpt	1873	Se	02	01	03
Devilleurre	Ufysse	F	Dr	1878	Au	31	01	05	Dixon			Mr	1874	De	30	01	04
Devine			Mr	1871	Jn	02	01	03	Dixon	Archibald			1876	Ap	25	01	05
Devine	Bernard		Mr	1871	Jn	04	01	03	Dixon	George			1874	Se	10	04	02
Devine	Martin			1871	Jl	07	01	06	Dixon	Giles			1874	Jl	26	01	04
Devine	William			1872	Jn	23	01	05	Dixon	Henry	M		1879	Au	21	05	01
Devinney	William	M		1841	Jl	21	03	05	Dixon	Jason		Hon	1873	Mr	28	01	02
Devoto	A			1878	Se	22	04	03	Dixon	L	V	Jud	1878	Se	26	01	04
Devoto	D			1878	Se	12	01	03	Dixon	Louis	L	Mr	1842	Jn	29	03	05
Devoto	D			1878	Se	22	04	03	Dixon	Martha	F	Mrs	1860	Ja	14	03	02
Devries	Rosa			1879	Au	21	01	01	Dixon	William			1878	Jn	08	04	07
Dew	J	C	Mr	1871	No	22	01	01	D'Lagnel	Julius	A	Col	1840	Jn	24	03	04
Dewing	Henry		Hon	1872	Oc	10	01	04	Doaks	Johnny			1878	Se	20	01	05
Dewitt	WashingtonJ		Dr	1852	Mr	19	03	07	Doane	Harmon			1875	Fe	19	01	04
Dewolf	J	M		1876	Jl	09	01	05	Dobbins	Samuel	J	Mr	1840	De	09	02	06
Dexter	William			1878	Jl	23	04	06	Dobelstein	Daniel	E		1872	Ap	23	01	04
Dickens	Charles			1870	Jn	23	02	04	Dobson	James	N	Mr	1875	De	08	03	01
Dickens	Charles			1870	Jl	13	03	01	Dobson	Neely		Col	1831	My	18	03	05
Dickens	Sam		Dr	1870	Oc	13	01	01	Dodd	A	M	Mr	1867	No	19	03	02
Dickens	Thomas		Col	1870	Se	30	01	01	Dodd	Ann			1839	Ja	02	03	04
Dickenson	Elizabeth	M		1879	Jn	26	08	05	Dodd	Sally	A	Mrs	1852	Au	13	03	07
Dickey	Kirkwood		Mr	1834	Ap	22	03	04	Dodd	Thomas	D	Mrs	1824	De	14	03	01
Dickey	Thomas		Mr	1874	Au	05	04	03	Dodge	Emeline		Mrs	1843	Ja	25	03	03
Dickinson	Alexander	D	Cpt	1866	Se	25	03	03	Dodge	Emeline	B	Mrs	1843	Mr	22	03	05
Dickinson	Eliza			1840	No	11	03	02	Dodge	Fannie	A		1855	No	16	03	06
Dickinson	Eliza		Mrs	1840	Se	16	03	04	Dodge	George	J		1878	My	04	01	07
Dickinson	John		Dr	1835	Oc	06	03	05	Dodge	Horace	B	Mr	1872	My	25	04	02

Last	First	MI	Ttl	Yr	Mo	Day	Pg	Col	Last	First	MI	Ttl	Yr	Mo	Day	Pg	Col
Dodge	Israe		Cpt	1838	Au	29	03	04	Dorphin	Angela			1876	De	27	01	04
Dodge	M	K	Mr	1858	Ap	10	03	03	Dorrett	W	K		1878	Se	12	01	03
Dodge	Susan		Mrs	1859	No	26	03	02	Dorris	Martin	W		1849	Jn	14	03	04
Dodson	Elisha			1873	Mr	02	01	03	Dorriss	Robenia	T	Mrs	1842	Se	14	03	05
Dodson	George	W		1853	Jl	15	03	07	Dorsey				1873	Oc	28	01	04
Dodson	Mary	T	Mrs	1871	Se	21	04	04	Dorsey	Fannie			1878	Se	05	01	03
Dodwell	A	F		1878	Oc	11	01	03	Dorsey	Morris	H		1878	Jl	06	02	04
Doe	Billy			1878	Fe	22	04	04	Dortch	Mary	B	Mrs	1872	Ap	10	04	05
Dogan			Pvt	1876	Jl	09	01	05	Doryer	William			1873	Se	07	01	03
Doherty	William	A	Esq	1852	Mr	26	03	06	Dosier			Mrs	1873	Jn	03	01	03
Dohlman	John			1876	My	27	01	04	Doster	Edmund		Mr	1833	No	20	03	05
Dolan	Infant			1872	De	18	01	02	Dotle	James		Mr	1866	Oc	09	03	02
Dolan	James			1879	Au	20	01	01	Dotson	Adams			1877	Se	20	04	03
Dolan	Lizzie			1879	Au	12	01	02	Dotter	Marcus		Mr	1875	Ja	17	04	03
Dolan	M			1878	Se	22	04	03	Dotter	Marcus		Mr	1875	Ja	19	04	02
Dolan	Mary	E		1879	Au	28	01	01	Doty	Henry			1879	Ja	11	01	04
Dolan	Willie			1879	Au	14	01	01	Doubleday	George			1879	Se	19	01	01
Dolive	Robert			1879	Jn	15	04	04	Doubletooth	Jack			1875	Ja	03	01	05
Dolive	Robert			1879	Jn	15	08	02	Dougal	George	W	Col	1872	My	17	02	04
Dolive	Robert			1879	Jn	17	08	02	Dougal	T	A	May	1878	No	19	01	02
Dolley	Samuel	F	Bro	1873	Ja	28	01	05	Dougherty	Annie			1879	Au	26	01	01
Dolley	Samuel	F	Mr	1873	Ja	22	04	03	Dougherty	James	B		1875	Ap	13	01	04
Dolley	Samuel	F	Mr	1873	Ja	22	04	05	Dougherty	Patrick			1874	My	30	01	04
Dolova	Sister			1878	Se	07	01	03	Doughty	Thomas			1877	De	16	01	07
Dolton	John	E		1843	Mr	01	03	06	Douglas	A	O	Mr	1873	Fe	23	01	03
Dominick			Con	1872	No	22	01	03	Douglas	Donald	M		1878	Ap	21	04	06
Donahoe			Pol	1872	Oc	24	01	06	Douglas	Emely		Mss	1832	Fe	08	03	05
Donahoe	John			1871	My	24	01	03	Douglas	Francis		Mr	1820	No	04	03	01
Donahue			Ofc	1872	No	26	01	02	Douglas	Hugh			1876	Ja	16	01	04
Donald	J	V	Jr	1878	Oc	09	01	04	Douglas	John		Mr	1835	De	29	03	02
Donaldson				1878	Se	22	04	03	Douglas	Mary	J		1877	No	24	03	01
Donaldson			Maj	1871	Jn	28	01	05	Douglas	Rose		Mss	1873	Mr	11	01	05
Donaldson	Alexander			1872	De	12	01	04	Douglass			Ofc	1871	Ap	26	01	03
Donavan			Mrs	1879	No	11	01	01	Douglass	B	W		1860	De	01	03	01
Donelson	Andrew	J	Maj	1837	Ja	31	03	05	Douglass	E	L	Mr	1872	My	24	01	03
Donelson	Corinne		Mss	1868	No	17	03	03	Douglass	Elizabeth		Mss	1829	Se	02	03	01
Doneth	Dominco			1874	Ja	08	01	02	Douglass	Henry		Mr	1839	Oc	16	03	05
Donhoff	F	A		1878	Se	22	04	03	Douglass	James	B	Mr	1846	Ja	19	03	01
Donnelly	David			1872	Jn	23	01	06	Douglass	John			1841	Mr	31	03	05
Donnelly	George			1878	Au	22	01	04	Douglass	Marian		Mrs	1857	Se	12	03	04
Donnelly	Minnie	S		1878	Se	01	01	03	Douglass	Martha		Mrs	1847	Jn	05	03	04
Donnelly	Peter	H		1879	Se	23	01	01	Douglass	Mary		Mrs	1858	Jl	17	03	03
Donnelly	Phil			1874	Au	15	01	07	Douglass	W	F	Maj	1879	De	19	01	03
Donnelly	Phil			1877	De	28	01	05	Douglass	William			1859	Jl	02	03	02
Donnely	Edward		Frm	1877	No	25	01	04	Doulin	Michael			1875	Mr	17	01	05
Donner	F	W	Fns	1877	No	25	01	04	Dover	M	S		1870	Se	28	01	02
Donohue			Pol	1872	De	07	01	06	Dow	Frank	L		1875	Jn	19	03	01
Donohue	Samuel			1878	Au	02	04	04	Dow	John	M		1871	Jl	07	01	06
Donohue	Thomas			1870	Se	27	02	03	Dow	Robert			1878	Au	30	01	04
Donovan			Pvt	1876	Jl	09	01	05	Dowd	Anna			1879	Au	15	01	05
Donovan	John		Jr	1878	Au	27	01	04	Dowd	Thos			1879	Ja	15	04	05
Donovan	William			1872	De	28	01	04	Dowdle	Robert			1875	Jl	16	04	02
Donovan	William		Sea	1877	No	25	01	04	Dowell	Austin	W		1879	Au	16	01	01
Doole	Arthur	A	Frm	1878	Jl	11	01	05	Dowell	Robert			1878	Au	30	01	04
Dooley	Benjamin	F	Mr	1854	Jn	02	03	06	Dowell	Thomas			1878	Ap	06	01	05
Dooley	Elizabeth		Mrs	1837	De	12	03	03	Dowling	Thomas			1872	Au	28	01	04
Dooley	George		Mrs	1834	Fe	18	02	05	Downer	Charles	A		1852	Se	24	03	05
Dooley	James		Mr	1833	Au	28	03	04	Downey	John	C		1878	Au	10	01	05
Dooley	Mike			1878	Se	22	04	03	Downey	Joseph			1879	Au	05	01	01
Dooley	Nn	H		1844	Jn	19	03	01	Downey	Maggie			1879	Au	05	01	01
Dooley	Thomas	Col		1829	De	16	03	02	Downey	Thomas			1879	Au	15	01	01
Dooley	Thomas		Mr	1841	Mr	17	03	05	Downie	Ada			1878	Mr	29	04	04
Doolittle			Mss	1871	Se	26	01	03	Downing	Davis	J	Cpt	1871	Jl	18	01	05
Doran	Edward			1874	Ap	06	01	04	Downing	Joseph			1878	Au	14	04	02
Doran	John		Dr	1878	Ja	27	01	07	Downing	Lewis			1872	No	13	01	07
Doraschat	Joseph			1873	Se	07	01	03	Downing	Lewis		Chf	1871	Fe	08	04	02

Last	First	MI	Ttl	Yr	Mo	Day	Pg	Col	Last	First	MI	Ttl	Yr	Mo	Day	Pg	Col
Downs			Mrs	1878	Se	22	04	03	Dudley	William			1878	Ap	04	04	04
Downs	E		Mrs	1878	Au	10	01	03	Dudley	William			1878	Ap	20	01	06
Downs	James			1878	Se	22	04	03	Dudley	William		Mr	1825	My	31	03	01
Doyce	Thomas			1873	Au	01	01	04	Dufaure	Madame			1878	Ap	09	01	06
Doyle	A	G	Mr	1841	Se	01	03	03	Duff	Alex		Rev	1878	Fe	14	04	04
Doyle	Carrie			1879	Au	14	01	01	Duff	Catherine		Mrs	1867	Mr	05	03	04
Doyle	Edward		Rev	1879	Au	05	01	01	Duff	Martha	B		1851	Oc	24	03	07
Doyle	J	N		1873	No	04	01	03	Duff	Sarah		Mrs	1857	Jl	04	03	03
Doyle	J	N	Mrs	1873	No	04	01	05	Duffy	Daniel			1878	Au	28	01	03
Doyle	Jas			1878	Oc	08	01	03	Duffy	James			1878	Au	22	01	04
Doyle	Thomas			1874	Ap	27	01	04	Duffy	Mat		Mr	1878	No	16	04	02
Drake	A	W		1873	Jn	17	01	03	Duffy	Mathew	A		1878	No	17	04	01
Drake	A	W	Mrs	1873	Jn	17	01	03	Duffy	Patrick		Mr	1873	Jn	20	01	03
Drake	Child			1873	Jn	17	01	03	Dugan	Jasper			1871	De	21	01	02
Drake	Dress	H	Gen	1879	Au	12	05	01	Dugan	Jasper			1871	De	21	01	04
Drake	E	H	Dr	1874	No	17	01	04	Dugan	John		Eng	1878	Au	08	01	05
Drake	E	R	Mrs	1873	Jn	17	01	03	Dugan	William	C	Mr	1841	Jn	02	03	02
Drake	Oscar			1878	Oc	15	01	03	Dugger	S			1870	My	04	03	01
Drake	Peter			1878	No	15	01	03	Duke	Joshia	J	Dr	1835	Mr	31	03	05
Drake	Samuel	A	Col	1836	Oc	25	03	05	Dukes	Robert			1878	Se	22	04	03
Draper	James		Mr	1836	Jn	28	03	04	Dulong	Frank		Mrs	1877	Se	20	04	03
Draper	James	B		1874	My	07	04	02	Dumas				1874	Au	08	04	04
Drath	Kate			1876	Mr	02	04	03	Dumas				1874	Au	12	04	03
Drayper	Ben			1878	Oc	13	01	03	Dumas	A			1878	Se	11	01	05
Drayton	Chas	T		1879	Se	27	01	01	Dumhoffe	Henry			1879	Oc	04	01	02
Drayton	Henry			1872	Jl	31	01	06	Dunbar	Robert	T	Col	1839	No	27	03	05
Drenan			Pvt	1876	Jl	09	01	05	Duncan				1871	Jn	02	01	03
Drennen	Catherine		Mrs	1858	De	25	03	03	Duncan			Mrs	1873	Se	07	01	03
Drennen	Emily	R	Mrs	1844	Se	04	03	05	Duncan	Anna	B		1878	Se	22	04	03
Drennen	John		Col	1855	No	02	02	02	Duncan	Arthur			1871	Au	11	01	04
Drennen	Margaret	H		1837	My	16	03	03	Duncan	C	A		1878	Se	22	04	03
Drennen	Narry	C		1871	Ja	20	04	02	Duncan	Charles	D		1854	Oc	27	03	05
Drennen	Will			1875	Jl	15	04	02	Duncan	James		Mr	1853	Fe	25	03	06
Drennen	William			1875	Jl	13	04	02	Duncan	Joseph			1871	My	23	01	02
Drennen	Willie			1875	Jl	14	04	03	Duncan	Lizzie		Mrs	1857	Oc	24	03	02
Drew	Cinderella			1872	No	30	01	03	Duncan	William	C	May	1877	De	20	01	05
Drew	Daniel			1879	Se	21	04	01	Dundas	Robert			1819	De	11	03	03
Drew	Harmon	S	Jud	1870	Jl	16	04	03	Dundon	W	W		1873	Se	02	01	03
Drew	Ida		Mss	1873	My	10	02	03	Dungee	Thomas	H		1872	Au	25	01	04
Drew	Mollie	B		1860	My	05	03	01	Dunham	George		Mr	1874	No	04	01	05
Dreyfus				1873	No	18	04	03	Dunham	George		Mrs	1874	No	04	01	05
Dreyfus	Sam			1878	Oc	01	01	04	Dunham	Jno			1877	De	22	01	06
Driscoil	Martin			1877	Oc	17	03	01	Dunk	Micheal		Ldm	1877	No	25	01	04
Driscoll	Daniel	D		1871	De	23	01	02	Dunkel	Thomas			1879	Jn	25	01	03
Driskell	Peter	W		1866	Oc	16	03	08	Dunkles	James			1872	Au	24	01	06
Dristle	Siegfred			1877	Oc	18	01	06	Dunlap	Thomas		Eng	1878	No	14	04	02
Driver	George		Mr	1873	Mr	15	01	06	Dunn				1873	Se	20	01	03
Driver	George		Mrs	1873	Mr	15	01	06	Dunn			Mr	1874	Jl	12	03	01
Driver	J	J		1873	Jn	17	04	04	Dunn	Anderson			1878	Oc	10	01	03
Drolete	Maria			1876	De	27	01	04	Dunn	Anna	P	Mss	1836	Oc	11	03	04
Drope	Eliza		Mss	1835	Au	11	03	06	Dunn	B	H	Bro	1872	Ap	28	04	05
Drose			Mr	1876	Oc	12	01	02	Dunn	David			1874	Ap	01	01	05
Drumm	Jode			1873	De	07	01	04	Dunn	Edward	H	Mr	1836	Se	27	03	05
Drury	Mattie			1878	Au	21	01	04	Dunn	Icabod		Mrs	1821	Oc	06	03	04
Drury	Mollie	G		1873	Fe	08	04	04	Dunn	Ichabud		Mr	1828	Ja	01	03	05
Drutson			Mrs	1877	Se	15	01	05	Dunn	J			1830	Mr	09	03	03
Du Val	E	W	Maj	1830	Se	22	03	04	Dunn	James			1821	Oc	06	03	04
Dubois	John	V	Col	1879	Au	01	05	01	Dunn	Lewis		Mr	1832	Oc	17	03	04
Dubois	Nicholas			1879	Au	16	01	03	Dunn	Margaret		Mrs	1845	No	03	03	03
Ducan				1873	Oc	15	01	02	Dunn	Michael			1872	Mr	12	01	04
Duchassin			Mrs	1828	Se	23	03	02	Dunn	P	R		1878	Se	17	01	05
Dudgeon	Fredrick			1875	My	21	01	04	Dunn	Patrick			1878	No	23	01	02
Dudley				1877	No	16	01	06	Dunn	R	T	Dml	1873	Au	10	01	02
Dudley	E	L	Mrs	1879	Jn	11	08	02	Dunn	Richard		Mr	1840	Jn	03	03	05
Dudley	Ethelbert	L	Jr	1879	My	08	08	05	Dunn	Thomas		Mrs	1871	Jl	06	01	04
Dudley	Susie	W		1879	Fe	18	04	06	Dunn	William			1874	Mr	26	04	04

Last	First	MI	Ttl	Yr	Mo	Day	Pg	Col	Last	First	MI	Ttl	Yr	Mo	Day	Pg	Col
Dunnigan	John		Mrs	1879	Au	01	01	03	Easly	Kate	E		1860	Jl	21	03	01
Dunsbach	Catherine			1879	Au	21	01	03	Eason	Felix	G	Bro	1871	Mr	10	04	04
Dunsbach	Kate			1879	Jn	28	01	02	East	Alfred			1872	Ja	31	04	03
Dunwell	George			1878	Au	03	04	07	Eastburn	Manton		Bp	1872	Se	13	01	04
Duny	Joseph	C		1833	Se	11	03	05	Eastley			Dr	1878	Oc	31	04	02
Dupanloup			Bp	1878	Oc	24	01	06	Eastman	David			1874	Ap	21	01	06
Dupont			Mrs	1877	No	07	03	01	Easton			Mr	1872	Au	08	01	05
Duprat	Hyoalite			1879	Au	01	01	01	Easton	John		Mr	1878	Se	20	01	05
Dupuy	Alfred		Mr	1839	De	25	03	01	Easton	John	B		1879	Se	06	01	01
Dupuy	J	J	Mr	1871	No	08	04	06	Easton	Philip	L	Mr	1832	Fe	08	03	05
Duran	George			1873	Au	31	01	04	Easton	Rufus		Col	1834	Jl	29	03	03
Durell	Louise		Mss	1874	Jn	19	01	06	Eaton	Annie			1877	No	29	01	07
Durger	Thomas			1873	Ja	14	01	07	Eaton	Frank			1873	Mr	26	01	02
Durham	Ben			1879	Se	13	01	01	Eaton	Mary	J	Mrs	1851	Oc	10	03	07
Durham	Joseph			1877	Oc	30	01	06	Eaton	Rudolph			1879	Jn	26	05	01
Durrit	William			1872	Oc	30	01	03	Eaton	Samuel			1870	My	04	03	01
Durtlee	Lafebre			1877	No	07	01	05	Eave	Mary	A		1878	Au	30	01	04
Dusold	Mary			1879	Au	16	01	01	Eayers	Georgette	M		1878	Au	13	04	05
Dutton	Henry	W		1875	Ap	16	01	03	Eazily			Mr	1877	No	24	03	02
Dutton	Margaret		Mrs	1852	Oc	08	03	06	Ebrich	Fred			1873	Oc	19	04	03
Dutton	Thomas	J		1870	Jl	26	04	04	Echols	Albert			1879	Oc	19	01	01
Duty	George	G	Esq	1834	My	27	03	04	Echter	W	A	Mrs	1874	My	21	01	01
Duty	Jane		Mrs	1834	Fe	18	02	05	Eckart	Ida	J		1871	Se	10	04	02
Duval	Harriet	T	Mrs	1841	Fe	03	03	02	Eckerson	Adelaide		Mss	1840	Ja	01	03	04
Duval	Perry		Dml	1873	No	08	04	04	Eckert	F	F		1878	De	08	01	01
Duvall	Thomas		Mr	1833	Au	07	03	05	Eckhart	Charles		Mr	1873	Ja	03	01	03
Dwight	Addie		Mss	1871	Jn	24	01	02	Eckman	Andrew			1874	Ja	31	01	03
Dwyer	Michael			1879	Au	12	01	01	Eddington	Aug			1878	Se	22	04	03
Dye			Pvt	1876	Jl	09	01	05	Eddington	Haley	S	Esq	1850	Mr	15	03	06
Dye	Catharine			1843	Au	16	03	05	Eddington	William	B		1836	Au	30	03	01
Dye	Squier		Mrs	1850	Au	16	03	07	Eddy	Abbott			1874	Jl	07	01	08
Dyer	A	B	Gen	1874	My	26	02	02	Eddy	T	M	Rev	1874	Oc	08	01	06
Dyer	William		Nr	1832	De	05	03	05	Edelstine	Lyon		Mr	1840	Se	16	03	04
Dyeus	Labna			1852	De	17	03	07	Edgeman	William	M		1871	Oc	03	01	02
Dyke	Albert	S	Mr	1842	Au	10	03	05	Edger	Harrison			1878	Se	28	04	05
Dyke	George	E		1844	Se	25	02	04	Edgerton	James			1879	Jl	06	01	03
Dyke	Robert		Mr	1873	My	10	02	03	Edington	James		Mrs	1837	Se	05	03	04
									Edmond	John			1874	Ja	08	04	03
									Edmonds	Martha	N	Mrs	1840	Fe	26	03	05
		E							Edmondson	John	H		1852	Au	06	03	06
									Edmondson	Samuel		Esq	1866	Oc	16	03	08
									Edmunds			Jud	1874	Ap	07	01	02
Eacker	Charley			1871	My	27	01	03	Edward	C	W	Cap	1874	My	12	01	06
Eagen	W	B	Jus	1878	No	30	01	01	Edwards				1871	My	31	01	02
Eagers	H	H		1871	Oc	01	01	05	Edwards			Mr	1872	Oc	29	01	04
Eagle	Dock			1873	No	08	04	02	Edwards	Alice	K	Mrs	1871	Se	28	04	04
Eagle	R	J		1873	No	08	04	02	Edwards	Ben			1875	No	27	01	04
Eagle	William			1873	No	08	04	02	Edwards	Bettie	A	Mrs	1860	Jl	28	03	02
Eakins				1874	Ap	07	03	01	Edwards	Charles			1878	Oc	18	04	02
Ealheart	Rodney		Mr	1840	Jl	08	03	04	Edwards	E	H	Mr	1871	Jn	11	04	04
Eames	John	O		1872	Au	24	01	06	Edwards	Jackson			1878	Ap	23	01	06
Eams			Mr	1875	Jl	11	03	01	Edwards	James			1878	Ap	20	01	06
Eanes	John	B	Mr	1879	Jl	09	08	06	Edwards	Jast			1878	Ap	04	04	04
Eanes	John	B	Mr	1879	Jl	10	05	01	Edwards	John			1873	Oc	30	01	03
Eanes	Lorena			1872	Se	07	01	04	Edwards	John			1879	Fe	15	01	04
Eanes	W	H		1879	Se	18	01	01	Edwards	Sarah		Mrs	1836	Jn	14	03	05
Earl	Mary		Mrs	1868	Se	22	03	06	Edwards	William		Mr	1824	Au	08	03	01
Early	Giles		Mr	1871	My	10	01	02	Edwin	Adams		Act	1878	Ja	09	03	02
Early	J	T		1878	Se	22	04	03	Egan	Dan			1874	Ap	19	01	03
Early	Joab		Col	1870	My	25	02	02	Egbert	Charlotte	D		1877	Ja	07	01	01
Early	John			1878	Au	22	01	04	Egden			Sgt	1876	Jl	09	01	05
Early	John		Bts	1874	Ja	08	01	02	Eggleston	Johnny			1858	De	11	03	02
Early	John		Rev	1873	No	11	01	01	Egner	Ephemia		Mrs	1858	My	29	03	04
Easler	B	H		1878	Se	22	04	03	Egner	Joseph			1845	De	15	03	01
Easley			Dr	1878	Oc	02	04	04	Egnew	Ruth	E	Mrs	1879	Au	29	01	01
Easley	Kate		Mrs	1860	Fe	18	03	03	Ehardt	Fredrick			1878	Ap	20	01	06

Last	First	MI	Ttl	Yr	Mo	Day	Pg	Col	Last	First	MI	Ttl	Yr	Mo	Day	Pg	Col
Ehrlow	George	W	Pro	1872	Au	06	01	05	Ellis	Redford		Esq	1837	My	02	03	03
Eichenbarger			Mr	1875	De	08	03	01	Ellis	Robert			1872	Jl	06	01	03
Eidler	John	D		1879	Oc	02	05	02	Ellis	S	B		1870	Fe	25	04	01
Eiseman			Pvt	1876	Jl	09	01	05	Ellis	S	M		1876	My	27	01	04
Eisner	Anna	E		1875	My	12	01	04	Ellis	Sara		Mrs	1871	Oc	19	01	03
Elannigan	Hugh		Mr	1852	Jl	09	03	06	Ellis	Silas	B	Mr	1870	Mr	05	04	02
Elbridge	M			1875	Jn	19	01	03	Ellis	Thomas	E		1841	De	08	03	02
Elcher	Conrad			1876	Ja	11	01	04	Ellis	William			1873	De	24	01	03
Elder			Mr	1873	Fe	01	01	05	Ellott			Mrs	1878	Se	22	04	03
Elder	Hontuse			1873	Au	22	01	02	Ellsworth	Edward	A		1837	No	14	03	05
Elder	L	M	Mr	1839	Oc	30	03	04	Elmer	Ed		Mr	1853	Au	12	03	07
Elder	M	N	Mr	1876	Jn	29	04	02	Elmore			Mr	1874	Jl	26	04	04
Elder	Robert			1874	My	03	01	07	Elsner	Herbert			1879	Se	24	01	01
Eldington	C			1878	Se	22	04	03	Elson	Francis			1873	Au	24	01	03
Eldridge	Amos			1878	Se	05	01	03	Elssher	J	E		1873	Se	28	01	05
Eldridge	Infant			1873	Jn	03	01	01	Elvandorf	Edwin			1876	Se	26	01	04
Eldridge	John	S		1876	Mr	26	01	05	Elwood	Charles			1878	No	27	01	03
Eleza	Nicholas			1873	Oc	19	04	03	Emand	John			1879	My	15	01	03
Elgin	Martin			1872	Jl	14	01	05	Emanuel	Victor		Kng	1878	Ja	10	01	03
Eliason	Mary	H	Mrs	1872	Jn	16	02	05	Emanuel	Victor		Kng	1878	Ja	11	01	06
Eliason	Mary	H	Mrs	1872	Jn	19	01	02	Emanuel	Victor		Kng	1878	Ja	15	01	05
Elkins	William	G		1879	Oc	12	01	03	Emanuel	Victor		Kng	1878	Ja	16	04	03
Ella	Ryan			1878	Se	05	01	03	Emanuel	Victor		Kng	1878	Ja	17	01	07
Ellar	John	P	Maj	1878	Se	11	04	06	Emanuel	Victor		Kng	1878	Ja	17	02	01
Eller	Catharine	E	Mrs	1850	Mr	29	03	06	Emanuel	Victor		Kng	1878	Ja	17	04	05
Ellerman	Albert	H		1879	Au	30	08	02	Emanuel	Victor		Kng	1878	Ja	18	01	05
Ellery	William			1820	My	20	03	04	Emanuel	Victor		Kng	1878	Ja	18	01	06
Ellet			Mrs	1878	Ja	09	03	02	Emanuel	Victor		Kng	1878	Ja	23	01	04
Ellioll	Hilliam	G	Mr	1831	Au	24	03	01	Emanuel	Victor		Kng	1878	Fe	01	01	06
Elliot			Jud	1879	Jl	08	01	03	Emanuel	Victor		Kng	1878	Fe	09	02	02
Elliot	A	F		1879	Ap	11	04	04	Emanuel	Victor		Kng	1878	Fe	10	04	06
Elliot	B	F		1879	Jn	20	05	02	Emanuel	Victor		Kng	1878	Fe	12	01	06
Elliot	Charles		Mr	1846	Fe	09	03	05	Emanuel	Victor		Kng	1878	Fe	21	01	05
Elliot	Charles	O		1857	Oc	31	03	03	Emberling	William			1874	No	21	01	02
Elliot	Fannie			1867	Oc	01	03	04	Emberson	George			1877	Oc	04	01	04
Elliot	George	B		1878	Se	14	01	04	Embree	Jordan	N	Hon	1870	Oc	13	04	02
Elliot	George	B		1878	Se	22	04	03	Embry	Arch			1872	Fe	08	04	02
Elliot	J			1871	Jn	25	01	05	Embry	Sallie	M	Mrs	1860	Se	01	03	02
Elliot	J	M	Jud	1879	Mr	27	01	03	Emerson	M	F	Sco	1877	No	25	01	04
Elliot	Joe	H		1878	Se	07	01	03	Emerson	M	F	Sco	1877	De	02	01	07
Elliot	John	M	Jud	1879	Mr	28	01	01	Emerson	Samuel	A	Esq	1851	Oc	03	03	03
Elliot	Katie		Mss	1879	Ja	08	04	05	Emery	Cambell	D	Col	1878	Mr	14	01	05
Elliot	L	Q	Mr	1878	No	06	02	02	Emily	Smith	E	Mrs	1837	Ja	03	03	04
Elliot	W	E		1878	Se	13	01	04	Emmet	Thomas	E		1878	Au	18	04	07
Elliot	William			1879	Au	30	05	01	Engels	Martha	S		1837	No	28	03	05
Elliott	Aaron	P	Mr	1832	Jn	13	03	04	Engleman	John		Col	1877	Se	12	01	05
Elliott	Charles			1871	Au	17	01	04	Engley	John		Mr	1878	Oc	18	02	01
Elliott	Charles		Dr	1852	Oc	08	03	06	Engley	John		Mrs	1878	Oc	18	02	01
Elliott	Elias	A	Mr	1822	Se	17	03	02	English	Ann	E	Mrs	1869	Oc	21	04	03
Elliott	Eugene	W	Cpt	1871	Se	05	04	02	English	Cyrus			1844	Au	07	03	05
Elliott	F	A	Mrs	1854	Se	22	03	07	English	Elizabeth	D		1876	De	23	04	04
Elliott	Fountain	C	Mr	1838	Oc	03	02	03	English	John			1879	Jn	24	05	03
Elliott	G	R		1878	Se	22	04	03	English	John		Esq	1821	De	29	02	01
Elliott	George	W		1862	Oc	18	02	04	English	Julia	A	Mrs	1871	Jn	08	01	04
Elliott	J			1871	Jn	25	01	05	English	Julia	A	Mrs	1871	Jn	10	04	04
Elliott	Robert			1835	Jl	07	03	04	English	Leona		Mss	1869	Oc	21	04	03
Elliott	William		Cpt	1878	Se	22	04	03	English	M	C	Mr	1852	Au	13	03	07
Ellis				1877	De	16	01	08	English	Maria			1879	Au	14	01	01
Ellis			Mr	1874	Jl	28	02	03	English	Noah	D	Hon	1871	Ja	22	03	01
Ellis			Mr	1877	Ja	03	01	05	English	Richard	T	Cpt	1871	Oc	14	01	02
Ellis	Alice			1870	Jl	31	04	04	English	William	W		1861	Jl	20	03	05
Ellis	Dwight			1876	Ap	19	01	05	Engras	Edward	L	Snr	1878	Oc	18	01	03
Ellis	Ellen	M	Mrs	1872	Fe	14	04	05	Engre			Pvt	1876	Jl	09	01	05
Ellis	H	D		1875	Mr	09	04	03	Ennalls	Bartholo		Mr	1825	Au	09	03	02
Ellis	John			1878	My	31	04	06	Ennis	James		Mrs	1873	Mr	09	01	05
Ellis	Rayborn			1878	Au	30	01	04	Ennis	John			1878	Se	18	01	07

Last	First	MI	Ttl	Yr	Mo	Day	Pg	Col	Last	First	MI	Ttl	Yr	Mo	Day	Pg	Col
Ensel	Henry	J		1879	Oc	22	01	01	Evans	John	J	Dra	1877	No	25	01	04
Ensign	E	W		1877	Oc	02	01	06	Evans	L	H		1878	Ap	24	04	04
Ephiras	Alexander		Gen	1875	Ap	15	01	05	Evans	Mary	J		1876	Mr	02	04	03
Eppes	John	W		1823	No	11	03	03	Evans	Nettie		Mss	1876	Ap	12	04	06
Epsy	Robert	L	Mr	1877	Se	12	01	05	Evans	P	W		1878	My	10	01	07
Epsy	Robert	L	Mrs	1877	Se	12	01	05	Evans	S	E	Dr	1840	Se	02	03	04
Erastous			Fat	1878	Se	01	01	03	Evans	Samuel		Cpt	1824	Jl	27	03	02
Erb	Jacob			1878	Se	22	04	03	Evans	Susan		Mss	1876	Ap	12	04	06
Erb	John			1878	Se	14	01	04	Evans	Thomas		Mr	1832	De	05	03	05
Erb	Pellip			1878	Se	22	04	03	Evarts	S	A	Mrs	1878	Au	18	04	07
Ergeton	Robert	L		1879	De	18	01	02	Evarts	William			1878	Ap	27	04	07
Erickson	John			1873	My	14	02	03	Evarts	William			1878	My	01	01	06
Erkhart	Fredrick			1878	Ap	04	04	04	Eve	Paul	F	Dr	1877	No	06	01	04
Erown	Charles		Mr	1872	Au	27	04	05	Eve	Paul	F	Dr	1877	No	08	02	01
Erskine	John			1878	Se	18	01	07	Everett	Charles			1878	Se	12	04	05
Erty	John			1878	Se	22	04	03	Everett	Isaac			1873	Ja	19	01	06
Ervin	William			1878	Oc	17	01	03	Everett	James	P		1874	Jl	12	01	04
Erwin	Edwin	L	Mr	1853	Mr	25	03	06	Ewell	R	S	Gen	1872	Ja	27	01	02
Erwin	Harriet	V		1852	Ap	30	03	07	Ewing	E	B	Hon	1873	Jn	25	02	02
Erwin	James			1876	Ja	16	01	04	Ewing	Frank			1878	Au	27	01	04
Erwin	James		Esq	1853	Ja	14	03	06	Ewing	George		Mr	1871	Jn	28	01	03
Erwin	John		Mr	1851	Oc	10	03	07	Ewing	Henry		Maj	1873	Jn	15	04	02
Erwin	John	M	Rev	1840	No	25	03	05	Ewing	Henry		Maj	1873	Jn	17	01	01
Ery	James	D		1879	Jn	01	01	02	Ewing	Henry		Maj	1873	Jn	17	01	04
Escozo	Katie			1879	Au	02	01	03	Ewing	Patrick			1837	Jn	06	02	06
Eshman	Andy			1874	Jn	30	01	06	Ewing	Thomas			1878	Jl	03	04	06
Eskridge	Cornelius	B	Mr	1830	Mr	30	03	01	Ewing	Thomas		Hon	1871	Oc	28	01	04
Eskridge	Gerard	B	Mr	1822	Jl	16	03	01	Ewing	Thomas		Hon	1871	Oc	29	02	02
Eskridge	Ignotiud	P	Dr	1834	Jn	17	03	05	Ewing	William			1830	Mr	09	03	03
Eskridge	Thomas	P	Hon	1835	De	15	03	01	Eycke	Martin			1878	Se	22	04	03
Espinoza			Gen	1875	Jl	20	03	01	Eyke	M		Mrs	1878	Se	07	01	03
Esselman			Dr	1873	Oc	02	04	02	Eyke	Martin			1878	Se	12	01	03
Essert	Johanna			1871	Fe	18	01	01	Eyre	George		Mr	1872	Se	10	02	06
Essleman			Dr	1873	Oc	04	04	02	Eyrich	Adolph		Rev	1878	Se	06	01	05
Estabrook	Juba		Dr	1851	Au	01	03	06									
Estabrook	Sarah			1851	Au	01	03	06									
Esterbrook			Mrs	1867	Se	17	03	03									
Esterhazy	Charles			1874	Ja	08	01	02					**F**				
Esterhazy	Charles		Pri	1873	Se	13	01	02									
Estes	Walter	D		1878	Fe	23	01	05	Faber			Mr	1873	Oc	15	01	02
Estill	Henderson		1842	Au	17	03	06		Faber	William	L		1873	De	20	04	04
Estill	James		Mr	1836	De	06	03	05	Fagan				1852	Se	17	03	05
Estinger	W	R		1879	Oc	15	01	01	Fagan	E		Mrs	1869	My	04	03	01
Estlin	R	W	Mr	1876	My	11	01	01	Fagan	Mary			1872	De	12	01	04
Eston	Elizabeth	A		1857	Au	22	03	04	Fagan	Mary	A		1872	De	13	01	01
Etheridge	Jim			1879	Au	29	01	02	Fagan	Stephen		Mr	1840	Jn	17	03	01
Eugels	Peter			1878	Se	22	04	03	Fagen	Charles			1878	Au	27	01	04
Eustis	George			1872	Mr	17	01	05	Fahey	John		Rev	1879	Au	07	01	01
Eustis	William		Mr	1825	Mr	22	03	01	Fahold			Pvt	1876	Jl	09	01	05
Evans			Dr	1878	My	12	01	06	Fair			Col	1871	Jn	11	02	03
Evans			Mr	1875	Mr	28	01	01	Fair	J	B		1878	Se	22	04	03
Evans	Albert		Col	1872	De	21	01	01	Fairchild				1878	Se	22	04	03
Evans	Andrew			1876	Ap	12	04	06	Fairchild	Fannie			1855	No	16	03	06
Evans	Belfast	M		1874	Au	20	04	07	Fairchild	John	H		1873	Au	20	01	05
Evans	Benjamin	F	Bro	1870	Au	10	03	01	Fairchild	Remsay			1876	Mr	04	04	04
Evans	Bud			1878	Au	11	01	04	Fairchild	William			1878	Se	21	01	04
Evans	C	M		1877	De	16	01	07	Faires	J	B		1878	Se	11	01	05
Evans	C	M		1877	De	18	01	08	Falconer	Thomas			1878	Se	10	01	03
Evans	Clark			1874	Jn	23	01	06	Falen	John	W		1878	Se	22	04	03
Evans	Curran			1876	Ap	12	04	06	Falk	Lizzie			1879	De	06	01	02
Evans	Franklin	B		1874	Fe	21	01	01	Falkenburg	Sophia			1879	Au	31	01	01
Evans	Gilead			1879	Au	13	05	02	Falkner	J			1871	My	21	02	02
Evans	Isaiah			1878	My	11	01	07	Falley	John			1871	Au	23	01	03
Evans	J	N		1872	Jl	06	01	01	Fallon	John			1872	Jl	21	04	02
Evans	John			1876	Mr	04	04	04	Falls	Lizzie			1878	Se	04	01	03
Evans	John	J		1879	Mr	14	01	02	Falls	Rachel			1878	Se	22	04	03

Last	First	MI	Ttl	Yr	Mo	Day	Pg	Col	Last	First	MI	Ttl	Yr	Mo	Day	Pg	Col
Falls	Walter		Cpt	1874	De	12	01	02	Featherston	W	G		1871	De	10	01	02
Fancher	James		Mr	1867	Fe	19	03	06	Feeny	Mike			1878	Se	22	04	03
Farbish	E	E		1878	Oc	01	04	02	Feild	Jane	M	Mrs	1873	Ja	14	01	07
Farbish	E	E		1878	Oc	02	04	04	Feldtner	Gus			1876	Fe	16	01	05
Farley				1871	Jl	25	01	03	Fell	Edward			1878	Se	01	01	04
Farley			Sgt	1876	Jl	09	01	05	Fell	John	C	Maj	1873	No	23	01	03
Farley	Maria			1835	Oc	27	03	06	Feller	Louise			1879	Ap	08	03	01
Farmer	James			1872	Ap	26	01	02	Fellows	Charles	M		1870	Jn	11	04	04
Farmer	Sallie			1878	Se	28	01	05	Felton	John			1875	Ap	18	01	05
Farmington	William	H		1879	No	12	05	01	Fennel	Calvin			1872	No	21	02	03
Farr			Mr	1870	Oc	12	01	01	Fennel	F	M	Dr	1878	Se	18	04	04
Farr	Howard		Shr	1878	No	20	01	01	Fenner	Richard	H	Dr	1823	Se	30	03	01
Farragut			Adm	1870	Oc	01	01	01	Fenslea	Susie			1878	Se	22	04	03
Farrall	Mike			1878	Oc	18	01	03	Fenton	Joseph			1876	Mr	04	04	04
Farreily	Mary	F		1840	Oc	21	03	06	Fenwick	John			1878	Se	25	01	04
Farrel	Patrick			1878	Se	01	01	03	Ferdinand				1878	Ja	09	03	02
Farrell	Daniel			1835	Ja	20	03	05	Ferebee	George	W	Esq	1838	Ap	11	03	03
Farrell	Hugh	O		1878	Se	22	04	03	Ferebee	Hannah	P	Mrs	1833	De	25	03	02
Farrell	Martha			1878	Oc	18	04	04	Ferguson			Mrs	1832	Ja	25	03	04
Farrell	Mary			1878	Au	22	01	04	Ferguson	A	B		1878	Se	19	01	04
Farrell	Mattie		Mrs	1878	Oc	17	01	04	Ferguson	A	W		1878	Se	19	01	04
Farrell	Thomas			1874	Jn	02	01	05	Ferguson	Alex			1875	Mr	04	04	03
Farrelly	P	A	Lt	1851	Au	22	03	06	Ferguson	C	W		1878	Se	18	01	07
Farrelly	Arbadoo	L	Mrs	1865	Se	30	03	04	Ferguson	Elijah			1875	Fe	16	04	02
Farrelly	Mary		Mrs	1833	Ap	17	03	04	Ferguson	Elijah		Col	1875	Fe	17	01	02
Farrent	Walter			1878	Au	22	01	04	Ferguson	George			1879	De	12	05	01
Farrington	Levi			1871	De	20	01	04	Ferguson	Gus			1878	Ap	20	04	03
Farrington	Rufus	M	Maj	1850	Au	30	03	07	Ferguson	H	W		1878	Se	22	04	03
Farris	J	W	Dr	1878	Se	28	01	05	Ferguson	James		Mr	1834	Oc	14	03	03
Farris	Robert			1875	Ap	14	01	03	Ferguson	Joseph			1879	De	12	05	01
Farriss	Amanda	K	Mrs	1878	Fe	08	04	06	Ferguson	Joseph		Mr	1836	Ap	05	03	05
Farry	William			1872	No	15	01	03	Ferguson	Margaret	D		1832	No	21	03	05
Fasig	Levi			1879	Ap	01	01	03	Ferguson	Mary			1841	Jn	09	03	05
Fass	Samuel	S		1879	Au	07	01	02	Ferguson	William		Sir	1878	Ja	09	03	02
Fatherly	Harriet	M	Mrs	1861	Mr	09	03	03	Fergusos	Jack			1873	Jl	26	11	03
Faucett	John		Jud	1876	Oc	12	02	04	Fern	Fanny			1872	Oc	12	01	03
Faulkner			Mr	1872	Ja	09	01	01	Fern	Fanny			1872	Oc	12	01	04
Faulkner	J			1871	Ja	14	04	02	Fernandes	Juan			1830	Fe	16	02	04
Faulkner	Jacob			1853	Se	30	03	07	Fernandez	Augustin			1871	Se	23	01	03
Faulkner	Laura			1841	Se	08	03	05	Fernandez	Francisco			1875	Jn	22	01	04
Faulkner	Mary	J		1841	Se	08	03	05	Feron	Bernard			1878	Ap	27	04	07
Faulkner	Minnie	P		1866	Se	25	03	03	Feronilly			Mr	1873	Ja	23	01	05
Faulkner	S	C	Mrs	1871	Jn	25	01	06	Ferrell	Benjamin			1873	De	02	04	03
Faulkner	S	C	Mrs	1871	Jn	29	01	04	Ferrell	Mary		Mrs	1833	My	08	02	03
Faulkner	Sanford	C	Col	1874	Au	05	01	01	Ferrier	A			1878	Se	22	04	03
Faulkner	Sanford	C	Col	1874	Au	05	04	05	Ferris	Isaac	H	Rev	1873	Jn	18	01	04
Faulkner	Satly		Mrs	1857	Ja	31	03	03	Ferry			Sen	1875	No	27	01	01
Faulkner	William	H		1862	De	27	02	02	Fessenden	William	P	Sen	1869	Se	10	02	02
Fause	V			1878	Se	22	04	03	Fethke	Louis		Mrs	1873	Ja	01	01	04
Faust	J	W	Cpt	1879	Se	24	08	03	Fick				1872	Ja	16	01	03
Faust	John	W		1879	Se	25	08	06	Fick				1872	Ja	18	01	03
Faust	John	W	Cpt	1879	Se	24	08	06	Fick	Charley			1873	Jn	08	02	03
Favor	George			1872	Se	29	01	05	Fick	H	W	Cpt	1871	Au	13	01	05
Favre	George			1872	Se	13	01	05	Ficke	Charles		Mr	1873	Jn	03	01	01
Fawcett	Amy			1877	Se	12	01	05	Field	Abner		Maj	1831	Se	14	03	04
Fawcett	Benjaman			1868	Oc	27	03	06	Field	Charles	W		1837	Jl	11	02	06
Faxon	Herman			1873	Oc	19	01	04	Field	Mildred			1872	Se	26	04	02
Fay	James	D		1879	Au	09	05	01	Field	Mildred			1872	Se	27	04	02
Fay	Martin			1878	Ja	15	01	07	Field	Mildred			1872	Se	28	01	04
Fay	Patrick			1872	De	15	01	06	Field	Mildred	T		1839	Jl	03	03	03
Fazzi	Louis			1879	Au	30	01	01	Field	Richard			1873	Oc	10	01	02
Fbler	E			1878	Se	22	04	03	Fields	John			1878	Se	10	01	05
Feach	James			1871	No	05	01	03	Fields	Mollie		Mss	1879	Jl	17	08	02
Feagler	Ellsworth			1878	Mr	06	04	05	Fields	Richard		Mr	1875	Jn	30	01	04
Fealt	Henry			1871	Ap	22	01	03	Fields	Thomas		Cpt	1834	Mr	18	07	05
Fearns	William			1877	Ja	05	01	04	Fields	Tip			1874	No	12	01	06

Last	First	MI	Ttl	Yr	Mo	Day	Pg	Col	Last	First	MI	Ttl	Yr	Mo	Day	Pg	Col
Figneras			Mrs	1874	Ap	24	01	03	Fisher	Thomas	P		1878	Mr	29	01	05
Figueras			Prw	1874	Ja	08	01	02	Fisk			Col	1872	Fe	17	01	04
Filkins			Mr	1875	Jl	10	01	05	Fisk	James			1872	Fe	02	01	03
Fillebrown	Samuel		Mr	1833	No	13	03	04	Fisk	James		Col	1872	Fe	29	01	03
Fillingim	Samuel		Esq	1834	Mr	04	03	04	Fisk	James		Jr	1874	Ap	27	01	04
Fillingin	Easter	P	Mrs	1859	Mr	05	03	01	Fisk	James		Jr	1873	Oc	10	01	03
Fillingin	Mary	C		1859	Mr	05	03	01	Fisk	Jim			1872	Au	28	01	04
Fillmore			Prs	1874	Mr	10	01	05	Fisk	Jim			1872	De	19	01	03
Fillmore	Albion	W		1840	Oc	28	03	05	Fisk	Jim			1876	No	22	03	02
Filmore			Prs	1874	Mr	11	02	02	Fisk	Jim		Col	1873	Ja	05	01	03
Filmore			Prs	1874	Mr	13	01	02	Fisk	Jim		Col	1873	Ja	07	01	02
Filmore	Isaac			1874	Ap	08	04	04	Fisk, Jr	James			1872	Ja	09	01	01
Fimple	Isaac		Mr	1876	De	27	04	02	Fisu	Thos		Esq	1823	Fe	11	03	01
Finch	Harry			1873	My	06	01	02	Fitchenal	Lauenia		Mss	1841	De	15	03	05
Findley	Jennie			1878	Se	22	04	03	Fitzgerald			Mr	1872	Mr	23	01	05
Findley	Pattie		Mrs	1879	Fe	18	03	02	Fitzgerald			Mrs	1871	Jl	29	01	03
Findley	William		Mr	1821	Jn	16	03	01	Fitzgerald	W	C		1878	Jl	31	01	04
Finerty			Mr	1875	Mr	30	01	05	Fitzpatrick	David		Col	1873	Mr	26	02	04
Finker	Mary			1872	Ja	05	01	03	Fitzpatrick	William			1879	Au	03	05	02
Finley			Cck	1878	Oc	01	04	05	Fizy	Jean	J		1878	No	07	01	06
Finley	Annie			1878	Se	22	04	03	Flack	Clara			1878	Se	22	04	03
Finley	Helen			1878	Se	24	01	06	Flack	L	B		1878	Se	22	04	03
Finley	Lewis			1875	Mr	06	04	03	Flack	T	J		1878	Se	22	04	03
Finley	Randolph		Mr	1836	Jn	21	03	05	Flack	W	J		1878	Se	22	04	03
Finley	W	F		1874	Ap	04	01	05	Flagg	Sumner		Mrs	1876	De	19	01	04
Finley	William			1872	No	30	01	03	Flago	Fannie			1879	Au	09	01	01
Finn	Edward	T		1841	Oc	13	03	04	Flaherty	Micheal			1878	Ja	15	01	07
Finn	Richard	C		1842	Ja	12	03	03	Flaherty	Morgan			1878	Ja	15	01	07
Finn	Robert	F		1845	Oc	13	03	04	Flanagin	Harris			1874	Oc	25	04	04
Finnerty	Jas			1877	De	22	01	05	Flanagin	Harris			1874	Oc	27	04	05
Finney	Alfred		Rev	1829	Jl	29	03	04	Flanakin	Polly		Mrs	1835	Jl	07	03	04
Finney	Lee		Cpt	1876	Jn	14	01	03	Flanigan	Matthew			1876	Ap	12	04	06
Finnick	J	M		1878	Se	22	04	03	Flannery	Mike			1878	Se	22	04	03
Finnick	L	D	Mrs	1878	Se	22	04	03	Flannigan	Ed			1878	Se	22	04	03
Finnie	F	H		1879	Au	19	01	01	Flarvey	James		Bro	1874	Ja	25	04	06
Finnie	William	S		1877	De	08	01	07	Flatley	Ed			1879	Jl	27	01	01
First	R	F		1878	Se	22	04	03	Fleming	H	W	Mr	1840	Oc	07	03	04
Firth	F	R	Maj	1872	Jn	20	01	05	Fleming	Jesse		Mss	1878	No	05	01	03
Fiseer	Harriet			1875	Ap	30	01	04	Fleming	John	B	Dr	1832	Jn	06	03	05
Fish			Maj	1871	Fe	18	01	01	Fleming	Pat		Mrs	1878	Oc	01	01	05
Fish			Mr	1871	No	16	01	03	Fleming	Robert		Mr	1831	Jn	01	03	04
Fish	Adelaide			1860	Au	25	03	01	Fleming	W	L		1838	No	28	03	05
Fish	David		Maj	1833	My	08	02	03	Flems			Mr	1873	Ja	14	01	04
Fish	John			1876	No	24	04	05	Fleshing	Anna			1879	Au	16	01	03
Fishback	Thomas			1872	Au	27	01	04	Fletch	Elizabeth			1879	Au	07	01	01
Fisher				1871	Mr	07	04	04	Fletch	Jacob			1879	Jl	29	01	01
Fisher				1878	Se	22	04	03	Fletcher			Mss	1876	Mr	30	03	01
Fisher			Mss	1872	De	27	01	02	Fletcher	Caleb	L	Bro	1868	My	19	02	07
Fisher	C	M	Mr	1876	Se	20	03	01	Fletcher	Carrie			1879	Se	12	08	06
Fisher	Charles		Mr	1835	Se	01	03	06	Fletcher	Carroll			1868	No	17	03	03
Fisher	Ella			1875	Fe	11	04	05	Fletcher	Crawford		Cpt	1876	Oc	26	02	04
Fisher	Henrietta			1875	My	02	01	04	Fletcher	Daisy			1878	Au	04	04	07
Fisher	Henry		Mr	1868	Jn	16	03	05	Fletcher	Francis		Mss	1876	Mr	22	03	01
Fisher	Jacob		Mr	1829	De	30	03	02	Fletcher	Henry	C	Col	1879	Se	05	05	02
Fisher	James			1873	Fe	06	01	01	Fletcher	Maggie			1878	Mr	23	04	05
Fisher	James		Mrs	1879	No	07	01	02	Fletcher	Penelope			1859	Jl	16	03	01
Fisher	James	L	Mr	1834	Fe	25	03	03	Fletcher	Richard			1873	Fe	13	04	03
Fisher	Joe	T	Mr	1878	Oc	16	04	02	Fletcher	Thomas	B		1879	Jl	17	08	06
Fisher	John			1873	Jl	27	01	04	Flette	John	W		1878	Ja	04	01	06
Fisher	John		Mr	1835	Fe	03	03	04	Flevry	J	W		1873	Au	19	01	02
Fisher	Louisa	C	Mss	1859	Au	27	03	02	Flint			Mar	1876	No	15	01	02
Fisher	Nancy	E		1839	No	20	03	03	Flint			Mar	1876	No	17	04	04
Fisher	O	S	Col	1874	Au	18	01	07	Flint	C	W	Mr	1867	No	19	03	02
Fisher	Otis		Lt	1820	Jl	15	03	04	Florence	Isaac			1879	No	18	07	01
Fisher	Patrick			1878	Se	22	04	03	Flournoy	Ann		Mrs	1835	Mr	17	03	06
Fisher	Susannah		Mrs	1874	Ja	01	01	04	Flournoy	Mary			1857	No	07	03	02

Last	First	MI	Ttl	Yr	Mo	Day	Pg	Col	Last	First	MI	Ttl	Yr	Mo	Day	Pg	Col
Flournoy	Notley	N	Esq	1837	No	28	03	05	Fort	Joseph	J		1867	Oc	29	05	06
Flournoy	Rosa		Mrs	1876	Mr	21	04	06	Fort	R	W		1878	Se	12	01	06
Flournoy	T	C	Col	1876	Ap	04	01	01	Fortenberry	Absalom		Bro	1872	Jl	31	04	05
Flournoy	Vaux			1874	De	22	01	03	Fortenberry	Henry	M	Mr	1872	Au	01	01	06
Flower	Mamie			1871	Oc	11	04	05	Fory	Elic	F		1872	Jn	22	01	04
Flowns	Jeff			1878	Se	05	01	03	Foster				1871	Jl	11	01	03
Floyd	John	S		1873	Fe	19	01	06	Foster	Arthur			1873	No	21	01	02
Flthian	Hester	F		1878	Se	22	04	03	Foster	Brooker			1875	Fe	28	04	03
Flutey	James			1873	My	25	04	05	Foster	George	H		1841	Fe	03	03	02
Flynn			Mr	1871	Se	06	01	03	Foster	J	W	Mr	1873	My	29	02	03
Flynn	A	D	Mr	1871	No	11	01	01	Foster	Jeff	D		1879	Au	26	01	01
Flynn	Ben			1878	Se	22	04	03	Foster	Jennie			1879	Se	06	01	01
Flynn	D	P		1878	Se	01	01	03	Foster	John		Mrs	1872	De	08	01	05
Flynn	John			1873	My	08	02	04	Foster	John		Prs	1872	Se	03	01	04
Flynn	Patrick			1871	De	22	01	02	Foster	John	J	Gen	1874	Se	03	01	08
Flynn	Thomas			1872	No	09	01	02	Foster	Josiah		Mr	1871	Ja	07	02	03
Flynn	Thomas			1875	De	08	04	03	Foster	Logan	R	Mr	1837	De	19	03	05
Flynt	Stephen	C	Bro	1870	Se	24	04	03	Foster	R	A	Mrs	1872	De	05	01	06
Foe	Daniel			1873	Mr	22	01	02	Foster	Samuel		Mr	1871	Mr	12	03	01
Fogardy	Phillips		Mrs	1870	No	12	01	02	Foster	W	C	Mrs	1879	De	07	01	03
Fogarty	Cancelot		Mr	1878	Ap	12	01	07	Foster	William			1879	Mr	06	04	03
Fogarty	Cancelot		Mrs	1878	Ap	12	01	07	Foster	William		Mr	1871	Ap	05	01	03
Foley			Bp	1879	Fe	19	01	03	Fountain	Matthew		Mr	1879	Jl	27	08	06
Foley			Bp	1879	Fe	26	01	06	Fountain	Wade			1873	No	11	03	01
Foley			Cor	1876	Jl	09	01	05	Fourbach	William			1876	Fe	16	01	05
Foley	Catherine		Mss	1873	My	10	02	03	Fournoy	Emma			1850	Se	27	03	01
Foley	John			1878	Mr	17	01	06	Fowe	Alden			1872	No	26	01	02
Foley	Minnie		Mrs	1879	Oc	16	01	01	Fower	Absalom			1859	Se	10	02	08
Foley	Morgan			1872	Ap	13	01	02	Fowler			Cpt	1876	My	19	01	04
Foley	T	P	Dml	1870	My	04	03	01	Fowler			Mr	1875	De	05	01	06
Fooks	Hiram			1878	Jl	13	01	06	Fowler	Absalom		Col	1859	Jn	11	02	03
Foote	G	W	Dr	1875	Oc	08	05	02	Fowler	Dick		Cpt	1876	My	26	01	03
Fooy	John	H	Maj	1832	No	14	03	04	Fowler	Doc			1872	De	29	01	06
Forbes	Charles			1879	Au	03	01	01	Fowler	Elizabeth		Mrs	1834	De	09	03	02
Forbes	Elma			1879	Au	14	01	01	Fowler	Elvina	D		1842	Oc	26	03	06
Forbes	J	G	Dr	1878	Se	26	01	04	Fowler	Flora		Mrs	1873	Fe	06	04	05
Forbes	Kate			1879	Au	16	01	01	Fowler	Gus		Cpt	1878	Au	11	01	04
Forbes	Nettie			1879	Au	14	01	01	Fowler	Henry	M	Maj	1878	Se	14	01	04
Forbes	William	E		1879	Au	01	01	01	Fowler	J	J		1878	Se	05	01	03
Forbett	Henry	W	Lt	1871	Jl	18	01	05	Fowler	J	S	Mrs	1873	Fe	08	04	04
Force	F	H		1878	Oc	19	02	04	Fowler	John	H	Hon	1873	No	23	04	02
Force	John			1873	No	07	01	03	Fowler	Milton		Mrs	1849	Fe	08	03	04
Ford	James			1878	Jn	21	04	02	Fowlkes	Daniel	A		1879	Se	07	01	01
Ford	James			1878	Jn	25	04	02	Fox	Charlie			1874	Jn	17	01	05
Ford	John	B	Esq	1851	Au	22	03	07	Fox	John		Jud	1874	Mr	24	04	03
Ford	Levi	P		1837	Au	29	03	04	Fox	John		Jud	1874	Mr	31	04	03
Ford	Mose		Mar	1872	Jn	04	01	02	Fox	John	W	Jud	1874	Mr	22	04	03
Ford	S	S	Col	1872	Jn	02	01	02	France	Jenny			1878	Ja	31	01	07
Ford	Sam			1877	No	08	01	06	France	Shirley	H		1879	Au	15	05	02
Ford	Samuel	S	Bro	1872	Jn	05	04	05	Frances	Henry		Maj	1840	Mr	11	03	05
Ford	William	E		1878	Au	29	04	07	Francis			Mr	1872	Mr	06	04	02
Foreham			Mr	1872	De	24	02	04	Francis	Charles			1872	Ja	30	04	03
Foreman	William			1878	Se	22	04	03	Francis	Colvin			1876	Fe	13	01	04
Forrest	Bedford		Gen	1877	Oc	30	01	05	Francis	E	S		1878	Se	22	04	03
Forrest	Bedford		Gen	1877	Oc	31	01	05	Francis	E	S	Pro	1878	Se	13	01	04
Forrest	Bedford		Gen	1877	Oc	31	02	01	Francis	Hannah			1875	My	04	03	01
Forrest	Bedford		Gen	1877	No	01	04	04	Francisco	Peter			1831	Mr	02	03	05
Forrest	Bedford		Gen	1877	No	04	02	02	Francola	F			1878	Se	22	04	03
Forrest	Edwin			1872	De	15	01	05	Frank	Cyrus			1879	Se	20	01	03
Forrest	Emily			1873	My	29	01	04	Frank	Sol			1878	Se	01	01	03
Forrest	N	B		1878	Ja	09	03	02	Frank	Texas			1877	Oc	07	01	05
Forsyth	John			1871	Jl	13	01	03	Frankel				1873	No	18	05	03
Forsythe	George			1879	De	02	01	03	Franklin	Alexander			1879	Au	19	01	01
Fort	James			1878	Se	06	01	05	Franklin	Eleanor		Mrs	1831	De	21	03	04
Fort	Jas			1878	Se	07	01	04	Franklin	F	E		1870	Se	29	01	02
Fort	Joseph	B		1866	No	13	03	03	Franklin	George			1874	Fe	08	03	01

Last	First	MI	Ttl	Yr	Mo	Day	Pg	Col	Last	First	MI	Ttl	Yr	Mo	Day	Pg	Col
Franklin	George			1878	Jn	13	01	06	Fryer	Camandra		Mrs	1851	De	05	03	07
Franklin	John			1874	Mr	29	01	07	Fugh	W	T		1878	Oc	15	01	03
Franklin	John		Sir	1877	De	23	03	02	Fugua	C	F	Mr	1852	Oc	08	03	06
Franklin	Johnny			1873	De	07	01	04	Fulding	Isaac			1879	My	29	01	02
Franklin	Nancy		Mrs	1853	Se	09	03	06	Fulgham	George	S	Mr	1874	Oc	08	04	07
Franklin	Thomas		Esq	1837	Fe	07	03	04	Fuller			Mrs	1874	No	28	04	04
Franklin	Thomas	B	Mr	1829	No	03	03	01	Fuller	Arab		Mr	1825	Mr	08	03	01
Franks			Mr	1876	Oc	12	01	02	Fuller	B	F		1878	Se	08	01	03
Fraver	Louis			1879	Fe	01	04	03	Fuller	Perry			1871	Ja	12	01	01
Frazer	Elizabeth	H	Mrs	1836	No	15	03	02	Fuller	Samuel	W	Jud	1873	Oc	26	01	03
Frazier	Ruth			1878	Se	22	04	03	Fuller	Willeam	H		1877	De	30	01	07
Frebis	Malvina			1873	Oc	26	04	04	Fullerton	C		Mrs	1878	Se	01	01	03
Fredrick	Dent			1874	Ja	08	01	02	Fullerton	Nathaniel		Hon	1872	Oc	30	01	03
Freedman			Mrs	1878	Se	01	01	03	Fulsom	Sampson		Col	1872	Fe	16	04	02
Freedman	Henry			1878	Se	04	01	03	Fulton	A			1879	Jn	28	01	02
Freedman	Lula			1878	Se	05	01	03	Fulton	D		Col	1878	Se	06	04	02
Freeedman	Infant			1878	Se	01	01	03	Fulton	D		Mrs	1878	Se	06	04	02
Freeland	Jasper			1879	Se	24	05	01	Fulton	David		Esq	1843	Au	09	03	06
Freels	Edward		Mr	1841	Ja	06	02	04	Fulton	David	C		1869	Se	26	04	04
Freels	John		Mr	1825	No	22	03	04	Fulton	David	M	Col	1878	Se	10	04	07
Freels	William			1879	Ja	23	04	03	Fulton	E	A	Mr	1871	Au	09	01	01
Freeman	Anne	Y		1855	Jn	22	03	06	Fulton	Edward	P		1870	Se	27	04	04
Freeman	Frances	A	Mrs	1851	Oc	10	03	07	Fulton	Edward	P		1870	Se	28	04	04
Freeman	H			1872	Oc	18	01	05	Fulton	Edward	P	Bro	1870	Se	28	04	04
Freeman	Hamlia		Maj	1842	Au	17	03	06	Fulton	Edward	P	Sgt	1870	Se	27	04	03
Freeman	Infant			1879	My	03	01	03	Fulton	Elizabeth		Mrs	1829	De	16	03	02
Freeman	Oscar			1875	No	27	01	04	Fulton	Hickory			1839	My	01	03	05
Freeman	P	A	Mrs	1867	Se	17	03	03	Fulton	Isabel	H		1851	Mr	21	03	05
Freeman	Richard			1878	De	06	01	01	Fulton	John	D		1865	Au	05	03	02
Freeman	Richard	N		1874	Se	23	04	02	Fulton	John	T	Dr	1842	Se	07	05	04
Freer	Mary	A	Mrs	1866	Oc	23	02	07	Fulton	Maria	E		1839	Ap	10	03	03
Freibolin	Christian		Mr	1872	Mr	13	01	03	Fulton	Mary	J		1835	My	19	03	04
Freidering	J		Mr	1871	De	08	01	03	Fulton	Matilda	F		1835	Fe	17	05	05
Freisch	Mary	I		1867	No	19	03	02	Fulton	Matilda	F	Mrs	1879	Ja	15	04	06
French			Cor	1876	Jl	09	01	05	Fulton	Wallace			1873	Jn	26	04	05
French	Edwin			1878	Se	19	01	07	Fulton	William	R		1863	Jl	04	02	03
French	Henry		Lt	1874	Ja	30	01	04	Funch	Christian	F		1879	De	18	01	02
French	W	S	Mas	1877	No	25	01	04	Furbush	Emma			1879	Jl	11	08	02
Frenzle	Julius	A		1872	Au	13	04	06	Furguson	P	L	Mrs	1857	Mr	14	03	04
Freret	George	A	Mr	1871	Jn	06	01	04	Furlong	William			1876	Oc	08	01	02
Fresaur	Henry			1869	Se	04	02	03	Furst	Sam			1860	Oc	23	02	07
Freshett	Infant			1875	My	15	04	04	Furtherston	Arnold		Jr	1878	Se	12	01	06
Fretwell	William			1878	Au	11	01	04									
Frey	Daniel			1873	Mr	22	01	02									
Friedel	George	W		1868	Ja	21	03	04					**G**					
Friedhoff	Tanna			1871	Au	09	01	03									
Friedhoff	Katarina			1870	Oc	12	01	02									
Friedland	Isaac			1878	Jl	12	04	06	Gabe	B			1878	Se	04	01	03
Friel	James			1879	Au	25	01	02	Gabriel			Sis	1873	Oc	01	01	04
Friend	Henry			1875	My	12	01	04	Gade	John			1877	No	09	04	02
Friend	Henry		Mrs	1875	My	14	01	04	Gaetz	Henry		Mrs	1877	No	11	01	06
Friente	George	R		1876	Jn	08	01	06	Gaff	Jacob			1875	De	01	01	03
Frink	B	B		1874	No	26	01	04	Gaffney	John			1873	Fe	15	04	01
Fristch	Fred			1877	De	15	01	06	Gage	C	N		1876	De	31	01	05
Fritz				1876	De	21	01	03	Gage	Clarence			1877	Ja	03	01	04
Fritz	Henry			1872	No	23	01	04	Gaillard	John		Sen	1826	Ap	11	02	03
Fritz	Lucy	E		1878	Au	30	01	04	Gainer	Jesse	C	Hon	1856	No	29	03	03
Frolich	Henry			1874	Ap	19	01	03	Gaines	Augustus	W		1856	Oc	18	03	06
Froman	Peter			1878	No	12	01	03	Gaines	Barbara	B		1836	De	27	03	03
Frost	Samuel			1876	My	27	01	05	Gaines	Ben	P	Mr	1878	No	21	04	05
Frothingham	Nathaniel		Mr	1825	Mr	22	03	01	Gaines	Edmond	P	Gen	1849	Jn	21	02	03
Fruley	J	C		1879	Mr	16	01	02	Gaines	J	J	Dr	1874	Au	02	03	03
Frunevenson	Charles			1879	Oc	04	05	01	Gaines	Mary			1852	Mr	05	03	06
Fry			Cap	1873	No	15	01	01	Gaines	Mary	T		1856	Oc	13	03	06
Fry	Ann	P		1837	De	05	03	05	Gaines	Richard	M	Gen	1871	Au	16	04	03
Frye	Joseph	F		1879	Au	16	01	03	Gaines	Richard	M	Mr	1866	Fe	24	03	03

Last	First	MI	Ttl	Yr	Mo	Day	Pg	Col	Last	First	MI	Ttl	Yr	Mo	Day	Pg	Col
Gaines	Samuel	J		1846	Fe	09	03	05	Garland	Josiah		Col	1871	Se	05	01	06
Gaines	Sarah	E		1855	Oc	19	03	06	Garland	Mary		Mrs	1879	Oc	12	01	03
Gaines	William	F		1860	Jn	16	03	01	Garland	Rufus	K	Mr	1833	Jl	24	02	03
Gaither	Ransom			1872	Se	21	02	06	Garland	S	V	Mrs	1877	De	25	04	02
Gaither	Ransom			1872	Se	25	01	02	Garland	S	V	Mrs	1877	De	27	04	01
Gall	H			1873	Oc	15	01	02	Garland	S	V	Mrs	1877	De	27	04	02
Gallager	Ambrose			1873	De	02	04	02	Garland	Sarah	V		1877	De	28	04	04
Gallagher	Ambrose			1873	De	02	04	04	Garner	Charles			1872	Se	28	01	04
Gallagher	Charles			1878	Se	08	01	04	Garner	Charles			1872	Oc	05	01	05
Gallagher	George	A		1878	Se	28	04	03	Garner	Josie			1879	Oc	05	01	01
Gallagher	George	A		1878	Oc	01	04	06	Garner	Sam			1875	Oc	15	01	03
Gallagher	George	A	Maj	1878	Se	26	04	04	Garner	William	W	Bro	1875	Ja	12	04	07
Gallagher	George	A	Maj	1878	Se	26	04	06	Garr	A		Mr	1871	Ap	13	04	02
Gallagher	James	C		1875	Fe	26	04	03	Garrett	Curtis			1871	De	21	01	02
Gallagher	Margaret	M	Mrs	1858	De	04	03	03	Garrett	Curtis			1871	De	21	01	04
Gallagher	William			1878	Oc	02	02	05	Garrett	John	J	Mr	1873	Mr	09	01	06
Gallaghers				1876	De	29	01	03	Garrett	Rolla			1871	Jl	12	01	06
Gallahan	Jno			1878	My	01	01	06	Garrett	Virginia	L	Mss	1858	De	11	03	02
Gallaway			Jud	1873	Mr	11	01	05	Garrett	William			1871	Jl	22	01	03
Gallaway	Morton	G	Col	1873	Oc	15	04	04	Garrette	Jesse	B	Hon	1853	Fe	11	03	06
Gallaway	William	J	Mr	1838	Ja	31	03	04	Garrette	Susan	A		1853	Fe	11	03	06
Galligan	Patrick			1878	Mr	27	01	07	Garrison	James		Dr	1820	No	25	03	04
Gallion	George	W	Mr	1859	Fe	19	03	02	Garrison	James		Ldy	1820	No	25	03	04
Galloway	A	D		1876	De	13	04	06	Garrison	V	D		1868	Ap	07	03	04
Galloway	Charles	A	Esq	1853	Au	19	03	05	Garrison	William	L		1879	My	24	05	01
Galloway	David	F		1850	Se	06	03	07	Garrison	William	L		1879	My	28	05	02
Galloway	David	W	Esq	1850	No	29	03	06	Garritt	Marilla	E		1857	Ap	11	03	04
Galloway	E	C	Mr	1867	Ja	15	02	08	Garrity	John			1872	No	26	01	02
Galloway	James	B		1844	Au	14	03	05	Garry				1873	Se	04	01	03
Galloway	Margaret	A	Mrs	1857	Jl	18	03	03	Garry	Bridget			1878	Se	22	04	03
Galloway	Mary	F	Mrs	1872	Fe	02	04	03	Garry	M	E		1878	Se	22	04	03
Galloway	Richard	L	Mr	1858	My	15	03	04	Gartnal	John			1875	Jn	22	01	04
Galloway	Samuel		Hon	1872	Ap	11	01	04	Garvey	W			1877	Oc	05	04	05
Galloway	Virginia			1871	Se	24	01	03	Garvin	J		Mr	1836	Jn	21	03	05
Galtz	Benjamin			1878	Ja	17	04	05	Garwood	Infant			1876	De	14	04	01
Galvin			Pvt	1876	Jl	09	01	05	Gary	Pat			1878	Au	17	04	02
Gamble	Robert		Bro	1874	Ja	22	04	05	Gassoway			Mr	1875	Ja	21	04	03
Gamble	Thomas			1878	De	25	01	01	Gaston	James			1872	My	01	01	01
Gamblin	Mary	J		1834	Ap	08	03	04	Gaston	Leroy		Rev	1878	Ja	08	04	04
Gammon	Alice			1874	Ap	12	01	02	Gates			Dsh	1873	Oc	03	04	03
Gammon	G	W		1879	De	21	01	01	Gates			Mr	1873	Au	16	03	01
Ganger				1876	My	12	01	05	Gates			Mr	1875	Ap	06	01	03
Gann	Justis	L		1879	Se	27	04	04	Gates	Jacob	H		1872	No	28	01	04
Gannon	Patrick			1878	Au	08	01	05	Gates	Rap			1878	Se	22	04	03
Gantt	Dick			1879	Ja	10	04	03	Gates	S	M	Mrs	1878	Se	11	01	05
Gantt	Dick			1879	Ja	11	04	03	Gates	Steuben	G	Mr	1833	Jl	03	03	03
Gantt	Laura	V	Mrs	1868	Oc	27	03	06	Gatewood	Steven	D		1879	Jl	25	05	02
Gantt	Robert	S	Col	1871	De	02	04	05	Gatland	J			1878	Se	22	04	03
Gantt	Robert	S	Hon	1871	De	02	01	01	Gatlin	Gilbert			1873	Jn	10	01	05
Gantt	Robert	S	Hon	1871	De	03	04	02	Gatlin	Scotia		Mrs	1852	Ja	16	03	06
Gantt	Robert	T		1867	No	26	02	08	Gatty	James			1878	Oc	01	01	04
Garcia			Mr	1875	Jn	26	01	02	Gaumer			Mss	1874	Au	08	01	06
Gard	Jeremiah		Mr	1842	Jn	01	03	04	Gavin	J	D	Cpc	1877	No	25	01	04
Gardenhire	Nicholas	C		1872	De	19	02	03	Gavthier	J	E		1878	Jl	31	01	04
Gardiner	George	A		1879	Oc	15	02	01	Gawn	John			1879	Oc	10	01	01
Gardiner	J	E	Cpt	1850	Jl	05	03	06	Gay	Infant			1878	Mr	16	01	06
Gardiner	James		Mr	1874	Oc	08	01	06	Gay	Lucius			1878	Se	22	04	03
Gardner	H	C		1878	Se	22	04	03	Gay	Peter	W	Hon	1874	Oc	08	01	06
Gardner	John	H		1876	No	09	01	04	Gaynoon	Sarah	J	Mrs	1877	Oc	05	04	06
Gardner	W	H		1878	Se	10	01	03	Gazzola	John			1874	Ap	09	01	04
Gardner	W	W	Mr	1874	De	11	04	03	Gbison	Wash			1874	No	26	04	02
Garland	A	H	Jr	1878	My	14	04	02	Gearheart	John			1877	Oc	21	01	05
Garland	A	H	Jr	1878	My	14	04	07	Geary			Gov	1873	Fe	09	01	06
Garland	Annie			1879	Oc	12	01	03	Geary	A	W		1866	Oc	16	02	05
Garland	Emma			1862	Jn	14	02	04	Geary	J	W		1874	Ja	08	01	02
Garland	Jennie			1860	Se	29	03	02	Gee	John	C		1878	Se	22	04	03

Last	First	MI	Ttl	Yr	Mo	Day	Pg	Col	Last	First	MI	Ttl	Yr	Mo	Day	Pg	Col
Geess	Mary	A		1878	Au	30	01	04	Gibson	Thomas	J	Mr	1848	My	18	03	04
Geing	S	B		1878	Se	22	04	03	Gibson	William	A		1878	My	01	04	05
Geizcke	G	T		1871	Fe	26	01	02	Gibson	William	R	Mr	1842	Au	17	03	06
Gellman	E	E		1878	Ja	17	04	05	Giddings	Laura		Mss	1869	Ja	26	03	02
Gelsey	Peter		Ald	1874	Ap	09	01	04	Gilbert			Pvt	1876	Jl	09	01	05
Genar	Bridget		Mrs	1875	Jn	01	01	04	Gilbert	Augustus	P		1871	Jl	18	01	05
Genbrou	Joseph			1879	De	16	01	03	Gilbert	Clinton			1871	Jl	20	01	05
Genevily	Rigault		Adm	1873	My	06	01	02	Gilbert	Clinton			1871	Jl	27	01	05
Genine	Camille			1879	Au	22	01	01	Gilbert	Frank			1874	De	08	03	01
Genner	Emile			1878	Se	22	04	03	Gilbert	Gilbert			1878	Se	22	04	03
Gennewine	George			1879	Au	30	01	01	Gilbert	John	W	Esq	1851	Jl	04	03	06
Gentry	John			1870	Oc	25	01	01	Gilbert	Milton			1879	Oc	12	01	03
Gentry	Thomas			1870	Oc	23	04	02	Gilbert	N	W		1872	Oc	18	01	05
Geoghan	John			1878	My	31	04	06	Gilbraith	Andrew	J	Mr	1837	Jl	25	03	04
George	Gaines		Dr	1872	Jl	10	01	07	Gilchrist	Martha	A	Mrs	1844	Au	14	03	05
George	John		Mr	1873	Jn	24	01	03	Giles	Alberta	M		1862	Se	20	02	05
George	John	M		1853	Mr	11	03	06	Giles	G	B		1830	Mr	09	03	03
George	John	M	Mr	1848	Ap	06	03	03	Giles	John		Mr	1851	Jl	11	03	06
George	John	M	Mr	1856	Jn	14	03	06	Giles	Joseph	M	Mr	1879	Jl	09	08	02
George	Loui			1873	Ja	14	01	07	Giles	Lizzie	E		1860	Oc	27	03	01
George	Loui		Esq	1872	De	20	04	03	Giles	Sarah	M		1853	Fe	11	03	06
George	Mary	J		1846	Oc	05	03	03	Gill	Annie			1878	Se	22	04	03
George	Mattie			1877	Ja	03	01	04	Gill	George		Rev	1848	Mr	23	03	03
Gerard	Emile			1875	Jl	10	01	05	Gill	William	G	Mrs	1878	Oc	15	01	03
Gere			Mrs	1871	Ap	26	01	03	Gill	William	K		1871	No	03	04	05
Gerges			Bp	1874	Fe	10	01	06	Gillespie			Dr	1878	Se	05	01	04
Gerrarie	Michael			1872	De	15	01	05	Gillett				1877	De	02	01	07
Gerry	Elbridge		Vpr	1875	De	02	02	02	Gillett	Aaron		Esq	1836	03	22	03	05
Gerry	Hollis		Dr	1822	No	05	02	01	Gilliard	Caroline			1879	Oc	11	01	01
Gerstenberg	H			1871	Ja	22	01	01	Gillihand	John			1879	Au	15	01	01
Gertrude			Sis	1878	Se	22	04	03	Gilliland	E	C	Mrs	1871	Jn	23	01	01
Gesler	Henry			1874	Mr	27	01	02	Gilliland	Sammie			1871	Jn	23	01	01
Getlray	Maria	L		1876	De	27	01	04	Gillis	Alex			1877	Oc	21	01	06
Getshell			Mrs	1878	Se	22	04	03	Gillis	J	J	Mrs	1879	De	16	08	03
Getz	Francis		Mrs	1879	Au	10	01	01	Gillis	Nead			1878	Ja	04	04	02
Getz	George			1879	Au	17	01	01	Gillis	Nead			1878	Ja	06	04	04
Getzell	Lizzie			1879	Au	10	01	01	Gillispie	Sallie			1866	No	27	03	02
Geyer	Anna	M	Mrs	1876	Fe	08	04	02	Gillman	E	E		1878	Ja	17	04	05
Geyer	John		Mr	1873	Jn	27	01	03	Gillman	William			1878	Ja	17	04	05
Geyer	Peter		Rev	1873	Jn	27	01	03	Gilman	Benjamin		Mrs	1873	My	10	02	03
Ghio	John	B		1879	Oc	11	01	01	Gilmartin	Felix			1878	Se	25	01	04
Gibbons	Walter			1879	Mr	14	01	04	Gilmore	Jane	V		1875	De	01	01	03
Gibbs			Mr	1873	Ja	16	02	03	Gilmore	John			1874	Ja	08	01	03
Gibbs			Mr	1874	Ja	31	04	03	Gilmore	John			1878	Au	30	01	04
Gibbs	Fred			1878	Au	30	01	04	Gilmore	William	H		1878	My	04	01	03
Gibbs	George			1871	Jl	20	01	05	Gilroy	Hugh			1870	Oc	26	01	01
Gibbs	George			1878	Au	30	01	04	Gingerich	David		Mr	1878	Ap	17	01	05
Gibbs	Sarah	J		1876	De	29	04	01	Gingerich	David		Mrs	1878	Ap	17	01	05
Gibbs	Seth			1874	Oc	28	01	06	Ginges	Joseph	E	Rev	1874	Fe	13	01	03
Gibbs	Walter			1874	Ap	18	01	04	Ginnis	Laura			1878	Au	30	01	04
Gibner	James			1879	No	26	01	03	Ginocchio	Ella	B	Mrs	1879	No	25	08	02
Gibson	Caroline	L	Mrs	1878	Se	03	04	05	Ginocchio	John		Mr	1878	Ja	12	04	01
Gibson	Caroline	L	Mrs	1878	Se	05	04	06	Ginocchio	John		Mr	1878	Ja	12	04	07
Gibson	D	E	Dr	1878	Oc	03	01	03	Gist	R	C		1878	Se	22	04	03
Gibson	E	W		1878	Se	17	01	04	Gist	Sarah	J		1878	Oc	31	01	04
Gibson	Edwin		Mr	1837	Oc	31	03	05	Given	John		Mrs	1872	Ap	02	01	04
Gibson	James			1879	Au	22	01	03	Glaber	James			1873	My	14	01	02
Gibson	John		Dr	1834	Jn	17	03	05	Glas	John	A		1879	Oc	30	01	03
Gibson	John		Mr	1836	Fe	02	03	05	Glasgow	Samuel			1874	Jn	26	01	06
Gibson	Laurie			1849	My	31	03	04	Glasier	Alice	F		1875	Ap	02	04	06
Gibson	Laurie			1853	Ja	21	03	04	Glasier	Nona		Mss	1872	Jl	02	04	05
Gibson	Mary			1873	My	17	01	03	Glass	D	M		1871	No	11	01	01
Gibson	Matilda			1834	Au	19	03	03	Glass	Joseph	B	Mr	1870	Se	24	03	01
Gibson	Nathan			1878	Se	22	04	03	Glass	Matt	E		1878	Se	24	01	04
Gibson	Philander		Mr	1840	Se	23	03	06	Glazier	Mag	C	Mrs	1863	Ja	31	02	02
Gibson	Robert			1877	Ja	27	01	04	Glazier	Marcellus			1873	Mr	29	01	02

Last	First	MI	Ttl	Yr	Mo	Day	Pg	Col	Last	First	MI	Ttl	Yr	Mo	Day	Pg	Col
Gleason	Alfred	J	Mr	1831	Se	21	03	04	Goodwin	James		Maj	1878	Mr	16	01	06
Gleason	M	J	Mrs	1878	Se	11	01	05	Goodwin	Lou			1873	Jn	03	01	03
Gleason	M	J	Mrs	1878	Se	22	04	03	Goodwin	Samuel			1878	Mr	30	01	06
Gleason	Stephan			1878	Au	06	01	06	Goodwin	Samuei	B	Dr	1853	Ap	29	03	07
Gledhill	C	H		1878	Oc	16	01	03	Goodwin	U	S		1878	Se	12	01	06
Glelsher	John			1878	Oc	04	01	03	Goodwin	W	T		1878	Oc	04	01	03
Glenn			Mr	1859	Ja	01	03	01	Goodyear	C	B		1875	Ja	05	01	04
Glenn			Mr	1859	Ja	01	03	01	Goos	Frank			1878	Au	30	01	04
Glenn	Caroline			1879	Oc	03	01	01	Gorbold	Virginia			1873	Oc	19	04	03
Glenn	John			1879	Au	21	08	02	Gordan				1872	Fe	20	01	02
Glennan	B	T		1878	No	17	01	03	Gordon			Mr	1875	Jn	26	01	03
Glesston	R		Mrs	1878	Oc	18	01	03	Gordon			Mrs	1872	Fe	20	01	02
Gleyson	Pleasent	A	Bro	1870	Au	27	03	01	Gordon			Mrs	1876	Ja	01	01	05
Glick			Mrs	1872	Jn	12	01	03	Gordon	A	M	Lt	1868	Fe	04	03	05
Glover	Joe		Mr	1874	Fe	01	03	01	Gordon	Almond		Mrs	1873	Jn	17	01	05
Glynn	Michael			1871	Ap	22	01	03	Gordon	Henry			1872	Mr	22	01	02
Glynn	Thomas			1878	Ja	15	01	07	Gordon	Ida		Mss	1875	Se	29	01	03
Glynne	J	L		1873	De	24	01	03	Gordon	Infant			1873	Jn	17	01	05
Gninnell	Moses	H		1877	No	25	01	07	Gordon	Isham	B	Esq	1828	Au	27	03	02
Gobbart	Isiah			1878	Ap	10	01	07	Gordon	Jane		Mrs	1878	Se	24	04	07
Goble	Ephraim			1830	Mr	09	03	03	Gordon	Joe	H		1879	Se	17	01	01
Goble	James		Mrs	1873	My	10	02	03	Gordon	Missouri			1878	Se	22	04	03
Godbold	Elizabeth		Mrs	1870	Fe	15	02	02	Gordon	Newton			1866	Oc	09	03	02
Godbold	Virginia		Mss	1873	Oc	15	01	03	Gore	Infant			1874	No	28	01	05
Godioe				1878	Ja	04	04	06	Goree	Don			1874	Ap	04	01	01
Godley	Crawford			1875	My	20	04	03	Gorham	Charles	E		1878	De	27	01	02
Godsey	Susan	C	Mss	1873	No	18	01	02	Gorman	Infant			1874	Mr	18	03	01
Goebets	Jane		Mrs	1879	Oc	08	01	01	Gorman	Patrick			1878	Se	22	04	03
Goelit	Peter			1879	No	25	04	01	Gorum	William	M	Sir	1875	Mr	17	01	02
Goeway	H	M		1878	Se	22	04	03	Gosdlet	William			1878	Se	26	01	04
Goewey	H	M		1878	Se	14	01	04	Gosie			Mrs	1878	Au	30	01	04
Goff	H	C		1874	My	19	01	07	Goslee	James		Cap	1875	Ap	03	01	05
Goff	Nancy		Mss	1872	My	11	01	02	Goss				1873	Oc	04	01	03
Goforth	John			1860	Jn	16	03	01	Gotleib	Albert			1875	My	27	01	04
Going	S	B		1878	Se	10	01	03	Gotschalt			Mrs	1878	Se	04	01	03
Going	S	B		1878	Oc	02	04	04	Gough	H	K		1878	Ap	17	03	01
Goldcamp	Frank			1879	Se	30	01	01	Gould	Josiah		Hon	1872	De	19	01	01
Golden	Patrick		Pvt	1876	Jl	09	01	05	Gould	Josiah		Hon	1872	De	19	02	04
Goldkamp	Dora		Mrs	1879	Au	23	01	01	Gould	L	D		1873	De	18	01	03
Goldsborough			Ram	1878	Ja	09	03	02	Gould	Lillian			1873	Fe	06	01	01
Goldsborough	John		Cdr	1878	Ja	09	03	02	Gould	M	B		1879	De	28	01	03
Goldsmith	George	W		1874	Au	21	01	07	Gould	W	B	Cap	1874	Jn	13	01	01
Golladay	S			1878	Oc	03	01	04	Gould	W	D		1875	Jl	07	03	01
Gollia	Mary	R	Mrs	1858	Ap	17	03	03	Gould	William			1878	Ja	16	01	06
Golostee	Johanna			1875	Jn	19	01	03	Goulding	William	J	Dr	1841	De	15	03	05
Gonaghen	Owen			1878	No	22	05	02	Gove	Janet			1878	Oc	01	01	06
Gooch	Lady			1879	No	11	07	01	Graffis	John	A		1871	Au	20	01	05
Gooding	John			1878	Au	29	01	04	Graham			Mr	1876	De	23	01	02
Gooding	Sarah	A		1841	Se	22	03	04	Graham	Andrew		Mr	1836	My	31	03	04
Gooding	William			1878	Mr	07	01	06	Graham	Eliza			1879	Au	14	01	01
Goodloe	Frank			1878	Oc	09	01	06	Graham	Frank	D		1878	Au	08	01	05
Goodman			Esq	1870	Se	22	03	01	Graham	Frederick	A	Mr	1843	Au	02	03	05
Goodman	Calvin		Mr	1867	No	12	05	02	Graham	George		Esq	1830	Se	08	03	05
Goodman	Eliza		Mrs	1867	No	12	05	02	Graham	James			1873	Fe	12	01	05
Goodman	Zack			1872	Fe	06	01	03	Graham	James			1878	Ap	04	04	04
Goodrich			Mr	1871	Se	09	01	03	Graham	Jerry			1872	No	19	01	02
Goodrich	Carris			1878	Se	22	04	03	Graham	John		Esq	1820	Se	23	03	04
Goodrich	Charles			1873	Jl	13	01	02	Graham	John		Rev	1879	Au	02	05	01
Goodrich	Charles		Mr	1841	Oc	20	03	06	Graham	John	E	Esq	1845	De	29	03	03
Goodrich	Hellen	V		1839	No	20	03	03	Graham	Mattie			1878	Se	05	01	03
Goodrich	John		St	1878	Ja	18	01	05	Graham	Moses		Esq	1821	Mr	31	03	03
Goodrich	Lemuel	H		1854	Oc	06	03	06	Grahem	John	H	Com	1878	Mr	17	04	05
Goodrich	Patrick	H		1839	No	20	03	03	Gramling	Mary			1876	De	12	04	02
Goodwin	Eber			1877	Se	12	01	05	Grange	William			1873	Mr	22	01	02
Goodwin	Edward	L		1878	Fe	22	04	05	Granger	Edward	J		1870	De	06	01	03
Goodwin	Fannie	A	Mss	1868	Fe	18	03	04	Granger	Peterson			1871	Ap	22	01	03

Last	First	MI	Ttl	Yr	Mo	Day	Pg	Col	Last	First	MI	Ttl	Yr	Mo	Day	Pg	Col
Granger	Peterson		Mrs	1871	Ap	22	01	03	Gray	Victory		Mss	1836	Jn	14	03	05
Grant	Arthur			1875	Jn	15	04	04	Gray	Waller			1878	Se	22	04	03
Grant	Diebald			1871	Jl	19	01	03	Gray	William	C		1850	My	24	03	06
Grant	Fannie			1858	Oc	09	03	03	Grayson	E			1872	Ja	16	01	02
Grant	G	H		1878	Se	22	04	03	Greasley	Joseph		Mr	1851	Mr	14	03	07
Grant	George			1872	No	14	01	04	Greathouse	Daniel		Mr	1836	Ap	05	03	05
Grant	George			1878	Ap	27	04	07	Greathouse	Gabriel		Mr	1829	Mr	18	03	02
Grant	Jesse			1874	Ja	08	01	02	Greaves			Gen	1872	My	26	01	05
Grant	Jesse	R		1873	Jl	01	01	04	Gregg	J	J	Maj	1878	Ap	20	01	06
Grant	Jos			1878	Se	22	04	03	Greek	Roger			1874	Ap	25	01	06
Grant	Louis			1878	Se	04	01	03	Greeley	Horace			1872	No	30	01	01
Grant	Louten			1878	Se	01	01	03	Greeley	Horace			1872	No	30	01	03
Grant	William			1874	Ap	18	01	04	Greeley	Horace			1872	No	30	01	04
Grant	William			1879	Oc	02	01	01	Greeley	Horace			1872	No	30	01	05
Grant	William		Mr	1837	Oc	17	03	05	Greeley	Horace			1872	No	30	02	02
Granwell	Nancy			1875	De	05	01	07	Greeley	Horace			1872	No	30	02	03
Grapneau	Julius			1866	De	03	02	07	Greeley	Horace			1872	De	01	01	01
Grappole	Francis			1876	No	14	01	04	Greeley	Horace			1872	De	01	01	03
Grasen	Henry		Mr	1878	Mr	17	04	04	Greeley	Horace			1872	De	01	01	04
Grasen	Henry		Mrs	1878	Mr	17	04	04	Greeley	Horace			1872	De	01	01	05
Gratiot	Henry			1836	My	31	03	04	Greeley	Horace			1872	De	04	01	02
Gratiot	Paul	M	Mrs	1871	De	03	04	02	Greeley	Horace			1872	De	04	01	03
Gratiot	Victoria	A	Mss	1853	Se	09	03	06	Greeley	Horace			1872	De	05	01	01
Grattan	Henry			1820	My	20	03	04	Greeley	Horace			1872	De	05	01	02
Grau	Frank			1878	Au	30	01	04	Greeley	Horace			1872	De	05	01	03
Gravel	Elizabeth			1876	De	27	01	04	Greeley	Horace			1872	De	05	01	04
Gravel	John			1874	Se	17	01	04	Greeley	Horace			1872	De	05	01	05
Graves			Mr	1872	No	20	01	04	Greeley	Horace			1872	De	05	01	06
Graves	David			1871	De	30	01	02	Greeley	Horace			1872	De	05	02	03
Graves	Frank	E		1879	Se	04	01	01	Greeley	Horace			1872	De	06	01	05
Graves	George	V		1879	Au	30	01	01	Greeley	Horace			1872	De	07	02	02
Graves	Margaret		Mrs	1856	No	15	03	04	Greeley	Horace			1872	De	07	02	04
Graves	Richard		Jud	1836	Se	13	03	04	Greeley	Horace			1872	De	08	01	04
Graves	Robert		Mrs	1879	No	04	05	02	Greeley	Horace			1872	De	11	01	03
Graves	William	B		1871	Ja	22	03	01	Greeley	Horace			1872	De	15	04	04
Gravett	Sarah	F	Mrs	1878	Mr	01	04	05	Greeley	Horace			1872	De	18	02	03
Gravety	B	F		1878	Ap	27	04	08	Greeley	Horace			1873	Ja	24	01	05
Gravier	John	B	Mr	1839	No	27	03	05	Greeley	Horace			1874	No	17	01	05
Gravier	Victoire		Mme	1828	No	25	03	02	Greeley	Horace			1879	Jn	28	05	02
Gravitte	Jesse			1858	De	11	03	02	Greeley	Horace		Mrs	1872	No	08	02	04
Graw	Jacob			1877	De	16	01	05	Green	A	L	Rev	1874	Jl	17	01	03
Gray			Pvt	1876	Jl	09	01	05	Green	A	R	Dr	1878	Se	06	01	05
Gray	Bernard			1878	Jl	12	04	05	Green	Charley			1879	Au	13	01	01
Gray	Charles			1871	Jl	28	01	04	Green	Duff		Gen	1875	Jn	20	01	04
Gray	Charles		Dr	1874	Au	20	01	07	Green	G			1876	De	12	01	01
Gray	George			1874	Jl	19	02	03	Green	Harriet	L	Mrs	1850	Ap	05	03	06
Gray	George	W		1871	Jl	07	01	05	Green	Henry	A		1878	Jl	10	04	06
Gray	George	W	Cpt	1879	Se	16	05	02	Green	Hiram		Mr	1825	Fe	01	03	01
Gray	Henry			1875	Ja	14	01	03	Green	J			1878	Se	22	04	03
Gray	J	D		1873	Mr	18	04	04	Green	J	S		1878	My	29	04	07
Gray	Jacob		Maj	1837	Ja	10	03	04	Green	James			1878	Se	01	01	03
Gray	Jacob		Mr	1837	Ap	04	03	05	Green	James	S	Sen	1870	Ja	28	03	01
Gray	Katie	A	Mss	1878	No	05	01	07	Green	Jennie			1879	Au	12	01	02
Gray	Maria	E		1851	Oc	31	03	07	Green	John			1871	No	06	01	03
Gray	Marietta			1872	Ja	03	01	02	Green	John			1875	My	11	04	04
Gray	Martha	A		1852	Jl	23	03	06	Green	John			1875	My	11	04	05
Gray	Mary		Mrs	1867	No	05	07	02	Green	John		Law	1875	My	11	04	03
Gray	Mary	A	Mrs	1857	Mr	16	03	02	Green	John	A	Gen	1872	Jn	25	01	05
Gray	Mathew		Cap	1837	No	14	03	05	Green	John	M		1859	My	14	03	01
Gray	Polly	A		1836	My	31	03	04	Green	Linton	J		1867	Ap	02	03	04
Gray	Robert			1878	De	01	01	02	Green	Lou	E		1878	Se	04	01	03
Gray	Sampson		Mr	1834	No	11	03	04	Green	Matthew	Mac		1877	No	25	01	04
Gray	Sherrard		Esq	1836	Fe	16	03	05	Green	Melinda		Mrs	1871	My	07	04	02
Gray	Thomas			1871	Mr	24	01	01	Green	Moses			1879	Oc	12	01	03
Gray	Thomas	W	Esq	1852	Ap	02	03	06	Green	Moses	P		1870	Oc	23	01	01
Gray	Victory			1836	My	31	03	04	Green	Nat	S	Cpt	1878	Oc	02	01	04

Last	First	MI	Ttl	Yr	Mo	Day	Pg	Col	Last	First	MI	Ttl	Yr	Mo	Day	Pg	Col
Green	Nat	S	Mrs	1878	Oc	02	01	04	Griffith	Samuel			1873	Oc	07	01	03
Green	Richard			1878	Mr	02	01	04	Griffith	Thomas		Maj	1830	Fe	16	03	04
Green	Richard			1878	Mr	13	01	06	Griffith	Walter	G		1872	No	26	01	02
Green	Sam			1877	De	05	01	04	Griffy	Susan		Mrs	1857	Jl	11	03	03
Green	Thomas	W		1879	Oc	07	01	01	Grifith	John	W		1878	Mr	17	01	06
Green	Thurman			1871	Se	23	01	03	Griggs	Mary	A	Mrs	1835	My	12	03	03
Green	W	H		1878	Se	22	04	03	Griggs	Squire		Mr	1837	Jn	13	03	04
Green	W	L		1879	Mr	20	01	05	Grigsby	Mary			1878	Se	05	01	03
Green	W	W	Cpt	1874	Ap	20	04	05	Grill	Nicholas		Mr	1838	Jl	11	03	04
Green	Wiley	B		1865	De	30	03	01	Grimes			Sen	1872	Fe	09	01	02
Green	William			1877	De	21	01	06	Grimes	Anna			1875	Ap	04	01	02
Greene			Cpt	1871	Ap	09	01	05	Grimes	Anna			1875	Ap	05	01	02
Greene	Fred	M	Mr	1873	Jn	25	03	01	Grimes	John			1875	Jn	23	01	03
Greene	Henry			1879	Oc	29	01	03	Grimes	L	A	Rev	1873	Mr	16	01	06
Greener	John		Mr	1871	My	14	01	08	Grinder	Jerdon			1871	Fe	12	03	01
Greenland	Eugene			1871	De	08	01	02	Grinder	Jesse		Col	1878	My	30	03	01
Greenleaf	A	W		1878	Mr	02	01	03	Grinnan	Charles	J		1870	My	04	03	01
Greenlock				1872	My	30	01	04	Grinnell	Henry			1874	Jl	02	01	04
Greenlock	George			1872	My	30	01	04	Grisham	John		Esq	1835	Jl	28	03	04
Greenlock	George		Mrs	1872	My	30	01	04	Grisler	August			1878	Ap	28	01	04
Greenpur	Fred			1878	Se	05	01	03	Grisler	Hannah			1878	Ap	28	01	04
Greenwalt	Ann		Mrs	1821	Se	22	03	01	Gristine	Lyman			1879	Au	09	08	04
Greenwood	Adaline	A	Mrs	1860	De	15	03	01	Griswold	John	A	Hon	1872	No	01	01	03
Greenwood	J	R		1872	Oc	12	01	04	Griswood	C	A		1878	Se	22	04	03
Greenwood	Morell			1841	Jn	23	03	02	Griswood	J	W		1878	Ap	07	01	06
Greer	James		Mrs	1851	Se	05	03	06	Gritzch	Fred		Mr	1871	Ap	09	01	05
Greer	W	M	Mr	1876	Se	20	03	01	Gross	Fred			1878	Au	08	01	05
Greetsbeck			Col	1879	My	22	03	01	Gross	Mary	T		1837	Au	15	03	04
Greever	Benjamin	W	Bro	1873	Mr	07	01	06	Grosvener	Thomas	W		1871	Oc	22	01	04
Gregory	D	D	Rev	1874	Se	17	01	05	Grosvenor	Thomas	W	Gen	1871	No	05	01	03
Gregory	James			1876	De	10	01	04	Grote	F	R		1878	Ap	26	01	07
Gregory	Mary	J	Mrs	1867	Oc	15	02	08	Grover	Fred			1878	Se	05	01	03
Gregory	W		Cdt	1872	Fe	06	04	03	Grover	N	D	Gen	1875	Jn	18	01	04
Gregory	W	R		1878	Ja	24	03	01	Groves				1878	Se	05	01	03
Greig	Thomas			1878	Ap	19	01	06	Gruelle	Sarah	F	Mrs	1839	Jl	17	03	04
Grennell	George		Jud	1877	No	22	01	07	Gruson	Nannie		Mss	1873	Mr	04	01	04
Greshan	John			1871	De	31	01	04	Gual	Pedro			1819	De	18	03	02
Greshman	Frank	B		1878	Ja	24	03	01	Gueigel	Annie			1879	Oc	22	01	01
Gressom	Louis			1879	Au	06	01	01	Guernsey	Porter			1878	De	15	01	01
Grey	Emily	M		1868	Mr	31	03	04	Guerrazzi	F			1874	Ja	08	01	02
Grey	M	J	Mrs	1879	Se	18	01	01	Guiber	Wille	P		1868	Au	25	03	07
Grider	Jesse		Col	1878	My	22	01	08	Guibor	Louisa		Mrs	1869	Oc	24	04	02
Grier	L	C	Hon	1872	Jn	07	01	06	Guilbault	Leo			1876	De	27	01	04
Grier	P		Mr	1840	Oc	28	03	05	Guilleroy	Dreux			1873	Au	21	01	04
Grifaith	George			1877	Oc	06	01	06	Guilleroys	Augastin			1873	Au	21	01	04
Griffen	Francis	M	Mr	1872	Jn	30	04	05	Guiry	John			1867	Au	27	03	02
Griffen	William			1878	Se	01	01	03	Guisky	Gustave			1876	Ja	01	01	01
Griffin			Pvt	1876	Jl	09	01	05	Guizaide			Cpt	1877	De	28	01	05
Griffin	A	Q		1878	Se	22	04	03	Gumberts	Abraham			1873	Au	23	01	04
Griffin	Ed			1876	De	12	01	01	Gumbleton				1871	My	21	01	06
Griffin	Hohn			1878	Se	05	01	03	Gunn	George	H	Dr	1871	Jl	18	01	05
Griffin	Jennie			1873	De	27	01	03	Gunn	William		Mrs	1840	Jn	17	03	01
Griffin	Joshua			1875	Mr	13	01	03	Gunn	William	W		1838	Jl	18	03	04
Griffin	Louis			1879	Oc	10	01	01	Gunning	Richard	C	Cpt	1872	Se	27	01	03
Griffing	Cornelius			1878	Fe	06	01	08	Gunter	James		Mr	1872	Au	20	01	04
Griffing	Cornelius			1878	Fe	07	04	04	Gunter	William		Bro	1874	Fe	13	04	06
Griffing	Cornelius			1878	Fe	08	01	05	Gunther	Susannah		Mrs	1833	Jn	12	03	01
Griffing	Cornelius			1878	Fe	08	02	01	Gurley	H	H	Jud	1832	Ap	25	03	05
Griffing	Thomas		Mr	1832	Se	19	03	03	Gusmont	Jennie			1878	Au	29	01	04
Griffith			Mrs	1824	De	14	03	01	Guthrie	H	W		1872	Jl	16	01	04
Griffith	Ben			1878	No	22	05	02	Guttenburg	Bernhard			1878	Oc	06	01	03
Griffith	George			1874	No	19	01	05	Guy			Mrs	1873	Mr	16	01	05
Griffith	Henry			1868	Ap	21	03	05	Gwynne	N	P		1871	Mr	02	01	01
Griffith	Henry		Pg	1868	My	19	02	07									
Griffith	John	A		1858	Au	21	03	05									
Griffith	Joseph		Mr	1867	Ja	29	03	04									

Last	First	MI	Ttl	Yr	Mo	Day	Pg	Col	Last	First	MI	Ttl	Yr	Mo	Day	Pg	Col
									Hall	John	A		1878	Oc	06	01	03
									Hall	Mary	A		1855	Se	07	03	04
		H							Hall	Matilda		Mrs	1879	No	13	08	03
									Hall	R	M	Col	1874	Jl	21	01	06
Haas	Perry			1873	Au	19	01	03	Hall	Robert	T	Mr	1875	My	02	04	05
Hables	B		Dr	1878	Oc	04	01	03	Hall	Rosa			1878	Se	22	04	03
Habrity				1877	De	02	01	07	Hall	S	Z	Mrs	1879	No	14	08	02
Hacke	James	H		1871	De	29	01	02	Hall	Sallie			1878	Oc	17	01	03
Hackett	John			1878	No	22	01	01	Hall	Sarah		Mrs	1878	Oc	10	01	03
Hackett	John			1879	De	27	05	02	Hall	William			1878	Se	28	01	05
Haddock	Jacob	C		1878	Au	20	01	04	Hall	William		Esq	1838	Se	19	03	05
Haddock	John			1878	Ja	03	01	05	Halleck			Gen	1872	Ja	12	01	03
Hadfield	George		Dr	1870	My	04	MY	04	Halleck			Gen	1872	Ja	26	01	03
Hadley	George		Pro	1877	Oc	17	04	05	Halleck	W			1874	No	04	01	05
Hadley	James			1871	Fe	28	01	02	Halley	Richard		Dr	1841	Jn	30	03	02
Hadley	James		Pro	1872	No	15	01	04	Halliburton	Thyrza		Mrs	1875	Ap	30	04	05
Hagan	James		Dr	1860	De	01	03	01	Halliday	A			1878	Au	29	01	03
Haganbach	George			1878	No	19	01	02	Hallisdall			Pvt	1876	Jl	09	01	05
Hagen	William			1875	Oc	02	04	04	Hallman	Charles	P		1879	Se	28	01	01
Hagen	William			1879	Jn	27	05	02	Halloran	John			1872	Se	10	01	03
Hager	Charles			1875	My	11	04	05	Hallovan	John			1872	Se	08	01	05
Hager	Mary	E		1872	Ap	26	04	04	Halloway	George			1872	No	27	01	04
Hagerman	Infant			1878	Ja	22	01	07	Halm	Frederick			1871	Jl	15	01	05
Hagerty			Mrs	1870	Se	30	01	01	Halsh	Tom		Eng	1878	My	07	04	05
Haggerty	M	C		1879	Mr	06	01	05	Halstad	W			1878	Au	27	01	04
Hahn	Conrad	P	Frm	1877	No	25	01	04	Halstead	Jack		Mrs	1879	Au	10	08	06
Hahn	J	H		1879	Au	22	01	01	Halstead	Peel			1871	Jl	04	01	03
Hahn	Moses			1878	Au	22	01	04	Halstead	Peter			1872	Ja	27	01	03
Haight	Henry			1878	Se	03	04	04	Halsted				1871	No	11	01	03
Haight	Mark			1872	De	27	01	03	Halsted	Jack			1878	My	15	04	06
Hail	Elizabeth		Mss	1859	My	28	03	01	Haltenback	Theodore		Mr	1878	My	01	01	06
Hail	Susan		Mrs	1859	My	28	03	01	Haltenback	Theodore		Mrs	1878	Mr	01	01	06
Haines	Charles	E		1879	Au	17	01	01	Haltom			Mrs	1874	Ja	29	04	02
Hainey	James	M	Mrs	1873	Mr	16	01	06	Halton	Jake			1878	Ap	20	04	03
Hairline	Jacob	E		1879	Au	09	05	01	Halton	Thomas			1879	Mr	18	01	06
Hairston	Samuel	H	Esq	1870	My	04	03	01	Ham	John	H	Bro	1872	Mr	13	04	05
Halbert	Henry		Esq	1877	Ja	13	04	04	Ham	Samuel			1879	Se	02	05	01
Hale				1876	Jn	11	03	01	Hamarie	Mollie			1879	Jl	23	01	02
Hale				1876	Jn	22	04	02	Hamblin	Isaac		Snr	1859	Oc	01	04	01
Hale	David	E		1839	My	01	03	04	Hamblin	Sarah			1871	Se	28	01	03
Hale	George	G		1876	My	12	01	02	Hames	Thomas	J	Bro	1869	De	25	02	03
Hale	H	B	Esq	1873	Jl	30	01	03	Hamilton			Pvt	1876	Jl	09	01	05
Hale	Hetty			1879	Se	16	01	01	Hamilton	Charles			1878	Se	04	01	03
Hale	John	C		1876	My	30	04	03	Hamilton	Charles			1878	Se	05	01	03
Hale	John	C		1876	Jn	27	04	02	Hamilton	Charles	A		1879	Jl	18	05	01
Hale	John	P		1873	No	21	01	03	Hamilton	Emile			1878	My	25	04	06
Hale	John	P	Hon	1873	No	22	01	01	Hamilton	Frank			1873	My	10	02	03
Hale	John	P	Sen	1874	Ja	08	01	02	Hamilton	George		Qum	1877	No	25	01	04
Hale	Johnny			1876	Se	24	04	02	Hamilton	George	A		1871	Se	20	01	04
Hale	Joseph	K		1873	Oc	15	01	03	Hamilton	James			1878	Au	18	02	04
Hale	Sarah	N	Mrs	1879	My	02	01	02	Hamilton	James		Esq	1826	Fe	07	03	02
Hale	Thomas	B	Col	1862	Se	06	02	05	Hamilton	James	A	Cpt	1878	Ap	14	04	04
Haley	Thomas			1873	My	10	02	03	Hamilton	James	W	Lt	1837	Ja	17	03	05
Halford			Dr	1873	Jl	12	01	09	Hamilton	Jas			1878	Ap	05	04	02
Hall			Cap	1873	Oc	19	01	03	Hamilton	Joseph	P		1874	No	04	01	05
Hall			Cpt	1873	My	17	02	02	Hamilton	Nannie	J	Mrs	1869	Fe	24	02	04
Hall			Dr	1871	Jn	10	01	02	Hamilton	Robert			1876	My	27	01	05
Hall			Dr	1872	Fe	20	01	04	Hamilton	S			1878	Se	22	04	03
Hall			Mss	1873	Au	05	01	03	Hamilton	W	F		1876	No	19	04	03
Hall	Ezra			1877	No	04	01	04	Hamilton	William			1872	De	25	01	02
Hall	Frank			1879	Oc	15	01	01	Hamilton	William			1873	De	03	04	02
Hall	Fredrick			1878	Jn	04	04	04	Hamland	John	D	Clk	1877	De	06	01	06
Hall	H	G		1873	No	18	04	03	Hamlet	Henry			1879	My	10	08	02
Hall	Infant			1876	Fe	25	04	02	Hamlet	John		Mr	1877	Ja	23	02	03
Hall	John			1871	No	11	01	03	Hamlin	Jesse			1871	Mr	11	03	01
									Hammeck				1871	Jn	10	01	01

Last	First	MI	Ttl	Yr	Mo	Day	Pg	Col	Last	First	MI	Ttl	Yr	Mo	Day	Pg	Col
Hammer	Theo			1873	De	07	01	04	Hanson	M	J		1878	Se	05	01	03
Hammerie	M		Mrs	1879	Jl	29	01	01	Hanson	Thomas	M	Cpt	1871	Oc	22	01	03
Hammit	Isaac			187	Jl	30	04	06	Hanson	William			1878	Au	30	01	04
Hammock	Bob			1878	Se	18	01	04	Haralson	Herndon		Maj	1852	Au	06	03	06
Hammock	Robert			1879	No	21	08	04	Harbach	F	P		1879	Oc	29	05	02
Hammock	William	M	Mr	1859	Jn	18	02	03	Harbert			Mr	1871	Ap	11	01	03
Hammond	Benjamin			1874	My	21	04	02	Harbest	S	P		1873	Au	09	01	03
Hammond	Charles		Esq	1840	Ap	29	03	03	Harbor	D	C		1879	Se	06	01	01
Hammond	Gordon	P		1860	Jl	28	03	02	Hardaker	Harry			1876	No	02	01	02
Hammond	John	N		1859	Ja	01	03	02	Hardee			Gen	1873	No	09	01	02
Hammond	Peter			1878	Ap	12	01	06	Hardee	James	H	Gen	1876	De	16	01	04
Hamner	C	S		1879	Se	19	01	01	Hardee	W	J	Gen	1874	Ja	08	01	02
Hamner	William	H		1879	Se	13	01	01	Harden	Henry			1878	Se	22	04	03
Hampstead	E	R	Mrs	1873	Se	16	04	06	Harder	Alfred			1871	Jn	30	01	02
Hampton	Wade		Gen	1835	Mr	10	03	05	Hardester	Charley			1875	Ap	13	03	01
Hampton	Wade		Mr	1822	Jl	16	03	01	Hardin	Ellen		Mrs	1828	My	28	03	01
Hamstein	Laura			1878	Se	22	04	03	Hardin	Johnathan			1846	No	30	03	05
Hancock	John	A		1872	Ja	25	01	01	Hardin	Jonathan		Mrs	1831	Ja	26	03	01
Hancock	Peter			1830	Oc	06	02	01	Hardin	Joseph		Col	1826	Se	05	03	01
Hancock	Richard			1830	Mr	09	03	03	Hardin	Richard			1871	De	19	04	03
Hancock	Wiley	L		1873	Fe	23	04	08	Harding	Billy		Unc	1876	No	22	04	02
Hand	James		Cpt	1875	Jn	11	01	03	Harding	W	G		1878	Oc	03	01	03
Hand	Simmons			1872	My	15	01	03	Hardwick			Mrs	1872	No	30	01	03
Hanes	R	Y		1878	Se	22	04	03	Hardwick	Garland		Esq	1852	De	24	03	06
Haney	Cara	P		1872	Oc	30	01	05	Hardwick	George			1872	No	30	01	03
Haney	Cara	P		1872	Oc	31	01	07	Hardy	George	W		1869	Oc	20	04	03
Haney	Sarah		Mrs	1858	Ap	17	03	03	Hardy	James	S		1869	Se	10	04	02
Haney	Timothy		Esq	1858	Ap	17	03	03	Hardy	Marian		Mrs	1851	No	21	03	06
Hanford	J			1878	Jl	19	01	04	Hardy	N	T	Cpt	1878	No	19	01	04
Hanford	Samuel			1878	No	23	01	02	Hare	Henry			1878	Se	22	04	03
Hanford	Tom			1878	No	23	01	01	Hare	Mary	A		1878	Oc	31	01	04
Hanger	Fannie	A	Mss	1873	Mr	25	01	03	Harebricge	H			1872	Ja	20	01	03
Hanger	Fannie	A	Mss	1873	Mr	26	01	02	Harelson	Mary	E		1847	Fe	20	03	01
Hanger	Lizzie	B		1859	Oc	29	03	02	Harland			Dr	1878	Se	22	04	03
Hanger	Matilda	J	Mrs	1865	Jl	08	03	03	Harley	Breckinridge	A		1857	Jl	18	03	03
Hanger	Matthew	C		1872	Ap	09	04	02	Harley	Dick			1870	No	24	02	03
Hanion				1877	De	02	01	07	Harley	Walter	C		1870	Au	17	02	03
Hanks	Alexander			1877	Oc	31	02	03	Harley	Walter	S		1878	Ja	16	01	04
Hanks	Alexander			1877	No	09	03	02	Harman	Lizzie			1878	Au	30	01	04
Hanks	Fleetwood		Mrs	1876	Ap	09	02	04	Harmon	Rock			1874	Ap	23	01	03
Hanks	Malinda			1874	Jn	13	01	07	Harness	William	B	Esq	1834	Mr	11	03	05
Hanks	Millende			1836	Oc	25	03	05	Harney			Maj	1869	Ja	30	02	04
Hankson	John	P	Gen	1876	De	28	01	04	Harney			Maj	1869	Jl	27	02	03
Hanley	C	G		1878	Oc	03	01	05	Harniss	Jacob			1877	De	30	01	06
Hanley	Edward			1878	Oc	08	01	03	Harold	Abner		Mr	1834	Oc	28	03	04
Hanley	Martin			1871	Au	20	01	05	Harold	Abner		Mr	1835	Se	22	03	05
Hanly	Jane	L	Mrs	1836	Au	16	03	06	Harold	Emily		Mrs	1872	My	29	01	02
Hanly	Phil			1873	Au	08	03	02	Harp	Fannie	E		1872	Oc	01	01	04
Hanman	Josiah			1879	Au	08	08	05	Harper	Bettie			1871	Se	12	01	04
Hann	Conrad			1871	Ja	07	04	04	Harper	Fletcher			1878	Ja	09	03	02
Hanna	Fisher			1878	Se	22	04	03	Harper	Frank			1871	Au	17	01	04
Hanna	Lula		Mss	1879	Oc	22	01	01	Harper	Fred	W		1858	Mr	20	03	03
Hanna	Mary	S	Mrs	1870	No	02	01	02	Harper	Jaccob			1871	Se	12	01	04
Hannafan				1873	Au	26	04	04	Harper	James			1878	Se	04	01	03
Hannay	James			1874	Ja	08	01	02	Harper	John			1875	Ap	25	02	02
Hanneburg	Jas			1878	Se	22	04	03	Harper	John			1875	Ap	28	01	01
Hanns	Henry			1878	Se	01	01	04	Harper	John			1875	My	01	02	02
Hansbrough	Alfred	S	Mr	1826	Au	15	03	03	Harper	L		Mr	1872	Mr	07	01	04
Hanscom	A		Esq	1830	Fe	23	03	05	Harper	R	B	Dr	1871	Au	31	01	02
Hansen	Edward		Pvt	1876	Jl	09	01	05	Harper	Silvester	P		1874	Ap	30	04	06
Hanslon			Mr	1876	No	04	01	04	Harpham	Martha	V	Mrs	1867	Oc	29	05	06
Hanslon	Charles			1878	Se	04	01	03	Harpman	Fred			1879	Se	25	01	01
Hansman	John	S		1877	Oc	03	01	06	Harrall	Abner		Mrs	1842	Se	28	03	02
Hanson			Mss	1878	Jl	07	01	06	Harrel	William	J		1878	Au	28	04	02
Hanson	A	C		1875	Mr	30	01	05	Harrell	Ben		Mr	1873	Jn	19	03	01
Hanson	L			1873	No	18	05	03	Harrell	G	T	Shr	1878	Oc	09	04	03

Last	First	MI	Ttl	Yr	Mo	Day	Pg	Col	Last	First	MI	Ttl	Yr	Mo	Day	Pg	Col
Harrell	Joe			1873	Se	13	01	03	Harrison	Henry			1879	Se	21	01	01
Harrell	John	S		1836	Ap	26	03	05	Harrison	J	S		1878	Jn	04	04	07
Harrell	Nancy			1870	No	26	02	03	Harrison	J	S	Hon	1878	My	31	01	05
Harrell	Patsy		Mss	1873	Jn	19	03	01	Harrison	James	H		1849	Ja	25	03	04
Harrington			Lt	1876	Jl	07	01	03	Harrison	Lina			1879	Se	10	01	01
Harrington			Pvt	1876	Jl	09	01	05	Harrison	R	D		1872	Ap	25	01	03
Harrington	Alfred		Mr	1839	Au	21	03	05	Harrison	R	D	Hon	1872	Ap	23	01	04
Harrington	Bartley		Maj	1835	Ja	27	03	05	Harrison	W	H	Prs	1875	De	02	02	02
Harrington	H	M	Lt	1876	Jl	09	01	05	Harrison	Wiley			1873	My	07	04	02
Harrington	John		Maj	1829	Se	30	03	01	Harrison	William			1871	Jn	10	01	02
Harrington	Kate		Mrs	1871	My	10	04	04	Harrison	William	G	Esq	1853	Fe	18	03	06
Harris				1872	Mr	07	01	05	Harrity	Huga		Cbm	1877	No	25	01	04
Harris				1876	Ap	21	01	03	Harrity	Thomas			1870	Oc	04	01	02
Harris			Col	1874	De	30	01	04	Harrow			Mrs	1872	My	25	01	03
Harris			Dr	1876	No	09	01	04	Hart	Billy		Mr	1874	Se	26	04	03
Harris	Allen			1874	Au	04	01	07	Hart	Billy		Mr	1874	Se	10	04	03
Harris	Arthur	H	Att	1873	Se	11	01	02	Hart	Green			1873	De	27	02	04
Harris	Ben	A	Mr	1872	Mr	26	01	02	Hart	Harry			1878	Au	24	01	03
Harris	Bob			1874	Mr	18	03	01	Hart	John			1871	Se	23	01	03
Harris	C	J		1874	Au	14	01	07	Hart	John			1875	Ap	24	01	03
Harris	Carey	A	Esq	1842	Jl	06	03	02	Hart	L	W		1877	Ja	03	01	04
Harris	Charles		Cpt	1840	De	16	03	03	Hart	Seymour		Mr	1835	No	24	03	03
Harris	Charles	G	Mr	1850	No	22	03	06	Hart	Sivay		Mss	1832	Au	15	03	05
Harris	Charles	G	Mr	1850	De	06	03	06	Hart	W	N		1879	Au	24	01	01
Harris	D	C	Mrs	1879	Se	02	08	03	Hartegan	Willaim			1872	Mr	17	01	05
Harris	Daniel			1875	Jn	06	03	01	Harter	Michael			1872	Se	22	01	05
Harris	Dick			1874	Jn	04	01	06	Hartley	J	B		1873	Se	04	01	02
Harris	Duke	H	Mr	1834	Mr	11	03	05	Hartman			Mr	1875	Jl	07	03	01
Harris	Edwin			1876	De	16	04	01	Hartman	Amanda		Mss	1872	Mr	23	01	04
Harris	Ehas		Ldm	1877	No	25	01	04	Hartman	Conrad			1878	Mr	22	01	06
Harris	Ehas		Ldm	1877	De	02	01	07	Hartman	George	W		1878	My	15	04	03
Harris	Esther		Mrs	1829	Se	23	03	01	Hartman	John	W	Mr	1874	Oc	03	04	08
Harris	Frank			1871	Au	24	02	03	Hartman	Thomas			1878	Oc	15	01	03
Harris	Frank			1876	Ap	21	01	03	Hartt	Edwin			1879	Se	23	01	03
Harris	George	D	Mr	1839	Au	14	03	05	Hartung			Gen	1878	Ja	03	04	06
Harris	George	M	Lt	1873	My	16	01	03	Harvey				1876	De	21	01	04
Harris	Henrietta		Mrs	1875	De	02	04	05	Harvey	Clarke			1878	Oc	04	01	03
Harris	Henry			1879	No	05	08	05	Harvey	Edward			1879	De	23	01	01
Harris	Ira		Sen	1875	De	03	01	06	Harvey	George			1872	Ja	31	04	02
Harris	J	C	Dr	1879	Jl	22	01	02	Harvey	J	B		1876	De	30	01	02
Harris	J	P		1878	De	12	04	05	Harvey	James	B		1877	Ja	03	01	05
Harris	John			1872	Se	25	01	02	Harvey	John			1858	Oc	23	03	04
Harris	John	C	Cap	1837	Se	26	03	05	Harvey	John	H	Mr	1873	Jn	20	04	05
Harris	Jordon			1878	Au	30	01	04	Harvey	Joseph			1876	De	28	04	02
Harris	Kattie		Mrs	1878	Mr	15	01	06	Harvey	Mary			1878	No	06	01	06
Harris	Mamie			1878	Se	22	04	03	Harvey	Peter			1878	Ja	09	03	02
Harris	Mat			1878	Se	22	04	03	Harvey	Peter		Cpt	1878	No	05	01	04
Harris	Mattie		Mrs	1878	Oc	27	01	04	Harvey	Walter		Lt	1878	Oc	11	01	03
Harris	Minnie			1875	De	08	04	03	Harvick	Nicholas		Mr	1837	Ja	31	03	05
Harris	Moses			1871	Fe	16	03	01	Harvill	Fannie	L	Mrs	1859	Au	20	03	02
Harris	R	J	Cpt	1878	Ja	08	04	04	Harwood	Chas			1878	Ap	14	04	06
Harris	Randolph			1874	Au	08	04	04	Hasberg	Nancy			1878	Se	24	01	06
Harris	Richard			1873	Se	12	01	04	Hascall	H	S	Hon	1876	No	21	04	02
Harris	S	O	Col	1836	De	27	03	03	Hascall	H	S	Mr	1876	No	17	04	03
Harris	Sarah	M	Mrs	1874	Jl	16	01	07	Hascall	H	S	Mr	1876	No	18	04	04
Harris	Stephan	R	Dr	1879	Ap	29	01	03	Haskell	Daniel	N		1874	No	14	01	05
Harris	Susan		Mrs	1840	Ap	29	03	03	Haskell	Rachel			1878	Au	22	01	04
Harris	Thomas			1871	Jn	23	01	03	Haskins	America		Mss	1872	Ja	16	01	02
Harris	William			1872	Mr	26	01	04	Haskins	Marshall			1879	Au	03	01	01
Harris	William			1874	Oc	31	02	02	Hasler	Infant			1879	Jn	07	08	01
Harris	William	G		1874	Au	08	04	04	Hastings			Mr	1871	Au	29	01	03
Harris	Willie			1878	Se	22	04	03	Hastings	William	K		1876	Oc	28	01	03
Harrison			Pvt	1876	Jl	09	01	05	Hatcher				1871	Jn	10	01	02
Harrison	Axley			1875	Mr	31	01	06	Hatcher	J	J		1878	Oc	03	01	03
Harrison	Elizabeth		Mrs	1852	My	07	03	07	Hatcher	Samuel	A		1879	Au	01	01	01
Harrison	George			1878	Oc	06	01	03	Hatchett	E	G	Esq	1867	Oc	22	04	08

Last	First	MI	Ttl	Yr	Mo	Day	Pg	Col	Last	First	MI	Ttl	Yr	Mo	Day	Pg	Col
Hatchkin	Ebenezer		Rev	1867	No	12	05	02	Hays	Samuel	H	Col	1872	Ja	04	01	02
Hatfield			Mr	1872	Au	14	01	04	Hays	Samuel	M	Bro	1872	Ja	18	04	04
Hatfield	John			1871	My	26	01	03	Hays	Steven			1876	Ap	12	04	06
Hatfield	William		Shr	1872	Jn	13	01	05	Hays	William	N	Mr	1848	Ja	27	03	03
Hatheway	Ed		Mrs	1879	Ap	12	04	05	Hayward	George			1872	Oc	23	01	04
Hatter	John	C		1873	Jn	15	01	04	Haywood				1874	Ap	10	01	05
Hauck	James	S	Jr	1879	Se	09	01	01	Haywood	George			1872	Oc	24	01	06
Hauck	Mary	E		1879	Se	09	01	01	Haywood	John		Hon	1827	Fe	06	03	01
Haught			Dr	1879	Fe	26	01	06	Hazeltine	Elta			1878	Ja	08	01	06
Haunstein	Enil			1878	Se	22	04	03	Hazelton	Peter			1870	Oc	16	01	02
Hausinger			Md	1873	Au	26	01	03	Hazen	William	C		1872	Ap	26	01	01
Havemeyer		May		1874	De	01	01	03	Hazieton	A		Jud	1879	De	21	01	02
Hawes	William	R		1879	No	07	01	02	Hazlett	G	B		1875	Mr	16	01	03
Hawkins			Mar	1872	Ap	21	01	05	Hazlett	Jacob		Mr	1828	Se	23	03	02
Hawkins	Alvan	S		1878	Oc	13	01	03	Hazy	Kelley			1878	Oc	31	01	06
Hawkins	Chester	A		1853	Mr	11	03	06	Head	Elizabeth		Mrs	1840	Au	05	03	05
Hawkins	E	W	Mr	1872	Jl	09	01	02	Head	J	M		1875	De	04	01	06
Hawkins	Eliza	J		1876	Ap	02	04	07	Head	Jno	W	Con	1879	Ap	08	02	02
Hawkins	George	A		1838	No	21	03	05	Head	John	W	Hon	1874	No	10	01	04
Hawkins	James		Mr	1829	Mr	25	03	03	Headington	Elliot		Mr	1844	My	29	03	03
Hawkins	Jas	R		1877	No	24	01	07	Heads	Jasper			1879	Au	23	05	01
Hawkins	Mary		Mrs	1834	No	18	03	05	Heady	Francis			1878	Se	28	01	04
Hawkins	Samuel		Mr	1872	No	05	01	04	Heady	J	J	Dr	1878	Se	24	01	04
Hawkins	Samuel		Mrs	1872	No	05	01	04	Heald	Lucy		Mrs	1853	Au	19	03	05
Hawkins	Sylvia		Mrs	1844	Jl	24	03	04	Healy	R			1877	Oc	25	01	06
Hawkins	William	J	Cpt	1869	No	28	02	03	Heard	Columbus			1878	Se	24	01	06
Hawkins	Willie	B		1869	Se	25	04	01	Heard	Jesse			1879	Au	08	01	01
Hawks	J		Esq	1872	De	20	01	04	Heard	John	H		1868	Fe	25	02	08
Hawks	Julia	A		1875	Mr	14	01	03	Heard	Mary	F		1858	Oc	23	03	03
Hawley	Daniel			1878	Se	01	01	03	Heard	Mary	F		1868	Fe	25	02	08
Hawley	E	P	Mrs	1878	No	05	01	03	Hearde	J	E		1878	Oc	03	01	03
Hawley	Isaac	C		1878	Oc	08	01	03	Hearn	Ella			1879	Jn	20	05	01
Hawley	Patrick			1873	Fe	04	01	04	Hearn	H	B	Dr	1873	De	27	02	04
Hawrush	Curtis			1848	Ja	27	03	03	Heath	J	W		1878	Se	18	01	07
Haws	Julia			1874	My	28	01	06	Heath	John			1874	Jl	19	01	04
Hawthorne	Alfa		Mrs	1879	No	11	01	03	Heath	Richard	K	Mr	1822	Fe	09	03	03
Hawthorne	Nathaniel		Mrs	1871	Mr	02	01	02	Heaton	W	W	Cj	1877	De	27	01	05
Hay	Francis		Md	1874	Fe	08	01	04	Heenan	John	C		1873	Oc	29	01	02
Hayden	Ella	C		1858	Oc	23	03	04	Heenan	John	C		1873	De	07	01	04
Hayden	Jeremiah	D	Maj	1826	Jn	27	03	02	Hefferman	James			1879	Oc	04	01	02
Hayden	John			1878	Au	10	01	03	Hefferman	Jerry			1878	Au	27	01	04
Hayes	C	H		1877	De	11	01	05	Hefford	John	B		1875	Jn	06	03	01
Hayes	J			1878	Se	26	01	04	Heggle			Pvt	1876	Jl	09	01	05
Hayes	Mary			1878	Se	01	01	03	Heidel	R	B		1878	Oc	20	01	03
Hayes	Mathias		Cmc	1877	No	25	01	04	Heill			Mrs	1873	De	31	01	03
Hayes	Oliver			1871	Jn	23	01	03	Heilman	John	C	Mr	1852	De	10	03	06
Hayle	James	T		1879	Jl	19	05	01	Heilman	M	W	Mrs	1840	Jl	22	03	03
Haymaker	J	S	Col	1871	No	30	01	03	Heiser	Henry			1873	Oc	18	01	03
Hayne	Nancy	C		1867	Ja	08	01	02	Heiskell	Margaret		Mrs	1837	Jn	20	03	06
Hayne	Nancy	M	Mrs	1867	Ja	08	01	02	Heitman	Charlotte		Mrs	1876	Se	28	04	06
Haynes	A	J	Cpt	1869	Jl	27	02	03	Heitman	Will			1876	No	04	04	05
Haynes	Landon	C	Hon	1875	Fe	19	01	04	Heldrich	Father		Rev	1878	Oc	25	01	04
Haynes	Mamie			1878	Au	29	01	04	Heller	Burt			1874	Au	26	01	07
Haynes	Sarah		Mrs	1851	My	16	03	07	Helm	J	B		1874	Ja	25	01	04
Haynes	William		Mr	1850	Oc	18	03	06	Helmer				1876	Jl	09	01	05
Haynie	Benjamin			1858	De	25	03	03	Helmer	Charles	D	Rev	1879	Ap	30	05	01
Haynie	Mary	J		1842	Jl	13	03	04	Hemmerly	John			1878	Se	22	04	03
Haynie	Maryann	E		1859	Jn	18	02	08	Hempstead	Albert			1847	Au	12	03	03
Haynie	Sammie	G		1872	No	14	01	04	Hempstead	B	F	Esq	1853	Se	09	03	06
Haynie	Seth			1859	Ja	01	03	02	Hempstead	Lena			1855	Jn	08	03	06
Haynie	Urban		Mr	1832	Oc	17	03	04	Hempstead	O	H		1878	Se	10	01	03
Haynie	William		Esq	1853	Oc	28	03	07	Hempstead	Shelby			1873	Au	13	04	05
Hays	Catherine			1877	Se	14	01	07	Hencke			Mrs	1875	My	12	01	06
Hays	Eliza			1876	Ap	12	04	06	Henderson				1876	Mr	31	04	03
Hays	Jack		Col	1849	Jn	21	02	03	Henderson	Alexander			1831	Au	17	03	05
Hays	John		Sea	1877	No	25	01	04	Henderson	Alford	C	Mr	1855	Mr	09	03	06

Last	First	MI	Ttl	Yr	Mo	Day	Pg	Col	Last	First	MI	Ttl	Yr	Mo	Day	Pg	Col
Henderson	Catherine	E	Mss	1878	Se	03	04	05	Herdon	Dabney		Dr	1870	No	04	03	01
Henderson	Catherine	F	Mss	1878	Se	01	04	06	Herdon	W	C	Dr	1878	Se	14	01	05
Henderson	Cora			1873	Oc	17	04	07	Herdson			Dr	1878	Se	13	01	05
Henderson	Eliza		Mrs	1870	Au	14	03	01	Herman	Frank			1871	Jl	11	01	06
Henderson	Joseph		Mr	1842	De	14	03	03	Herman	Max			1878	Se	22	04	03
Henderson	Mary	A		1837	Jn	06	02	06	Hernandez	M			1878	Au	22	01	04
Henderson	Mary	B	Sis	1859	De	10	03	01	Hernesson	Pauline			1878	Se	22	04	03
Henderson	Morris		Rev	1877	Oc	28	02	02	Hernsteger	B		Rev	1878	Oc	19	01	05
Henderson	R			1878	Se	04	01	03	Heron	John			1876	De	05	04	04
Hendricks	Christopher			1871	No	16	01	03	Heron	John	T		1878	Ja	15	04	01
Hendren	Dollie		Mss	1876	My	10	01	05	Herring	D	S	Lt	1836	Au	02	03	05
Hendren	William			1875	Oc	01	04	04	Herring	Ichabod		Bro	1869	De	25	02	03
Hendrick	W	E		1874	De	18	04	06	Herriott	George	R	Cpt	1873	Fe	21	04	03
Hendricks				1877	Ja	24	01	05	Herroid			Mr	1873	De	24	01	03
Hendricks			Mr	1871	My	10	01	01	Herron	Bertha			1876	De	19	02	04
Hendricks			Mrs	1873	My	10	02	03	Herron	Fielding		Bro	1870	Jl	17	03	01
Hendricks	Ann	E		1879	Au	31	01	01	Herron	Isaac			1872	Se	28	01	03
Hendricks	Infant			1872	Se	07	01	04	Herron	John	T		1878	Ja	19	04	02
Hendricks	N	H		1875	Fe	17	01	07	Herschel	John	W	Mr	1871	My	14	01	08
Hendricks	Rosa			1879	Au	06	01	01	Herzberge			Eng	1877	De	29	01	05
Hendricks	Samuel		Mr	1879	No	06	05	02	Hesse			Mrs	1871	Fe	28	01	01
Hendricks	Samuel		Mrs	1879	No	06	05	02	Hesse	John			1871	Fe	28	01	02
Hendrickson	John			1878	Se	15	01	06	Hesser	Fredrick			1878	Ap	14	04	06
Hendrickson	Thos		Col	1878	Oc	27	04	06	Hester	H	M	Mrs	1872	Jn	16	04	07
Hendrix	Henry	B	Cpt	1870	My	04	02	02	Hesterley	Mary	A	Mrs	1843	Fe	01	03	04
Hendrix	William			1877	Se	23	01	04	Heston	W	J	Dua	1873	Oc	15	02	03
Hendrixon	Henry			1874	De	05	01	04	Hetzch	Fritz			1879	Au	12	01	01
Henley	Robert		Cpt	1828	De	09	03	01	Hewett	H	S		1874	Ap	05	01	03
Henn	John	E	Mr	1876	Ap	12	04	04	Hewett	Mike			1878	Se	17	01	04
Henn	John	E	Mr	1876	Ap	12	04	07	Hewett	Peter			1878	Au	30	01	04
Hennessey	James	A	Rev	1875	Oc	12	01	02	Hewitt	Jennie		Mrs	1878	Oc	09	01	03
Hennessey	Patrick			1868	Mr	31	03	04	Hewson	M	F		1872	De	31	01	03
Hennessy	John			1879	Jl	29	01	03	Heyman	Howard			1878	Se	01	01	03
Henniger	Rose			1878	Oc	31	01	04	Heymann	H			1878	Se	01	01	03
Henning	Charles			1871	De	19	04	03	Hezekiah	F	W		1878	Ap	21	04	06
Henny	Julia		Mrs	1878	Oc	10	01	03	Hezekiah	Fred	W		1878	Ap	21	04	04
Henri	Charles		Pro	1874	Ap	08	04	06	Hezetish	Emma			1871	Fe	14	01	01
Henry	Ann		Mrs	1823	De	23	03	03	Hibbard	J			1875	Jl	07	03	01
Henry	Ben			1878	Ap	28	04	04	Hibbert	John			1872	Jn	23	01	04
Henry	Catherine		Mrs	1850	Fe	08	03	06	Hibbets	Emma			1878	Ap	24	04	05
Henry	Charles			1872	Ap	21	04	01	Hibbets	Marget			1878	Ap	24	04	05
Henry	Cross			1879	Oc	12	01	01	Hibbette	J	L	Dr	1873	No	18	04	03
Henry	Frank	B		1879	My	01	08	05	Hibbler	Lewis			1875	No	27	01	04
Henry	Frank	B		1879	My	04	08	03	Hickerson	L			1878	Se	22	04	03
Henry	George	M		1878	Au	06	01	06	Hickery	Walter			1860	De	01	03	01
Henry	Henry	J	Bro	1872	Ja	24	01	04	Hickey			Mr	1871	Au	26	01	04
Henry	Isaac	N	Esq	1821	Fe	17	03	01	Hickey	C	A	Mrs	1874	Ap	25	01	03
Henry	John	A		1830	Se	08	02	05	Hickey	Catherine		Mrs	1879	Ap	08	01	02
Henry	Joseph			1878	Oc	13	01	05	Hickey	Elizabeth		Mrs	1876	Se	22	03	01
Henry	Joseph		Pro	1878	My	14	04	06	Hickey	Michael			1872	Jl	18	01	04
Henry	Joseph		Pro	1878	My	22	03	01	Hickman	John			1873	Ja	21	01	03
Henry	Mary	E	Mrs	1845	My	26	03	05	Hickman	William	P	Mr	1842	Au	24	03	06
Henry	Robert			1871	De	27	01	03	Hicks			Jud	1871	Jl	02	01	01
Henry	William		Mr	1835	My	26	03	05	Hicks			Jud	1871	Jl	19	01	02
Henry	Willie	P		1866	Ja	20	03	03	Hicks	Ada			1879	Jl	30	01	01
Henshaw	John	P	Rev	1852	Au	13	03	07	Hicks	E	M		1879	No	23	01	03
Hensley	Lydia	E		1849	Jl	12	03	05	Hicks	George			1878	Se	22	04	03
Hensley	Robert	L		1871	De	23	04	05	Hicks	George	B		1873	My	03	01	05
Hensley	Rose	P	Mrs	1871	My	23	01	04	Hicks	J	L		1875	Jn	27	03	01
Henson			Mr	1817	Jl	30	01	06	Hicks	James			1872	Jn	08	04	02
Henson	John			1878	My	05	01	05	Hicks	Jane		Mss	1877	Ja	03	04	05
Henthorn	Nimrod	E	Mr	1871	My	16	01	02	Hicks	Jesse	E		1851	Se	26	03	06
Hentley	Lena			1878	Oc	01	01	05	Hicks	John		Dr	1878	Se	19	01	04
Her	N	C		1873	Se	28	01	05	Hicks	Leon			1870	No	15	04	05
Herbert				1878	Se	22	04	03	Hicks	Leona	L		1870	No	15	04	05
Herdon			Dr	1877	Oc	17	04	05	Hicks	Minnie	D		1867	Jl	23	02	08

Last	First	MI	Ttl	Yr	Mo	Day	Pg	Col	Last	First	MI	Ttl	Yr	Mo	Day	Pg	Col
Hicks	William			1872	Ap	24	01	01	Hinds	Jahn		Maj	1838	Au	08	03	04
Hicks	William			1872	Ap	26	01	02	Hinds	John		Mr	1833	Jl	03	03	03
Hicks	William		Col	1869	Au	26	02	03	Hinds	Margaret			1879	Se	07	01	01
Hicky	John			1876	Oc	31	01	04	Hine	Jonas			1879	Mr	14	01	04
Hide	Clarke		Mr	1868	Se	22	03	06	Hines	Ed			1879	Fe	12	01	02
Hiern	R			1878	Oc	04	01	04	Hines	Edward			1871	My	31	01	02
Hiesland	W	P		1879	Oc	05	01	01	Hines	Jacob			1871	Jn	10	01	01
Hiestand			Mss	1872	Oc	02	01	08	Hines	John	A	Cpt	1878	Ja	15	01	07
Higbee				1873	De	07	01	01	Hines	Martin			1878	Ja	15	01	07
Higbee	E	Y	Rev	1871	De	12	01	03	Hines	Micheal			1878	Ja	15	01	07
Higby	Angeline			1878	Se	22	01	05	Hines	Owen			1874	Ja	14	02	03
Higgins			Mrs	1871	My	10	01	02	Hines	Owen			1878	Ja	15	01	07
Higgins	Andy	R		1878	Se	17	01	06	Hines	Thomas			1878	Ja	15	01	07
Higgins	J	M		1879	Oc	07	01	01	Hines	Thomas		Mr	1871	My	13	01	03
Higgins	Robert	B		1872	Mr	07	01	05	Hinkson	Samuel	H	Maj	1834	De	23	03	04
Higgins	William			1878	Se	22	04	03	Hinsbrell	Joseph			1876	Oc	06	01	01
Hight	Frank			1879	De	27	05	01	Hinse	W	B	Col	1878	Oc	21	01	03
Hightower	David			1878	Se	01	01	03	Hinton	Hugh	C	Esq	1841	Jl	21	03	05
Hilcher	Hiram			1879	Au	23	01	01	Hipple	Joseph			1871	Se	12	01	04
Hiley	John			1833	No	13	03	04	Hislett	George	C		1876	Oc	28	01	03
Hill			Frm	1878	Fe	14	01	08	Hitchcock	Samuel	A		1873	No	25	01	02
Hill			Mr	1872	Jl	13	04	02	Hitcher	C	H		1879	Au	26	01	01
Hill	Arthur			1878	Se	01	01	03	Hite	W			1876	De	12	01	01
Hill	Eli	S	Maj	1858	Oc	09	03	03	Hitt			Mr	1878	Ja	20	03	02
Hill	Elizabeth		Mrs	1866	Oc	16	03	08	Hitzfield	Will			1878	Se	22	04	03
Hill	Emma			1879	Se	18	01	01	Hixon	Benjamin		Mr	1836	No	29	03	05
Hill	George			1871	Jl	09	01	05	Hixon	Lucus		Dr	1830	Au	18	03	01
Hill	George			1871	Jl	11	01	06	Hobart	John	H	Dr	1830	Oc	20	03	01
Hill	George			1879	Se	10	01	01	Hobb	William			1878	Jl	19	01	04
Hill	George		Gen	1849	Fe	22	03	05	Hobbs				1874	Ap	14	03	01
Hill	George		Mr	1873	My	20	01	04	Hobbs	Lilly			1869	Se	24	04	01
Hill	Issac	D		1876	No	01	01	04	Hockersmith			Mrs	1876	Ja	29	04	03
Hill	Jacob		Mrs	1870	No	01	01	01	Hodge	William		Sea	1877	No	25	01	04
Hill	James	F		1859	Au	27	03	01	Hodge	William		Sea	1877	De	02	01	07
Hill	John			1876	Oc	28	01	03	Hodges				1878	Se	22	04	03
Hill	John	W	Bro	1871	Oc	26	04	04	Hodges	A	M		1878	Mr	12	01	06
Hill	Margaret		Mrs	1876	Ap	13	04	05	Hodges	Andison		Bro	1872	Ja	05	01	04
Hill	Moses		Aon	1878	Ap	14	04	02	Hodges	B	M		1878	Se	22	04	03
Hill	Moses		Mrs	1878	Ja	03	04	01	Hodges	Dock			1875	Ap	30	01	04
Hill	Nettie		Mss	1873	My	10	02	03	Hodges	E		Mrs	1878	Se	22	04	03
Hill	Paul	C	Mr	1870	Ja	12	04	02	Hodges	Mittie			1875	Ap	30	01	04
Hill	Rowland		Sir	1879	Au	28	01	03	Hodges	Rose			1879	Se	17	01	01
Hill	Sam			1878	Se	04	01	03	Hodges	W	P	Dr	1878	Se	05	01	03
Hill	Sam	E		1874	Mr	22	04	03	Hodges	W	R	Dr	1878	Se	05	01	03
Hill	Samuel			1871	Jn	02	01	03	Hodgson			Lt	1876	Jl	07	01	03
Hill	Samuel			1874	Mr	20	04	03	Hodgson			Lt	1876	Jl	09	01	05
Hill	T	J		1872	Jn	01	04	03	Hodson	Julius	A		1870	My	04	03	01
Hill	Thomas	J		1872	My	31	04	02	Hoehre	Max	H		1878	Fe	24	01	05
Hill	Thomas	T	Bro	1869	De	25	02	03	Hoffan	Annie	M	Mss	1879	Se	24	08	02
Hill	W	A		1878	Se	22	04	03	Hoffheimer			Mr	1871	My	20	01	03
Hill	William	W		1878	My	30	01	06	Hoffman			Dr	1873	My	10	02	03
Hillen	Thomas		Mr	1840	Oc	28	03	05	Hoffman			Jud	1877	No	18	04	05
Hills	Nick			1879	Au	15	01	03	Hoffman	Fred		Sea	1877	No	25	01	04
Hillsman	Sophia	M	Mrs	1873	Ja	08	01	05	Hoffman	John		Mr	1874	Ap	11	04	03
Hillyer	Giles	M	Col	1871	Ap	29	02	02	Hoffman	John	P		1879	Au	31	01	01
Hilscher	Elizabeth		Mrs	1879	Au	19	01	01	Hoffman	Max	F	Md	1874	Mr	22	01	03
Hinchman	Oscar			1875	Mr	11	01	03	Hoffman	Murray			1878	My	09	04	04
Hincks	William			1879	Jl	25	05	01	Hofstatter	Nettie	C		1879	Jl	18	08	06
Hind	C		Mrs	1878	Jl	19	01	04	Hogan			Cor	1876	Jl	09	01	05
Hinderliter	Jesse		Mr	1834	Jl	29	03	03	Hogan	A	O		1878	Se	07	01	04
Hinderliter	Sophia		Mrs	1831	Jn	01	03	04	Hogan	Charley			1872	My	08	04	02
Hindman			Mr	1874	De	11	04	03	Hogan	Fred			1879	Oc	19	08	03
Hindman	Thomas			1874	Ap	15	01	04	Hogan	James			1827	Se	25	03	01
Hindman	Thomas	C	Gen	1868	Se	29	02	01	Hogan	Jane		Mrs	1842	Se	07	05	04
Hindman	Thomas	C	Gen	1874	Ap	27	04	04	Hogan	John			1872	Mr	26	01	05
Hinds	Isabella	J	Mrs	1840	Se	23	03	06	Hogan	John			1875	Jn	29	04	03

Last	First	MI	Ttl	Yr	Mo	Day	Pg	Col	Last	First	MI	Ttl	Yr	Mo	Day	Pg	Col
Hogan	John			1875	Jl	02	04	03	Holt	O	H		1878	Se	05	01	04
Hogan	Matthew		Mr	1842	Jn	22	03	04	Holtzclaw	Howard			1879	Fe	08	01	02
Hogan	Nancy		Mrs	1824	Ja	27	03	01	Holtzman	George	W	Mr	1852	Oc	15	03	06
Hogan	Sarah		Mrs	1853	Fe	11	03	06	Holtzman	Henry	B		1865	Jl	22	03	01
Hogden	James			1878	Se	22	04	03	Holtzman	William	F	Mr	1866	Au	18	02	01
Hoge	John			1879	Au	16	05	01	Holy	David		Dr	1839	My	08	03	05
Hoge	William			1871	Jl	18	01	02	Homan	Annie			1875	Ja	12	04	07
Hogeboon	Henry		Jus	1872	Se	13	01	04	Homel	P	W		1871	No	14	01	02
Hogin	Jas			1879	Fe	12	01	02	Homer	William	H	Lt	1829	De	09	03	03
Hogue	Tatlor			1872	My	25	01	01	Honck	Sarah	A	Mrs	1851	Oc	10	03	07
Hohemyer			Sgt	1876	Jl	09	01	05	Honey	William	P	Bro	1869	Jn	12	02	03
Hohlen	Amelia			1878	Se	05	01	03	Honsinger	Wilo	M		1873	Jn	11	01	04
Holcomb	Harrison		Mr	1842	Mr	16	03	02	Hood	Anna	M	Mrs	1879	Au	29	05	02
Holcomb	John	R	Rev	1876	De	20	02	05	Hood	John	H		1879	Se	11	01	01
Holcomb	R	W		1878	Oc	21	01	03	Hood	Thomas			1875	Jn	02	03	01
Holcomb	William	P		1872	Fe	24	01	05	Hood	Thomas			1878	Se	10	01	03
Hole	Richard		Jr	1872	Au	20	01	06	Hood	Thos	B		1878	Se	22	04	03
Holford	Neal		Mr	1876	Fe	18	02	04	Hood	Tom			1874	No	21	01	03
Holford	Neill		Mr	1876	Fe	20	04	03	Hood	William			1830	Se	08	02	04
Holford	W	W		1875	Oc	12	01	03	Hooe	William	T		1871	De	24	04	01
Holiby				1874	Mr	11	03	01	Hook	James	H	Lcl	1841	De	22	03	05
Holland			Mr	1873	My	02	01	04	Hooker			Gen	1879	No	02	01	03
Holland	Henry		Sir	1874	Ja	08	01	02	Hooker			Gen	1879	No	06	01	03
Holland	John			1878	My	25	04	06	Hooker	Joseph		Gen	1879	No	05	05	01
Holland	John		Wdc	1877	No	25	01	04	Hooley	James			1879	Jl	04	05	01
Holland	T	P		1878	Oc	13	01	03	Hoon	M	S	Mss	1878	Oc	04	01	03
Hollander	Bonnie	E	Mss	1879	Jl	25	01	01	Hoon	William	J		1878	Oc	02	01	04
Hollander	Fred			1879	Au	08	01	01	Hooper	Alanson		Mr	1850	Jl	05	03	06
Hollander	Robert			1879	Au	12	01	02	Hooper	Charles	F		1878	Mr	15	01	05
Hollbert	John			1874	My	03	01	07	Hooper	J		Mr	1878	Mr	21	02	03
Hollenburg	B	A	Mrs	1878	Au	28	01	03	Hooper	Magdaline		Mrs	1877	Ja	04	04	04
Holleran	John			1876	Mr	14	04	05	Hoover			Mr	1874	No	07	04	03
Holliday	Julia		Mrs	1872	Oc	11	01	06	Hoover	Jacob			1870	Se	20	04	04
Hollingswort	M			1878	Se	04	01	03	Hoover	Jacob		Mr	1838	Jn	13	03	03
Hollins	George	N	Cdr	1878	Ja	20	01	06	Hoover	William	S		1874	Jl	01	01	05
Hollis	William	M		1868	Mr	03	03	05	Hooz	William			1877	De	30	01	07
Hollman	Louis			1878	Se	11	01	06	Hope	Elis		Mrs	1873	My	10	02	03
Hollman	William			1877	Oc	06	01	06	Hope	George			1878	Se	22	04	03
Hollman	William		Mrs	1877	Oc	06	01	06	Hope	Jenny		Mss	1871	Au	26	01	05
Hollohan				1873	Au	02	01	02	Hope	William	W		1871	Mr	28	03	01
Hollowell	Forrest			1879	Au	28	01	01	Hopkins	A	W	Dr	1877	Ja	06	01	03
Hollowell	George			1878	Jl	23	04	03	Hopkins	Daniel		Mr	1856	Au	16	03	05
Hollows	John			1874	Jl	07	01	06	Hopkins	F	G	Esq	1843	Au	16	03	05
Hollshan				1873	Au	03	01	06	Hopkins	Florence			1879	Au	14	01	01
Holly	John			1879	Au	02	01	01	Hopkins	John			1873	De	27	01	03
Holly	Katie			1879	Au	08	01	01	Hopkins	John			1874	Ja	08	01	02
Holly	Micheal			1879	Au	08	01	01	Hopkins	John	D	Pro	1877	Oc	17	04	05
Holman	Carolina			1878	Se	22	04	03	Hopkins	Mark			1878	Mr	30	01	06
Holman	Henry			1879	Oc	07	01	01	Hopkins	Mark			1878	Mr	31	01	06
Holman	Mary			1879	Au	24	01	01	Hopkins	Samuel			1820	Ja	22	03	01
Holmes	Arthur		Mrs	1872	Jl	27	01	04	Hopkins	Samuel		Gen	1820	Ja	22	03	01
Holmes	Basil			1873	De	07	01	04	Hopotsky	Edward			1879	Se	27	01	01
Holmes	David		Gov	1832	Se	26	03	03	Hopper	Henrietta			1853	My	20	03	07
Holmes	George			1875	Jl	01	01	04	Horan	Katie		Mss	1879	Au	01	01	03
Holmes	Henry			1878	Se	04	01	03	Horant	Mary			1878	Oc	02	01	05
Holmes	J		Mrs	1879	Oc	16	01	01	Hord	R	C	Jud	1874	Fe	13	01	04
Holmes	W	I	Mr	1874	Mr	21	04	02	Horgan	Conrad			1878	Oc	23	01	06
Holson			Mrs	1871	Oc	03	01	03	Horn	Buffalo			1878	Jn	19	04	05
Holst			Mrs	1878	Se	22	04	03	Horn	Calvin	J		1879	Oc	28	05	02
Holst	Theo			1878	Se	25	01	04	Horn	Dan		Mrs	1872	My	23	01	04
Holston	Nehemiah			1875	Oc	02	01	03	Horn	Jack			1877	De	15	01	06
Holt				1877	No	01	02	02	Hornberger			Jud	1871	Jl	06	01	04
Holt	Elias			1872	My	31	01	01	Horne	Jefferson	V	Maj	1857	De	19	03	03
Holt	John	A		1878	Oc	03	01	03	Horner	Julia		Mrs	1833	Oc	02	03	04
Holt	Mollie		Mss	1871	De	24	01	03	Horner	Patty		Mrs	1831	No	28	03	05
Holt	Mollie		Mss	1872	Ja	09	01	01	Horner	William	B	Col	1838	My	09	03	05

Last	First	MI	Ttl	Yr	Mo	Day	Pg	Col
Hornet			Pvt	1876	Jl	09	01	05
Horrell	William	Y		1877	Se	16	04	06
Hort	Herman			1878	Se	22	04	03
Horton	Chas			1871	Jl	19	01	02
Hosrins	William		Mrs	1871	No	06	01	02
Hoss	James			1873	No	18	04	03
Hoss	Nathan			1873	No	18	05	03
Hotchkiss	Fred			1878	Ja	17	04	05
Hotchkiss	Giles	W		1878	Jl	06	02	04
Hotter	Lizzie			1879	Au	07	01	01
Houck	J	S		1879	Se	05	01	01
Houck	J	S	Mrs	1879	Se	12	01	01
Hough	Charles			1874	Mr	17	02	03
Hough	H	W	Hon	1878	Fe	16	01	06
House	David	P		1879	Au	02	01	10
House	Irwin		Rev	1875	My	21	01	03
House	John			1879	Jn	15	01	02
Houseman	W	L	Msa	1877	No	25	01	04
Houstadt	Bella			1870	Se	27	02	03
Houstin	Martin			1879	Ja	17	01	03
Houston	John			1873	Se	23	03	02
Houston	John	P	Maj	1838	My	23	03	03
Houston	Sam		Cap	1874	My	09	01	01
Houston	Sam		Cap	1874	My	09	04	03
Houston	Sam		Cpt	1875	My	11	04	02
Houston	Sam		Mrs	1870	Oc	12	03	01
Houston	Samuel		Cpt	1875	My	09	04	03
Houston	Taylor			1871	De	07	01	01
Hovey			Mr	1874	Ap	23	01	03
Howard				1877	Oc	12	01	04
Howard				1877	De	19	01	06
Howard				1878	Ja	05	01	06
Howard				1878	Fe	03	01	07
Howard			Jud	1877	De	28	01	06
Howard			Jud	1878	Se	12	04	05
Howard			Mr	1873	Au	22	01	03
Howard			Mr	1876	Oc	06	04	02
Howard			Mr	1877	No	24	03	01
Howard	B	F	Col	1865	Oc	21	03	03
Howard	Barry			1878	Se	22	04	03
Howard	C		Mrs	1878	Oc	06	01	03
Howard	Charlette		Mrs	1879	Se	16	05	01
Howard	Clara			1859	Mr	19	03	01
Howard	D	B		1878	Oc	13	01	05
Howard	James		Cpt	1876	Oc	15	01	02
Howard	M	J	Mrs	1878	Oc	15	01	03
Howard	Moses			1870	Mr	11	04	01
Howard	N	P	Law	1870	My	04	03	01
Howard	Phillip	R		1873	No	04	01	04
Howard	Solomon			1874	Ja	08	01	02
Howard	Solomon		Mr	1834	Au	05	03	03
Howard	Washington			1876	Ap	12	01	02
Howard	Wiley			1871	Jl	06	01	04
Howard	William			1871	Jl	06	01	04
Howard	William			1873	Au	16	01	03
Howard	William		Rev	1876	Se	23	01	01
Howard	William	P		1862	Jl	12	02	05
Howe			Mr	1822	Jn	11	03	01
Howe	Edward	C	Mr	1878	De	20	04	03
Howe	George		Dr	1871	Au	03	01	05
Howe	George		Mrs	1871	Au	03	01	05
Howel	John		Col	1847	Oc	28	03	04
Howell			Mr	1877	De	04	03	04
Howell	Adlisa		Mrs	1874	Ap	26	04	08
Howell	D	R	Cpt	1877	No	13	01	05
Howell	George			1878	Se	06	01	06
Howell	Henry		Mr	1875	My	05	04	03
Howell	Margaret	W	Mrs	1859	Oc	01	03	02
Howell	Nelson			1871	Fe	25	04	04
Howell	P	J	Mrs	1867	Ap	02	03	04
Howell	Philo			1857	No	14	03	03
Howell	Samuel	W		1842	No	16	03	04
Howell	W	J	Shr	1878	Se	06	04	02
Howerton	Carrell		Mr	1852	De	31	03	06
Howerton	F	F	Mr	1872	Au	31	01	03
Howerton	Fannie	A	Mrs	1871	Au	25	04	02
Howgood	James		Col	1870	No	12	01	02
Howlett	W	T	Mr	1873	My	27	02	03
Hubbard	A	W	Jud	1879	Se	23	05	01
Hubbard	G	F	Dr	1877	Ja	06	01	04
Hubbard	H	W	Dr	1877	Ja	30	01	07
Hubbard	Saray			1871	De	28	01	02
Hubert				1871	Mr	04	01	02
Hubuck	Hawry			1871	Jl	19	01	03
Huchardt	W	S		1879	Au	17	01	03
Huddleston	Corrie			1873	Fe	11	02	04
Huddleston	Jas	K		1878	No	17	02	04
Hudgens	Ambrose		Mr	1838	De	12	03	05
Hudgens	John		Mr	1828	Se	23	03	02
Hudgens	Lewis	D		1833	Se	11	03	05
Hudgens	Lucinda			1835	Oc	27	03	06
Hudgins	Eliza			1840	Se	16	03	04
Hudman	William			1878	Oc	04	01	03
Hudson	Bob		Mr	1877	De	08	04	03
Hudson	Henry			1872	My	24	01	03
Hudson	Henry		Jud	1873	Jn	05	01	02
Hudson	James	B	Mr	1855	De	14	03	06
Hudson	John	R		1858	Oc	23	03	03
Hudson	Joshua		Mr	1866	Oc	09	03	02
Hudson	Leo			1873	Jn	07	01	02
Hudson	Martha	T		1849	Jn	21	02	04
Hudson	Mary		Mrs	1852	De	24	03	06
Hudson	Monroe			1868	Ap	07	03	04
Hudson	Sidnor	T		1875	Jn	29	04	02
Hudson	William			1878	Se	22	04	03
Hudson	William	J		1874	Fe	14	02	03
Huehes	J	E	Mrs	1878	Au	22	01	04
Huerta			Col	1872	Jl	12	01	04
Huesey	Marion			1879	Au	17	05	01
Hueson	Jacob	V		1879	Ja	05	01	02
Huff	Isaac		Mr	1873	Jn	27	01	02
Huff	M	W		1878	Oc	06	01	03
Hufford	Thos			1878	Oc	06	01	03
Hugey	Ellen			1878	Oc	18	01	06
Hugey	Georgia			1878	Oc	18	01	06
Hughes			Mss	1878	Se	22	04	03
Hughes			Pvt	1876	Jl	09	01	05
Hughes			Sgt	1876	Jl	09	01	05
Hughes	Ann			1879	Se	11	01	01
Hughes	Benjamin			1871	No	19	01	04
Hughes	Garrison	P	Mr	1857	Mr	07	03	04
Hughes	George	T		1872	Se	13	01	05
Hughes	John			1878	Au	30	01	04
Hughes	John		Gen	1830	Mr	09	03	05
Hughes	John	J		1878	Fe	14	04	05
Hughes	Johnnie			1878	Fe	14	04	02
Hughes	Louisa	S	Mrs	1860	Ap	21	03	01
Hughes	Marshall			1878	Mr	13	01	06
Hughes	Marshall		Dsh	1878	Mr	02	01	04

Last	First	MI	Ttl	Yr	Mo	Day	Pg	Col	Last	First	MI	Ttl	Yr	Mo	Day	Pg	Col
Hughes	Mary	F	Mrs	1859	Jn	18	02	08	Huss	John			1875	Oc	16	01	04
Hughes	William	H		1878	Au	23	01	03	Hutchens	A	V	Maj	1879	Fe	27	01	04
Hughey	Freeman			1876	Mr	02	04	03	Hutchinson	Ben	F	Cpt	1876	Oc	12	01	02
Hughs	Sarah	E	Mrs	1839	Se	04	03	04	Hutchinson	R	B		1879	Oc	15	01	01
Huitt	Nancy		Nrs	1835	My	12	03	03	Hutchinson	Robert			1878	Se	22	04	03
Hujubs	Matilda			1876	Fe	18	01	04	Hutchinson	Robert		Jud	1878	Se	13	01	04
Hukins	F			1878	Se	05	01	03	Hutson	Fredonia			1858	No	06	03	02
Huldy	Infant			1878	Au	10	01	03	Hutt	Alice	S		1845	No	10	03	02
Huldy	James		Mrs	1878	Au	10	01	03	Hutt	Henry			1840	Jl	08	03	04
Huling	Marcus		Esq	1839	Au	07	03	04	Hutt	Mary	E		1847	Fe	27	03	03
Hull				1874	Ap	14	03	01	Hutt	Mittie		Mss	1859	Jl	30	03	01
Hull	C	B		1872	Ap	13	01	02	Hutt	Rinaldo	D	Mr	1840	Jl	08	03	04
Hull	Jane	L	Mrs	1879	Jn	12	01	03	Hutt	Virginia	C		1842	Au	17	03	06
Hull	M	L	Mrs	1879	Jn	14	05	01	Hutt	William	S	Jud	1855	Mr	09	03	06
Hull	William		Gen	1826	Ja	10	03	03	Hutton	Srella		Mss	1876	Oc	25	01	04
Hull	William	H		1877	Se	15	04	05	Hutton	Thomas			1878	Ja	24	03	01
Hulsey	Marion			1879	Se	16	08	02	Hyatt	Joe			1875	Fe	19	01	04
Hummel	Jacob			1876	De	03	01	05	Hyde	Ben		Mrs	1872	Mr	20	01	02
Hummel	Robert	J		1856	Jl	19	03	06	Hyde	Harry	L		1869	Au	03	02	05
Hummel	William		Jr	1873	Fe	05	01	07	Hyde	John			1878	Se	22	04	03
Humphrey	John			1875	Jn	04	01	03	Hyer	Henry			1872	Se	22	01	05
Humphrey	Joseph	R	Bro	1876	Oc	05	04	04	Hyland	Frank	B	Mrs	1871	Au	23	01	04
Humphreys	Ben		Jr	1878	Oc	09	01	04	Hynds	William	A	Mr	1833	Se	25	03	02
Humphreys	John			1879	Jl	04	05	01	Hynes	Joe			1872	Jn	18	01	04
Humphreys	William		Col	1828	Se	09	03	01	Hynes	Joseph		Ldm	1877	No	25	01	04
Humphries	Levi		Mr	1838	Au	08	03	04	Hynman	Leon			1879	Mr	06	01	06
Huneway	James			1878	Fe	03	01	06	Hynson	Eliza	A	Mrs	1845	Ja	26	03	04
Hunt	Andrew	J	Mr	1835	Se	22	03	05	Hynson	R	E		1875	Oc	06	01	02
Hunt	Benjamin	S	Mr	1822	Jl	30	03	02	Hyoms			Ltg	1875	Jn	26	01	03
Hunt	Dorcas		Mrs	1839	De	25	03	01	Hyronemous			Mr	1874	De	30	01	04
Hunt	G	A	Dr	1879	Se	06	01	01	Hyslop	Sarah	E	Mrs	1872	Fe	06	01	03
Hunt	Jack			1877	De	19	01	06									
Hunt	Jack		Mr	1877	De	22	01	04									
Hunt	Jack		Mrs	1877	De	19	01	06									
Hunt	Jack		Mrs	1877	De	22	01	04									
Hunt	James			1879	Au	27	01	01				**I**					
Hunt	James	J		1836	My	24	03	05	Ide	George	B	Rev	1872	Ap	18	01	03
Hunt	James	S	Mr	1834	Ap	15	03	05	Ide	William			1878	Mr	22	04	04
Hunt	Laura	F		1878	Se	01	00	00	Iglauer	L			1878	Oc	04	01	03
Hunt	Lizzie			1872	No	30	01	03	Igoe	Patrick			1879	Au	16	01	01
Hunt	Mary		Sis	1873	No	22	04	05	Illing	Charles			1876	Jn	23	01	06
Hunt	Selka			1878	Au	30	01	04	Illrum	Peter	A	Mr	1838	Jl	11	03	04
Hunt	W	B		1878	Se	14	01	04	Imbeau			Mme	1824	Mr	09	03	01
Hunt	W	H		1871	Fe	28	01	01	Imbeau	Paul		Mr	1856	Fe	09	03	07
Hunt	William	G	Esq	1833	Au	28	03	04	Imbeau	Pierre		Mr	1838	Jl	18	03	04
Hunter				1871	Fe	25	04	04	Imboden	M	J	Mrs	1876	Ap	19	02	04
Hunter	Ben			1879	Ja	11	01	02	Impy	Joseph		Mr	1871	My	03	01	01
Hunter	Dora			1872	Mr	21	04	05	Ingalls			Dr	1878	Se	05	01	03
Hunter	George			1874	De	08	01	02	Inge	Elijah	S	Maj	1838	Au	22	03	04
Hunter	Henry			1879	Au	06	01	03	Ingersoll	Ralph	J		1872	Au	27	01	03
Hunter	Infant			1874	Jl	30	01	03	Inglish	William	K	Cpt	1853	Mr	11	03	06
Hunter	John	W		1842	Ja	05	03	03	Inglish	William	K	Cpt	1853	Mr	25	03	06
Hunter	Mary	I		1845	Oc	27	03	03	Ingraham	Lotta			1878	Se	18	04	04
Hunter	Pleasant		Mr	1851	No	14	03	07	Ingraham	Robert		Car	1877	No	25	01	04
Hunter	Sammy			1879	Mr	11	01	04	Ingraham	Robert		Car	1877	De	02	01	07
Hunter	Samuel			1879	Mr	07	04	04	Ingraham	Thomas			1876	Oc	08	01	02
Hunter	William	F		1875	Se	29	04	02	Ingram			Cpt	1870	Se	20	04	04
Hunter	Willie			1878	Se	22	04	03	Ingram	Lilly			1879	Oc	07	01	01
Huntington	William	S		1872	Mr	27	01	05	Inlow	Mary	J	Mrs	1867	Au	20	02	08
Huntley				1876	Se	27	01	01	Inman	Ahib			1875	Ap	15	04	03
Huntsman	Hannah			1872	Mr	05	01	02	Inman	William	A	Bro	1870	Ja	06	02	03
Huribut	Johanna			1878	Jl	19	04	05	Inscore	Thomas			1877	De	25	03	02
Hurley	John			1876	Fe	25	04	04	Inverness			Duc	1873	Au	03	01	05
Hurst	Ada			1879	Se	02	01	01	Irby	J	J		1878	Oc	04	01	03
Hurst	Henry			1878	Se	04	01	03	Irby	J	J	Mrs	1878	Oc	04	01	04
Husky	Thomas			1836	No	01	02	02	Iriby	Saunders			1878	Se	24	01	04

Last	First	MI	Ttl	Yr	Mo	Day	Pg	Col	Last	First	MI	Ttl	Yr	Mo	Day	Pg	Col
Irvin	William			1872	Se	27	01	02	Jackson	George	N		1875	Jl	17	01	02
Irvin	William	A		1834	Mr	11	03	05	Jackson	Green		Blm	1877	No	25	01	04
Irving	A			1876	Oc	06	01	05	Jackson	Infant			1879	Au	12	01	02
Irving	John	W		1879	Ja	10	01	02	Jackson	James			1878	Se	04	01	03
Irving	Louis			1874	Ja	13	03	01	Jackson	James	A	Maj	1873	Oc	23	04	04
Irving	Michael			1871	Jl	12	01	06	Jackson	John		Mr	1821	Au	18	03	01
Irving	O	P		1871	Mr	29	01	03	Jackson	Mary			1878	Se	04	01	03
Irwin	C	L	Mrs	1875	Ap	17	01	05	Jackson	Minervil			1878	Se	01	01	03
Irwin	David		Maj	1836	Se	27	03	05	Jackson	Phil			1878	Se	22	04	04
Irwin	E	F	Mrs	1878	Se	22	04	03	Jackson	R	L		1878	Se	22	04	03
Irwin	James			1876	Mr	02	04	03	Jackson	Robert			1879	My	29	03	01
Irwin	Jesse			1879	Jn	22	05	02	Jackson	Seaborn	W	Mr	1873	Jn	20	04	02
Irwin	John	K		1878	Se	17	01	04	Jackson	Stonewall			1870	Fe	22	04	01
Irwin	Mary	E		1836	De	06	03	05	Jackson	Stonewall			1870	Fe	23	03	01
Irwin	Patrick			1878	Ap	27	04	07	Jackson	Susan			1876	Ap	12	04	06
Irwin	Samuel			1878	My	22	04	05	Jackson	Thomas		Esq	1855	Se	14	03	06
Irwin	Sophia		Mrs	1879	Au	13	01	01	Jacobi	Theodore			1879	Oc	22	01	01
Irwin	Susan			1879	Se	10	01	01	Jacoble	Henry			1851	De	05	03	07
Isaac	George			1879	Jn	29	01	03	Jacobs	Delia			1879	Oc	15	01	01
Isaacs	Charles	K		1879	Oc	18	01	01	Jacobs	E	C		1878	Se	20	01	04
Isaacs	Mary	J		1858	Oc	09	03	03	Jacobs	Joseph		Esq	1837	Ja	10	03	04
Isadore	Matilda			1878	Se	12	01	03	Jacobs	Phillip			1871	Se	06	01	04
Ishtannubbee	Gibson			1876	Ap	21	01	03	Jacobson	Abraham			1878	Au	08	04	06
Ishtannubbee	Gibson			1876	Ap	22	01	03	Jacoby	J	C		1878	Oc	10	01	03
Isom	Jonathan		Dr	1830	Jl	28	03	04	Jacol	Anthony			1872	Au	20	01	06
Ives			Mr	1874	Oc	08	01	04	Jacoway	Thos			1879	My	07	08	02
Ives	Edwin	A		1872	Ap	12	01	04	Jacoway	Tom			1878	Au	08	04	03
Ives	Leila			1861	My	25	03	03	James				1877	Oc	04	01	06
Ives	Robert			1879	Jl	03	05	01	James			Sgt	1876	Jl	09	01	05
Ives	Samuel	M		1879	Ja	26	04	04	James	Abner		Mr	1877	Se	27	01	05
Ives	Thomas		Mr	1877	Jn	17	04	02	James	Abner		Mrs	1877	Se	27	01	05
Iveson	John			1879	Ja	12	01	04	James	Albert			1876	No	24	04	03
Izard	Elizabeth	C	Mrs	1826	Se	12	03	01	James	Burgess			1879	Oc	11	08	03
Izard	George			1831	Jl	20	03	04	James	Charles		Bro	1872	Se	25	01	04
Izard	George		Gov	1828	No	25	03	01	James	Charley	A		1871	No	08	04	06
									James	D	S	Cpt	1876	Fe	10	04	03
									James	David	W		1842	De	21	03	04
									James	Enestine			1868	Oc	27	03	06
	J								James	F	B		1878	Ja	19	01	07
									James	Ferdinand	A	Esq	1853	No	11	03	05
									James	Henry			1879	Oc	14	01	01
Jabine	Eugene		Mr	1869	Oc	08	02	03	James	Henry		Mr	1825	My	17	03	01
Jabine	Eugene		Mr	1869	Oc	08	04	01	James	Jesse			1879	No	05	05	01
Jabine	John	N		1873	Jl	31	04	05	James	Jesse		Mr	1874	Mr	24	04	04
Jabine	Lucien		Mr	1871	Se	23	04	05	James	John			1879	Jn	15	01	02
Jack	Infant			1879	My	25	02	01	James	Margaret		Mrs	1833	Jn	05	03	02
Jack	James	F		1867	My	21	03	03	James	Samuel			1879	Oc	19	01	02
Jackson				1876	Ja	30	01	04	James	Savilla		Mrs	1867	Oc	08	03	03
Jackson				1876	Jn	16	04	01	James	Thomas	A	Esq	1850	Mr	15	03	06
Jackson			Blm	1877	De	02	01	07	Jameson	Belle		Mrs	1875	Jl	18	01	03
Jackson			Dr	1878	Jl	21	02	06	Jameson	Presley			1857	Jl	11	03	03
Jackson			Mr	1877	Oc	07	04	02	Jameston	Andrew	C	Mr	1879	Fe	11	04	02
Jackson			Mrs	1875	My	20	01	05	Jamieson	Harriet	M	Mrs	1854	Se	01	03	07
Jackson			Mrs	1878	Se	22	04	03	Jamison	Elizabeth	S	Mrs	1849	My	31	03	04
Jackson			Mrs	1878	Se	22	04	04	Jamison	George		Esq	1836	Ap	19	03	05
Jackson	A			1878	Se	22	04	04	Jamison	Rebecca	B		1867	Oc	22	04	08
Jackson	Alford			1874	Fe	14	02	02	Janderson	Samuel		Col	1874	De	22	01	02
Jackson	Anderson			1878	Se	04	01	03	Janes	Ellen	T	Mrs	1869	Oc	08	02	03
Jackson	Augustus	M		1878	Jl	07	01	06	Janes	John	G	Mr	1836	Oc	04	03	06
Jackson	Ben		Col	1878	Au	27	01	04	Jankson	Joseph	H		1873	Mr	30	01	03
Jackson	D	L		1849	Jn	07	03	02	Jarbis	Warren		Mr	1851	My	23	03	06
Jackson	Dick			1874	De	13	04	03	Jarine	Jane			1874	Oc	24	04	07
Jackson	Dick			1874	De	15	04	02	Jarrett			Mrs	1875	Jn	15	01	03
Jackson	Emma			1879	Au	29	01	01	Jarvis				1878	Se	22	04	03
Jackson	Emma	K		1867	Se	17	03	03	Jarvis	Jake			1870	Oc	20	01	01
Jackson	Enoch		Mr	1873	Fe	01	04	04	Jasper	Jacob			1873	My	30	01	03
Jackson	George			1876	De	12	01	01									

Last	First	MI	Ttl	Yr	Mo	Day	Pg	Col	Last	First	MI	Ttl	Yr	Mo	Day	Pg	Col
Jasper	Maurice			1872	Jn	29	01	02	Johnson				1871	Au	20	01	05
Jay	James			1870	No	12	01	02	Johnson				1874	Ja	08	04	03
Jay	James	E		1858	Jn	05	03	03	Johnson			Mr	1871	My	05	01	02
Jay	Jane		Mrs	1860	Se	08	03	02	Johnson			Mr	1871	Se	09	01	03
Jay	John			1876	Mr	04	04	04	Johnson			Mr	1871	De	09	04	03
Jay	John		Mr	1829	Jn	24	03	04	Johnson			Mr	1875	Jn	24	03	01
Jay	Jonia	E		1859	Oc	15	03	01	Johnson			Mr	1877	Oc	09	04	01
Jay	Joshua	B		1870	No	12	03	01	Johnson	Alice			1872	De	04	02	03
Jay	William	R	Mr	1858	Jn	05	03	03	Johnson	Alida	P		1879	My	13	08	04
Jayline	William			1878	Oc	02	01	05	Johnson	Amelia		Mrs	1874	Mr	05	04	05
Jebrocney	Simon			1832	Oc	31	03	01	Johnson	Andy		Prs	1874	Mr	15	01	01
Jefferies	D	H	Dr	1830	Au	11	04	01	Johnson	Audre			1875	Ap	18	01	05
Jefferson	Lizzie			1878	Fe	10	01	04	Johnson	Benjamin			1831	My	18	03	05
Jefferson	Thomas		Mr	1826	Au	08	03	01	Johnson	Benjamin	S	Esq	1857	My	02	02	01
Jeffery	Jehoida		Hon	1846	De	05	03	04	Johnson	Billy			1874	Mr	17	03	01
Jeffries	George			1872	Fe	23	01	04	Johnson	C	M		1874	Jl	19	02	03
Jeffrey	Ananda			1878	Se	22	04	03	Johnson	Charles			1875	Jl	10	03	01
Jeffries	Samuel			1853	De	16	03	06	Johnson	Charles		Mrs	1872	No	03	01	04
Jeffry	Robert			1877	De	27	01	05	Johnson	Charles	C		1840	Jl	01	03	05
Jemise	A			1878	Se	22	04	03	Johnson	Charley			1872	Fe	17	01	01
Jenkins				1877	Oc	13	01	05	Johnson	Clarence			1873	Fe	02	01	04
Jenkins			Mr	1860	De	01	03	01	Johnson	Cyrus	R		1870	Se	13	04	03
Jenkins			Mrs	1877	Oc	13	01	05	Johnson	Dick			1871	Au	10	01	05
Jenkins			Sgt	1877	Oc	13	01	05	Johnson	Ed			1871	Ap	25	01	02
Jenkins	Ellis	T	Mar	1871	Fe	21	01	02	Johnson	Edward			1872	Fe	04	01	04
Jenkins	Ellis	T	Mar	1871	Fe	22	01	01	Johnson	Edward			1878	Se	22	04	03
Jenkins	Fannie	L		1878	Mr	27	04	05	Johnson	Edward		Gen	1873	Mr	05	01	05
Jenkins	Fanny		Mrs	1878	Mr	13	04	04	Johnson	Elias	R		1876	Ap	12	04	06
Jenkins	Frank		Mr	1872	Ja	21	04	02	Johnson	Elizabeth		Mrs	1841	Fe	10	03	02
Jenkins	Frank	W		1872	Ja	25	04	02	Johnson	Estelle		Mrs	1879	Se	03	05	02
Jenkins	G	W	Mr	1872	No	01	01	03	Johnson	Euclid	L	Esq	1846	Ja	19	03	01
Jenkins	G	W	Mrs	1872	No	01	01	03	Johnson	Frank			1874	Ap	11	01	02
Jenkins	Henry			1878	Se	22	04	03	Johnson	Frank			1874	Jl	21	04	03
Jenkins	Henry			1878	Se	22	04	04	Johnson	Frank			1875	Ap	10	04	02
Jenkins	J	S		1878	Ap	09	01	06	Johnson	G	V	Esq	1855	My	11	03	06
Jenkins	John			1879	Jl	31	05	02	Johnson	George			1840	Oc	07	03	04
Jenkins	Mary	E		1871	No	28	01	03	Johnson	George	J		1840	Mr	04	03	04
Jenkins	Thos		Sea	1877	No	25	01	04	Johnson	George	J	Mr	1840	Fe	26	03	05
Jennings	J	T	Mr	1876	Mr	26	04	05	Johnson	Harrison			1872	Fe	18	01	04
Jennings	R	H		1876	Ap	12	04	06	Johnson	Harry			1878	Ap	13	04	05
Jennings	Rowley	S	Lt	1839	De	25	03	01	Johnson	Henderson			1871	Au	11	04	02
Jerome	George			1879	Se	30	01	01	Johnson	Henry			1878	Au	25	01	04
Jesson	Jerold			1878	Se	04	01	03	Johnson	Hill			1878	Se	12	01	03
Jessup	Alfred	D	Jr	1876	Jn	09	01	02	Johnson	Hugh			1879	My	29	01	02
Jester	John		Bro	1873	Se	16	04	06	Johnson	Hugh		Mr	1877	De	06	04	05
Jetton	R	H		1871	Se	02	01	04	Johnson	Infant			1879	Ja	23	04	04
Jewell	H			1873	Jn	15	01	04	Johnson	Infant			1879	Ja	28	04	05
Jewell	Martin			1870	Oc	20	01	01	Johnson	Isaac			1875	Ja	14	04	03
Jewitt	Chas		Dr	1879	Ap	04	01	06	Johnson	Isaac		Mr	1853	Ja	21	03	04
Jim	Black			1873	Oc	04	01	03	Johnson	Isaac		Mr	1874	Oc	09	04	04
Joanson	Thomas		Hon	1878	Mr	27	04	04	Johnson	Isiphena			1831	Jl	20	03	04
Joanson	Thomas		Jud	1878	Mr	26	04	02	Johnson	James			1879	Au	07	05	01
Joanson	Thomas		Jud	1878	Mr	26	04	05	Johnson	James		Col	1826	Se	05	03	01
Jobe	R	S		1879	Se	17	01	01	Johnson	James	M		1867	Oc	15	02	08
Jobe	S	M		1878	Oc	03	01	03	Johnson	James	R		1837	No	21	03	05
Jobe	S	M		1878	Oc	06	01	03	Johnson	James	R	Col	1862	Mr	01	02	01
Joblin	Willie			1876	Jl	08	02	04	Johnson	James	W		1874	Ja	08	01	02
Jock	Stillinger			1879	Mr	02	01	04	Johnson	Jilson	P	Col	1879	Jn	15	08	05
Joely	Melina			1876	De	27	01	04	Johnson	Jim			1873	Jl	15	01	03
John			Kng	1873	Oc	30	01	03	Johnson	Joel		Mr	1840	De	30	03	03
John			Kng	1874	Ja	08	01	02	Johnson	John			1878	Se	22	04	03
John	Annie			1879	Oc	07	01	01	Johnson	John		Sea	1877	No	25	01	04
John	Monroe	E		1878	Se	04	01	03	Johnson	Lewis	B	Mr	1871	Ap	09	01	05
John	Sam			1879	Oc	12	01	01	Johnson	Louis			1879	Au	26	01	01
John	Walter			1873	Ja	17	04	02	Johnson	Louis	C	Mrs	1846	Oc	05	03	03
Johns	William			1876	No	14	04	04	Johnson	Maggie		Mrs	1879	No	01	08	02

Last	First	MI	Ttl	Yr	Mo	Day	Pg	Col
Johnson	Maggie		Mrs	1879	No	04	08	05
Johnson	Mary			1866	No	13	03	03
Johnson	Mary			1874	Ja	31	04	04
Johnson	Mary			1878	Se	04	01	03
Johnson	Mary	M	Mrs	1873	Mr	20	01	03
Johnson	Matilda			1857	Jl	04	03	03
Johnson	Matilda		Mrs	1874	Oc	02	01	01
Johnson	Melton			1878	Ap	13	01	06
Johnson	N	C		1871	My	09	01	03
Johnson	N	C		1871	My	10	04	04
Johnson	P	J	Dr	1876	Se	20	03	01
Johnson	Peyton		Mrs	1879	My	10	08	03
Johnson	Precilla		Mrs	1836	Ja	19	03	04
Johnson	R	T		1879	Se	12	01	01
Johnson	R	W	Hon	1879	Jl	27	08	06
Johnson	R	W	Hon	1879	Au	10	04	03
Johnson	R	W	Hon	1879	Au	12	04	03
Johnson	R	W	Hon	1879	Au	12	04	04
Johnson	R	W	Hon	1879	Au	13	04	04
Johnson	Reverdy			1876	Fe	11	01	03
Johnson	Reverdy			1876	Fe	12	01	05
Johnson	Reverdy			1876	Fe	15	02	03
Johnson	Robert			1879	Oc	10	01	01
Johnson	Robert		Mr	1836	Au	23	03	05
Johnson	Robert	J		1874	De	02	01	06
Johnson	Robert	K		1874	Ja	06	01	05
Johnson	Robert	W	Col	1879	Au	05	05	03
Johnson	Robert	W	Hon	1879	Au	26	04	03
Johnson	Robert	W	Sen	1879	Au	06	04	04
Johnson	Robert	W	Sen	1879	Au	26	04	01
Johnson	Ruth	A		1875	My	08	01	02
Johnson	Sarah		Mrs	1873	Au	23	04	03
Johnson	Sarah	F	Mrs	1862	Au	16	02	06
Johnson	Sarah	F	Mrs	1868	Mr	10	03	04
Johnson	Sevier			1859	Jl	09	03	01
Johnson	Simon		Col	1872	Mr	02	01	04
Johnson	Sinkler		Mr	1859	Ap	02	03	01
Johnson	Solomon		Mr	1855	Mr	16	03	06
Johnson	Sonny			1873	De	07	01	04
Johnson	Stanley			1875	Se	28	04	02
Johnson	Susan			1873	Oc	26	04	04
Johnson	Thomas			1872	De	15	01	05
Johnson	Thomas			1878	My	22	02	05
Johnson	Thomas			1879	Jl	25	08	06
Johnson	Thomas			1879	Se	13	05	01
Johnson	Thomas		Mr	1851	Jn	20	03	05
Johnson	Thomas		Mr	1878	Ja	13	02	03
Johnson	Thomas	C		1878	Se	18	01	07
Johnson	Thomas	P		1862	Jn	14	02	05
Johnson	W	H		1879	Au	30	01	01
Johnson	W	M		1879	Oc	26	01	01
Johnson	Warren	B		1867	Se	17	03	03
Johnson	William			1871	Ja	17	01	01
Johnson	William			1871	Ap	25	01	02
Johnson	William			1878	Se	22	04	04
Johnson	William			1879	Ap	22	01	02
Johnson	Wilson	P		1879	Jn	11	05	01
Johnson	Wyley			1873	Fe	20	01	01
Johnson	Zuleika			1867	Se	10	03	03
Johnston	Edward			1878	Se	01	01	03
Johnston	Samuel	H	Mr	1856	Ap	19	03	05
Johnston	Thomas		Cj	1872	De	07	01	06
Johnston	Thomas		Lt	1835	Ja	20	03	05
Johnston	Thomas	N		1878	Oc	09	01	03
Johnston	Thomas	W	Mr	1833	Ja	23	03	01
Johnston	W	R		1878	Au	08	01	05
Johnston	William	F	Hon	1872	Oc	27	01	02
Joliebois			Mr	1870	Oc	12	01	02
Jolly	J	W		1878	Se	04	01	04
Jones				1871	My	31	01	02
Jones				1876	Ap	06	04	06
Jones				1878	Fe	05	04	03
Jones			Dr	1877	Ja	05	04	01
Jones			Mr	1874	Jl	26	01	04
Jones			Mrs	1875	Ap	09	04	05
Jones			Mrs	1875	Ap	10	04	04
Jones			Mrs	1875	Ap	11	04	05
Jones	A	P	Com	1878	My	25	04	04
Jones	Abbie			1870	My	27	04	02
Jones	Ada			1871	Jl	16	04	01
Jones	Adolphus	D	Md	1858	Oc	23	03	03
Jones	Albert	G	Cpt	1878	Se	18	01	06
Jones	Amos		Mr	1850	Ap	19	03	07
Jones	Asa		Mr	1872	Jl	06	01	01
Jones	B	F	Dr	1876	De	29	04	03
Jones	Bennett			1872	Ap	27	01	03
Jones	Bennett			1872	Jl	02	01	05
Jones	Bennett			1872	Jl	03	01	03
Jones	Bill			1876	Oc	28	04	05
Jones	Buck			1873	De	09	04	02
Jones	Burrell		Mr	1828	Oc	07	03	01
Jones	C			1878	Se	22	04	04
Jones	Caroline	L	Mrs	1858	Oc	23	03	03
Jones	Charles		Mr	1867	My	14	03	04
Jones	Charles	E	Col	1870	Mr	16	03	01
Jones	Charlie			1871	Mr	07	04	05
Jones	Chas			1878	Se	22	04	03
Jones	Clayton		Mr	1859	Se	17	03	02
Jones	Constable			1878	Mr	30	07	06
Jones	Daniel			1878	No	03	01	03
Jones	David			1871	My	20	01	03
Jones	David			1871	My	21	01	05
Jones	David			1872	Mr	27	01	03
Jones	David			1872	Mr	30	01	01
Jones	Dempsey		Mrs	1873	Jn	03	01	03
Jones	E	H		1838	Jn	06	03	05
Jones	Ed			1878	Oc	27	01	04
Jones	Ed	C		1878	Oc	15	01	03
Jones	Edward		Mr	1838	My	30	03	03
Jones	Eliza		Mrs	1839	My	08	03	05
Jones	Evan		Rev	1872	Se	03	01	02
Jones	F	C		1860	De	01	03	01
Jones	Frank			1871	Se	07	02	02
Jones	Frank			1871	No	04	01	03
Jones	Frank			1871	No	04	01	05
Jones	George		Cnv	1877	No	25	01	04
Jones	Harry	P		1879	Ja	14	04	06
Jones	Hattie			1878	Jn	09	04	07
Jones	Infant			1879	Oc	12	01	03
Jones	J	H	Mr	1875	Oc	07	04	02
Jones	J	L		1875	Ap	01	01	06
Jones	J	S	Dr	1877	De	30	01	06
Jones	J	W	Bro	1870	Ja	23	04	02
Jones	Jackson			1873	Jl	01	01	04
Jones	Jacob		Mr	1822	De	17	03	01
Jones	Jacob		Mr	1831	Jn	08	03	04
Jones	James	A	Mr	1875	Jn	09	02	02
Jones	James	C		1858	Oc	30	03	02
Jones	James	M		1857	Se	05	03	03
Jones	Jim			1875	Fe	25	01	02
Jones	John			1877	De	16	01	07
Jones	John			1879	My	22	01	03

Last	First	MI	Ttl	Yr	Mo	Day	Pg	Col	Last	First	MI	Ttl	Yr	Mo	Day	Pg	Col
Leming			Shr	1879	Au	21	01	03	Levy	Victor			1873	No	18	04	03
Lemmera	Henry			1878	No	06	01	06	Lewis				1872	Ap	05	04	02
Lemmon	Frank			1876	Ja	23	01	06	Lewis				1874	Ja	08	04	03
Lemon	G	C		1879	Oc	23	01	02	Lewis				1876	No	14	01	01
Lemon	George	P	Cpt	1846	No	30	03	05	Lewis			Mr	1871	My	26	04	02
Lemon	James		Col	1833	Au	28	03	04	Lewis			Pvt	1876	Jl	09	01	05
Lemon	Matilda		Mrs	1832	Ja	18	03	05	Lewis	Andrew	J		1879	Oc	10	01	01
Lemon	Sally		Mrs	1829	Oc	20	03	01	Lewis	Anna	M	Mrs	1852	Oc	01	03	05
Lemon	Samuel		Mr	1831	Ja	05	03	05	Lewis	Arvareni	S		1850	Au	30	03	07
Lemonds	James	M	Cpt	1871	Oc	01	03	01	Lewis	Charles			1851	Se	12	03	07
Lemons	James		Mrs	1878	Jn	26	01	07	Lewis	Charles	W		1873	No	18	05	03
Lemons	James		Mrs	1878	Jn	26	03	01	Lewis	Didimus		Dr	1877	No	20	04	06
Lemor			Pvt	1876	Jl	09	01	05	Lewis	Dock		Mr	1878	Se	17	01	05
Lemoyne	G	W	Col	1867	Au	27	02	08	Lewis	Edward	W		1852	Jl	30	03	06
Lemoyne	P	P	Mrs	1863	Au	22	02	03	Lewis	Eli	J	Col	1833	De	25	03	02
Lenahen	Mariah			1879	Jl	03	01	01	Lewis	Elise			1868	Se	22	03	06
Lenmon	Hugh			1879	Ap	22	01	02	Lewis	George	W	Bro	1869	De	25	02	03
Lenox	Dicy		Mss	1834	Fe	18	02	05	Lewis	Harriet		Mrs	1832	My	16	03	03
Lenox	Flora		Mrs	1870	Ja	19	02	03	Lewis	Henderson			1834	Ap	08	03	04
Lenox	William		Mr	1831	Se	14	03	04	Lewis	Henri			1874	Oc	31	04	02
Lensing	Frank	H		1879	Se	18	05	01	Lewis	Henry			1873	Jn	08	02	04
Leon	Thomas	A	Mr	1876	Mr	14	01	05	Lewis	J	C		1871	My	23	01	01
Leonard			Con	1878	Mr	23	01	05	Lewis	J	R	Dr	1858	Jn	05	03	03
Leonard	F	W		1879	Se	09	05	01	Lewis	James	C	Mr	1871	My	07	04	02
Leonard	Fannie	M		1867	Se	17	03	03	Lewis	James	N		1862	De	20	02	01
Leonard	Issac			1878	Se	12	01	03	Lewis	Jane	S	Mrs	1853	Fe	04	03	04
Leonard	Thos			1878	Au	13	04	02	Lewis	Jerome	B		1867	De	17	03	04
Leopoid	S			1879	De	23	01	02	Lewis	John	H		1872	Fe	20	01	04
Leozanet			Rev	1873	Oc	10	01	02	Lewis	Laura			1879	Oc	12	01	01
Lephiew	William	J		1868	Mr	17	03	05	Lewis	Louisa	M	Mrs	1859	Jl	16	03	01
Lephiew	William	J		1868	Mr	24	03	04	Lewis	Maggie	L		1877	Ja	03	01	04
Lepper	Charles			1871	Se	08	01	03	Lewis	Malinda	H	Mrs	1853	Ja	28	03	07
Lepper	Lewis			1871	Se	08	01	03	Lewis	Margrett	E	Mrs	1870	My	07	02	04
Leroy			Lcj	1869	My	11	02	02	Lewis	Mary		Mrs	1824	My	04	03	02
Leroy	Frankie			1876	Mr	04	04	04	Lewis	Mary	E		1841	Fe	10	03	02
Leroy	James	H		1878	Oc	06	04	06	Lewis	Mary	F	Mrs	1858	De	04	03	03
Leroy	James	H		1878	Oc	08	04	06	Lewis	Moses			1874	My	26	04	02
Leroy	Joseph			1877	No	18	01	04	Lewis	Moses			1875	My	20	04	03
Lersey			Mr	1873	Mr	11	01	07	Lewis	Moses			1879	Au	13	01	01
Lescher	G	J		1874	De	16	04	02	Lewis	Moses			1879	Au	14	01	01
Lescher	Walter	G		1879	Au	26	08	06	Lewis	Nathaniel		Mr	1852	Oc	15	03	06
Leshan	Kate		Mss	1871	Oc	29	01	04	Lewis	Nathaniel	J		1862	Mr	01	03	06
Leshan	Mike	A		1878	Se	22	04	03	Lewis	Rebecca			1834	Au	26	03	05
Leslie	Clara		Mrs	1867	De	17	03	04	Lewis	Robert	A	Bro	1870	Ap	29	02	04
Leslie	Infant			1878	Se	14	01	06	Lewis	Ruth	R	Mrs	1853	Ja	14	03	06
Lessing	Linie		Mrs	1867	Oc	08	03	03	Lewis	Sarah			1820	Ja	08	03	01
Lester	Nathan		Gen	1839	Au	21	03	05	Lewis	Sarah		Mrs	1820	Ja	08	03	01
Lester	Noah		Maj	1820	Jn	24	03	01	Lewis	Sarah	E		1852	Mr	12	03	07
Lester	Scott			1872	My	14	01	02	Lewis	Susan		Mss	1852	No	05	03	03
Lettler	John			1877	De	30	01	07	Lewis	William			1878	De	04	01	02
Lettrim			Erl	1878	Ap	03	01	05	Lewis	William		Gen	1825	Ja	25	03	01
Letz	John			1871	No	14	01	02	Lewis	William		Mr	1824	Oc	05	03	02
Level	Child			1875	Ap	11	04	04	Lewis	William		Mr	1829	Oc	20	03	01
Level	Jacob		Mrs	1875	Ap	11	04	04	Lewis	William	P		1849	Au	23	03	04
Leverett	S	G		1873	Se	28	01	05	Lewis	Willis		Mr	1852	No	12	03	04
Leverett	W	W	Mr	1874	No	13	04	05	Lewre	John			1875	My	20	01	02
Leverett	W	W	Mr	1874	No	14	04	02	Libby	C	H		1878	Oc	24	01	04
Leverrier				1878	Ja	09	03	02	Libby	Lewis	M		1879	Jl	08	01	02
Leverson	Charles	S		1874	Jn	18	01	07	Liddell	John		Gen	1870	Fe	24	02	01
Levert	Fannie			1878	Au	21	01	04	Liddell	John	R	Gen	1870	Fe	26	03	01
Levezonet	J		Rev	1873	Oc	17	02	02	Lide	Sarah	E	Mss	1859	Jl	09	03	01
Levi	Harris		Mrs	1872	Au	30	01	05	Lieben	Albert	H		1878	Se	22	04	03
Levinson	A	C	Mrs	1878	Se	22	04	03	Lieber	Francis			1872	Oc	04	01	05
Levur	Losie			1878	Se	22	04	03	Liebig			Bar	1874	Ap	22	01	04
Levy	Ash			1870	My	04	03	01	Liebig	Justus	V		1874	Ja	08	01	02
Levy	M	D	Mrs	1871	My	19	01	03	Lienberry	Lavina	K		1878	Jl	19	01	04

Last	First	MI	Ttl	Yr	Mo	Day	Pg	Col	Last	First	MI	Ttl	Yr	Mo	Day	Pg	Col
Kearney	John			1879	Au	24	01	01	Kelly	George			1878	Se	22	04	03
Keary	Martin		Col	1878	Se	11	01	06	Kelly	I			1878	Se	22	04	03
Keating	M	J		1872	My	25	01	03	Kelly	J			1878	Au	30	01	04
Keating	M	T	Dr	1878	Oc	20	01	03	Kelly	James			1873	No	15	03	01
Keating	Mike			1879	Ja	03	04	04	Kelly	James			1879	Au	28	01	03
Keatis	Henry		Snr	1858	Oc	09	03	03	Kelly	Joe			1879	Au	26	01	01
Keattes	Henry		Snr	1878	Mr	14	04	04	Kelly	Joseph		Mrs	1876	De	31	01	06
Kebeart	John			1878	Se	22	04	03	Kelly	Josephine			1876	Se	21	01	03
Kecher	John			1878	Ap	07	01	04	Kelly	M			1873	Se	28	01	05
Kedding	Anny			1876	Mr	04	04	04	Kelly	Martin			1878	Se	01	01	03
Keeby	J	H	Dr	1879	Se	20	08	03	Kelly	Mary			1871	Au	20	01	05
Keeder	Pernecia		Mss	1836	My	31	03	04	Kelly	Mary			1878	Mr	03	01	03
Keefe	Annie			1878	Se	04	01	03	Kelly	Mary		Mrs	1836	Fe	23	03	06
Keefe	Timothy			1879	Se	16	01	01	Kelly	Thomas	H		1867	Oc	29	05	06
Keel	E	T		1879	Oc	14	01	01	Kelly	William			1873	Fe	05	01	07
Keeling	Mary			1879	Mr	20	01	05	Kelly	William		Hon	1834	Se	23	03	05
Keemer	William			1875	Jn	27	03	01	Kelney	Frank			1877	Oc	06	01	06
Keene				1874	Ja	08	01	02	Kelsey	Charles			1873	Au	31	01	03
Keene	Lewis			1871	Se	09	01	04	Kelsey	Charles	G		1873	Oc	30	01	03
Keenon	Catherine			1878	Ap	14	01	05	Kelsey	J	E	Mr	1840	Au	05	03	05
Keesacker	Elizabeth		Mrs	1842	Ap	20	03	01	Kemp	August			1872	Mr	01	01	05
Keesee	James	P	Esq	1837	No	21	03	05	Kemp	John			1872	Mr	03	01	01
Kehoe	Archie	R		1879	Se	23	01	01	Kempner	Amelia		Mss	1870	Jn	03	03	01
Kehoe	Mike			1872	Mr	21	01	05	Kempner	Amelia		Mss	1870	Jn	05	01	03
Kehoe	Peter	M		1879	Au	28	01	01	Kenching	William			1876	Se	23	01	03
Keifer			Pvt	1876	Jl	09	01	05	Kendall	Clifford	L		1858	Oc	23	03	03
Keiley	Mary			1878	Oc	27	01	04	Kendall	Nellie			1878	Se	22	04	03
Keily	M			1878	Se	22	04	03	Kendrick	Austin		Esq	1832	Oc	24	03	02
Keith	Alexandar		Snr	1877	De	27	04	06	Kendrick	Daniel		Mr	1830	Jl	14	03	02
Keith	Davis		Mrs	1879	Se	12	01	01	Kendrick	Peter			1876	Oc	13	01	03
Keith	Minerva		Mrs	1850	Jl	05	03	06	Kendricks	Thomas			1876	Ap	12	04	06
Keithley	C	V	Woc	1877	No	25	01	04	Keni			Mr	1836	Se	27	03	05
Keley	William	J	Bro	1872	Oc	08	01	05	Kennaday	Mollie			1879	Oc	10	01	01
Kellam	Jane		Mrs	1839	De	11	03	04	Kennan	Frank			1871	Jl	09	01	05
Kelleam	Eliza		Mrs	1832	Au	22	03	01	Kenneday	James	A		1872	Au	01	01	08
Kelleam	James		Mrs	1825	Jn	21	03	01	Kennedy				1877	De	16	01	07
Kelleam	Smith		Mr	1838	My	16	03	04	Kennedy	J	P	Sec	1870	Au	24	02	03
Kellean	Elizabeth		Mrs	1839	Oc	02	03	01	Kennedy	James			1873	Au	03	01	04
Kelleher	John			1878	Se	22	04	03	Kennedy	James	A		1872	Au	01	01	08
Kellenburger			Mrs	1873	My	02	01	04	Kennedy	James	W		1871	De	27	01	03
Keller	A	J		1879	Ja	14	01	03	Kennedy	Jeremiah		Mr	1878	No	05	01	03
Keller	Master			1878	Oc	09	01	04	Kennedy	Jeremiah		Mrs	1878	No	05	01	03
Kelley				1877	De	02	01	07	Kennedy	John			1879	Jl	26	01	01
Kelley	Edward			1875	Jl	11	01	05	Kennedy	John	P	Mr	1870	Au	27	02	03
Kelley	George		Mr	1867	No	19	03	02	Kennedy	Martin			1876	Jn	20	04	03
Kelley	Mary			1876	De	15	01	03	Kennedy	Micheal		Ldm	1877	No	25	01	04
Kelley	Mary			1878	No	01	01	04	Kennedy	N	B		1876	No	18	01	03
Kelley	William	C		1877	Oc	16	04	04	Kennedy	S	T	Maj	1878	Au	11	03	07
Kellog	Curtis	A		1878	Mr	03	01	05	Kennedy	Samuel			1868	Ja	21	03	04
Kellogg				1870	No	23	01	01	Kennedy	William	W		1877	Ja	21	04	05
Kellogg	Benjamin			1848	Jl	20	03	04	Kenneilly	Bridget	F		1877	No	16	01	06
Kellogg	Carl			1871	Oc	05	04	03	Kennell	Lizzie			1878	Se	22	04	03
Kellogg	Marion			1835	Ap	21	03	05	Kennett	Alice			1878	No	02	01	05
Kellogg	Rebecca		Mrs	1838	Fe	21	03	04	Kennett	Dixon			1878	My	02	01	06
Kellogg	W	P		1873	My	27	01	02	Kennett	Luther	M	Hon	1874	Ap	19	02	03
Kellum	Rebecca		Mrs	1875	Ap	25	04	05	Kenney	J	M		1878	Oc	03	01	04
Kelly				1878	Fe	08	04	04	Kenney	Rachael	C	Mrs	1859	Ap	23	03	01
Kelly			Mr	1872	De	12	01	04	Kenny	George			1858	Se	11	03	04
Kelly	A	J		1873	De	27	02	04	Kent	Edward		Gov	1878	Ja	09	03	02
Kelly	Amos			1879	Se	24	01	02	Kent	George	W		1873	My	10	02	03
Kelly	Australian			1873	Se	06	04	02	Kenzie	Charles	M		1871	My	02	01	03
Kelly	Bill			1874	My	07	01	05	Keogh			Col	1876	Jl	07	01	03
Kelly	Charles		Cpt	1834	Jn	03	03	04	Keogh	M		Col	1876	Jl	09	01	05
Kelly	Edward			1872	Ja	20	01	03	Keohol			Mr	1875	Jl	07	03	01
Kelly	Elder	W		1869	Ap	22	02	04	Keon	James			1872	Au	20	01	06
Kelly	Frank			1875	Ap	14	01	03	Kephart	Sarah	E	Mrs	1872	No	21	01	05

Last	First	MI	Ttl	Yr	Mo	Day	Pg	Col	Last	First	MI	Ttl	Yr	Mo	Day	Pg	Col
Kerferie	Mollie			1878	Se	22	04	03	King				1876	My	17	02	05
Kerferle	Jos			1878	Se	22	04	03	King			Cor	1876	Jl	09	01	05
Kergan	John			1874	No	03	01	05	King			Mar	1871	Se	29	01	04
Kerman	George		Mr	1830	De	22	03	05	King			Pvt	1876	Jl	09	01	05
Kern	R	C	Dr	1872	Jn	04	04	02	King	Alfred	R	Mr	1867	Jn	11	01	08
Kernan	T	R		1879	Jl	23	01	02	King	B	F		1872	Ja	11	04	05
Kernell	Nannie			1878	Se	22	04	03	King	Charles	A		1847	My	29	03	05
Kerns	William	H	Mrs	1879	Se	23	07	01	King	Cynthia	V		1855	Se	14	03	06
Kerr	Alex	A		1878	Oc	13	01	03	King	Elizabeth		Mrs	1829	Se	02	03	01
Kerr	J	M		1878	Se	22	04	03	King	F	A	Mr	1860	Oc	27	03	01
Kerr	J	W	Mrs	1875	Mr	16	01	05	King	Foster			1879	Ap	26	04	04
Kerr	Joseph			1874	De	17	01	04	King	Francis	C		1874	No	11	01	01
Kerr	William	M		1876	Oc	11	01	03	King	George			1847	Jn	05	03	04
Kerrand	J	M		1878	Se	11	01	05	King	Harry			1874	Jl	22	01	05
Kessel	Mary		Mrs	1879	De	09	05	01	King	James			1879	Au	30	01	01
Kessier	Joseph			1870	Se	27	02	04	King	John			1878	Ja	15	01	07
Kester	Susie			1878	Se	22	04	03	King	John			1879	My	27	05	01
Ketcham			Gen	1871	De	03	01	04	King	John		Col	1869	De	22	02	03
Ketcham	D		Maj	1828	Se	23	03	02	King	John		Col	1870	Ja	18	04	02
Ketchman	W	P		1878	Se	24	01	06	King	John		Maj	1869	De	12	02	02
Ketchum			Gen	1871	Jl	18	02	02	King	John	B		1855	Se	14	03	06
Ketchum	William		Col	1871	Jl	18	01	05	King	L			1878	Oc	13	01	04
Kettell	Joshia		Bro	1870	Au	18	02	03	King	Mildred		Mrs	1858	Oc	23	03	03
Key			Mr	1871	Jn	24	01	02	King	P	H	Maj	1872	Oc	17	01	03
Key	G	W	Sq	1873	My	08	04	05	King	Patrick			1878	Ja	15	01	07
Key	J	L		1878	Mr	07	04	05	King	Peter			1875	Mr	16	01	03
Key	M	A	Mrs	1879	Oc	09	01	01	King	R	T	Mrs	1875	My	28	01	02
Key	Maggie		Mss	1879	Oc	09	01	01	King	Rufus		Gen	1876	Oc	15	01	02
Key	Samuel	D	Maj	1871	Mr	07	04	04	King	Thomas			1874	De	29	01	05
Key	Watson			1878	Se	22	04	04	King	Wiley		Mr	1872	Ja	20	01	01
Key	William			1870	Oc	06	03	01	King	Wiley		Mrs	1872	Jn	13	02	04
Keyer	Martin			1878	Se	07	01	03	King	William			1875	Ja	14	04	03
Keys	J			1879	Se	20	01	03	King	William		Mr	1874	Oc	03	04	05
Keyton	John			1873	Se	19	01	03	King	William	A	Bro	1858	Jl	31	03	03
Kibbe	Dr			1878	Se	25	01	04	King	William	R	Mr	1858	Jn	05	03	03
Kibler	William	R	Md	1870	Jl	14	03	01	King	William	R	Vpr	1875	De	02	02	02
Kick	W			1873	No	21	01	03	King	William	T	Mr	1874	Jn	12	01	06
Kidd			Mr	1825	Au	15	03	02	King	Willie			1877	De	27	04	02
Kidd			Mrs	1873	Fe	11	02	03	Kingman	A		Jr	1878	Se	10	01	03
Kidd	Oswald		Cpt	1878	Mr	23	01	06	Kingsbury	Frederick	B		1856	Au	23	03	06
Kidder	Laura	R	Mrs	1870	Mr	06	04	01	Kingsbury	G	P	Lt	1839	Au	07	03	04
Kiers	Frederick			1840	De	16	03	03	Kingsbury	Harriet	R	Mrs	1858	Se	18	03	03
Kilbourne	E	G	Hon	1873	Mr	15	01	07	Kingsbury	Mary	A		1856	Au	23	03	06
Kilder	Dave			1877	No	15	01	05	Kingsbury	Thomas	B		1856	Oc	25	03	05
Kile			Mrs	1878	Se	22	04	03	Kingsbury	Tommy	B		1865	Oc	14	03	03
Killberry	Thomas			1876	Ja	15	01	06	Kingsland			May	1873	Ja	14	01	07
Killian	Milus		Dr	1868	My	12	03	03	Kingsley	Benjamin			1873	My	08	04	02
Kilpatrick	D		Jr	1878	Se	22	04	03	Kinkead	Adam	D	Mr	1825	Au	23	03	01
Kilty	August	H	Ram	1879	No	12	01	03	Kinkead	Laura	F		1879	De	02	08	05
Kimball	J	B	Eng	1879	My	20	01	03	Kinkhead	William			1835	Fe	10	03	04
Kimball	J	M		1871	My	10	04	04	Kinman	Perry		Mr	1868	My	19	02	07
Kimball	J	M	Mr	1871	My	09	01	03	Kinmon	Jane		Mrs	1846	Au	17	03	05
Kimball	J	M	Mrs	1871	My	09	01	03	Kinnear	Jas	A	Mr	1867	My	21	03	03
Kimball	James			1871	Ja	20	01	01	Kinnehan			Dsh	1876	Fe	16	04	03
Kimbell	Ann	M	Mss	1838	Oc	03	02	03	Kinney				1876	De	29	01	02
Kimbell	Easter			1877	No	01	04	02	Kinney				1878	Se	22	04	03
Kimbell	John	D		1867	Se	17	03	03	Kinney	Samuel		Lt	1835	De	29	03	02
Kimbell	Josephine	D	Mrs	1870	My	25	04	02	Kinsbury	Kate	P		1865	Oc	14	03	03
Kimbro	Levi		Mr	1840	Ja	08	09	04	Kinsman	B	W	Lt	1832	My	30	03	05
Kime				1874	Au	12	01	07	Kinsolvin	Charles		Mr	1866	De	18	02	08
Kincade	William	J		1875	My	09	01	04	Kinsolvin	Charles	C	Mr	1867	Ja	01	01	04
Kincaid	Isabella		Mrs	1834	Fe	18	02	05	Kinter	C	W	Mrs	1873	My	10	02	03
Kincaid	Samuel			1873	Se	25	01	03	Kinzie	Robert	A	Maj	1873	De	17	02	03
Kindell	Walter			1879	Jn	15	01	02	Kirby	Leonard			1878	Mr	05	01	05
Kine	Bridget			1878	Se	22	04	03	Kirby	Timothy			1876	Ja	11	01	05
King				1872	Jn	13	02	04	Kirchner	William			1872	Oc	26	01	03

Last	First	MI	Ttl	Yr	Mo	Day	Pg	Col	Last	First	MI	Ttl	Yr	Mo	Day	Pg	Col
Kirk			Mr	1871	Oc	20	04	03	Kolb	Fred		Frm	1879	Ap	20	01	02
Kirk	John	M	Mr	1875	Ap	28	04	02	Kone	Peter			1870	Mr	08	04	01
Kirk	Johnnie		Mr	1875	Ap	28	04	02	Kooher	Joseph			1879	No	01	01	02
Kirk	Thomas			1877	Oc	04	01	04	Kooper	Elizabeth		Mrs	1877	Ja	04	01	07
Kirkendall				1870	Se	22	03	01	Koors	Henry			1872	De	25	01	01
Kirkland	Harry			1878	Au	30	01	04	Kopp	George		Mrs	1876	Se	22	03	01
Kirkland	Jared	P		1877	De	11	01	05	Kornfeldt	Henry			1879	Se	26	01	01
Kirkland	Louis	M		1879	Se	02	01	01	Korsine	Frank			1875	Ja	03	01	05
Kirkpatrick			Mr	1835	Oc	27	03	02	Kortrecht	Charlie			1872	Au	22	01	04
Kirkwood	Henry	C		1859	Jn	04	03	01	Kortreicht	Charles		Jud	1878	Se	25	01	04
Kirkwood	John		Dr	1874	Jl	07	03	01	Kosh	William	J		1878	Se	22	04	03
Kirkwood	Joseph			1878	Au	15	01	06	Kraft	Peter			1878	Se	22	04	03
Kirkwood	Robert			1872	Jn	23	01	05	Kraft	Toney			1873	Fe	15	04	01
Kise	Reuben		Gen	1872	No	23	01	03	Kraly	Father		Rev	1878	Oc	08	01	03
Kister	Samuel			1879	De	30	05	01	Kramer			Mr	1875	Mr	07	01	03
Kitchen	H			1878	Se	22	04	03	Kramer			Mrs	1875	Mr	07	01	03
Kitler				1878	Se	04	01	03	Kramer	Charles			1874	Oc	20	01	06
Kitteredge	Benjamin		Dr	1839	Ap	24	03	03	Kraus	William			1878	Oc	06	01	03
Kittrell	E	D		1868	Ap	07	03	04	Krause	Clara		Mss	1866	No	13	03	03
Klaetich	John			1878	Au	28	01	03	Krause	John		Mr	1856	Mr	15	03	06
Klaferry	Pat			1875	Fe	21	01	05	Krause	Sue		Mrs	1873	Jl	25	01	04
Klaus	Estella	C		1872	De	05	01	06	Kreamer	Annette			1875	Mr	25	01	04
Kleiner	Josephine			1878	Se	01	01	03	Kreamer	Daniel	S		1875	Mr	25	01	04
Klenan	Thomas			1878	No	20	01	03	Kreamer	Daniel	S	Mrs	1875	Mr	25	01	04
Klenan	Thomas		Mrs	1878	No	20	01	03	Krebs	Adelheide		Mrs	1875	Mr	09	04	03
Klien	John			1878	Au	27	01	04	Krebs	Adelheide		Mrs	1875	Mr	09	04	06
Kliffort	John	H		1878	Oc	25	01	06	Krebs	Adelheide		Mrs	1875	Mr	10	04	02
Kline	Abbie			1872	Oc	15	01	03	Krebs	Adelheide		Mrs	1875	Mr	14	04	07
Kline	Fred		Mrs	1876	Oc	22	01	01	Kregman	H	C		1878	Se	24	01	04
Kline	Fredrick			1878	Jl	21	01	05	Krepps	Solomon	G	Gen	1833	Au	14	03	03
Kline	James			1871	Oc	03	01	02	Kringer	Frank			1878	Se	25	01	05
Klump	John			1873	No	18	04	03	Kritner	C	W	Mrs	1873	My	10	02	03
Knapp	Adam			1877	Oc	03	03	01	Krous	George			1878	Oc	18	01	03
Knapp	Betty		Mss	1866	Ja	06	03	03	Krumpelman	Ben			1879	Ja	28	01	04
Knapp	James			1878	Ja	25	01	06	Krunich	Anthony			1879	Oc	03	01	03
Knapp	Myra	E		1860	Se	01	03	02	Krust	Dora		Mrs	1871	My	10	04	04
Kneehouse	Henry			1872	Mr	16	01	05	Kugler	George	W	Mr	1842	Ja	05	03	03
Kneeland	Burr			1875	Jl	04	01	03	Kuhnzier	Joseph			1877	De	16	01	07
Knight				1876	Jn	22	01	04	Kumpe	Angie		Mrs	1873	No	09	04	04
Knight	Andrew			1878	Se	05	01	03	Kumpe	Frank			1871	Fe	26	04	05
Knight	Andy			1878	Se	05	01	03	Kumpe	Frank			1871	Mr	01	01	03
Knight	Jos		Mrs	1878	Oc	09	01	03	Kumpe	M	L	Mrs	1873	No	11	04	05
Knight	W	R	Bro	1869	De	25	02	03	Kumpe	Tommie	M		1873	My	25	04	06
Knightley	Adalaide			1873	Se	02	01	03	Kundig			Gen	1879	Mr	09	01	03
Knightley	William			1873	Se	02	01	03	Kunkell	Godfrey			1874	Ja	01	01	04
Knighton	Barney			1873	Au	31	04	04	Kuntz	George	S		1879	Se	03	05	01
Knighton	Barney	A		1875	No	24	04	03	Kurkwood	Lydia		Mrs	1878	Oc	11	04	06
Knobel	Minika	P		1867	Oc	15	02	08	Kuster	Gustave			1871	No	02	01	04
Knode	O	B	Dr	1872	Oc	03	01	03	Kuykendail	Benjamin		Mr	1835	Jl	14	03	02
Knowland				1873	Oc	15	04	03	Kuykendall	Dempsey		Mr	1824	Fe	23	03	02
Knowland	Thomas			1872	Jl	17	01	04	Kuykendall	James	M	Esq	1836	Fe	23	03	06
Knowlton	L		Col	1878	Se	22	04	03	Kuykendall	Joseph		Mr	1828	My	21	03	01
Knox	George			1871	Se	15	01	03	Kuykendall	Moses		Mr	1828	Jl	30	03	01
Knox	Hugh		Esq	1835	Mr	17	03	06									
Knox	Lydia		Mrs	1832	Jl	11	03	04									
Koch	A			1878	Jl	16	04	02									
Koch	W			1878	Oc	04	01	03									
Koefe				1874	Fe	10	01	06		**L**							
Koen	Anna	B		1878	My	17	01	06	Labsaring			Pvt	1876	Jl	09	01	05
Koers	Herman	L		1879	Se	27	08	06	Lacey	A	T	Cpt	1878	Se	22	04	03
Koffman	Katie		Mrs	1878	Au	22	01	04	Lacey	John	C		1879	Fe	18	03	02
Koffman	R		Mrs	1878	Au	22	01	04	Lackie	Paul	L		1869	Jl	31	02	03
Kohifelt	Iryina			1878	Se	22	04	03	Lacomil	Pierce			1874	Jn	19	01	06
Kohl	Jean	G	Mr	1871	Jn	08	01	03	Lacourse	Martha	E	Mrs	1868	My	19	02	07
Kohlhepp	John			1879	Oc	08	01	01	Lacroix	Isaac			1879	Oc	01	01	01
Kohn	Paul			1878	Se	22	04	03	Lacy	A	T	Cpt	1878	Se	13	01	04

Last	First	MI	Ttl	Yr	Mo	Day	Pg	Col	Last	First	MI	Ttl	Yr	Mo	Day	Pg	Col
Lacy	Anna	A	Mrs	1844	Mr	20	03	04	Langdon	John			1820	Ja	22	03	01
Lacy	Edgar	M	Cpt	1839	My	22	03	03	Langdon	John		Hon	1820	Ja	22	03	01
Lacy	John	W	Mr	1835	Jn	23	03	04	Langer	William			1878	Ja	09	01	06
Lacy	Tabittha		Mrs	1853	Jl	15	03	07	Langes				1877	No	02	01	05
Lafayette			Gen	1834	Jl	08	03	03	Langford	Jack			1872	Jn	06	02	03
Lafferty	Bettie			1872	De	13	01	04	Langham	Angus	L	Maj	1834	Se	02	03	03
Lafferty	Betty		Mrs	1871	No	15	04	02	Langley	A	P		1876	Ap	22	01	04
Lafferty	James			1875	Ap	25	01	04	Langley	James	M	Mr	1851	Jn	20	03	05
Lafferty	John			1872	No	30	01	03	Langley	John		Cpt	1831	No	09	03	05
Lafferty	Lucinda		Mrs	1840	Ap	15	03	04	Langley	Michael	J		1875	Mr	28	01	02
Lafferty	Mary			1870	Jn	18	04	04	Langley	Moses			1871	Se	22	04	02
Laflamm	J	R		1879	Ja	24	04	05	Langley	W	A		1878	Se	22	01	05
Lafourche	William		Mrs	1878	Oc	03	01	05	Langley	William			1872	De	28	01	01
Lagoria	Gus			1879	Oc	19	01	01	Langly	Joseph			1872	Fe	08	04	03
Lagretta	Joseph			1879	Oc	07	01	01	Langtree	Caleb			1874	Ja	28	04	04
Laguere	John	A		1878	Se	05	01	03	Langtree	Caleb			1874	Ja	29	04	02
Laing	Tommy			1878	Au	13	04	05	Langtree	Caleb		Mr	1874	Ja	28	04	03
Lake	John			1879	Jn	15	01	02	Langtree	Virginia	C		1852	No	19	03	06
Lake	Winn			1874	My	31	04	04	Langworth	W	E		1871	Oc	24	01	03
Lalanne	Pierre			1879	Au	29	01	01	Lanier	Edmund		Cpt	1872	Fe	27	01	03
Laman	George			1879	Se	28	08	04	Lanier	P	E	Gen	1879	Fe	14	01	04
Lamb	B			1875	My	02	01	03	Lanigan	M			1878	Se	22	04	03
Lamb	Daniel	G		1873	Jn	06	01	02	Lank	Louis	M		1874	Mr	03	01	05
Lamb	Elizabeth		Mrs	1869	Mr	11	02	06	Lankford	Fred			1874	Mr	24	03	01
Lamb	Jacob			1876	Oc	04	01	01	Lankin	W			1879	Jl	17	01	03
Lamber	Leonard	P		1878	Se	25	01	04	Lannigan	James			1875	My	06	03	01
Lambert	Charles	A		1873	Se	07	01	03	Lanns	James			1879	Se	04	01	01
Lambert	Henry	B	Mr	1840	Se	02	03	04	Lanprey			Mrs	1873	Fe	01	01	05
Lambert	James			1876	Ap	13	01	02	Lansam	Martha			1873	Au	23	04	03
Lambinet	Emil			1878	Ja	04	01	04	Lanxton	Nancy		Mrs	1873	Mr	08	01	05
Lambrie	Dimitry			1878	Se	14	01	06	Lapham	Charles	E	Mr	1868	Se	29	03	02
Lamgan	Maggie			1878	Au	30	01	04	Larches			Mrs	1871	My	10	04	04
Lammerson	Valentine		Dr	1874	Jn	17	01	05	Larentz	L	M		1878	Se	01	01	03
Lampley	Mary	A	Mrs	1873	Ja	04	01	02	Large	Jack			1878	Au	21	01	04
Lampley	Mary	A	Mrs	1873	My	10	01	01	La Rigne	Charles		Mgr	1875	Jl	13	01	02
Lancaster	Charlie			1871	Au	22	01	02	Larkin	Henry	A		1878	No	12	01	03
Lancaster	Parson	J		1874	Ja	27	02	02	Larkin	Thomas			1875	Jn	06	03	02
Lancaster	Robert			1879	Se	13	08	02	Larman			Cpt	1871	Jl	23	01	05
Lance	James			1879	Ja	07	04	04	Laroe	Henry		Mrs	1879	Jl	04	05	01
Lancer	Peter	R		1870	Oc	18	01	01	Larquier	Joseph	M	Mr	1826	Mr	21	03	01
Lancott				1874	Au	14	01	07	Larquier	Oliver		Mr	1826	Mr	21	03	01
Lancy	William			1848	Ja	13	03	05	Larrus			Ser	1877	Oc	20	01	05
Landon	Hattie	A	Mss	1869	Jn	16	02	04	Larsen	Ida			1879	Se	09	01	01
Landrum	Herbert	S		1878	Se	13	01	04	Larson	Lars			1873	Ja	08	01	04
Landrum	Herbert	S		1878	Se	22	04	03	Larv	Elizabeth		Mrs	1858	Oc	23	03	04
Landrum	John	D		1878	Se	26	01	04	Lash	Geroge			1877	Oc	14	02	03
Landseer	Charles		Mr	1879	Jl	27	04	01	Lass	John			1878	Jl	19	01	04
Landseer	Edwin		Sir	1874	Ja	08	01	02	Lastor	Thos	M		1877	Oc	25	04	05
Landsey	Corlton		Mr	1831	Mr	09	03	01	Latfroqua			Ser	1875	No	25	01	06
Landsey	James		Rev	1831	Mr	09	03	01	Latham				1876	My	17	03	01
Landy				1878	Se	22	04	03	Latham	Robert		Maj	1820	No	25	03	04
Lane	C	W	Mr	1878	De	14	01	01	Lathan	Phebe		Mrs	1837	Ja	10	03	04
Lane	C	W	Mrs	1878	De	14	01	01	Lathrobe	Bengamin		Eng	1878	Oc	20	01	04
Lane	Charles	G	Jud	1873	Ja	08	01	05	Lathrop	A	D	Mr	1872	Ja	10	04	02
Lane	Chas	M	Sea	1877	No	25	01	04	Lathrop	J	W		1876	Oc	14	01	01
Lane	George			1878	Se	11	01	05	Latimer	Celia		Mrs	1826	Oc	10	03	02
Lane	George			1878	Se	22	04	03	Latimer	Witherel		Mr	1838	No	28	03	05
Lane	H	B		1878	Se	04	01	03	Latith	John			1878	Au	28	01	03
Lane	Infant			1878	De	14	01	01	Latling	Richard		Esq	1830	Ja	09	03	05
Lane	Infant			1878	De	14	01	01	Latrimonille	Lemaire			1879	Au	21	01	03
Lane	Ira			1878	Se	22	04	03	Lattermore	Griswold		Mr	1829	Oc	06	03	01
Lane	John			1878	Fe	16	01	08	Lattimore	W	K	Cdr	1873	Mr	16	01	06
Lane	Josiah			1872	Mr	20	04	02	Latting	Richard		Esq	1830	Mr	02	03	05
Lane	Susan	E	Mrs	1868	Ap	07	03	04	Laty	J	W	Mrs	1873	My	10	02	03
Langals	Thomas			1878	Ap	09	01	06	Lauenstein	Charles		Dr	1879	Jl	18	05	01
Langdon	Horace			1879	Mr	22	01	04	Laughlin	Harry			1878	Se	03	04	05

Last	First	MI	Ttl	Yr	Mo	Day	Pg	Col	Last	First	MI	Ttl	Yr	Mo	Day	Pg	Col
Laura	William			1876	Fe	16	01	05	Lee	Julia			1873	Se	28	04	05
Lauratt	Marquis	C		1874	Ja	08	01	02	Lee	Limerick			1876	Fe	08	04	04
Laurell	Carrie			1878	Se	04	01	03	Lee	Lula			1870	Jl	17	04	04
Laurens	Henry			1874	Ap	18	03	01	Lee	Mary		Mrs	1870	Jn	22	04	02
Laurie	Elizabeth	B	Mrs	1849	My	24	03	04	Lee	Mary	C	Mrs	1873	No	09	01	03
Lavallee	Della			1876	De	27	01	04	Lee	Mary	D		1879	Se	13	01	01
Lavallee	Georgianna		1876	De	27	01	04		Lee	Mollie		Sis	1870	Jn	30	04	03
Lavallee	Lussena			1876	De	27	01	04	Lee	Morton			1879	Jl	10	01	01
Lavergne	John		Mr	1830	Ja	26	03	03	Lee	Phil		Col	1875	Jl	13	01	02
Lavert			Mme	1878	Ja	09	03	02	Lee	Phillip			1878	Se	17	01	06
Lavine	George			1874	Mr	18	01	05	Lee	R	S	Mrs	1874	Ja	08	01	02
Law	Allen			1873	De	24	01	04	Lee	Robert	E	Gen	1870	Oc	13	01	01
Law	W	J		1876	Oc	24	01	04	Lee	Robert	E	Gen	1870	Oc	15	01	01
Lawerence	A	V		1877	Oc	31	01	05	Lee	Robert	E	Gen	1870	Oc	15	02	02
Lawernce	C	S	Bro	1869	De	25	02	03	Lee	Robert	E	Gen	1870	Oc	16	01	01
Lawernce	John	R		1872	Mr	10	01	05	Lee	Robert	E	Gen	1870	Oc	19	01	02
Lawes	William	C	Jud	1870	No	11	01	02	Lee	Robert	E	Gen	1870	Oc	19	01	03
Lawhorn	E	W		1878	Oc	03	01	03	Lee	Robert	E	Gen	1870	Oc	19	04	04
Lawley	Edward			1873	Au	03	01	05	Lee	Robert	E	Gen	1870	Oc	21	02	03
Lawrence			Mr	1872	Jl	16	04	02	Lee	Robert	E	Gen	1870	Oc	22	02	02
Lawrence	A	W		1878	Ja	13	01	07	Lee	Robert	E	Gen	1870	Oc	25	04	02
Lawrence	Effingham			1878	De	10	01	01	Lee	Robert	E	Gen	1870	Oc	29	04	04
Lawrence	L	N		1878	Fe	02	04	06	Lee	Robert	E	Gen	1870	No	24	01	01
Lawrence	Mary	S	Mrs	1871	Ap	07	01	03	Lee	Stephen		Mr	1852	Jl	30	03	06
Lawrence	R	S		1879	Se	30	01	01	Lee	Thomas		Mr	1878	Mr	30	03	01
Laws	L			1878	Se	22	04	03	Lee	William			1872	No	26	01	02
Lawson	Charlotte		Mrs	1854	Jn	02	03	06	Lee	William	E		1879	Se	13	01	01
Lawson	David			1875	Mr	17	01	04	Leeber			Dr	1872	Oc	08	01	05
Lawson	James		Maj	1855	Ja	19	03	07	Leech	R		Mrs	1878	Se	22	04	03
Lawson	Willam			1846	Ap	06	03	03	Leedon	Jack			1878	No	23	01	02
Lawson	William			1872	Ja	26	01	02	Leek	Joseph		Mr	1874	No	03	01	04
Lawton	J	M		1873	No	18	04	03	Leek	Joseph		Mrs	1874	No	03	01	04
Layton	Bob			1879	No	11	01	01	Lees	Joseph			1875	Jn	06	03	02
Layton	C	A		1874	Ja	25	01	05	Lefave	Felix		Mr	1850	My	17	03	07
Lazarus	Jacob			1878	No	05	01	03	Lefave	John		Mr	1837	Ja	10	03	04
Lea	Soloman			1876	Ap	12	04	06	Lefavre	Mary	A	Mrs	1875	Jn	19	04	04
Leach				1877	De	29	01	07	Lefere	Morgan		Mr	1850	Jl	05	03	06
Leach	William			1876	Ap	21	01	03	Leferre	Theresa		Mrs	1842	No	09	03	04
Leach	William			1876	Ap	22	01	03	Lefeve	Peter		Mr	1822	Jl	30	03	02
Leadbetter	Winnie	C		1875	Oc	12	01	02	Lefevre	Etienne		Mr	1851	My	16	03	07
Leake	Earnest	P		1879	Au	21	01	01	Lefevre	John	C	Mr	1853	Jl	22	03	07
Lear	Infant			1821	No	03	03	01	Lefeyre	Amerose		Mr	1846	Ja	12	02	06
Leare	E	A	Mr	1874	Ap	05	03	01	Lefeyre	Thurza		Mss	1846	Ja	12	02	06
Learned	W	W		1877	De	08	01	07	Lefils	Arman			1868	Mr	31	03	04
Leary	Cornelius			1872	Jl	21	04	02	Leflore	Benjamin			1876	De	20	02	05
Leavitt			Jud	1873	Mr	16	01	06	Leftridge				1878	Fe	15	01	08
Leavitt	D	W	Mrs	1850	My	24	03	06	Leftwich	Granville		Cpt	1824	Se	28	03	01
Leavitt	H	H	Jud	1874	Ja	08	01	02	Legate			Mr	1835	De	08	03	02
Leavitt	Lewis	F		1874	Se	27	04	06	Legate	Charles	S	Mr	1834	De	09	03	02
Lebezque	J	B	Mrs	1878	Oc	09	01	03	Legate	Sally		Mrs	1829	Mr	25	03	03
Lecoq	Mamie			1879	Se	09	01	01	Leggett	M	D		1873	Oc	18	01	04
Ledbetter	John			1878	Mr	17	04	01	Legitimist	Defrankhn			1877	No	15	01	06
Ledbetter	Joseph			1874	Ap	20	01	02	Legley	Thos			1878	Mr	03	01	05
Ledwidge	Susie			1878	Oc	18	04	06	Legorint	Thomas			1878	Se	22	04	03
Lee				1876	Ja	11	01	04	Leich	John			1878	De	04	01	01
Lee	A	N		1879	Oc	01	01	02	Leith	David		Hon	1871	Jl	18	01	05
Lee	Arthur	T	Col	1879	De	30	05	01	Leiwellyn	Anrdew			1878	Ap	09	01	06
Lee	Berry			1878	Se	22	04	03	Lejoure	John			1877	De	21	01	06
Lee	C	E		1878	My	15	04	03	Leland	Ella		Mss	1871	Jl	04	01	03
Lee	Charles			1871	Au	15	04	05	Leland	Henry			1877	De	07	01	07
Lee	Charlie			1875	My	25	04	02	Leland	Simon			1872	Au	06	01	05
Lee	H	H		1873	No	18	05	03	Leland	William	W	Maj	1879	Au	10	01	03
Lee	J	F		1878	Jn	27	01	06	Lellavre	C	O		1878	Oc	19	01	03
Lee	John			1872	Jl	04	01	05	Leman	George	W		1878	Se	01	01	03
Lee	John			1878	Mr	31	01	06	Leman	Nellie	J		1878	Au	27	01	04
Lee	Joseph	W		1879	Se	06	01	01	Leman	T	A		1876	No	15	04	03

Last	First	MI	Ttl	Yr	Mo	Day	Pg	Col	Last	First	MI	Ttl	Yr	Mo	Day	Pg	Col
Leming			Shr	1879	Au	21	01	03	Levy	Victor			1873	No	18	04	03
Lemmera	Henry			1878	No	06	01	06	Lewis				1872	Ap	05	04	02
Lemmon	Frank			1876	Ja	23	01	06	Lewis				1874	Ja	08	04	03
Lemon	G	C		1879	Oc	23	01	02	Lewis				1876	No	14	01	01
Lemon	George	P	Cpt	1846	No	30	03	05	Lewis			Mr	1871	My	26	04	02
Lemon	James		Col	1833	Au	28	03	04	Lewis			Pvt	1876	Jl	09	01	05
Lemon	Matilda		Mrs	1832	Ja	18	03	05	Lewis	Andrew	J		1879	Oc	10	01	01
Lemon	Sally		Mrs	1829	Oc	20	03	01	Lewis	Anna	M	Mrs	1852	Oc	01	03	05
Lemon	Samuel		Mr	1831	Ja	05	03	05	Lewis	Arvareni	S		1850	Au	30	03	07
Lemonds	James	M	Cpt	1871	Oc	01	03	01	Lewis	Charles			1851	Se	12	03	07
Lemons	James		Mrs	1878	Jn	26	01	07	Lewis	Charles	W		1873	No	18	05	03
Lemons	James		Mrs	1878	Jn	26	03	01	Lewis	Didimus		Dr	1877	No	20	04	06
Lemor			Pvt	1876	Jl	09	01	05	Lewis	Dock		Mr	1878	Se	17	01	05
Lemoyne	G	W	Col	1867	Au	27	02	08	Lewis	Edward	W		1852	Jl	30	03	06
Lemoyne	P	P	Mrs	1863	Au	22	02	03	Lewis	Eli	J	Col	1833	De	25	03	02
Lenahen	Mariah			1879	Jl	03	01	01	Lewis	Elise			1868	Se	22	03	06
Lenmon	Hugh			1879	Ap	22	01	02	Lewis	George	W	Bro	1869	De	25	02	03
Lenox	Dicy		Mss	1834	Fe	18	02	05	Lewis	Harriet		Mrs	1832	My	16	03	03
Lenox	Flora		Mrs	1870	Ja	19	02	03	Lewis	Henderson			1834	Ap	08	03	04
Lenox	William		Mr	1831	Se	14	03	04	Lewis	Henri			1874	Oc	31	04	02
Lensing	Frank	H		1879	Se	18	05	01	Lewis	Henry			1873	Jn	08	02	04
Leon	Thomas	A	Mr	1876	Mr	14	01	05	Lewis	J	C		1871	My	23	01	01
Leonard			Con	1878	Mr	23	01	05	Lewis	J	R	Dr	1858	Jn	05	03	03
Leonard	F	W		1879	Se	09	05	01	Lewis	James	C	Mr	1871	My	07	04	02
Leonard	Fannie	M		1867	Se	17	03	03	Lewis	James	N		1862	De	20	02	01
Leonard	Issac			1878	Se	12	01	03	Lewis	Jane	S	Mrs	1853	Fe	04	03	04
Leonard	Thos			1878	Au	13	04	02	Lewis	Jerome	B		1867	De	17	03	04
Leopoid	S			1879	De	23	01	02	Lewis	John	H		1872	Fe	20	01	04
Leozanet			Rev	1873	Oc	10	01	02	Lewis	Laura			1879	Oc	12	01	01
Lephiew	William	J		1868	Mr	17	03	05	Lewis	Louisa	M	Mrs	1859	Jl	16	03	01
Lephiew	William	J		1868	Mr	24	03	04	Lewis	Maggie	L		1877	Ja	03	01	04
Lepper	Charles			1871	Se	08	01	03	Lewis	Malinda	H	Mrs	1853	Ja	28	03	07
Lepper	Lewis			1871	Se	08	01	03	Lewis	Margrett	E	Mrs	1870	My	07	02	04
Leroy			Lcj	1869	My	11	02	02	Lewis	Mary		Mrs	1824	My	04	03	02
Leroy	Frankie			1876	Mr	04	04	04	Lewis	Mary	E		1841	Fe	10	03	02
Leroy	James	H		1878	Oc	06	04	06	Lewis	Mary	F	Mrs	1858	De	04	03	03
Leroy	James	H		1878	Oc	08	04	06	Lewis	Moses			1874	My	26	04	02
Leroy	Joseph			1877	No	18	01	04	Lewis	Moses			1875	My	20	04	03
Lersey			Mr	1873	Mr	11	01	07	Lewis	Moses			1879	Au	13	01	01
Lescher	G	J		1874	De	16	04	02	Lewis	Moses			1879	Au	14	01	01
Lescher	Walter	G		1879	Au	26	08	06	Lewis	Nathaniel		Mr	1852	Oc	15	03	06
Leshan	Kate		Mss	1871	Oc	29	01	04	Lewis	Nathaniel	J		1862	Mr	01	03	06
Leshan	Mike	A		1878	Se	22	04	03	Lewis	Rebecca			1834	Au	26	03	05
Leslie	Clara		Mrs	1867	De	17	03	04	Lewis	Robert	A	Bro	1870	Ap	29	02	04
Leslie	Infant			1878	Se	14	01	06	Lewis	Ruth	R	Mrs	1853	Ja	14	03	06
Lessing	Linie		Mrs	1867	Oc	08	03	03	Lewis	Sarah			1820	Ja	08	03	01
Lester	Nathan		Gen	1839	Au	21	03	05	Lewis	Sarah		Mrs	1820	Ja	08	03	01
Lester	Noah		Maj	1820	Jn	24	03	01	Lewis	Sarah	E		1852	Mr	12	03	07
Lester	Scott			1872	My	14	01	02	Lewis	Susan		Mss	1852	No	05	03	03
Lettler	John			1877	De	30	01	07	Lewis	William			1878	De	04	01	02
Lettrim			Erl	1878	Ap	03	01	05	Lewis	William		Gen	1825	Ja	25	03	01
Letz	John			1871	No	14	01	02	Lewis	William		Mr	1824	Oc	05	03	02
Level	Child			1875	Ap	11	04	04	Lewis	William		Mr	1829	Oc	20	03	01
Level	Jacob		Mrs	1875	Ap	11	04	04	Lewis	William	P		1849	Au	23	03	04
Leverett	S	G		1873	Se	28	01	05	Lewis	Willis		Mr	1852	No	12	03	04
Leverett	W	W	Mr	1874	No	13	04	05	Lewre	John			1875	My	20	01	02
Leverett	W	W	Mr	1874	No	14	04	02	Libby	C	H		1878	Oc	24	01	04
Leverrier				1878	Ja	09	03	02	Libby	Lewis	M		1879	Jl	08	01	02
Leverson	Charles	S		1874	Jn	18	01	07	Liddell	John		Gen	1870	Fe	24	02	01
Levert	Fannie			1878	Au	21	01	04	Liddell	John	R	Gen	1870	Fe	26	03	01
Levezonet	J		Rev	1873	Oc	17	02	02	Lide	Sarah	E	Mss	1859	Jl	09	03	01
Levi	Harris		Mrs	1872	Au	30	01	05	Lieben	Albert	H		1878	Se	22	04	03
Levinson	A	C	Mrs	1878	Se	22	04	03	Lieber	Francis			1872	Oc	04	01	05
Levur	Losie			1878	Se	22	04	03	Liebig			Bar	1874	Ap	22	01	04
Levy	Ash			1870	My	04	03	01	Liebig	Justus	V		1874	Ja	08	01	02
Levy	M	D	Mrs	1871	My	19	01	03	Lienberry	Lavina	K		1878	Jl	19	01	04

Last	First	MI	Ttl	Yr	Mo	Day	Pg	Col	Last	First	MI	Ttl	Yr	Mo	Day	Pg	Col
Liewellyn	Amos			1879	De	03	05	02	Lloyd	William	A	Dr	1859	Mr	05	04	01
Liles	David			1871	Se	29	01	04	Lloyd	Willis			1879	Mr	14	01	02
Lillard			Con	1872	Jl	11	04	03	Lobdeil	Daniel	G		1875	Jl	10	01	05
Lillard			Con	1872	Au	20	04	03	Lobo	Charles			1876	Ja	11	01	04
Linbauch	Benjamin		Mr	1845	Oc	06	03	04	Lock	R	A		1871	Fe	18	01	01
Linburg	Anton			1875	Ap	18	01	05	Lock	Will			1874	No	17	01	05
Lincecum	Green	B		1833	No	13	03	04	Lock	Will			1874	No	18	04	02
Lincoln			Mr	1875	Jn	08	01	02	Lockard	John			1879	Jl	25	01	01
Lincoln	George	S	Mr	1842	Mr	23	03	02	Lockard	W	W		1879	Se	07	01	01
Lincoln	Thomas			1871	Jl	18	01	05	Locke	Susan	W	Mrs	1867	Au	20	02	08
Lindeley	William	R		1837	Oc	10	03	05	Lockert	Eleanor		Mrs	1840	Jl	22	03	03
Lindenbower			Jud	1871	Fe	05	03	01	Lockert	James		Mr	1829	Ja	27	03	01
Linder	Augusta			1877	De	22	01	06	Lockert	John	J	Mr	1836	Jn	14	03	05
Linderman	J	H		1872	Ap	13	01	02	Lockert	Priscilla		Mss	1823	Ja	28	03	02
Lindley	R	A	Dr	1878	Oc	01	01	05	Lockert	William	S	Col	1847	Ja	30	03	03
Lindon	Robert			1879	Se	09	01	01	Lockhart	Calvin		Mr	1878	Fe	13	04	03
Lindsay	Jasper			1879	Se	03	05	02	Lockhart	Charles			1861	Mr	02	03	02
Lindsay	Owen			1876	Fe	13	01	04	Lockwood	George		Mr	1879	Ja	11	04	04
Lindsey	Asa	S		1879	Ap	26	04	04	Lockwood	Legrand			1872	Fe	25	01	04
Lindsey	Catharine		Mrs	1831	Mr	16	03	05	Lockwood	Lulu			1879	Oc	05	01	01
Lindsey	E	B	Bro	1870	No	22	04	04	Lockwood	Ollie			1879	Au	30	01	01
Lindsey	Eli		Rev	1834	My	13	03	05	Loeb	Henry			1878	Se	20	01	04
Lindsey	Frank			1879	Au	22	01	01	Loeb	Jacob			1878	Se	22	04	03
Lindsey	J	A		1870	No	26	01	02	Loeb	Lilly			1874	Oc	21	04	02
Lindsey	Peter	G	Mr	1839	Mr	13	03	04	Loeder	M	J		1879	Oc	16	01	01
Lindsey	Seldon			1879	Ap	08	04	04	Loeffel	C			1878	Se	22	04	03
Lindsey	Thomas	N		1877	No	24	01	06	Loeschmeyer	William			1878	Au	22	01	04
Lindsey	Thomas	N	Col	1877	No	23	01	02	Lofland	Charles		Esq	1851	Ja	17	03	07
Lindsey	W	T		1878	Se	22	04	03	Logan			Dml	1875	Jl	01	03	01
Lindway	Chas			1878	Se	01	01	03	Logan	David		Mr	1835	Se	01	03	06
Ling	John			1878	No	05	01	03	Logan	David	D	Mr	1833	My	29	03	04
Ling	Lucy			1878	Se	22	04	03	Logan	James		Col	1859	De	24	02	08
Lingham			Mr	1876	Oc	12	01	02	Logan	James	W	Mr	1835	Jl	21	03	06
Lingheist	Aug		Cag	1877	No	25	01	04	Logan	Massey			1833	My	15	03	04
Lingifelt				1877	No	18	01	05	Logan	Matthew	T	Col	1845	Jn	09	03	03
Lingo	Robert			1877	No	01	04	02	Logan	Nancy	A	Mrs	1840	Jn	24	03	04
Lins	Chris			1878	Jl	19	01	04	Logan	Rachel		Mrs	1852	Ap	16	03	06
Linscott	A	H		1859	My	21	02	08	Logan	Robert	A	Esq	1852	Mr	05	03	06
Linsey	Caleb		Mr	1826	No	28	03	01	Logan	Sarah		Mrs	1833	No	06	03	05
Linsey	Wesley			1873	Au	12	04	05	Logan	Sarah		Mrs	1841	De	29	03	03
Linton	John			1848	Fe	10	03	04	Logan	Thomas	G	Bro	1870	Jl	16	03	01
Lippi	Luigi			1871	My	26	04	02	Logan	W	C	Mr	1873	Mr	25	01	01
Lippincott	R	H		1872	Oc	18	01	05	Lognea			Bp	1872	Oc	01	01	04
Lisle	Edward			1872	Ap	26	01	04	Logo	Charles			1878	Se	22	04	03
Lissenbee	L	W		1871	Se	09	01	04	Lomax	Halsom			1870	No	12	01	02
Lissenbee	L	W	Mr	1871	Se	06	04	02	Long				1872	Ja	09	01	01
List	Thomas	H		1878	Jl	28	01	06	Long	A			1878	Se	22	04	03
Litchfield	David		Esq	1831	My	04	03	05	Long	A	B		1870	No	03	01	01
Little				1876	Se	20	03	01	Long	A	J		1873	Se	07	03	01
Little	Joseph	C		1840	De	30	03	03	Long	Chaney			1878	Fe	24	01	05
Little	Lucinda		Mrs	1854	My	12	03	05	Long	H	C		1871	Ap	22	01	03
Little	Nancy		Mrs	1840	De	30	03	03	Long	Ira			1878	Jl	06	03	01
Little	R	B		1877	Se	30	01	04	Long	Joseph			1871	Se	10	01	05
Littlewood	Fredrick			1878	Au	10	01	03	Long	Martha	D	Mrs	1821	Mr	31	03	03
Litty	Willie			1878	Se	05	01	03	Long	Martha	H		1866	Oc	23	02	07
Livingston	Edward		Hon	1836	Jn	14	02	05	Long	Moses			1878	De	06	01	01
Livingston	Fanny			1878	Au	30	01	04	Long	N	S		1871	Jn	25	01	05
Livingston	Joe			1876	Ap	12	04	06	Long	Patrick		Mrs	1872	Oc	01	01	05
Livingston	Robert		Mr	1837	Jn	27	03	03	Long	William			1879	Jl	01	05	01
Livingston	Stanley		Dr	1874	Ap	19	01	05	Longacre	James			1879	De	12	01	03
Livingston	William		Jud	1871	Se	09	01	04	Longham	Jane	L	Mss	1840	Au	19	03	05
Livingstone			Md	1874	Mr	25	01	02	Longham	Thos		Cxs	1877	No	25	01	04
Livingstone			Md	1874	Ap	01	01	02	Longley	John			1873	Fe	11	04	05
Llewellyn	W	B		1871	Jl	08	04	02	Longstreet	A	B	Hon	1870	Jl	22	03	01
Lloyd				1871	My	31	01	02	Longworth	Langdon			1879	Ja	16	04	07
Lloyd	Clemans		Mr	1878	Ap	06	01	05	Longyear	John	W	Jud	1875	Mr	13	01	03

Last	First	MI	Ttl	Yr	Mo	Day	Pg	Col	Last	First	MI	Ttl	Yr	Mo	Day	Pg	Col
Lonsdale	G	G	Mrs	1878	Se	21	01	04	Luster	Betty			1878	Se	01	01	03
Lonsdale	J	G	Snr	1878	Oc	03	01	03	Lutz	Calvin			1878	No	19	01	02
Lord			Dr	1876	Jl	09	01	05	Lutz	Jacob			1878	Au	30	01	04
Lord	John			1878	Mr	22	01	05	Lutz	John			1879	Oc	18	01	01
Lore			Rev	1875	Jn	22	03	01	Lychestenste	M	H		1872	Se	13	01	04
Lore	Charles			1872	Oc	15	01	03	Lyde	Dick			1871	Mr	14	02	03
Lorenzi	F			1879	Jl	22	01	02	Lyman	O	A	Rev	1872	Ja	20	01	03
Loring	F	U		1871	No	14	01	02	Lynch	Barney		Frm	1878	Se	21	01	07
Lorman	Alexander			1872	Ja	20	01	03	Lynch	Dennis			1879	De	06	05	01
Lothrop	Albert		Mr	1825	Jl	05	03	01	Lynch	Edward		Mr	1850	Mr	01	03	06
Lotshaw	John			1877	Oc	07	01	04	Lynch	Edward		Qug	1877	No	25	01	04
Louden	Jane			1841	Jn	09	03	05	Lynch	George		Mrs	1878	Se	17	01	06
Loughborough	James	M		1877	Ja	07	04	03	Lynch	Jack			1872	My	11	01	03
Louis	Marcus			1876	Fe	17	01	02	Lynch	James			1878	Jl	14	01	06
Loury	Tom			1872	Jn	08	01	02	Lynch	John		Mrs	1878	Au	10	01	03
Love			Mr	1874	Ap	17	04	04	Lynch	Johnny			1878	Se	10	01	03
Love	Dolly		Mrs	1873	Se	16	01	01	Lynch	Julia	A	Mss	1859	Jn	04	03	01
Love	Franckes	M	Mrs	1840	Jn	10	03	05	Lynch	Maggie			1878	Au	11	01	06
Love	Frank			1871	No	03	01	02	Lynch	Mary			1878	Au	27	01	04
Love	Harry			1878	Ap	21	01	05	Lynch	Mary		Mrs	1878	Au	11	01	06
Love	John			1876	No	04	01	04	Lynchy	M			1871	Se	27	01	03
Love	Joseph		Mr	1831	Au	24	03	01	Lynde	James		Hon	1876	Jl	01	01	04
Love	Robert			1874	Ap	29	01	02	Lyng	Jandine	T		1842	Ja	05	03	03
Love	William			1878	No	20	01	01	Lynn	Bengiman			1877	No	11	01	04
Lovejoy	James	A	Hon	1852	De	24	03	06	Lynn	Lizzie		Mrs	1878	Ja	20	03	01
Lovell	Mary	J	Mrs	1871	Mr	26	01	04	Lynn	Maggie			1879	Au	05	05	01
Lovely	Perais		Mrs	1842	Fe	16	03	01	Lynn	Mary			1875	Ja	03	01	06
Lover	Louis			1874	Jn	26	01	06	Lyon	J	E		1871	Jl	01	01	03
Loveridge	S	M		1871	Jl	20	01	05	Lyon	James	E		1871	Jn	24	01	02
Lovering	Georgiana			1872	No	05	01	04	Lyon	John	E		1878	Ap	12	01	06
Loving	Sam			1878	Jn	06	01	06	Lyon	Matthew		Col	1822	Au	13	03	02
Low	George	A	Mr	1835	Se	22	03	05	Lyon	Matthew		Gen	1839	Mr	13	03	04
Lowe	Bernard	B	Esq	1858	Ja	23	03	03	Lyon	Sidney	S	Maj	1872	Jn	25	01	05
Lowe	Robert	M		1878	Jl	16	01	04	Lyons	Dan			1879	Oc	08	01	01
Lowenstein				1874	Ap	11	01	04	Lyons	James			1871	No	01	01	03
Lowery	J			1879	Au	29	01	01	Lytle	John	C	Maj	1840	Ja	22	03	01
Lowery	Josephine			1879	Au	31	01	01	Lytton	Edward	B		1873	Ja	19	01	06
Lowery	Tom			1872	Jl	31	02	04	Lytton	Edward	B	Sir	1874	Ja	08	01	02
Lowinsohn	L		Rev	1878	Oc	06	01	03									
Lowry	Henry	B		1872	Mr	07	01	05									
Lowry	James		Mr	1835	Au	04	03	05				**M**					
Lowry	Steve			1874	Fe	24	01	04									
Lowry	Steve			1874	Fe	25	01	05									
Lowry	Steve			1874	Fe	26	01	01	Maas				1877	De	29	01	06
Lowshe	William			1878	Jl	10	01	06	Mabbet	William			1820	Ja	08	03	01
Loyd	Priscilla	W	Mr	1841	Ap	28	03	05	Mabbet	William			1820	Ja	22	03	01
Lucarrini	J		Frm	1878	Se	21	01	04	Mabbet	William		Mr	1820	Ja	08	03	01
Lucas	Bakely	J		1878	Oc	06	01	06	Maberry	George	W	Bro	1875	Ap	06	04	02
Lucas	Henry	C	Mr	1869	Oc	09	03	01	Maberry	George	W	Col	1875	Mr	05	04	02
Lucas	James	H		1873	No	11	01	03	Mace	Dan			1874	Fe	22	01	06
Lucas	James	H		1874	Ja	08	01	02	MacHemer			Mrs	1875	Mr	25	01	04
Lucas	John	B	Hon	1842	Se	14	03	05	Machldo			Ser	1877	Oc	20	01	05
Lucas	Walter	R		1879	Se	02	01	01	Machot	Eugene			1878	Oc	03	01	03
Luce	Jas		Cpt	1879	Jl	11	05	01	Machot	Minnie			1878	Oc	03	01	03
Lucky	Monroe		Mrs	1878	No	28	04	03	MacKall	T	F	Mrs	1878	Se	25	01	04
Lucus	William			1878	Oc	27	01	04	MacKey	Alfred			1871	Oc	29	01	03
Luder	Robert			1870	Oc	12	01	01	MacKey	Elizabeth			1873	My	10	02	03
Ludlow	Thos	W		1878	Jl	19	01	03	MacKey	Emma			1876	Ap	12	04	06
Luecke	Archibald	C		1870	Oc	27	01	02	MacKey	Louisa			1874	Ap	25	01	06
Lugo	Diego			1877	De	25	01	07	MacKey	Robert			1878	Ja	03	04	06
Lum			Dsh	1878	No	28	01	01	Mack			Gen	1871	Jn	25	01	05
Lumpkin	E	F	Mr	1855	Fe	09	03	04	Mack	Charles			1876	Ja	15	01	06
Lunalilo			Mr	1874	Fe	21	02	02	Mack	Patrick			1878	Au	28	01	03
Lunn	Phil	H		1878	Se	18	01	07	Mackin	Eliza			1878	Se	22	04	08
Lusby	James	O		1867	Oc	15	02	08	Macklin	Jack			1879	Au	09	01	01
Lusignani			Mr	1873	My	16	01	02	MacLin			Dr	1860	De	01	03	01

Last	First	MI	Ttl	Yr	Mo	Day	Pg	Col	Last	First	MI	Ttl	Yr	Mo	Day	Pg	Col
Maclehart	E		Mss	1878	Se	22	04	03	Malloy	F			1879	Ap	22	01	02
Macnori			Col	1871	De	19	01	03	Mallvius			Fat	1878	Se	22	04	03
Macomb			Cdr	1872	Au	17	01	04	Malone				1873	Au	14	03	01
MacReady	Charles	W		1873	My	09	02	04	Malone	Eliza			1834	Jl	08	03	03
MacRey	Micheal			1877	De	30	01	06	Malone	George	H	Mr	1835	Fe	10	03	04
Macy				1874	Ap	09	01	05	Malone	Johnny			1877	No	13	04	03
Macy	Hugh			1871	Jl	19	01	03	Malone	Mary	A		1835	Jn	30	03	05
Madden	John			1871	No	15	01	03	Malone	Milton			1873	No	29	01	05
Madden	Mollie			1879	Se	18	01	01	Malone	Ned			1878	Se	22	04	03
Maddison	John			1878	Au	23	01	03	Malone	P	J		1878	No	08	04	06
Maddox	Thomas		Mr	1829	Oc	06	03	01	Malone	P	J	Mr	1878	No	07	04	07
Madera	Wells		Mrs	1878	Jn	14	04	09	Malone	Sarah		Mrs	1834	Jl	22	03	03
Madigan	Pat			1875	Jl	08	03	01	Maloney	Annie			1879	Au	17	01	03
Madison				1877	Oc	27	04	06	Maloney	Con			1872	De	27	01	03
Madison	G	F	Col	1868	Oc	13	03	06	Maloney	Hanna			1878	Se	22	04	03
Madison	James		Col	1878	No	20	04	04	Maloney	Lizzie			1879	Oc	15	01	01
Madison	James		Mr	1836	Jl	36	03	05	Maloney	Mary		Mrs	1879	Oc	14	01	01
Madison	Walter			1878	My	04	04	03	Maloney	P			1878	Se	04	01	03
Maffatt	Sadie		Mrs	1872	De	27	01	02	Maloue	L			1878	Se	22	04	03
Magee	W	N		1879	Jn	03	06	01	Mancher	A			1878	Se	22	04	03
Magevney	Eugene			1873	Oc	01	01	04	Manchester	Luman		Mr	1824	Oc	26	03	01
Magg	George			1878	Se	22	04	03	Mangas	Annetta			1878	Au	29	01	04
Magness	David			1851	Oc	10	03	07	Manice	Edward	M		1877	De	06	01	05
Magness	John		Esq	1842	Oc	12	03	05	Manley	Charles			1873	Mr	29	01	01
Magness	Morgan		Col	1871	Se	16	01	03	Manley	Margaret			1879	Se	28	01	01
Magness	Morgan		Col	1871	Se	20	04	04	Manley	Mary	C	Mrs	1871	Mr	18	04	05
Magness	Morgan		Hon	1871	Se	08	01	03	Manly			Mrs	1833	Fe	27	03	05
Magness	Patsey		Mrs	1832	Mr	21	03	05	Mann	Judd			1879	Oc	18	05	01
Magness	Perry		Mr	1848	Fe	24	03	04	Mann	Thomas	J		1872	Jn	20	04	05
Magness	Robert			1837	Jn	27	03	03	Manning	Patrick			1875	Jl	07	01	01
Magruder	John	B	Gen	1871	Mr	04	02	03	Manning	Patrick		Mr	1876	De	22	04	02
Magruder	Ogden	C		1854	No	10	03	06	Manning	T	H		1878	Oc	19	04	02
Maguire	Douglass			1857	Oc	31	03	02	Mannix				1877	De	23	01	04
Maguire	J	J	Mrs	1878	Se	19	01	04	Mannler	C	V		1878	Se	20	01	04
Maguire	Michael			1877	De	27	01	04	Mansfield	George			1879	De	05	01	03
Maguire	Mollie			1878	My	22	04	05	Mansford	W	J		1873	Oc	11	01	03
Mahaffey	George			1879	Se	18	01	01	Manshare	M	P		1870	Oc	29	01	01
Mahan	D	H	Pro	1871	Se	17	01	04	Manson	John			1878	Jn	13	03	01
Mahan	Mary	A		1870	Jl	15	04	04	Mantifriore	Leonard			1879	Se	07	05	01
Mahan	W	H		1878	Au	16	04	05	Manzoni	Alesander			1874	Ja	08	01	02
Maher	Mike			1878	Se	05	01	03	Mapes	Alice		Ms	1871	No	06	01	03
Mahon	Henry		Col	1834	No	04	03	05	Marcey	Ira	T		1879	Ap	09	01	01
Mahoney			Mr	1871	My	07	01	06	March	Dree		Mr	1871	Se	10	01	04
Mahoney			Pvt	1876	Jl	09	01	05	March	Dree		Mrs	1871	Se	10	01	04
Mahoney	D	A		1879	No	06	05	01	March	William		Mr	1840	Au	26	03	05
Mahoney	Thomas			1878	Oc	23	01	06	Marchall	Nancy		Mrs	1831	Ap	13	03	05
Mahoun	William			1879	Fe	26	01	06	Marchisa	Antonio			1879	De	25	01	01
Main			Mrs	1878	Se	22	04	03	Marcie	Jacob			1878	Oc	09	01	04
Mainard	Joshua	E		1877	Ja	27	04	06	Marcus	James			1870	No	03	04	03
Mainwarning	W	C		1878	Fe	26	01	04	Marcus	Rebecca		Mrs	1846	Ja	19	03	01
Maitland	Jones	R	Mr	1879	Au	23	08	02	Marcus	William			1834	De	09	03	02
Major	Edwin	W		1877	Ja	06	01	04	Marcus	William		Mr	1846	Ja	19	03	01
Major	Edwin	W	Mrs	1877	Ja	06	01	04	Mares	J			1878	Se	22	04	03
Major	Elwin	W		1877	Ja	13	02	05	Margage	Jeavetie			1878	Se	22	04	03
Majors	Ida		Mss	1873	Ja	22	01	05	Margham	John			1871	No	17	01	04
Majors	Richard			1879	Au	22	01	01	Marham	Bennie			1870	Fe	27	02	03
Majur	I	R		1878	Se	22	04	03	Marierson			Jud	1875	Jn	12	01	04
Malanski	Agnes			1875	Mr	17	01	02	Marinus	J	H		1879	Ja	14	04	06
Malanski	Constance			1875	Mr	17	01	02	Markley			Ald	1878	Mr	16	01	06
Malcom	George		Apc	1877	No	25	01	04	Markovitz			Col	1878	My	29	01	07
Malcom	George		Apc	1877	De	02	01	07	Marks	Birney			1873	My	21	02	02
Maley	Patsey	W		1878	Oc	04	01	03	Marler	George	W		1848	Ap	06	03	03
Malley	John	O		1872	Oc	22	01	05	Marler	John	C		1873	Au	13	01	03
Mallory	Edward		Hon	1868	My	19	02	07	Marlow	Charles			1872	Au	03	01	05
Malloy	Edward			1878	Se	18	04	04	Marlow	William			1837	My	16	03	03
Malloy	Edward			1878	Oc	29	01	05	Marquand	Leonard		Mrs	1872	Mr	12	01	03

Last	First	MI	Ttl	Yr	Mo	Day	Pg	Col	Last	First	MI	Ttl	Yr	Mo	Day	Pg	Col
Marquette			Mr	1873	My	14	02	03	Martin	Thomas	R		1878	Au	21	04	07
Marquette			Mrs	1873	My	14	02	03	Martin	William			1879	Jl	02	05	02
Marr	C	J	Mss	1866	Oc	23	02	07	Martin	William	C		1879	Ap	13	01	01
Marr	Jack			1871	Au	15	01	03	Martineau	Harriet			1876	Jn	30	01	06
Marray	Mattie	C	Mss	1857	Oc	24	03	02	Martinez	Francisce	P		1840	Mr	04	03	04
Marre	James			1878	Mr	31	04	02	Marvin	E	M	Bp	1877	No	27	01	04
Marrs	Samuel	L	Cpt	1876	No	23	03	01	Marvin	E	M	Bp	1877	No	28	02	01
Mars	M	M		1878	Fe	19	01	05	Marvin	E	M	Bp	1877	De	01	01	07
Marsh	Daniel	W		1835	Fe	10	03	04	Marvin	James	C	Col	1871	Mr	22	01	02
Marsh	Friedrick		Rev	1873	Fe	09	01	07	Marwell	D			1871	No	03	01	04
Marsh	Laura		Mss	1879	Au	16	05	01	Marx	Charles			1871	Se	23	01	03
Marsh	Richard		Cod	1878	Oc	09	01	07	Marzoul	Tony			1877	No	13	04	05
Marshall			Mss	1871	De	08	01	03	Maser			Mr	1875	My	11	01	02
Marshall	Bernard			1877	De	05	01	04	Masey	S	D	Mrs	1875	Mr	24	01	05
Marshall	E			1878	Se	17	01	04	Mason	E			1875	Ja	03	01	06
Marshall	E	C		1878	Se	18	01	07	Mason	Frank			1877	Se	30	01	05
Marshall	Edward	E		1879	Se	24	01	01	Mason	James	M	Hon	1871	Ap	30	01	06
Marshall	Edward	E	Mrs	1879	Se	24	01	01	Mason	James	M	Hon	1871	My	05	02	02
Marshall	Gilbert		Col	1847	Oc	14	03	04	Mason	Jay	R		1873	My	10	02	03
Marshall	Gilbert		Col	1852	Se	10	03	07	Mason	John			1873	Jn	06	01	02
Marshall	John			1871	Jl	06	01	04	Mason	Justin	P		1874	Ap	22	01	04
Marshall	Ralph			1878	Se	24	01	06	Mason	M		Maj	1837	Fe	28	03	05
Marshall	Samuel	D		1851	Ja	10	03	06	Mason	Mary	M		1831	Jl	27	03	05
Marshall	William		Mr	1833	Ap	17	03	04	Mason	Thomas	R		1875	Oc	12	01	03
Marston	George			1878	Oc	11	01	04	Mason	William	H	Mr	1837	Ja	24	03	04
Marten	Jos		Mac	1877	No	25	01	04	Mass	Richard			1875	My	09	01	04
Martier	William			1876	Ap	21	01	04	Masse	Delina			1876	De	27	01	04
Martin	Alice			1873	Au	19	04	06	Masse	Rosanna			1876	De	27	01	04
Martin	Andrew		Jud	1834	Se	23	03	05	Massel	Joseph			1878	Se	22	04	03
Martin	Anna	L		1873	My	20	01	04	Massengill	Henry		Mr	1839	Ja	30	03	02
Martin	Annie	L		1873	My	22	04	06	Massengill	Thomas		Mr	1833	Jl	24	02	03
Martin	Bessie			1876	No	02	01	05	Massey				1873	Oc	14	03	01
Martin	Carroll		Mr	1871	My	05	01	02	Massoft	Edward			1878	Ap	14	01	06
Martin	Catherine		Mrs	1879	Oc	15	01	01	Massram	Otto			1871	Se	08	01	04
Martin	Claibournet			1870	Jn	28	04	04	Masters	Martha	E		1856	De	20	03	04
Martin	Eli			1870	My	20	04	02	Matheny	W	H	Rev	1876	No	04	04	04
Martin	Elizabeth		Mrs	1835	My	26	03	05	Mathers	Thomas		Col	1839	De	11	03	04
Martin	George		Mrs	1874	De	02	01	05	Mathews			Mr	1874	No	29	02	03
Martin	George	W		1833	Jl	10	03	03	Mathews	Charles	J		1871	Jl	27	01	04
Martin	Georgine			1874	Ja	20	04	07	Mathews	Fannie	A		1878	Se	22	04	03
Martin	Green		Mrs	1875	Jn	29	04	03	Mathews	Julia		Mss	1876	My	21	01	05
Martin	Henrietta	L	Mrs	1868	Fe	25	02	08	Mathews	William			1878	Oc	25	01	04
Martin	Henry			1875	My	14	01	04	Mathias	Thomas		Mrs	1857	De	26	03	02
Martin	J	P		1879	Oc	04	08	06	Mathis	Laura	A		1867	Au	20	02	08
Martin	James	A		1866	De	11	02	07	Mathson			Cpt	1871	My	30	01	04
Martin	James	H	Mr	1825	Au	09	03	02	Matlock	Cass			1874	Jn	20	04	03
Martin	James	H	Mr	1826	Fe	28	03	01	Matlock	Thomas	B		1820	Mr	18	03	03
Martin	Jared	C		1857	No	14	03	03	Matthews			Mr	1873	My	06	04	03
Martin	John			1873	Jl	06	01	03	Matthews			Mrs	1872	Au	13	01	05
Martin	John		Hon	1840	De	02	03	04	Matthews	Catherina			1875	De	08	04	03
Martin	John	D		1823	Se	09	02	01	Matthews	Cifas			1878	Jn	25	01	05
Martin	John	D		1833	No	06	03	05	Matthews	Fannie			1878	Se	22	04	03
Martin	Jos			1878	Se	06	01	06	Matthews	Fannie		Mss	1878	Se	11	01	05
Martin	Jos		Mac	1877	De	02	01	07	Matthews	George	L	Mr	1874	Oc	02	04	06
Martin	Joseph		Mr	1841	Ap	21	03	06	Matthews	George	W		1879	Se	03	01	01
Martin	Juan			1873	De	24	01	03	Matthews	J	O		1879	Se	09	01	03
Martin	Lucas		Mr	1834	Ja	15	03	04	Matthews	John	A		1866	Oc	16	03	08
Martin	Mahala	C	Mrs	1840	Jl	22	03	03	Matthews	Malinda		Mrs	1853	Oc	07	03	07
Martin	Mary	E		1852	Jn	25	03	06	Matthewson	John		Mrs	1872	Au	07	01	04
Martin	Micheal			1878	No	05	01	03	Mattingly	Thomas		Mrs	1872	Jl	28	01	04
Martin	R	A		1872	My	01	01	03	Mauldin			Mr	1871	Jl	22	01	02
Martin	Robert	A		1827	Oc	09	03	01	Mauldin	Nancy		Mrs	1852	No	26	03	06
Martin	Sally	D	Esq	1852	Jl	16	03	07	Maupin	Jennings	A	Mr	1839	Se	04	03	04
Martin	Sheradhim			1879	My	29	01	02	Maurer	Erich	P		1878	Oc	13	01	03
Martin	Susan	B	Mrs	1876	Fe	27	04	05	Maurer	Nicholas			1879	Au	19	08	06
Martin	Thomas		Mrs	1878	Oc	11	01	04	Maurice	A		Hon	1878	Au	20	03	02

Last	First	MI	Ttl	Yr	Mo	Day	Pg	Col	Last	First	MI	Ttl	Yr	Mo	Day	Pg	Col
Maury	Edward		Eng	1878	Se	18	04	04	McBride	Thomas			1879	Oc	05	01	01
Maury	Robert	H	Jr	1870	My	04	03	01	McBurney	James			1875	My	23	01	02
Maxey				1876	Ap	08	02	03	McCabe	James			1878	No	05	01	03
Maxwell			Pvt	1876	Jl	09	01	05	McCabe	Mary			1872	De	12	01	04
Maxwell	Hugh			1874	Ap	01	01	02	McCabe	Samuel	E	Mr	1851	Ja	10	03	06
Maxwell	John	D		1879	Ja	16	04	09	McCafferty				1876	Oc	13	01	03
May	Anthony	F	Esq	1825	Au	30	03	01	McCafferty				1876	Oc	13	01	03
May	Frank		Ldm	1877	No	25	01	04	McCaffray	Peter			1871	Jl	20	01	05
May	Infant			1877	No	06	04	04	McCain	James		Cpt	1872	Jn	12	04	04
May	James			1871	Au	30	04	04	McCalla	John		Gen	1873	Mr	02	01	07
May	Susannah		Mrs	1852	Jn	11	03	07	McCallister			Mr	1874	Ja	31	04	02
Mayberry	George		Mr	1826	Jn	06	03	01	McCallum	Octavia	J		1866	Oc	30	02	07
Mayberry	John			1878	Se	11	04	07	McCallum	W	D		1878	Se	17	01	04
Maybin	Joseph	A		1876	My	16	01	01	McCalt	H			1878	Au	28	01	03
Mayer			Mr	1871	Jl	25	01	03	McCann				1878	Au	30	01	04
Mayer			Pvt	1876	Jl	09	01	05	McCann	Francis		Jr	1859	De	31	03	01
Mayer	John			1877	De	16	02	03	McCann	John			1875	Mr	04	04	03
Mayfield	James		Mr	1851	Ja	10	03	06	McCann	John			1879	Au	26	01	01
Maynadier	William		Col	1871	Jl	04	01	03	McCann	Willis		Mr	1836		03	29	03	06
Maynaier	William		Col	1871	Jl	18	01	05	McCarger			Mss	1878	Ja	17	04	05
Maynard	Auditor			1879	My	18	01	03	McCarley	Mollie	R		1868	Oc	27	03	06
Maynard	Johnny			1868	My	19	02	07	McCarly	Elizabeth		Mrs	1836	Jn	07	03	05
Maynor	Nathan	W	Mr	1835	My	26	03	05	McCarroll	Nathaniel		Mr	1835	Ap	07	03	06
Mayo	Doniel	K		1831	Fe	09	03	01	McCarroll	Sarah		Mrs	1867	No	19	03	02
Mayo	Earl			1872	Mr	19	01	04	McCarter	James	H		1872	De	27	01	03
Mayo	Earl			1872	Ap	26	01	04	McCarthy			Mr	1871	Au	16	01	04
Mayo	Margaret		Mrs	1858	Se	11	03	04	McCarthy			Pvt	1876	Jl	09	01	05
Mayo	William	J		1871	Oc	27	04	04	McCarthy	Charles			1878	Ja	16	01	05
Mays	Frank			1871	De	23	01	03	McCarthy	John			1873	Oc	24	01	03
Mays	James			1876	De	12	01	01	McCarthy	Lizzie			1878	Oc	20	01	03
Mays	Joshua			1876	Oc	28	04	01	McCarthy	Thomas			1873	Fe	04	01	04
Mazetia	Anna			1878	Se	22	04	03	McCarty			Mr	1872	My	11	01	03
Mazzina	Joseph			1872	Mr	12	01	04	McCarty			Mrs	1827	Mr	13	03	01
McAdams	Robert			1878	Mr	13	01	06	McCarty	Frank		Mrs	1871	Jl	02	01	05
McAdams	Robert			1878	Mr	15	01	06	McCarty	Sarah		Mrs	1878	Oc	13	01	04
McAfee	J	H		1878	Oc	27	01	04	McCarty	Thomas			1878	Se	22	04	03
McAlister	Charles			1874	Ja	08	01	02	McCauler	Robert			1878	Oc	19	01	06
McAlister	William			1875	Jn	26	01	07	McClagnin			Mr	1877	No	25	01	07
McAlister	William			1875	Jn	30	03	05	McClaine	G	W	Mrs	1876	Ja	06	04	04
McAlister	William			1875	Jl	01	03	05	McClane	Patrick			1879	Se	03	01	01
McAlister	William			1875	Jl	02	03	05	McCleary				1871	Jl	07	01	06
McAlister	William			1875	Jl	03	03	05	McClellan	J	A	Mrs	1879	Se	03	08	02
McAlister	William			1875	Jl	04	03	06	McClellan	William		Maj	1829	Jn	03	03	01
McAlister	William			1875	Jl	07	03	01	McClemments	Fred	1879		Au	31	01	01	
McAllister			Cpt	1869	Jl	27	02	03	McClendon	James			1877	De	16	01	07
McAllister			Mr	1869	Ja	30	02	04	McClerq	J	P		1878	Au	04	01	06
McAllister	Andrew		Mr	1851	My	23	03	05	McCloud	Henry	D		1873	Oc	15	01	02
McAllister	Hugh	M	Hon	1873	My	06	01	02	McCloud	John			1873	No	18	04	03
McAllister	John		Jr	1877	De	19	01	07	McCloy	J	W		1878	Se	22	04	03
McAllister	John		Mr	1835	Fe	10	03	04	McCluer	James		Lt	1838	My	30	03	03
McAlmont	C		Dr	1862	De	13	02	02	McClure	Albertine	E		1859	Ja	15	03	02
McAlpine	Cleburne			1875	Oc	13	01	01	McClure	Frank		Mr	1861	Ap	06	03	02
McAndrews	Micheal			1878	Mr	03	01	03	McClure	Latisha	M		1859	Ja	15	03	02
McArnish				1878	Se	22	04	03	McClure	Myra	H	Mss	1878	Oc	04	01	03
McArthur	James			1879	Ja	05	01	03	McClure	William	A		1879	Oc	05	04	03
McAuley	Barney			1873	Fe	04	01	04	McCoil	Mat			1874	Ja	06	02	02
McAvoy	William			1873	My	06	01	02	McCollister	William			1874	Fe	04	04	03
McBarnett	John		Cap	1874	Jn	23	04	02	McCollom	Frank		Cbs	1877	No	25	01	04
McBath	Claud	D		1875	Ap	17	04	06	McCombs	John	R	Mr	1873	Jn	20	04	02
McBath	George	D		1851	Au	15	03	07	McConanghey	Mary	R		1857	Se	26	03	03
McBride				1876	Oc	06	01	05	McConaughey	Albina		Mrs	1869	Au	31	02	03
McBride				1877	De	19	01	06	McConnaughey	George			1873	Ja	19	01	06
McBride				1878	Ja	05	01	06	McConnell				1874	Mr	11	03	01
McBride				1878	Fe	03	01	07	McConnell			Mrs	1878	Se	22	04	03
McBride	Charles			1878	Oc	13	01	04	McConnell	Andy			1878	Se	22	04	03
McBride	James			1879	Oc	15	01	01	McConnell	Hugh			1878	Ja	22	04	05

Last	First	MI	Ttl	Yr	Mo	Day	Pg	Col	Last	First	MI	Ttl	Yr	Mo	Day	Pg	Col
McConnell	Jesse		Mr	1839	Jl	24	03	04	McDaniel	William			1874	Jn	13	03	01
McConnell	John	B		1874	Ap	21	04	03	McDaniels			Mss	1871	Jn	06	01	03
McConnell	John	B	Cap	1874	My	01	04	04	McDermott	J	J		1878	Oc	24	01	04
McCook			Gen	1874	Mr	05	01	05	McDermott	John			1879	Au	26	01	01
McCook			Gen	1875	Fe	25	01	04	McDermott	Luke			1879	Au	08	05	01
McCook	Ed	S	Gen	1874	Ja	08	01	02	McDevitt	John			1871	No	19	01	05
McCook	Edwin		Gen	1873	Se	13	01	02	McDevitt	John			1871	No	21	01	03
McCooney	John			1878	Se	05	01	03	McDiarmid	Katie	J		1871	De	02	04	05
McCormick	Charles			1872	Oc	03	01	03	McDiarmid	Lillie			1871	No	18	04	04
McCormick	James			1872	Au	28	01	04	McDonald			Col	1878	Oc	15	01	03
McCormick	James		Mr	1835	Se	22	03	05	McDonald			Mr	1875	Mr	07	01	04
McCormick	Johanna		Mss	1871	Jl	09	01	06	McDonald			Mrs	1878	Fe	22	04	04
McCormick	John			1878	Mr	29	03	01	McDonald			Pvt	1876	Jl	09	01	05
McCormick	Martin			1873	Au	07	01	03	McDonald	A			1872	Oc	30	01	03
McCormick	Mary			1879	Au	30	01	01	McDonald	Chas	R		1879	Oc	25	01	01
McCormick	Sam		Cpt	1879	Jn	28	08	02	McDonald	J	W		1878	Se	17	01	04
McCormick	Sarah		Mrs	1878	Ja	13	01	05	McDonald	J	W	Mrs	1878	Oc	04	01	03
McCorry	William			1833	Se	25	03	02	McDonald	James			1876	Oc	08	01	02
McCortney	A	B		1877	De	13	01	06	McDonald	James		Cpt	1874	Ap	06	04	06
McCory	William	P	Dr	1833	No	27	03	04	McDonald	Jas	C	Mr	1861	Mr	09	03	03
McCotter	William	H		1874	Fe	06	01	05	McDonald	Mary	B		1879	Oc	02	01	01
McCourt	Henry		Apc	1877	No	25	01	04	McDonald	Robert	H		1866	Oc	30	02	07
McCowan	Gabreil		Mr	1870	Au	23	04	03	McDonald	William			1873	Oc	28	03	01
McCowan	Gabriel			1870	Se	03	04	04	McDonald	William	S		1866	Oc	02	03	01
McCowan	Gabriel			1870	Oc	28	04	03	McDonald	William	S		1866	Oc	30	02	07
McCowan	Simon	M		1856	Jn	07	03	05	McDonnell	John			1871	Au	10	01	05
McCowen	Elizabeth		Mrs	1852	Jl	16	03	07	McDonough	Bridgette			1879	My	09	04	01
McCoy			Mr	1827	My	25	01	01	McDougal	C	H		1878	Se	07	01	03
McCoy			Mr	1872	My	25	01	01	McDougal	Elias			1879	Au	30	01	01
McCoy	Arthur			1874	Ap	16	01	04	McDougall	Hugh		Cpt	1875	My	18	04	05
McCoy	Chas			1878	Se	17	01	05	McDowell	Jacob		Mr	1869	Mr	28	02	04
McCoy	John			1876	Jn	28	04	06	McEachern			Mr	1874	My	23	03	01
McCoy	Sarah	A	Mrs	1867	De	17	03	04	McElfresh	James			1878	Se	07	01	03
McCracken			Mr	1872	My	18	01	03	McElhaney	James		Mr	1873	Mr	22	01	02
McCraner	Katie			1875	Ja	08	04	05	McElhaney	James		Mrs	1872	No	24	01	04
McCraner	Katie		Mrs	1875	Ja	09	04	02	McElhaney	James		Mrs	1873	Mr	22	01	02
McCratha			Mr	1875	Mr	17	04	04	McElhany			Cpt	1873	Fe	11	01	06
McCraw	Pleasant		Esq	1851	Oc	03	03	03	McElmurry	Charity		Mrs	1831	Ja	26	03	01
McCraw	Pleasant	V		1859	Au	20	03	02	McElmurry	Eliz		Mrs	1830	De	29	03	04
McCray			Mr	1875	De	01	01	03	McElmurry	John		Mrs	1825	Au	30	03	01
McCrea	Thomas			1877	Se	28	01	05	McEloy	William			1877	Oc	30	01	06
McCready	W	C		1874	Ja	08	01	02	McElrath	J	J	Dr	1868	Ja	07	03	01
McCrubb	J	W	Cpt	1839	De	18	03	03	McElroy	John		Rev	1877	Se	14	01	07
McCubbin	William		Dr	1829	Jn	17	03	01	McElroy	Lizzie			1879	Au	15	01	01
McCudock	Ben			1878	Se	04	01	03	McElroy	Reuben			1876	No	14	03	01
McCudock	Ben		Mrs	1878	Se	04	01	03	McElroy	Thomas			1879	Au	28	01	01
McCue	Clarence			1876	Oc	18	01	04	McElroy	Thos			1879	Ap	22	01	02
McCullogh	Nancy	C	Mrs	1856	Ja	12	03	06	McEvoy	Robert			1878	Ap	20	01	06
McCullough	C	F	Mrs	1868	Mr	31	03	04	McEwan	Robert			1873	No	30	01	03
McCullough	William		Mr	1859	De	24	02	08	McEwen	John			1878	Oc	18	01	04
McCunn	John	H	Jud	1872	Jl	11	04	02	McFall	M			1873	Se	28	01	05
McCurdy	Samuel	M	Bro	1859	Jl	16	03	01	McFall	Mollie			1878	Se	22	04	03
McCurtain			Mr	1872	Mr	03	01	01	McFall	Wash			1878	Mr	09	04	02
McCurtain	Daniel		Cpt	1837	De	26	02	05	McFarland	John		Mr	1879	Ja	28	01	04
McCurtain	Thomas		Mr	1837	De	19	03	05	McFarland	John		Mrs	1879	Ja	28	01	04
McDaniel			Mrs	1874	Jn	13	03	01	McFarland	Thos		Qum	1877	No	25	01	04
McDaniel	Charley			1874	Jn	13	03	01	McFarlane	Catharine		Mrs	1853	Mr	04	03	06
McDaniel	Fran			1874	Jn	13	03	01	McFerran	T	C	Gen	1872	Ap	27	01	04
McDaniel	George			1873	Au	29	04	06	McFerson	James	H		1876	No	24	01	06
McDaniel	J	S		1879	Oc	16	01	01	McGann	Mary		Mrs	1875	Jl	08	04	04
McDaniel	James			1874	Ap	18	02	04	McGarrah	Matthew			1876	Oc	05	02	04
McDaniel	John			1874	Jn	13	03	01	McGarry	Micheal			1872	Mr	29	01	04
McDaniel	Maud			1874	Jn	13	03	01	McGarsh	Alonzo			1874	No	20	04	02
McDaniel	Samuel			1874	Jn	13	03	01	McGarth	Tom			1874	No	18	04	06
McDaniel	Sarah			1874	Jn	13	03	01	McGarvey				1878	Au	30	01	04
McDaniel	Susie		Mss	1871	Jn	03	01	03	McGary	Nancy	G	Mrs	1876	De	15	04	01

Last	First	MI	Ttl	Yr	Mo	Day	Pg	Col	Last	First	MI	Ttl	Yr	Mo	Day	Pg	Col
McGavock	F	G	Dr	1871	Se	21	01	03	McIntosh			Mr	1875	Fe	19	01	03
McGayon				1874	Fe	10	01	06	McIntyre	Duncan			1874	Mr	22	01	04
McGee			Mr	1871	Au	30	01	03	McIntyre	John			1877	No	24	04	05
McGee			Pvt	1876	Jl	09	01	05	McIver	G			1878	Oc	18	01	06
McGee	Charles			1878	Se	22	04	03	McKain	W	L	Dr	1872	De	31	02	02
McGee	Mary		Mrs	1878	My	25	02	04	McKamey	John		Mr	1826	Jl	18	03	02
McGee	Orpheus			1876	Ap	21	01	03	McKaney	R	K	Mr	1851	De	19	03	07
McGee	Orpheus			1876	Ap	22	01	03	McKanny	Robert	T		1878	Fe	08	01	08
McGee	Patrick			1872	Ja	05	01	02	McKay	Catherine			1878	Se	01	01	03
McGehee	James			1879	De	23	01	01	McKay	Donald	A		1878	Oc	18	01	03
McGerks	Alabama			1878	Se	04	01	03	McKean			Dr	1871	My	30	01	04
McGilbroy	M			1871	My	21	02	02	McKean	William	G	Cpt	1870	Ap	10	02	03
McGill	Charles			1879	Fe	14	01	04	McKean	William	K	Mr	1870	Mr	26	02	03
McGill	Edward			1877	Oc	07	04	05	McKee	George		Rev	1872	Ap	03	04	02
McGillas	A			1871	Jl	28	01	04	McKee	Isaac	B	Mr	1837	Fe	21	03	05
McGinnis	Sarah		Mrs	1837	No	16	03	03	McKee	Josiah	S		1870	Se	21	04	02
McGinuis				1877	Ja	23	04	04	McKee	William			1879	De	21	01	02
McGlassin	George		Maj	1822	Oc	08	03	01	McKeller				1873	Se	28	01	05
McGlynn	Pat			1872	Oc	06	01	04	McKendree	John	A		1868	Fe	18	03	04
McGonnegle	Harriet		Mrs	1836	Jn	28	03	04	McKenna	John			1874	No	04	01	05
McGovern	Hugh			1878	Jl	09	04	02	McKenor	Mary			1876	My	23	01	06
McGovern	Pat			1874	Ja	03	01	03	McKenzie				1878	Se	05	01	03
McGowan	J	G	Mr	1878	Oc	30	01	07	McKenzie	Alex			1871	Ap	22	01	03
McGracer	J			1876	Jl	09	01	05	McKenzie	Alexandar			1820	Jl	08	03	04
McGrane	Thomas			1879	Ja	23	04	05	McKenzie	John		Mr	1824	Se	21	03	01
McGrann				1878	Au	30	01	04	McKenzie	Mary		Mrs	1877	Oc	20	04	01
McGrath	Charles	R		1878	Oc	10	01	03	McKeon				1876	De	30	01	02
McGrath	Mike			1879	No	29	01	02	McKeon	Mary			1878	Au	28	01	03
McGregor	Flowers		Cpt	1872	Mr	26	01	02	McKeon	W	J		1878	Au	27	01	04
McGregor	Hugh			1878	De	25	01	01	McKinley			Mrs	1878	Se	22	04	03
McGrew	Charlie			1879	Ap	09	04	02	McKinley	Infant			1878	Se	22	04	03
McGruder	Henry			1878	Fe	20	04	02	McKinley	Matilda	C		1869	Jl	27	04	02
McGuffy	W	H		1874	Ja	08	01	02	McKinley	Sarah		Mrs	1822	Ap	16	03	01
McGuire			Mr	1871	Jl	16	04	02	McKinley	William			1879	Jn	29	01	03
McGuire	Andrew		Mr	1849	Se	27	03	05	McKinloy		E		1878	Se	22	04	03
McGuire	Buck			1875	Mr	16	01	03	McKinney			Lt	1876	De	24	01	04
McGuire	George		Mr	1872	Mr	09	01	03	McKinney			Mrs	1831	Mr	09	03	01
McGuire	Hugh			1876	Mr	03	03	01	McKinney	David	E	Esq	1830	Jn	01	03	05
McGuire	James			1879	Oc	18	05	01	McKinney	George	C		1851	Au	15	03	07
McGuire	John	F		1872	No	03	01	04	McKinney	Robert		Mrs	1821	No	03	03	01
McGuire	Mary	E		1862	Se	20	02	05	McKinney	Robert	J	Jud	1875	Oc	10	01	02
McGuire	Mary	J	Mrs	1845	Oc	06	03	04	McKinney	Russell			1876	De	13	04	02
McGuire	Micheal			1878	Jn	26	03	01	McKinnie	Mollie			1875	Jl	15	04	02
McGuire	Nettie		Mss	1871	My	16	01	02	McKinnon	John	B	Bro	1872	Se	27	01	04
McGuire	Thomas	J		1879	Se	12	01	01	McKinzie	S	A	Mrs	1878	Se	22	04	03
McGwire	Mike			1871	Mr	07	01	01	McKirm	J	M	Dr	1878	Se	22	04	03
McHenry	Archibald		Mr	1835	Mr	17	03	06	McKnight	J	W	Bro	1868	Ja	21	01	07
McHenry	Benjaman	F		1836	Au	23	03	05	McLain	John		Mr	1842	Oc	05	03	06
McHenry	Eliza	M	Mss	1834	De	02	03	02	McLain	John	B		1841	Ja	20	03	02
McHenry	George	W	Mr	1834	De	09	03	02	McLain	Mary		Mrs	1827	Oc	16	03	05
McHenry	Harriet		Mrs	1868	Ja	21	03	04	McLane	Neal		Esq	1822	No	26	03	04
McHenry	Henry		Mr	1836	De	27	03	03	McLaren	Lelie	K		1867	Oc	22	04	08
McHenry	J	H	Hon	1871	No	10	02	02	McLaughin	John			1873	Oc	29	01	03
McHenry	James	S	Mr	1826	Ja	24	03	03	McLaughlin			Mr	1871	Se	26	01	03
McHenry	John	B	Col	1846	Fe	02	03	03	McLaughlin	Flor			1878	Se	22	04	03
McHenry	Margaret		Mrs	1835	De	29	03	02	McLaughlin	James			1871	De	08	01	03
McHenry	Samuel		Mr	1829	Ap	22	03	01	McLaughlin	John			1879	Au	19	01	01
McHugh	Felix			1874	No	06	01	05	McLaughlin	Nicholas	M		1867	My	14	03	04
McHugh	Jason			1878	No	12	01	03	McLean	Daniel	M		1871	Jl	18	01	06
McHugh	Morgan			1879	Se	06	01	01	McLean	Hugh			1871	Jl	18	01	06
McHugh	William		Sea	1877	No	25	01	04	McLean	John			1872	Fe	04	01	04
McIlvaine			Bp	1873	Mr	30	02	03	McLean	John		Mr	1828	Au	27	03	02
McIlvaine			Bp	1873	My	10	01	02	McLean	Robert			1878	Se	06	01	05
McIlvaine			Bp	1873	My	16	01	03	McLean	William		Rev	1844	Se	18	03	05
McIlvane			Bp	1873	Mr	15	01	07	McLeed	Henry			1879	My	10	01	03
McIntosh			Lt	1876	Jl	07	01	03	McLellan			Cpt	1871	Oc	01	01	05

Last	First	MI	Ttl	Yr	Mo	Day	Pg	Col	Last	First	MI	Ttl	Yr	Mo	Day	Pg	Col
McLemorg	Elizabeth		Mrs	1836	Jl	12	03	04	McRae	Collin	J	Mr	1876	Ap	16	03	01
McLemosey	Dock			1875	Ap	23	04	02	McRae	Harriet			1876	Ja	18	04	04
McLendon	James			1877	De	18	01	08	McRea	William		Col	1833	Jn	05	03	02
McLendon	William	N	Mr	1851	Oc	31	03	07	McRehn	J			1877	De	30	01	07
McLeod	Noramn		Rev	1872	Jn	18	01	05	McSwine	Tom		Cpt	1872	Fe	06	01	02
McMackin	T	C	Gen	1875	Jl	15	04	03	McSwiney	Elizabeth		Mss	1829	Ap	22	03	01
McMahon	Barney		Mrs	1874	No	14	01	06	McSwiney	Mary	A	Mrs	1833	No	20	03	05
McMahon	Pat			1879	Au	24	01	01	McVey	F	S	Mr	1877	Oc	28	01	04
McMahon	Thomas			1879	Se	03	01	01	McVey	F	S	Mrs	1877	Oc	28	01	04
McMahon	W	H		1873	Oc	02	04	04	McVicar	Amanda		Mrs	1871	Au	10	04	02
McManaway	Milton	D		1871	De	27	01	03	McVicar	James			1872	Oc	01	01	04
McMann	Michael		Mr	1872	No	06	02	03	McWeen	Virginia		Mrs	1874	Mr	24	01	05
McManus	M	M		1871	Jl	09	01	05	McWells	D		Mr	1869	Ja	15	02	04
McMicheal	Martin			1879	Ja	07	04	05	McWilliams	C			1878	Se	01	01	03
McMicheal	Morton			1879	Ja	11	01	03	McWilliams	Catharine	E		1833	Oc	23	03	05
McMillen	Daniel			1878	Oc	04	01	03	McWilliams	F	A	Dr	1840	Ja	01	03	04
McMillin	Frazier			1851	Jn	13	03	07	McWilliams	James			1872	Se	25	01	04
McMillin	John		Mr	1830	Fe	02	03	04	McWilliams	James			1872	Oc	24	01	06
McMinn			Mrs	1870	Oc	04	01	02	McWilliams	James			1878	Se	12	01	05
McMorrin	Samuel		Mr	1854	Jn	02	03	06	McWilliams	Jeanette	S	Mrs	1839	Fe	13	03	02
McMullany	Robert			1878	Au	06	01	06	Mead	J	C		1878	Se	22	04	03
McMullen	James		Mrs	1878	Ja	04	01	05	Mead	James			1879	Au	02	01	01
McMurray	Sam			1879	Ap	22	01	02	Meade	George	W		1872	No	28	01	04
McNair			Mr	1831	Jn	22	03	01	Meade	George	Y	Gen	1872	No	07	01	04
McNair	Alexander		Col	1826	Ap	11	02	03	Meade	George	Y	Gen	1872	No	08	01	03
McNally	Frank			1876	Ap	28	01	05	Meade	George	Y	Gen	1872	No	10	01	05
McNally	John			1871	My	23	01	01	Meade	George	Y	Gen	1872	No	12	01	07
McNally	Mike			1879	Ja	04	04	02	Meade	George	Y	Gen	1872	No	19	01	04
McNamar	Hugh	M	Mr	1833	De	25	03	02	Meade	Thos			1877	Se	25	01	05
McNamara			Fat	1878	Se	28	01	04	Meador	Hattie	M		1871	Oc	22	04	04
McNamara			Mss	1871	Ap	22	01	03	Meador	Hattie	V		1871	Se	03	04	04
McNamara			Mss	1871	Ap	22	01	03	Meador	Mattie		Mrs	1871	Au	01	01	06
McNamara	John			1872	Au	23	01	03	Meagher			Fat	1878	Au	31	01	04
McNamara	Michael			1874	Fe	24	01	05	Meal	Elias			1872	Au	17	02	04
McNamara	Patrick			1872	My	16	01	03	Means	Isabella	A	Mrs	1858	Mr	27	03	02
McNamara	Peter			1878	De	27	01	02	Meara				1871	Jl	07	01	05
McNary	David			1872	De	20	01	03	Meara	Martin			1871	Jl	07	01	05
McNary	J	A	Rev	1878	Au	30	01	04	Mears	D	H		1875	My	01	01	03
McNash	W	J		1870	No	12	01	03	Mears	G	W	Dr	1879	My	21	05	02
McNeal			Mrs	1874	Mr	22	03	01	Meath	Lizzie			1879	Jl	27	01	01
McNeal	Neil		Mr	1857	Mr	07	03	04	Meath	Patrick			1879	Jl	23	01	02
McNeel			Mrs	1873	De	02	01	04	Meats	John		Mrs	1874	Jl	14	01	04
McNeely	Lucy	B		1868	Oc	06	03	06	Mechan	Margrett		Mrs	1878	Oc	31	01	06
McNeil	James			1872	Mr	10	01	04	Mechella	Jacob			1874	Ja	10	01	03
McNeil	James			1875	Se	28	01	03	Mecklin	Robert	W		1871	My	05	01	02
McNeill	Henry	C	Gen	1853	Ja	28	03	06	Medlin	George		Cck	1875	Ap	16	01	05
McNeilly	May		Mrs	1876	Oc	27	01	04	Meehet	C	L		1878	Oc	18	01	03
McNichol	Thos			1878	Se	22	04	03	Meek	John		Mrs	1842	Mr	16	03	02
McNicholas	John			1872	Mr	21	01	05	Meeks	A	H		1839	Ja	16	01	05
McNight	Austin			1878	Au	15	01	05	Meeks	Richard			1876	My	30	02	04
McNulta	Henry		Mr	1872	De	13	01	04	Meers			Jud	1873	Se	10	02	03
McNulta	Henry		Mrs	1872	De	13	01	04	Meers			Jud	1873	Oc	10	04	02
McNulty	Nellie			1879	Ja	18	04	07	Meers	Elisha		Jud	1873	Au	29	04	02
McNutt	Thos			1879	Fe	27	01	04	Megiveny	Micheal			1871	Oc	08	01	04
McOle	P	K		1874	Ap	19	01	04	Mehaffey	Boyd			1872	De	27	01	02
M'Conaugney	Robert			1858	Oc	02	03	04	Mehr			Mrs	1874	Fe	06	01	05
McPheeters	David		Mr	1856	Ap	05	03	06	Mehring			Dr	1878	Se	14	01	06
McPherson	Granville	D		1871	Ja	22	01	02	Meiggs			Mr	1877	Oc	20	01	04
McPherson	Henry			1877	Ja	03	04	01	Meiggs	Henry			1877	No	06	01	04
McPherson	J	B	Dr	1851	Ap	04	03	06	Meigs	Henry			1877	Oc	12	01	05
McPherson	Peyton			1873	Ja	16	04	04	Meigs	Henry			1877	Oc	16	02	01
McPherson	Sallie	F		1867	Oc	22	04	08	Meirs	Peter			1876	Fe	16	01	05
McPherson	Silas			1871	Jn	27	01	05	Mekegan	Mary	L	Mrs	1877	De	25	01	05
McPike	Abe		Cpt	1873	Ja	16	01	06	Meldrum	R	S	Mr	1874	Oc	22	04	05
McQueen	Dan			1878	Jn	28	03	07	Melivaine			Bts	1874	Ja	08	01	02
McQueen	William		Mrs	1874	Mr	20	04	02	Mellan	Robert			1878	Au	28	01	03

Last	First	MI	Ttl	Yr	Mo	Day	Pg	Col	Last	First	MI	Ttl	Yr	Mo	Day	Pg	Col
Mellen			Jud	1875	Jn	02	01	02	Miles	John			1877	De	22	01	05
Mellish	David	B		1874	My	26	02	02	Miles	Sarah	L	Mrs	1834	Au	26	03	05
M'Elmurry	John		Maj	1827	Ja	16	03	03	Milford			Maj	1878	Mr	07	01	06
Melton	James		Dsh	1877	Se	25	01	05	Mill	John	S		1874	Ja	08	01	02
Melvin	Lizzie	G		1858	Jl	31	03	03	Millen	R	B		1878	Au	27	01	04
Menees			Dr	1878	Se	17	01	04	Millen	William			1874	Mr	31	03	01
Menefee	Harriet		Mrs	1829	Se	23	03	01	Miller				1827	Ap	17	03	02
Menefee	Richard		Esq	1831	My	18	03	05	Miller			Mr	1870	Oc	21	04	03
Menefee	William	N	Dr	1874	Au	09	04	03	Miller			Mr	1874	Jn	07	04	03
Menifee	Richard	A	Mr	1871	Jn	06	01	04	Miller			Pvt	1876	Jl	09	01	05
Menken	N	D		1878	Se	03	01	03	Miller	A		Mr	1874	Ap	03	04	05
Mennenger	Minnie	W		1871	Ja	17	04	05	Miller	A	F	Lt	1875	Mr	10	01	05
Mentzell	James			1879	Au	14	01	03	Miller	Adeline	C		1872	Au	01	04	05
Mercedes			Qun	1878	Jl	06	03	02	Miller	Alexander			1875	Jl	09	03	01
Meredith	Johnathan			1872	Fe	27	01	03	Miller	Anderson			1878	Jn	12	04	06
Merguth	Charles			1876	Jl	04	04	02	Miller	Andy			1871	Se	01	01	04
Merguth	Charles			1876	Jl	04	04	03	Miller	Annie			1879	Au	13	01	01
Merinbar	Matthew			1876	Oc	03	01	03	Miller	August			1878	Au	30	01	04
Meriwether	William			1872	Jn	25	01	05	Miller	August			1879	My	09	04	01
Merksill	Adolph			1878	Jl	19	01	04	Miller	B	F	Mrs	1879	Jl	25	01	01
Merrell	Charles		Bro	1872	De	01	01	05	Miller	B	O	Mrs	1878	Se	01	01	03
Merriam	A	W		1874	Fe	19	01	05	Miller	Belle			1879	Se	07	01	01
Merrick	Hiram			1873	Se	11	01	04	Miller	Bernhard			1878	Au	08	01	05
Merrick	Micheal			1877	Oc	06	01	06	Miller	Charles		Bro	1875	Oc	06	04	04
Merril	Henry			1879	Se	17	05	02	Miller	Charles			1879	De	05	01	01
Merrill	John	M	Cps	1877	No	25	01	04	Miller	Charles	T	Sen	1871	Ja	05	01	01
Merrill	William			1878	Se	22	04	03	Miller	Clem			1876	Se	26	01	04
Merriman			Mrs	1873	My	10	02	03	Miller	D			1878	Se	22	04	03
Merritt			Mrs	1874	Ap	05	01	03	Miller	Daniel	S		1871	Se	02	01	04
Merritt	John	W		1878	No	17	01	03	Miller	David		Cpt	1833	Jl	03	03	02
Merriwether				1871	No	05	01	04	Miller	David		Cpt	1835	Se	29	03	06
Merriwether	M	J	Mr	1871	My	09	01	03	Miller	E	O	Mrs	1878	Se	18	04	04
Merriwett	William			1879	Se	10	01	01	Miller	Edward	T	Mr	1858	Oc	16	03	04
Meshane	John			1878	Se	22	04	03	Miller	Ellen		Mss	1878	Mr	24	01	06
Messenger	William			1876	De	24	01	04	Miller	G	F		1868	Ap	21	03	05
Metcalf			Ofc	1874	Ap	05	01	03	Miller	G	W	Qum	1877	No	25	01	04
Metcalf	James	W		1879	Oc	07	01	01	Miller	George			1875	Ap	24	01	03
Metcalf	Jason			1878	No	05	01	03	Miller	George		Mrs	1837	Oc	10	03	05
Mettell	Joe			1879	Ja	16	04	08	Miller	George	F	Bro	1868	Ap	28	03	05
Mettles	Andrew			1876	De	17	01	04	Miller	George	S		1878	Se	14	01	04
Metz	Charles			1872	De	27	01	03	Miller	George	S		1878	Se	22	04	03
Metzger	Maria	T	Mrs	1874	Se	10	04	04	Miller	Henry			1872	Se	17	01	04
Meyer	Andrew			1877	Ja	11	04	02	Miller	Henry		Mr	1836	Au	09	03	03
Meyer	Andrew			1879	Oc	14	01	02	Miller	Jacob		Cpt	1822	Ja	14	02	01
Meyer	Birdie			1877	Ja	03	01	04	Miller	Jacob		Mr	1873	Jl	17	04	03
Meyer	Fred		Lcl	1874	Jl	10	01	05	Miller	Jesse	R		1878	Fe	28	01	05
Meyer	Isaac			1877	Ja	03	01	04	Miller	Jimmy			1868	Au	04	03	06
Meyer	Lewis		Mr	1876	De	20	02	05	Miller	Joe			1878	Au	28	01	03
Meyers	Adolph			1878	Se	01	01	03	Miller	John			1872	Oc	08	01	05
Meyers	E	H	Rev	1876	Se	27	01	03	Miller	John			1872	De	15	01	05
Meyers	John		Cpt	1875	My	09	04	03	Miller	John			1877	De	12	01	04
Meyers	John		Cpt	1875	My	11	04	02	Miller	John	C		1878	Oc	06	01	03
Michal	Eliza			1878	Oc	08	01	03	Miller	John	H	Mrs	1879	Jn	18	01	02
Michar	Frank			1876	Fe	16	01	05	Miller	Kate			1862	Mr	08	02	06
Micheal	Gus			1878	Au	29	01	04	Miller	Lena			1874	Au	11	01	06
Michelet	Jules			1876	My	19	01	05	Miller	Lorenzo			1847	De	16	03	05
Mickle	Mattie	C		1860	Fe	18	03	03	Miller	Peter			1877	Oc	04	01	04
Middleton	Louis	A		1875	Mr	28	01	02	Miller	Peter			1879	Fe	19	01	03
Middleton	William			1840	De	16	03	03	Miller	Samuel		Dr	1853	Ja	21	03	04
Miehart	Susan			1878	Se	04	01	03	Miller	Sophia		Mrs	1878	Jl	21	01	05
Mier	John			1870	Au	14	04	02	Miller	Thomas		Bro	1872	Jl	02	04	05
Miese	Henry			1878	De	04	01	01	Miller	W	J	Cpt	1877	No	24	03	01
Milam			Mr	1872	De	04	02	04	Miller	William			1876	De	05	01	05
Milburn	Martha			1879	Oc	01	01	01	Miller	William			1878	Ja	25	04	03
Miles	Barzillia			1833	Au	14	03	03	Miller	William		Cpt	1878	Se	14	01	04
Miles	Frank			1874	Ap	07	02	03	Miller	William		Cpt	1878	Se	22	04	03

Last	First	MI	Ttl	Yr	Mo	Day	Pg	Col	Last	First	MI	Ttl	Yr	Mo	Day	Pg	Col
Miller	William	J		1875	Ap	28	01	05	Mitchell	R	W	Mrs	1878	Se	05	01	03
Milliken	John		Hon	1852	Ap	16	03	06	Mitchell	Rector			1875	Jl	08	04	04
Milliner	Joseph	L		1859	Ja	29	03	01	Mitchell	S	W	Bro	1871	No	21	04	05
Mills	A	H	Mr	1872	Mr	20	01	02	Mitchell	Sarah	J	Mrs	1846	Oc	05	03	03
Mills	Aaron	L	Mr	1852	Ja	09	03	06	Mitchell	Thomas	G		1877	De	20	01	05
Mills	Archie	E		1879	Se	09	01	01	Mitchell	Walter			1849	Se	06	03	04
Mills	Belle			1876	Ap	12	04	06	Mitchell	William			1878	My	03	04	05
Mills	Charles			1871	My	17	01	01	Mix	Mary	E	Mss	1844	Jn	19	03	01
Mills	Drake		Mrs	1872	Jl	06	01	02	Mixer	L	W	Mr	1872	Se	28	01	04
Mills	Isaac			1878	No	01	04	07	Mixer	Minnie		Mss	1877	Ja	03	01	04
Mills	James	E	Mr	1852	Jl	30	03	06	Moan	Henry	W		1877	Oc	09	01	05
Mills	John	R		1879	Jl	11	08	06	Moan	Infant			1877	Oc	09	01	05
Mills	McFarland		Dr	1875	Jl	02	03	01	Mocrann	Nellie			1878	Se	22	04	03
Mills	Sam			1877	De	22	01	05	Mode	Maria		Mss	1878	Au	22	01	04
Mills	Sarah		Mrs	1837	Ap	18	03	05	Moffat	Emily		Mrs	1817	De	07	01	03
Mills	Willaim	A	Esq	1874	My	02	04	02	Moffate	Sarah			1852	Mr	26	03	06
Millsaps	Betsey		Mrs	1824	De	14	03	01	Moffate	Sarah		Mrs	1852	Mr	26	03	06
Milner			Mr	1873	Oc	31	01	02	Moffatt	William			1878	Se	18	01	07
Milner	John			1851	De	19	03	06	Mofitt	John			1878	Au	30	01	04
Milthak	C	A		1878	Jl	31	01	04	Molen	Spike			1872	Au	10	01	06
Milton	Robert			1871	Ap	25	01	02	Moles	J	C	Col	1876	Oc	05	02	03
Milton	Robert		Mrs	1871	Ap	25	01	02	Molloy	David			1871	My	05	01	05
Mimms	Andrew			1872	Fe	27	01	01	Moloncy	Patrick			1877	Se	30	01	05
Mims	Etta		Mr	1872	Mr	03	01	01	Mona	Lucy		Mss	1871	Oc	29	01	03
Minchell	Manchell	R		1872	De	28	01	04	Monahan	John			1879	No	05	08	05
Mingle	George		Mrs	1877	De	25	01	05	Monezo	Christopher		Mrs	1874	Fe	25	01	05
Mingo	Tisho		Cpt	1841	My	26	03	02	Mongoon	Louis			1879	Oc	12	01	03
Minkwitz	E	A	Mrs	1878	Oc	01	04	07	Monroe				1876	Oc	14	01	01
Minor	C	L	Qum	1833	No	27	03	04	Monroe	Infant			1876	Mr	21	04	02
Minor	D	P		1878	Se	01	01	03	Monroe	Joseph	J	Col	1824	Au	10	03	01
Minthorne	F	A		1877	No	18	01	04	Monroe	Robert			1828	Se	09	03	01
Miriz	F			1878	Se	22	04	03	Monroe	Sarah		Mrs	1860	Jl	21	03	02
Mitchel	Adalaide	W	Mrs	1838	Jl	25	03	03	Monroe	Sarah		Mrs	1860	Au	04	03	02
Mitchel	John			1875	Mr	23	02	03	Montague	Grace			1870	No	12	01	02
Mitchel	John			1875	Mr	24	01	05	Montague	H	A		1878	Au	14	01	06
Mitchel	John			1875	Mr	25	01	05	Montague	H	G		1878	Au	21	01	05
Mitchel	John			1875	Mr	28	01	02	Monteith	Francis			1871	Jl	18	01	06
Mitchel	John			1875	Mr	30	01	03	Montgomery	A		Mr	1875	Jl	07	01	01
Mitchel	John			1875	Ap	03	01	06	Montgomery	Anthony			1878	Fe	20	04	02
Mitchell			Cpt	1839	Se	04	01	06	Montgomery	Anthony			1879	Au	24	08	04
Mitchell	A	R	Dr	1870	Mr	12	04	01	Montgomery	C	E	Mrs	1859	Jl	02	03	02
Mitchell	Caroline			1835	Se	29	03	06	Montgomery	Frederick	N		1848	Oc	05	03	05
Mitchell	Charles			1878	Au	28	01	03	Montgomery	George	E		1873	Oc	11	01	03
Mitchell	D		Jud	1875	Mr	30	01	04	Montgomery	Hugh		Maj	1835	Au	04	03	05
Mitchell	Daniel			1874	Jn	07	04	03	Montgomery	Isabella		Mr	1835	Jl	07	03	04
Mitchell	Daniel		Mr	1842	Jn	01	03	04	Montgomery	John			1878	No	22	01	01
Mitchell	Ed			1872	Se	08	01	04	Montgomery	Karl	F		1872	Ap	25	04	05
Mitchell	Elizabeth		Mrs	1849	Jl	19	03	04	Montgomery	Lens			1878	Au	11	04	06
Mitchell	Eudora		Mrs	1869	Se	07	02	04	Montgomery	Napolean	B		1831	Oc	05	03	05
Mitchell	George	D		1844	Oc	23	03	04	Montgomery	R	D		1872	Ap	25	01	03
Mitchell	Granda			1878	No	19	02	01	Montgomery	Richard		Mr	1830	De	29	03	04
Mitchell	Henry			1878	Ap	24	04	04	Montgomery	Thomas		Mrs	1875	Jl	07	01	01
Mitchell	Infant			1878	Se	22	04	03	Montgomery	Walter			1871	Se	03	01	04
Mitchell	Joe			1878	Se	22	04	03	Montgomery	William		Gen	1835	Au	11	03	06
Mitchell	John			1870	Jn	24	04	03	Montgomery	William	B	Bro	1876	De	05	04	04
Mitchell	John			1872	Au	10	01	05	Montogome	Richard	M	Col	1877	De	02	01	07
Mitchell	John			1875	Mr	21	01	02	Montogomery	BR		Dr	1878	Oc	10	01	03
Mitchell	John			1875	Ap	10	01	03	Montogomery	William			1878	Au	30	01	04
Mitchell	John	D		1878	Se	26	01	04	Montour			Mon	1874	Oc	22	01	05
Mitchell	Josephine			1878	Se	22	04	03	Moody			Mr	1867	Fe	19	01	08
Mitchell	Josie			1878	Se	22	04	03	Moody			Mr	1876	No	16	04	02
Mitchell	Margaret	A	Mrs	1879	Oc	21	08	05	Moody			Pvt	1876	Jl	09	01	05
Mitchell	Maria		Mrs	1840	Fe	19	03	04	Moody	F	H	Cap	1873	Oc	26	04	04
Mitchell	Mary	A	Mrs	1853	Mr	11	03	06	Moody	John			1871	My	16	01	05
Mitchell	Mollie			1878	Se	22	04	03	Moody	John			1874	Fe	04	01	05
Mitchell	Ollie			1879	Se	06	01	01	Moody	Mary			1879	Au	28	01	01

Last	First	MI	Ttl	Yr	Mo	Day	Pg	Col	Last	First	MI	Ttl	Yr	Mo	Day	Pg	Col
Moody	Mary		Mrs	1858	Oc	23	03	03	Moores	Fannie	B		1879	Au	28	04	01
Moody	S	N	Col	1875	Ja	03	01	06	Moorhead	Tilmon		Mr	1835	Jl	21	03	06
Moody	T	J		1871	Jl	20	01	05	Moors	Charles		Mrs	1832	My	30	03	05
Moon				1877	No	24	01	07	Moran	Charles			1876	Oc	15	01	02
Moon	Charles			1878	Jn	13	04	03	Moran	Martin			1879	Au	29	01	01
Moon	Edward			1879	Oc	15	01	01	Morand	Wiley		Mr	1873	Jn	25	03	01
Moon	Jimmy			1873	De	07	01	04	Mordecai	John	B		1873	My	11	01	02
Moon	John			1879	No	29	01	02	Mordecki				1873	Se	06	01	02
Moone			Pro	1870	Oc	23	01	01	More	Issac	D		1878	Mr	03	01	03
Mooney	Daniel		Col	1827	Jn	26	03	04	More	Sarah	C	Mrs	1839	Ja	30	03	02
Mooney	H			1871	Jn	23	01	03	Morehouse	Alfred	C	Mr	1873	Jn	22	04	06
Mooney	J	J	Rev	1878	Se	28	01	04	Moreland			Mrs	1872	Fe	14	01	02
Mooney	John		Mr	1878	Au	10	01	03	Moreland	J	C	Mr	1858	Oc	09	03	03
Mooney	John		Mrs	1878	Au	10	01	03	Moreland	Margaret		Mrs	1871	Ap	11	03	01
Mooney	Margaret		Mrs	1878	Au	10	01	03	Morgan			Mr	1871	No	16	01	03
Mooney	Mathew			1878	Au	10	01	03	Morgan			Mr	1872	Jl	13	04	02
Mooney	Thomas			1876	Se	28	04	02	Morgan			Mr	1874	Oc	07	01	05
Mooney	Thomas	J	Rev	1877	Se	15	01	06	Morgan			Mrs	1876	Ap	11	01	05
Moore				1871	Mr	11	03	01	Morgan	Betsey		Mrs	1835	Jl	21	03	05
Moore			Sis	1876	Fe	17	04	03	Morgan	Charles			1878	My	10	01	06
Moore	Adaline	J	Mrs	1868	Mr	17	03	05	Morgan	Christopher			1875	Ap	20	01	06
Moore	Bloomfield			1878	Jl	07	01	06	Morgan	David			1879	My	09	04	04
Moore	Calvin	S		1879	Se	04	01	01	Morgan	Dehlia			1878	Se	04	01	03
Moore	Charles	E	Esq	1852	Au	27	03	06	Morgan	John	B	Mr	1824	Au	17	03	01
Moore	Charles	G		1878	Se	22	04	03	Morgan	John	R	Mr	1840	Se	02	03	04
Moore	Dick			1878	Mr	03	01	05	Morgan	Johnson			1875	Ap	20	01	06
Moore	Dick		Coe	1878	Mr	02	01	05	Morgan	Martin			1875	Ap	20	01	06
Moore	Edward			1870	No	12	01	03	Morgan	Mary			1878	Jl	19	01	04
Moore	Edward			1873	Se	07	01	04	Morgan	Nancy			1879	Se	11	01	01
Moore	Elenor		Mrs	1861	Mr	30	03	02	Morgan	P	G		1873	Au	16	01	02
Moore	Elizabeth	W		1856	Se	06	03	06	Morgan	R			1873	My	22	01	02
Moore	Ellis			1872	De	29	01	05	Morgan	Rosalinda	M	Mrs	1858	My	01	03	03
Moore	Emma			1879	Au	23	01	01	Morgan	Sarah	R		1858	Au	14	03	04
Moore	Fannie	B	Mrs	1879	Au	24	01	01	Morgan	W	S	Rev	1878	My	08	01	07
Moore	Francis		Mr	1876	No	07	04	03	Morissey	John		Sir	1878	My	03	04	05
Moore	Frank	M	Mr	1873	Jl	29	01	04	Morrell	Charles			1877	De	16	01	08
Moore	George			1874	Jn	27	01	04	Morrin	Buckner	S		1879	De	17	01	02
Moore	Granville			1870	Se	22	04	02	Morris				1873	Oc	11	01	04
Moore	Henry			1879	Ja	01	04	08	Morris			Cor	1876	Jl	09	01	05
Moore	I	J		1878	Se	28	01	04	Morris	Alice			1879	No	15	01	02
Moore	J	L	Mr	1869	Au	06	04	04	Morris	Amos			1876	Fe	17	04	04
Moore	Jacob			1872	Au	29	01	02	Morris	Amos			1876	Mr	04	04	04
Moore	James	W	Rev	1873	Ja	30	04	05	Morris	Charles			1879	Se	05	05	02
Moore	James	W	Rev	1873	Fe	02	01	04	Morris	E	F	Mr	1871	No	15	01	04
Moore	Jesse			1878	Se	26	01	04	Morris	E	F	Mrs	1871	No	15	01	04
Moore	John			1871	Se	03	01	05	Morris	Eliza		Mrs	1840	My	13	03	01
Moore	John	T		1871	Mr	03	01	02	Morris	Henry			1879	Au	12	01	02
Moore	Joseph			1857	Oc	24	03	03	Morris	I	J	Pro	1878	Fe	12	04	02
Moore	Joseph		Mr	1840	Jn	24	03	04	Morris	I	N	Hon	1879	Oc	30	01	01
Moore	Katie			1879	Au	02	01	03	Morris	James			1878	Au	30	01	04
Moore	Lillie	U		1867	Oc	15	02	08	Morris	Joe			1878	Mr	23	04	02
Moore	Mary		Mss	1871	My	18	01	01	Morris	Kate			1878	My	15	01	06
Moore	Michael		Mr	1872	No	28	01	03	Morris	Kate		Mss	1878	My	12	01	06
Moore	Michael		Mrs	1872	No	28	01	03	Morris	N			1877	De	06	04	05
Moore	Phillip	G		1869	Mr	02	02	03	Morris	Old	M		1878	Se	24	01	06
Moore	R	C		1875	Ap	30	04	05	Morris	Samuel			1877	Ja	14	01	07
Moore	R	H		1879	Jn	28	01	02	Morris	Thomas	H		1872	Fe	18	01	04
Moore	Robert		Mr	1838	Jl	11	03	04	Morris	Thos			1878	My	07	04	05
Moore	Sallie			1873	Au	09	04	06	Morrison	Benjamin			1839	Oc	23	03	04
Moore	Samuel	E		1859	Au	20	03	02	Morrison	Channing			1878	Se	14	01	04
Moore	Sarah	A	Mrs	1873	Fe	28	04	04	Morrison	Channing			1878	Se	22	04	03
Moore	Sarah	A	Mrs	1873	Mr	15	04	05	Morrison	F	S	Mrs	1839	Jl	24	03	04
Moore	Virgil	P	Mr	1871	Au	20	04	04	Morrison	J			1879	De	05	01	03
Moore	William		Mr	1852	De	31	03	06	Morrison	J	J		1871	My	21	02	02
Moore	William	P		1874	Ja	20	04	07	Morrison	James		Mr	1845	My	12	03	04
Moore	William	P	Maj	1853	Mr	11	03	06	Morrison	Jas	C	Lt	1871	Jl	18	01	05

Last	First	MI	Ttl	Yr	Mo	Day	Pg	Col	Last	First	MI	Ttl	Yr	Mo	Day	Pg	Col
Morrison	Joshua		Maj	1857	No	14	03	03	Mueller	Christina			1878	Fe	16	04	05
Morrison	Murray		Jud	1871	De	28	01	03	Mueller	Infant			1879	Jn	14	08	05
Morrison	William		Mr	1827	Ap	17	03	01	Muer	Robert			1873	Se	05	01	02
Morrissey			Mr	1872	Se	07	01	04	Muffey	Samuel			1878	Se	22	04	03
Morrissey	John			1878	My	02	01	06	Muhlenbery			Rev	1878	Ja	09	03	02
Morrissey	John			1878	My	05	01	07	Mulbrandon	Frank			1879	Jl	10	01	03
Morrissey	Peter			1878	Se	22	04	03	Mulbrandon	Mary			1879	Au	03	01	01
Morrow	George	B		1857	No	14	03	03	Mulchay	John			1878	Se	15	01	05
Morse	Chas		Mrs	1878	Se	19	04	07	Mulihauen				1876	De	10	01	06
Morse	Hod			1871	Au	20	01	05	Mullarkey	Thomas			1878	Ap	24	03	01
Morse	Hod			1871	Se	01	01	03	Mullco	J	W		1878	Oc	03	01	03
Morse	Hod			1872	Ja	27	01	03	Mulleda	Henry	S		1876	My	16	01	01
Morse	John	B		1879	Mr	26	01	02	Mullegan	Thomas			1878	Se	22	04	03
Morse	John	H		1875	Jn	08	01	03	Mullen	Richard	W		1875	Mr	16	01	05
Morse	Samuel	B	Pro	1872	Ap	04	01	01	Mullendore	Roach			1872	No	08	01	03
Morse	Sidney	E		1871	De	24	01	04	Muller	Gotlieb			1879	Oc	23	01	03
Morse	Sidney	E		1871	De	27	01	03	Muller	James			1878	Oc	02	01	04
Mortimer	Charles			1873	My	17	01	03	Mullet	Samuel			1878	Mr	21	01	06
Morton			Mrs	1875	Oc	02	01	01	Mulligan	Richard			1878	Se	05	01	03
Morton			Sen	1877	No	22	02	02	Mullins	John			1871	Jn	25	01	05
Morton	A		Mrs	1878	Oc	19	01	03	Mullins	W	T		1879	Oc	12	01	01
Morton	Dave			1878	Au	03	01	06	Mullins	William			1871	No	06	01	03
Morton	Edward	C	Cpt	1873	Ja	04	04	05	Mullivan	M			1878	Se	04	01	03
Morton	Edward	C	Cpt	1873	Ja	14	01	07	Munber	Lyman			1872	Au	13	01	05
Morton	George	H	Mr	1842	Mr	02	03	02	Mundt	Clara			1874	Ja	08	01	02
Morton	J	K	Dr	1879	Fe	04	03	01	Mundy	John			1873	No	18	04	03
Morton	James			1878	Ja	16	01	06	Mundy	William			1874	Mr	27	01	02
Morton	O	P	Sen	1877	No	02	01	06	Munford	Frank	M	Mr	1878	Fe	20	03	01
Morton	O	P	Sen	1877	No	03	01	04	Munn	J	C		1874	My	03	04	02
Morton	O	P	Sen	1877	No	03	02	02	Munn	Jack			1879	Au	15	01	03
Morton	O	P	Sen	1877	No	04	01	03	Munn	John	R	Bp	1874	Fe	10	01	06
Morton	O	P	Sen	1877	No	06	01	03	Munroe	George			1876	Ap	12	04	06
Morton	O	P	Sen	1877	No	07	01	03	Munsey	W	E	Rev	1877	Oc	24	01	04
Morton	O	P	Sen	1878	Ja	09	03	02	Munter			Mr	1875	My	12	01	04
Moryan	Mark			1879	Se	25	01	01	Munter			Mrs	1875	My	12	01	04
Mosby			Col	1872	Au	08	01	05	Murchasia	Lotta			1878	Se	22	04	03
Mosby	James	H	Esq	1867	Oc	01	03	04	Murchison	Roderick	J	Sir	1871	Oc	24	01	03
Mosby	James	H	Esq	1867	Oc	08	03	03	Murff	Ellen		Mrs	1859	Au	13	03	01
Mosby	John	D	Mr	1842	Ja	12	03	03	Murphey	Thomas	T	Mr	1840	My	20	02	05
Mosby	John	W		1862	Mr	01	03	06	Murphy	A	W		1872	No	30	01	03
Mosby	John	W		1862	De	06	02	02	Murphy	Beranrd		Mr	1871	Oc	31	04	05
Mosby	Sarah		Mrs	1842	My	04	03	06	Murphy	Bernard		Mrs	1871	Oc	31	04	05
Moseby	James	H	Esq	1867	Oc	01	03	04	Murphy	Daniel	J	Esq	1871	No	17	04	04
Moseby	James	H	Esq	1867	Oc	08	03	03	Murphy	Daniel	P		1872	Fe	01	01	03
Moseley	James			1835	Au	11	03	06	Murphy	Eliza			1878	Se	01	01	03
Moseley	Jane	E	Mrs	1874	Ap	29	01	06	Murphy	Frank			1871	Oc	14	04	05
Moseley	Samuel			1819	De	04	03	01	Murphy	Frank			1873	Au	31	03	01
Moses	Matilda			1878	Se	14	01	04	Murphy	Frank			1878	Au	27	01	04
Moses	Samuel			1878	Se	01	01	04	Murphy	George			1869	No	10	03	01
Moses	Samuel			1878	Se	14	01	04	Murphy	Geraldine		Mss	1870	Oc	01	04	03
Mosobach	R	H		1872	Jl	25	04	05	Murphy	Henry			1878	Se	01	01	04
Moss			Pvt	1876	Jl	09	01	05	Murphy	Isaac		Mr	1830	Fe	16	03	02
Moss	David			1878	Au	30	01	04	Murphy	J	R		1872	No	30	01	03
Moss	Elizabeth		Mrs	1867	Au	20	02	08	Murphy	James			1875	My	19	01	04
Moss	Henry	C	Dr	1878	Fe	19	01	05	Murphy	James	J		1874	Au	13	04	07
Moss	James		Esq	1833	No	13	03	04	Murphy	Jane			1878	Se	22	04	03
Mossely	William		Mr	1832	Oc	10	03	04	Murphy	Jas		Cbc	1877	No	25	01	04
Motes	Henry	F	Bro	1870	No	22	04	04	Murphy	John			1878	Se	05	01	03
Motley	John	L		1877	Oc	21	01	05	Murphy	Johnnie			1872	Se	20	01	05
Motley	John	L		1878	Ja	09	03	02	Murphy	Johnny			1873	Jn	01	01	04
Motrebe	Frederick		Mr	1849	Ap	26	03	04	Murphy	Lawrence	S		1874	Se	27	04	06
Motsch	Charles			1877	Se	28	04	01	Murphy	Mary			1879	No	18	08	02
Moulding	John	W	Mr	1837	Jl	25	03	04	Murphy	Mary	E		1879	No	18	08	05
Moulton	Tom		Feg	1878	Se	07	01	05	Murphy	Mary	I		1866	De	03	02	07
Mower	John	C		1879	Mr	14	01	02	Murphy	Mollie			1878	Se	22	04	03
Mudd	John	G		1878	Se	05	01	03	Murphy	Muranda		Mrs	1837	Jn	06	02	06

Last	First	MI	Ttl	Yr	Mo	Day	Pg	Col	Last	First	MI	Ttl	Yr	Mo	Day	Pg	Col
Murphy	Pat			1876	Oc	05	02	03	Nash			Mr	1871	Au	18	01	01
Murphy	Patrick			1875	Mr	21	01	03	Nash	Anna	B		1854	No	17	03	07
Murphy	Thomas			1876	Oc	13	01	03	Nash	H			1873	De	18	01	03
Murphy	W	J		1875	Mr	13	04	04	Nash	Jack			1879	De	27	08	02
Murphy	W	J		1875	Mr	16	04	04	Nason	Daniel			1872	Mr	05	01	05
Murray			Mr	1872	Mr	27	01	03	Nathan			Mr	1872	Se	10	01	02
Murray	Alexander			1872	Jn	25	04	04	Nathan			Mr	1872	Se	12	01	01
Murray	Alexander		Com	1821	No	24	03	01	Nathan	Benjamin			1872	Se	24	01	03
Murray	Charles			1872	Ap	13	01	02	Nathan	Chas	H		1878	Se	04	01	04
Murray	Henry			1872	Mr	30	01	01	Nathan	J	P	Mr	1873	Ja	18	04	04
Murray	J			1871	Ja	14	04	02	Nathan	Samuel			1878	Se	25	01	04
Murray	J			1871	My	21	02	02	Nathans	Benjamin			1870	No	16	01	02
Murray	Joe			1875	My	20	01	03	Neal			Mrs	1878	Se	22	04	03
Murray	John			1878	No	12	01	03	Neal	Elias			1872	Au	17	02	04
Murray	John	R		1871	No	15	01	04	Neasom	Libbie			1878	Oc	25	01	04
Murray	John	W	Lt	1831	Mr	16	03	05	Neckere	Leon	D	Rev	1833	Oc	09	03	05
Murray	Joseph			1871	Se	23	01	03	Nedville	Elihu		Mr	1852	Fe	13	03	07
Murray	Margaret	M		1870	Au	30	04	04	Neel			Mr	1871	Jl	26	01	02
Murray	Mary	E		1837	Mr	14	03	02	Neely	Anthony	B	Mr	1828	Jl	30	03	01
Murray	Thomas		Esq	1836	03	22	03	05	Neely	Ed			1878	Se	22	04	03
Murray	William			1879	Au	17	01	01	Neely	Ellen	E	Mrs	1857	No	28	03	01
Murrell	Charles			1877	No	08	01	06	Neely	Rachel		Mrs	1829	De	23	03	02
Murrell	Henry			1876	Se	24	04	01	Neely	William		Esq	1827	No	13	03	04
Murry	Alfred		Esq	1829	Fe	10	03	02	Neff	Isaac			1879	My	15	01	03
Murry	Eliza	J	Mrs	1854	Jn	23	03	06	Neidig	F			1878	Se	13	01	04
Murry	Frank	D		1854	Jn	23	03	06	Neill	Gordon		Dr	1829	Se	16	03	01
Murry	Mary	H	Mss	1867	De	03	03	02	Neill	Lettitia		Mrs	1844	Au	14	03	05
Murtagh	Thomas			1878	Ja	24	01	04	Neill	William		Mr	1826	Se	05	03	01
Murtha	Hugh	M		1878	My	26	04	07	Neimeyer	George	F		1879	Jl	25	08	02
Murtha	Jennie		Mss	1875	Jl	18	04	04	Neimeyer	George	F		1879	Jl	25	08	06
Murtry	M	H		1879	Ja	23	04	06	Nelding	F			1878	Se	22	04	03
Mussner	Anna			1875	My	12	01	04	Neller			Pvt	1876	Jl	09	01	05
Myers			Mr	1859	Ja	01	03	01	Nelson				1873	Oc	04	01	03
Myers	Albert			1871	Jl	18	01	06	Nelson			Cpt	1878	Au	14	01	04
Myers	Carrie			1878	Se	08	01	05	Nelson			Dr	1878	Se	22	04	03
Myers	Francis			1878	Se	22	04	03	Nelson			Mrs	1872	Oc	24	01	06
Myers	John			1878	Jl	14	01	06	Nelson	Ann	E	Mrs	1869	Au	15	02	04
Myers	John		Cap	1874	Jn	24	01	01	Nelson	Charles		Esq	1870	Se	14	04	04
Myers	John		Cpt	1874	No	10	04	02	Nelson	Harry		Ldm	1877	No	25	01	04
Myers	Margaret		Mrs	1879	No	11	01	01	Nelson	J	L	Mrs	1878	Jl	09	04	01
Myers	Paul			1878	Jl	19	01	04	Nelson	James		Mrs	1872	Mr	20	01	04
Myers	Samuel			1874	Jn	24	01	06	Nelson	Martha			1878	Se	22	04	03
Myers	William			1878	Oc	15	01	03	Nelson	Mattie			1867	Au	27	03	02
Mynatt	Thos			1878	Se	22	04	03	Nelson	Mollie			1878	Au	27	01	04
Mynatt	William			1878	Se	22	04	03	Nelson	N		Jud	1878	Se	24	01	06
Mytinger	Lulu	E		1875	Se	28	04	03	Nelson	Neil			1876	Oc	01	01	03
									Nelson	Norborne			1838	Fe	14	03	05
									Nelson	Peter			1876	Jn	04	01	05
			N						Nelson	Reuben		Rev	1879	Fe	21	01	03
									Nelson	Samuel		Hon	1873	De	17	02	03
									Nelson	Samuel		Jus	1874	Ja	08	01	02
Nabors	Amanda			1879	Au	16	01	01	Nelson	T	W		1878	Oc	06	01	03
Nabors	James	M		1873	No	18	05	03	Nelson	Thomas		Mrs	1872	Oc	19	01	03
Nagie	David	A	Sen	1878	Mr	24	01	04	Nelson	Thomas	A	Jud	1873	Au	26	01	04
Nagle	Callie			1879	Oc	18	01	01	Nelson	Thomas	C	Esq	1857	De	05	03	02
Nagle	Tom			1873	Fe	08	01	06	Nelson	W	C		1879	Au	19	01	01
Nagle	Tom			1876	Ja	09	01	02	Nelson	William			1878	Au	28	01	03
Naht	Charles		Art	1878	Mr	03	01	03	Neltalon	Augustus		Md	1874	Ja	08	01	02
Nail	Morris			1872	Fe	08	01	03	Nepoleon			Emp	1875	Ja	10	01	05
Naile	J	H	Col	1878	Se	21	01	04	Neston	Joshua		Mr	1879	Au	13	01	03
Nale	John	H	Mrs	1878	Oc	11	04	02	Nettles	Charles			1859	Ja	29	03	01
Nale	Mary		Mrs	1878	Oc	11	01	03	Nettles	Eugenia	F	Mss	1851	Oc	31	03	07
Nance	Franklin			1873	Au	01	03	02	Nevill			Dml	1878	Jl	04	04	06
Nance	R	S		1878	Jn	08	04	02	Neville			Dml	1878	Jl	12	04	05
Narillo	John			1878	Oc	01	01	05	Neville	John		Dr	1876	No	25	04	01
Nash			Mr	1820	Se	30	03	03	Nevils	Thomas			1879	Oc	22	01	01

Last	First	MI	Ttl	Yr	Mo	Day	Pg	Col	Last	First	MI	Ttl	Yr	Mo	Day	Pg	Col
New	John	A	Maj	1879	Ja	18	04	03	Nixon				1877	No	24	01	06
Newan	Ida			1878	Se	01	01	03	Nixon	Agnes		Mss	1873	My	10	02	03
Newark	N	J		1873	Oc	16	01	01	Nixon	Charles			1873	My	17	01	03
Newberry	Julia			1879	Se	07	01	01	Noble	H	T	Col	1873	My	10	02	03
Newbert	William			1872	No	10	01	06	Noble	James		Gen	1831	Ap	13	03	05
Newbery	Wiley		Mr	1848	Ja	20	03	04	Noel	Baptist	W	Rev	1874	Ja	08	01	02
Newbury	Mark			1873	Fe	27	04	06	Noel	Beverly		Mr	1841	Jl	28	03	03
Newcomb	H	A		1878	Jn	03	04	07	Noel	George	H	Mr	1839	Jl	17	03	04
Newcomb	H	A		1878	Jl	03	04	07	Noel	Theo			1878	Se	22	04	03
Newcome	H	D		1874	Au	19	01	06	Noel	Washington		Mr	1840	Ap	08	03	03
Newey			Mr	1831	Fe	16	02	03	Nolan				1871	Ap	22	01	03
Newland	Ben			1872	No	30	01	03	Nolan	Mary			1879	Se	26	01	01
Newland	Rebecca		Mrs	1834	Ja	01	03	05	Noland				1873	Oc	26	04	04
Newland	William		Dr	1834	De	02	03	03	Noland	Lewis	B		1870	Fe	27	02	03
Newman	Abner			1875	Jl	07	01	02	Noland	Lewis	B		1870	Fe	27	03	01
Newman	Bernard			1878	Oc	09	01	04	Noland	Louis	B		1870	Fe	27	02	03
Newman	Charles			1876	Se	21	01	03	Noland	Louis	B		1870	Fe	27	03	01
Newman	James	R		1871	Se	02	01	04	Noland	Mary			1878	Au	25	01	04
Newman	Joe			1878	Fe	28	02	02	Noland	Noble	B		1859	Ja	01	03	02
Newman	Joseph			1872	Mr	12	01	04	Noland	R	W	Cpt	1841	No	24	03	04
Newman	Thomas	B		1873	My	17	01	03	Noland	Thomas	J	Esq	1857	Se	12	03	04
Newton			Mrs	1871	Au	13	01	06	Nolen	John			1870	Oc	19	01	03
Newton	Annie			1877	No	16	04	05	Nolly	Thomas			1878	Se	13	01	05
Newton	Annie			1877	No	20	04	06	Nolte	Henry		Mr	1872	Oc	13	01	03
Newton	Arabella	J	Mrs	1853	Se	09	03	07	Nolte	Henry		Mrs	1872	Oc	13	01	03
Newton	Arabella	J	Mrs	1853	Se	16	03	06	Nolton	Eugehia	W		1878	Se	22	04	03
Newton	Fannie	B		1876	Se	20	03	01	Nono	Pio		Poe	1878	Fe	09	01	08
Newton	James		Cpt	1862	Jl	12	02	05	Nono	Pio		Poe	1878	Fe	09	02	02
Newton	John		Mr	1822	De	03	03	01	Nono	Pio		Poe	1878	Fe	10	01	06
Newton	John	H		1878	Mr	14	01	05	Nono	Pio		Poe	1878	Fe	12	01	06
Newton	John	W		1857	Oc	03	02	02	Nono	Pio		Poe	1878	Fe	12	02	01
Newton	Mary			1875	De	05	01	07	Nono	Pio		Poe	1878	Fe	13	01	08
Newton	Mary		Mrs	1844	No	27	03	05	Nono	Pio		Poe	1878	Fe	14	01	07
Newton	Mary	E		1844	De	23	03	01	Nono	Pio		Poe	1878	Fe	15	01	05
Newton	Mary	E							Nono	Pio		Poe	1878	Fe	19	01	05
Newton	W	S	Cap	1837	Ap	11	03	05	Nono	Pio		Poe	1878	Fe	20	04	02
Nibit	Solomon		Mr	1820	No	25	03	04	Nono	Pio		Poe	1878	Fe	21	04	04
Nicalow	Catherine			1871	Jn	01	01	03	Norcross	Albert			1878	Oc	06	01	03
Nichall	P			1878	Se	22	04	03	Norcross	Jno	C		1878	Oc	06	01	03
Nichol	Ann			1862	Jl	12	02	05	Norell	Frank			1871	Au	15	01	03
Nicholas			Pri	1874	Ja	08	01	02	Norfork	Harry		Mrs	1877	No	04	01	06
Nicholas	Alexander		Mr	1852	Oc	08	03	06	Norfork	Henry		Mr	1877	De	22	01	04
Nicholas	Caladona	E	Mrs	1852	Oc	08	03	06	Norfork	Henry		Mrs	1877	De	22	01	04
Nicholas	James			1852	Oc	08	03	06	Norman	Jas			1878	Se	01	01	03
Nichols			Mr	1872	My	25	01	01	Norman	Sarah	H	Mrs	1840	Se	02	03	04
Nichols	Alonzo	J		1873	Au	07	01	03	Norris			Dr	1878	Se	13	01	04
Nichols	Leroy			1879	Ap	20	01	01	Norris			Mrs	1878	Se	05	01	03
Nichols	W	B	Snr	1878	Oc	20	01	03	Norris	B	W	Con	1873	Ja	28	01	04
Nichols	William	L		1878	Se	22	04	03	Norris	George	L		1830	Ap	20	03	05
Nicholson				1873	Au	02	01	02	Norris	Minnie	H	Mss	1868	My	19	02	07
Nicholson				1873	Au	03	01	06	Norris	Nancy		Mrs	1821	Mr	31	03	04
Nicholson			Cj	1876	Mr	24	01	01	Norris	Samuel		Esq	1856	Ap	26	03	06
Nicholson	J	J	Com	1839	Ja	16	01	06	Northern	William	F	Mr	1842	Fe	16	03	01
Nicholson	Joshua			1873	Jn	07	01	02									
Nicholson	Paul			1871	Jn	23	01	03									
Nicholson	Ribert			1878	Au	28	01	03	Norton			Mrs	1878	Ja	09	03	02
Nicholson	W	G	Mrs	1879	Oc	07	01	01	Norton	Chas	W		1879	Oc	25	01	01
Nickols			Son	1876	Ap	09	02	04	Norton	Daniel	S	Sen	1870	Jl	27	03	01
Nicks	John		Gen	1832	Ja	11	03	05	Norton	Dennis			1879	Au	27	01	01
Nicks	William		Bro	1869	Jn	15	02	04	Norton	Jacob	H	Mr	1840	Au	05	03	05
Nicodemus	Joseph	C		1878	Fe	28	01	05	Norton	James			1874	Mr	31	03	01
Nicrasl	Antonio			1877	De	04	03	04	Norton	John			1872	Fe	09	01	02
Nidrene	Alexander			1873	Au	21	01	04	Norton	John			1873	De	18	01	03
Niemeyer	Jacob		Mrs	1879	Fe	25	04	04	Norton	Joseph	W		1879	Jl	23	01	03
Niemeyer	Mattie		Mrs	1879	Fe	25	04	07	Norton	Lottie		Mss	1872	Ja	03	04	02
Nierosi	Antanio			1877	De	15	03	01	Norton	Richard		Cpt	1872	Oc	23	01	04
Ninchester	James		Gen	1826	Se	05	03	01	Norton	William			1876	Oc	22	01	01

Last	First	MI	Ttl	Yr	Mo	Day	Pg	Col	Last	First	MI	Ttl	Yr	Mo	Day	Pg	Col
Nortus	Alice			1878	Au	28	01	03	O'Conner	Maurice			1878	Mr	24	01	06
Norvell	Joshua		Esq	1821	Oc	20	03	01	O'Conner	T	D	Mr	1872	Ja	05	01	02
Norvelle	Mattie		Mrs	1878	Se	05	01	05	O'Conner	Wallace			1845	Ja	06	03	04
Norville	W	R		1878	Au	28	01	04	O'Connor	Ellen			1878	Se	22	04	03
Norwood			Mr	1872	Ja	09	01	01	O'Connor	John			1878	Se	22	04	03
Nostrand	E			1873	No	18	05	03	O'Connor	Wiliam			1877	No	01	04	02
Nothwang	Christian			1877	Ja	23	04	06	Oday	Peter			1879	Se	28	01	01
Notrebe	Charles	F	Mr	1841	Se	22	03	04	Oddie	Berrell	F		1873	Jn	14	01	04
Notrebe	Eugene		Col	1840	My	27	03	04	O'Dell	C		Mrs	1878	Se	22	04	03
Notrebe	Felicite			1821	Oc	13	03	04	Oder			Mr	1877	Se	18	01	05
Nourse	C	A		1879	De	06	05	01	Oder			Mrs	1877	Se	18	01	06
Novilsky	Annie			1878	Au	30	01	04	Odin	William			1876	Jn	23	01	06
Nowlan	Maria	M	Mss	1858	Mr	06	03	03	Odin	William		Mrs	1876	Jn	23	01	06
Nowland	Eva			1879	Au	12	01	01	O'Donnel	Mary			1879	Se	17	01	01
Nowland	Maria	M	Mss	1858	Fe	27	03	04	O'Donnel	Stephan	A		1878	Oc	04	01	03
Nowland	William		Cpt	1871	Fe	21	04	02	O'Donnel	Thos	W		1879	Oc	15	01	01
Nugent	Peter		Dr	1878	Se	22	04	03	O'Donnell	Dow		Sea	1877	No	25	01	04
Nugent	Richard			1878	Se	25	01	05	O'Donnell	John			1872	De	08	01	04
Null	John			1871	Ja	14	04	02	O'Donnell	John			1879	No	04	05	02
Null	John			1871	My	21	02	02	O'Donnell	Kane			1871	Se	09	01	04
Null	William		Esq	1839	Mr	06	03	05	O'Donnell	Kate			1879	Oc	04	01	01
Nunn	Infant			1874	Jl	12	04	02	O'Donnell	Micheal			1878	Ja	15	01	07
Nunn	John		Mr	1872	Jn	26	01	01	O'Donnell	William			1878	Se	22	04	03
Nutail	James			1878	Se	06	01	05	O'Fallen	Infant			1879	Au	08	08	02
Nutall	T		Mrs	1878	Se	07	01	04	Oearde	Ada			1874	Ap	02	04	06
Nutling	G	A		1878	Oc	13	01	03	Oebler	Alvia			1873	Au	13	01	04
Nutzell	Joseph			1879	Oc	24	01	01	Oechsteerich			Mrs	1878	Ja	25	04	04
Nye	S	L	Mr	1874	Ap	16	01	03	Oerrel			Con	1874	Au	04	01	07
									Officer	William	P		1852	Ap	23	03	07
									Officer	William	P	Mr	1851	Jn	27	03	05
									Offutt	George		Mr	1837	Au	15	03	04
	O								Ogburn	W	M	Bro	1868	Oc	13	03	06
									Ogden	Benjamin		Rev	1837	De	26	02	05
Oakley	A	M		1871	De	29	01	02	Ogden	Charles			1868	Mr	31	03	04
Oakley	Allen	W	Esq	1839	Au	14	03	05	Ogden	Charles		Bro	1868	Ap	07	03	04
Oakley	George		Maj	1829	Jn	24	03	04	Ogden	William			1877	Se	12	04	05
Oakley	Walter	D		1878	Se	01	01	03	Oglesby	Crispin			1876	Jl	02	01	04
Oates	O	H	Mrs	1867	Oc	01	03	04	Ogra	James			1873	My	18	01	01
Oates	Oliver	H	Col	1870	Mr	10	02	02	O'Hagen	Joseph	B	Rev	1878	De	28	04	04
Ober	Ratie			1878	Au	27	04	07	O'Haire	Elizabeth	E		1879	Oc	24	08	06
Obergon	Pablo		Don	1828	Oc	14	03	04	O'Hara	Daniel			1877	Oc	14	01	05
Obermeyer	Joseph			1878	Oc	10	01	03	O'Hara	Daniel		Cpt	1877	Oc	16	01	06
Oberst	William			1878	Se	01	01	07	O'Hara	William	M	Esq	1821	Jl	28	03	01
O'Brett	Father			1878	Se	12	01	06	Ohman	Olof			1879	Oc	22	01	01
O'Brien			Bp	1879	Au	02	05	01	Ohmer	Morris			1878	Oc	24	01	05
O'Brien	Ann			1878	Au	27	01	04	Oilverick	B	P		1878	Se	07	01	04
O'Brien	D	A	Rev	1873	Oc	11	01	03	Okonser	George			1879	Ap	05	04	03
O'Brien	John			1871	Se	26	01	03	O'Keefe	Mary			1878	Ja	29	03	01
O'Brien	John		Mr	1871	Jn	07	04	02	O'Keefe	P			1879	Oc	10	01	01
O'Brien	Lucius		Lt	1841	Fe	24	03	04	Oldham	Mary	A	Mrs	1867	My	28	03	04
O'Brien	Maggie		Mss	1873	My	10	02	03	Oldstein	C	G		1878	Se	18	04	04
O'Brien	W	S		1878	My	03	04	05	Oleary	Daniel	J		1867	Se	17	03	03
O'Brien	William			1879	Ja	23	04	05	O'Leary	Ellen		Mrs	1867	De	17	03	04
O'Brien	Willie			1878	Se	22	04	03	O'Leary	John			1878	Se	04	01	03
O'Bryan	Ann			1872	Ja	20	01	03	O'Leary	Martin			1879	Au	09	01	01
O'Callaghan	John			1859	No	05	03	02	O'Leary	Timothy			1871	Au	05	01	04
Ochiltree	William	B	Jud	1868	Ja	21	03	04	Olen	Beverly			1878	De	24	04	05
O'Connel	Daniel	L		1873	Mr	30	04	03	Oley	George			1878	Se	01	01	03
O'Connell			Pvt	1876	Jl	09	01	05	Oliphint	Georgia		Mrs	1878	No	02	04	03
O'Connell	Daniel	L	Mr	1874	Ap	01	04	05	Olive			Mrs	1874	Ja	08	01	02
O'Connell	James		Sir	1872	Jl	30	01	05	Olive	Zep			1878	Se	25	01	04
O'Connell	Oscar			1869	De	04	02	03	Oliver	B	P		1878	Se	06	01	05
O'Conner	Fannie		Mss	1876	Oc	12	01	02	Oliver	Edward		Mr	1838	De	05	03	04
O'Conner	James			1871	Oc	05	01	08	Oliver	John	M	Gen	1872	Ap	02	01	04
O'Conner	John			1878	Se	04	01	03	Olmstead	Frank			1872	No	15	01	03
O'Conner	Martin			1878	Jl	13	04	05	Olney	Jesse			1872	Au	15	02	05

Last	First	MI	Ttl	Yr	Mo	Day	Pg	Col	Last	First	MI	Ttl	Yr	Mo	Day	Pg	Col
Olsen	John			1873	Jn	06	01	02	Owen	John			1878	Au	30	01	04
Olson	Carrie		Mss	1871	Jn	28	01	04	Owen	John	A		1876	De	29	04	01
Olson	E	M	Ceg	1877	No	25	01	04	Owen	M	E	Mrs	1878	No	17	01	03
Oltman	W	F		1879	Au	28	01	01	Owen	Mary	A	Mrs	1838	Fe	14	03	05
O'Neal	Percy			1873	Au	12	01	02	Owen	Miles			1879	Au	14	01	01
O'Neil			Mr	1877	Oc	07	04	02	Owen	R	E		1871	My	21	02	02
O'Neil	Bridgett			1879	Se	12	01	01	Owen	R	G		1871	Ja	14	04	02
O'Neil	Infant			1878	Au	10	01	03	Owen	Robert	D		1878	Ja	09	03	02
O'Neil	James			1877	De	28	01	05	Owen	Susan	F		1839	Oc	30	03	04
O'Neil	John			1878	Oc	02	01	05	Owen	T	J		1835	No	10	03	05
O'Neill	John			1871	Au	11	01	04	Owen	William	M	Esq	1846	Se	28	02	06
O'Niell				1868	Mr	17	03	05	Owens				1873	Oc	21	04	02
Openhelmer			Bp	1879	Au	15	05	02	Owens			Mar	1872	Ap	21	01	05
O'Reilly	Lawrence			1878	No	16	01	04	Owens	Annie			1867	Oc	08	03	03
O'Reilly	Terence			1879	Oc	12	01	01	Owens	Anthony			1879	Se	09	01	01
Organ	John	N		1869	Jl	27	02	03	Owens	J	G		1872	Ap	26	01	02
Orman			Mrs	1870	Se	21	04	04	Owens	J	G	Dml	1872	Ap	24	01	01
Ormiston	George			1872	Ap	02	01	04	Owens	J	M	Dr	1874	Jn	23	04	02
Ormond	Jules			1873	Se	28	01	05	Owens	James			1879	Se	07	01	01
Ormond	Robert			1872	De	05	04	04	Owens	Jas			1878	Se	22	04	03
Ormsby	James			1874	Jn	26	01	04	Owens	John			1875	Mr	11	01	03
Ormsteader	J	D		1878	Oc	09	01	03	Owens	Maggie			1879	Se	10	01	01
O'Rourke				1877	No	16	01	06	Owens	Mary			1878	Se	22	04	03
O'Rourke	Micheal			1878	Mr	27	01	07	Owens	Pasa			1878	Se	22	04	03
Orr	James			1879	Au	16	01	03	Owens	Robert			1875	Se	28	04	02
Orr	Robert		Gen	1876	My	31	01	04	Owens	Thomas			1878	Oc	09	01	03
Orr	William	I	Dr	1821	Ja	20	03	04	Owens	William		Maj	1840	Jl	15	03	04
Orsdale	John	J		1873	Jl	29	01	05	Owens	William		Mr	1874	Se	24	02	02
Ortman	Barney		Mr	1871	Ap	09	01	05	Owens	Zack			1876	Jn	15	02	03
Orton	William			1878	Ap	24	04	04	Owl	White			1879	Ja	12	01	03
Orton	William		Hon	1878	Ap	23	01	06	Owne	Fritz	W		1850	Se	13	03	07
Orton	William		Hon	1878	Ap	25	04	04									
Orton	William		Hon	1878	Ap	26	01	07									
Orton	William		Hon	1878	My	08	02	02				**P**					
Orvilley	J	V	Rev	1873	Oc	07	01	04									
Osborn	John	P		1874	Fe	28	04	03									
Osborn	Susan	J	Mrs	1861	Mr	23	03	02	Pace	Mary		Mrs	1876	Oc	25	04	06
Osborne				1876	Jn	25	01	04	Pack	Jefferson		Hon	1851	Ja	03	03	06
Osborne	Elizabeth		Mrs	1871	De	05	04	04	Packard	C	M	Con	1870	Se	27	02	03
Osborne	Sandy			1878	Oc	13	01	04	Packer	Asa		Jud	1879	My	20	04	01
Osborne	William	H		1872	De	27	01	03	Padden	Luke			1872	Mr	23	01	04
Osburn	Mary	F	Mrs	1871	Oc	29	04	06	Page				1871	Jl	02	01	05
Osgood	S	D	Rev	1875	Jl	11	01	05	Page				1873	No	18	04	03
Osher	Patrick			1875	Ap	10	01	03	Page	Charles	A		1873	My	28	01	01
Ostman	Fritz			1879	Au	17	01	01	Page	Charles	T		1878	Se	17	01	06
Ostman	Wilhelma		Mrs	1879	Au	14	01	01	Page	Henry	C		1871	Jl	13	01	05
Ostmann	Johanna			1879	Au	15	01	01	Page	James	R	Jud	1873	Jl	06	03	01
Ostrander	Carrie			1874	Jl	08	01	06	Page	John	F		1878	Se	06	01	04
Ostrander	Charles		Mr	1837	Se	19	03	05	Page	Joseph			1871	Jl	18	01	06
Ostrander	John			1874	Mr	27	01	02	Page	Joseph		Mrs	1878	De	22	04	04
Ostwald	Catherina		Mrs	1852	No	26	03	06	Page	M	B	Mss	1878	Se	22	04	03
Otey	Easter			1879	Jl	30	01	01	Page	Nathaniel		Bro	1869	De	25	02	03
Otey	Mollie		Mss	1867	De	17	03	04	Pagels	Amelin		Mrs	1878	Se	05	01	03
Ott	Henry			1872	Au	20	01	06	Paige	Joseph			1878	Mr	16	01	06
Ottenheimer	Bareth			1877	Ja	26	04	05	Paine			Mr	1872	Au	27	01	04
Otto	A			1878	Se	01	01	03	Paine	George	N		1879	Se	14	01	01
Otto	Charles			1876	Ja	15	01	06	Painter	William			1877	Oc	02	01	05
Otto	George			1878	Se	05	01	03	Palermo	Francisco		Mr	1875	Mr	17	01	03
Outlaw			Mrs	1874	Fe	21	04	02	Palfrey	Fanny	A	Mrs	1878	Oc	13	01	04
Overbaugh	Aemen		Ldm	1877	No	25	01	04	Palfrey	Sidney		Mss	1878	Oc	09	01	04
Overton	Calvin	H		1859	No	05	03	02	Palmer	Dennis			1878	Se	04	01	03
Overton	Edward			1877	Se	22	04	03	Palmer	Dennis			1878	Se	05	01	03
Overton	Elizabeth		Mrs	1874	Ja	29	04	02	Palmer	G	E	Mrs	1877	Ja	03	01	04
Owen			Mss	1872	Jn	15	02	04	Palmer	H	L		1878	Oc	11	01	03
Owen	Cynthia	M	Mrs	1873	Mr	13	04	04	Palmer	Henry		Mr	1835	Jn	09	03	05
Owen	Hop			1878	Se	24	01	04	Palmer	John			1852	Au	20	03	07

Last	First	MI	Ttl	Yr	Mo	Day	Pg	Col	Last	First	MI	Ttl	Yr	Mo	Day	Pg	Col
Palmer	John		Mr	1852	Au	20	03	07	Parry	Richard			1878	Se	24	01	07
Palmer	John	J		1875	My	23	03	01	Parshall	David	C		1876	Jn	22	01	04
Palmer	L	G	Lt	1877	No	25	01	04	Parsons	F	M	Esq	1877	Oc	04	04	01
Palmer	L	G	Lt	1877	De	02	01	07	Parsons	William			1857	Ja	31	03	03
Palmer	L	P		1874	Ap	30	01	01	Partee	Hiram	A		1877	De	11	01	05
Palmer	Leven			1873	Au	23	01	03	Parthesius	Henry			1879	Jl	29	01	01
Palmer	Louis			1879	Au	09	01	01	Partlow	P		Mrs	1878	Se	22	04	03
Palmer	Nancy		Mrs	1834	Oc	28	03	04	Partridge	Dick			1876	My	26	01	03
Palmer	William			1879	Ap	13	01	01	Partridge	Isaac	C		1860	De	01	03	01
Palone	Andy			1872	Ap	20	01	02	Pascal			Gov	1878	Au	22	01	04
Panloona	Helene		Gd	1873	Ja	23	01	06	Pascal	Henry			1878	Se	22	04	03
Panormo			Mr	1872	Ja	26	01	30	Paschal	George			1878	Fe	17	01	03
Panormo			Pro	1872	Ja	28	01	03	Paschal	Susan	A		1846	My	04	03	05
Papeneau	Louis	J	Hon	1871	Se	27	01	04	Pasha	Daoud			1874	Ja	08	01	02
Paramour	Robert	P	Bro	1875	Se	28	04	03	Pasha	Moussa			1877	Oc	20	01	05
Pardee	Charles			1878	Ap	11	01	07	Pasley	William	H		1858	Jl	24	03	03
Parish	Albert		Mr	1872	No	06	02	03	Passner			Dsh	1878	Se	11	04	06
Parish	Brooks			1878	Au	28	01	03	Past	John	C		1876	Se	26	01	05
Park	Jas	G		1878	Se	22	04	03	Patch	Sam			1829	De	23	02	04
Parke	Lilly	M		1858	No	06	03	02	Patchel			Mrs	1878	Se	22	04	03
Parker	Chauncey	M		1867	Oc	08	03	03	Patchell	Jos			1878	Se	22	04	03
Parker	Emily	C	Mrs	1859	Oc	29	03	02	Patillo	J	A		1879	Ap	12	04	05
Parker	George	W		1879	Mr	12	04	07	Patillo	R	A	Dr	1878	Se	22	04	03
Parker	Jacob			1877	No	20	01	08	Patillo	R	F		1878	Se	22	04	03
Parker	Jacob	E		1878	Ap	12	01	07	Patrick	Cynthia	A	Mrs	1846	Fe	02	03	03
Parker	Jane	V	Mrs	1857	My	16	03	02	Patrick	Freeman	E	Hon	1857	Jl	18	02	01
Parker	Joel			1874	Ja	08	01	02	Patrick	John			1878	Se	08	04	05
Parker	Joel		Rev	1873	My	03	01	05	Patrick	John	W		1879	Au	21	08	03
Parker	John			1874	Ja	01	01	04	Patrick	W	H		1878	Ap	26	03	02
Parker	John			1878	Jn	13	01	06	Patta	Frank	O		1878	No	06	01	06
Parker	John		Col	1878	Oc	04	01	03	Pattan	E	L		1878	Au	28	01	03
Parker	John		Mrs	1874	Ja	01	01	04	Patten	Ada	L		1869	Oc	29	04	02
Parker	John	W	Mr	1837	My	09	03	04	Patterson				1871	Ap	23	03	01
Parker	M	F		1874	Ap	03	02	04	Patterson			Mr	1875	Mr	12	04	03
Parker	S	R		1877	Se	27	04	06	Patterson	Charles	H		1875	Jl	11	01	05
Parker	Samuel			1862	Au	16	02	06	Patterson	Croyden	F		1875	Jl	11	01	05
Parker	Samuel	H	Mr	1873	Fe	19	01	06	Patterson	J	G		1878	Oc	31	01	07
Parker	Samuel	S	Cpt	1835	Fe	17	09	05	Patterson	J	N		1878	No	01	01	06
Parker	Sarah	W	Mrs	1855	Jn	01	03	07	Patterson	James			1872	Jn	23	01	06
Parker	Thomas	G		1879	Ja	23	04	06	Patterson	James			1879	Jl	08	01	02
Parker	W	L	Apm	1878	Oc	20	01	03	Patterson	James		Mr	1879	My	27	08	04
Parker	William	B		1871	Oc	29	01	03	Patterson	John	C		1874	Ap	09	04	06
Parkes	George			1878	Se	05	01	03	Patterson	John	G		1868	Ja	21	03	04
Parkhurst	William	H		1876	Oc	17	04	03	Patterson	William			1871	Se	10	01	05
Parkman			Dr	1872	Jl	20	02	05	Patton				1878	Ja	20	03	02
Parks	C	D		1862	Jn	28	02	05	Patton	Robert		Mrs	1878	Oc	02	01	05
Parks	Carrie			1878	Au	30	01	04	Paul	W	P		1878	Se	22	04	03
Parks	George			1876	Se	24	01	02	Paul	William		Mr	1831	My	18	03	05
Parks	George		Mrs	1876	Se	24	01	02	Pauseburger			Mr	1874	Ja	11	01	03
Parks	John	D		1876	Fe	01	04	03	Paxton	Joseph		Dr	1829	Fe	13	03	03
Parks	John	D		1876	Mr	04	04	04	Paxton	William		Mr	1826	Se	19	03	01
Parks	Margaret		Mrs	1868	Mr	31	03	04	Payne				1873	Au	09	01	03
Parks	Robert			1868	Mr	03	03	05	Payne			Mr	1874	Ap	10	04	02
Parks	Susie			1878	Jl	21	04	07	Payne	Bessie		Mss	1873	My	10	02	03
Parks	Tillman	B		1851	No	21	03	06	Payne	Elizabeth		Mrs	1849	Fe	22	03	05
Parnell	Benjamin			1871	Jl	14	01	01	Payne	M			1878	Se	22	04	03
Parr	James	A		1876	My	04	01	01	Payne	May			1878	Se	01	01	03
Parr	Neoma		Mrs	1840	No	18	03	04	Payne	Minnie	B		1878	Se	22	04	03
Parradol	Minerva			1870	No	12	01	02	Payne	Natheniel	W	Dr	1867	Oc	01	03	04
Parring	J			1873	Au	22	01	03	Payne	Tom			1874	Fe	25	04	04
Parrish	Addie	P	Mrs	1872	Mr	05	04	06	Payne	Tom			1877	No	04	02	02
Parrish	Ella		Mss	1878	Oc	09	01	04	Payne	William			1876	No	04	01	04
Parrish	Howell	J		1840	Mr	11	03	05	Payne	William	H	Dr	1870	Se	15	04	05
Parrott	E	G	Ram	1879	My	13	05	01	Peabody	George			1870	Fe	18	01	02
Parrott	Robert	P		1877	De	25	01	05	Peabody	George		Mr	1869	De	04	03	01
Parrott	Washington			1872	No	30	01	03	Peabody	George		Mr	1870	My	26	03	01

Last	First	MI	Ttl	Yr	Mo	Day	Pg	Col	Last	First	MI	Ttl	Yr	Mo	Day	Pg	Col
Peabody	John	M		1878	Oc	04	01	03	Pennell	Julia			1875	Jl	13	04	03
Peach	William		Mr	1837	No	07	03	05	Penniman	Atherton	T	Col	1832	Jn	27	03	05
Peacock	George			1872	Jl	06	01	01	Pennington	D	W	Mrs	1848	Ap	20	03	03
Peake	William	H		1860	Ja	21	03	01	Pennington	George	A		1877	Ja	03	01	04
Pearce	Alexander			1879	Se	04	01	01	Pennington	Isaac		Esq	1832	My	02	03	05
Pearce	Eli			1877	De	16	02	04	Pennington	Isaac	J	Mr	1836	Se	27	03	05
Pearce	Ella	P		1867	No	05	07	02	Pennington	J	M	Mr	1874	No	12	04	02
Pearce	Hiram		Dr	1878	Se	20	01	04	Pennington	Jacob	W		1873	Fe	20	01	01
Pearce	Joseph			1879	Au	17	01	03	Pennington	James	M		1872	Ja	16	04	05
Pearce	Lizzie		Mss	1878	Se	24	01	06	Pennington	John	E	Mr	1843	Mr	01	03	06
Pears	Maud			1874	Jl	08	01	06	Pennington	Martha	A	Mrs	1857	No	14	03	03
Pearsoll	A			1878	Au	30	01	04	Pennington	William	D		1874	Ap	18	04	04
Pearson	Reed			1878	Oc	11	01	04	Pennington	William	D	Esq	1842	Fe	19	02	06
Pease	Fannie			1878	Au	22	01	04	Pennington	William	Q		1872	Ap	02	04	05
Peay			Maj	1872	No	22	01	03	Pennypacker	Albert		Mrs	1877	Oc	07	01	04
Peay	Ann	M		1838	Se	05	03	04	Pennypacker	Nathan			1877	Oc	06	01	06
Peay	Bettie	F	Mrs	1855	Jn	01	03	07	Pennywit	Phillip		Cpt	1868	Ja	14	03	05
Peay	Gordon	N		1867	No	26	02	08	Pentecost	Joseph		Col	1843	Mr	29	03	06
Peay	Gordon	N		1876	De	15	04	03	Pentland	Joe			1873	Fe	09	01	07
Peay	Gordon	N		1876	De	16	01	06	Penzstock	A	M	Ram	1876	Se	21	01	03
Peay	Gordon	N		1876	De	16	04	03	Peoples	George		Dr	1867	Jl	30	03	04
Peay	Gordon	N		1876	De	17	04	02	Peoples	Jesse			1878	Oc	04	01	03
Peay	Gordon	N		1876	De	23	04	04	Pepper	John	A		1878	Oc	03	01	03
Peay	Gordon	N		1876	De	24	02	05	Pepper	Mont			1872	Au	16	01	05
Peay	Gordon	N	Col	1876	De	15	01	01	Percefull	John		Mr	1852	Ja	09	03	06
Peay	Gordon	N	Col	1876	De	28	04	04	Percell	James			1878	Mr	05	01	05
Peay	Gordon	N	Hon	1876	De	16	04	04	Percelo	Turigi			1877	Se	30	01	04
Peay	Gordon	N	Hon	1876	De	24	02	04	Peregrine	David			1831	Jl	20	03	04
Peay	Gordon	N	Hon	1877	Ja	12	04	01	Pereifield	John		Mr	1835	Au	04	03	05
Peay	John		Mr	1838	Oc	10	03	04	Peres	J	J	Rev	1879	Oc	16	01	01
Peay	Juliet		Mrs	1847	Ap	03	03	04	Perfect	Ernest			1878	Se	22	04	03
Peay	Mildred	G		1832	Mr	28	03	05	Perizean	August			1876	De	15	01	03
Peay	Nicholas		Maj	1843	My	17	03	03	Perkins			Mr	1875	Mr	20	04	03
Peay	Sue			1859	Ja	29	03	01	Perkins			Pvt	1876	Jl	09	01	05
Peck	Asa		Gov	1879	My	20	01	03	Perkins	F			1878	Se	04	01	03
Peck	F	B		1878	Se	22	04	03	Perkins	F	W	Cpt	1871	Mr	08	01	02
Peck	James		Mgn	1878	Ap	23	01	07	Perkins	Jas			1878	Se	22	04	03
Peck	John			1874	Jl	01	01	01	Perkins	John		Mr	1871	My	24	01	03
Peck	Peter	G		1872	Ap	02	01	04	Perkins	John		Mrs	1871	My	24	01	03
Peck	Stephen			1875	Jl	10	04	04	Perodea	B	D		1878	Se	22	04	03
Peckham	George	W		1873	De	04	01	03	Perrin	George			1876	Ap	12	04	06
Peddy			Mss	1874	Fe	24	02	03	Perrino	Frank			1878	Jn	27	01	06
Peebles			Mr	1873	Fe	19	01	04	Perro	Joshua			1871	Jn	11	01	01
Peek	Charles	R		1866	Au	18	03	04	Perry	Alexander			1879	Oc	07	01	01
Pegram	Amelia		Mss	1872	De	24	01	03	Perry	Charles	E		1872	Oc	26	01	03
Pegram	Maggie			1872	Oc	29	01	03	Perry	D	C	Mr	1854	No	24	03	06
Peil	Bettie		Mss	1876	Oc	26	04	01	Perry	David			1871	Jl	28	01	04
Peil	Daniel			1868	De	20	02	04	Perry	J	S	Bro	1869	Se	16	02	03
Peirson	Salome	D	Mrs	1852	Oc	08	03	06	Perry	Mathew	C	Mrs	1879	Jn	15	01	03
Pelcher	Anthony			1878	Oc	04	04	07	Perry	Nathan			1878	No	16	01	03
Pelham	Richard		Mr	1834	Jl	29	03	03	Perry	Oliver	H	Com	1819	De	11	02	04
Pelham	Sarah	L	Mrs	1855	Mr	23	03	05	Perry	Sarah	S	Mr	1835	Au	04	03	05
Pelham	William	C		1834	Oc	07	03	03	Perry	Shadric			1871	Jl	18	01	01
Pelton	Benjamin			1846	Mr	02	03	03	Perryman	George		Mr	1851	Au	22	03	07
Pelton	James		Mr	1846	Fe	23	03	04	Pertues	Manuel		Mr	1844	Au	14	03	05
Pelton	Lucretia		Mrs	1836	Au	09	03	03	Pertui	Chevallier		Mgr	1820	De	09	03	01
Pemberton	Mattie		Mss	1873	Jn	21	04	06	Petereburger			Mrs	1873	My	10	02	03
Pemberton	William			1875	Oc	10	01	03	Peters			Con	1873	No	23	01	01
Pendergrass			Mr	1871	Jl	06	01	04	Peters	D	C	Mrs	1874	Ap	27	04	06
Pendergrast	Nicholas			1871	Jn	23	01	03	Peters	William			1878	Se	22	04	03
Pendleton			Dr	1872	Ap	02	01	01	Peterson			Dr	1872	Ap	06	04	02
Pendleton	Henry	F	Mr	1855	De	28	03	06	Peterson			Mr	1871	Fe	18	01	01
Pendleton	Robert		Mr	1838	No	14	03	03	Peterson	Swan			1877	De	25	01	06
Penington	William	Q		1874	Ap	18	04	04	Petist	Maria	C	Mrs	1841	Ap	21	03	06
Penn	J	W	Dr	1878	Se	18	01	07	Petit	Charles			1871	Jl	13	01	05
Penn	Lyttleton			1879	Se	27	01	01	Petitt	J	M		1859	Ja	01	03	02

Last	First	MI	Ttl	Yr	Mo	Day	Pg	Col	Last	First	MI	Ttl	Yr	Mo	Day	Pg	Col
Petterson	Martha			1878	Oc	18	01	03	Pickering	John			1877	Ja	03	01	04
Pettibone	Rufus		Hon	1825	Au	30	03	01	Pickering	William		Gov	1874	Ap	25	01	03
Pettigrew	Alice	R	Mrs	1870	Fe	20	03	01	Pickett	David	M		1839	Mr	06	03	05
Pettis	John			1879	Oc	01	01	01	Pickett	Margaret	A		1836	Jl	12	03	04
Pettis	Marshall			1876	Ap	12	04	06	Pickett	Mollie			1879	Se	25	01	01
Pettis	Mose			1879	Se	16	01	01	Pickett	Robert	C	Mr	1823	Mr	25	03	03
Pettit	William			1878	My	02	01	06	Pickney	Robert	F	Cdr	1878	Mr	15	01	06
Petty	John	T		1878	Oc	20	01	04	Piddon	Henriett			1871	Jl	20	01	05
Petty	John	T	Mrs	1878	Oc	20	01	04	Pierce	E	J		1875	Fe	28	04	03
Petty	Maggie			1878	Oc	20	01	04	Pierce	Enoch	J	Mr	1875	Jl	11	04	02
Petty	Mary			1878	Oc	20	01	04	Pierce	Franklin		Prs	1869	Oc	10	02	02
Petty	William	C		1873	Ja	21	01	03	Pierce	George			1871	Jl	30	01	06
Pettyjohn	John			1878	Au	10	03	01	Pierce	J	C		1873	Au	23	01	03
Petway	S			1878	Se	22	04	03	Pierce	Jas	F	Spc	1877	No	25	01	04
Peyton	Bailey		Hon	1878	Au	20	01	05	Pierce	Jas	F	Spc	1877	De	02	01	07
Peyton	Caroline			1877	Se	22	04	05	Pierce	Jerome			1878	Ja	05	01	07
Peyton	Cranen		Dr	1872	No	08	01	01	Pierce	Joseph			1879	Au	17	01	03
Peyton	Craven		Dr	1872	No	08	04	03	Pierce	Lovick		Dr	1879	No	13	04	01
Peyton	Craven		Dr	1872	No	09	04	03	Pierce	Nat			1877	Se	28	01	05
Peyton	Craven		Dr	1872	No	10	01	04	Pierce	William			1879	Jl	03	01	03
Peyton	Craven		Dr	1872	No	13	01	07	Piercy	F			1879	De	21	01	02
Peyton	Craven		Dr	1872	No	16	01	04	Pierdaso	Francis			1876	Se	30	01	03
Peyton	John		Rev	1873	Ja	14	04	04	Pifefer			Mr	1875	Jl	07	03	01
Peyton	Sallie	F	Mrs	1853	Se	23	03	07	Pigg	J	G		1873	Au	21	01	02
Pfarr	Philip			1875	My	27	01	06	Pike	Albert			1837	Fe	28	03	05
Pfeifer	Charles			1873	My	17	01	03	Pike	Albert		Mrs	1876	Ap	18	04	02
Pflugh	Fred		Eng	1878	Fe	14	01	08	Pike	Ben		Mr	1836	03	01	03	05
Phaorow	Phil			1878	Se	22	04	03	Pike	Clarence			1848	Fe	17	03	02
Phelman	James		Hon	1873	My	18	01	02	Pike	Isadore			1869	Jl	15	02	03
Phelps	Arthur			1878	Jn	15	04	02	Pike	Isadore		Mss	1872	De	10	04	04
Phelps	Arthur		Eng	1878	Jn	13	04	03	Pike	Mary	H	Mrs	1876	Ap	19	04	01
Phelps	Arthur		Eng	1878	Jn	15	04	07	Pike	S	N		1872	De	13	01	04
Phelps	C	O		1873	No	18	05	03	Pike	Samuel	N		1872	De	10	01	06
Phelps	Calvin		Snr	1870	Ap	10	02	04	Pilar	Marie	D		1879	Au	06	05	01
Phelps	Homer			1875	Ap	07	01	03	Pilch				1878	Se	22	04	03
Phelps	John	E		1878	Fe	03	01	06	Pillisman	Mary	I		1840	De	02	03	04
Phelps	R	A		1873	No	18	04	03	Pillow			Gen	1878	Oc	10	01	04
Philburn	Michael			1873	Jl	06	01	03	Pillow	Catharine		Mrs	1866	Oc	09	03	02
Philips	Parker		Jud	1871	Se	13	04	04	Pinckney	John			1872	Jn	05	02	04
Phillips			Pvt	1876	Jl	09	01	05	Pindall	Hannah	E	Mss	1874	Ap	06	04	06
Phillips	Augustus	E		1873	Oc	12	01	03	Pine	George		Ldm	1877	No	25	01	04
Phillips	Catherine			1879	Au	16	01	01	Pinkerton	Allan			1874	Mr	18	01	02
Phillips	Ezekiel			1872	Jl	06	01	01	Pinkney	Ninian		Col	1826	Ja	24	03	03
Phillips	George	A		1859	My	14	03	01	Pinn	H	E	Mr	1873	Oc	03	04	02
Phillips	Helena		Mss	1831	Se	14	03	01	Pinnel	Mollie	J		1879	Jl	02	08	06
Phillips	Infant			1821	No	03	03	01	Pinney	George			1878	Ja	17	04	05
Phillips	James		Mr	1831	Au	03	03	01	Pinson	R	A	Col	1873	My	18	01	02
Phillips	John			1874	Ap	25	01	06	Pinson	Richard	A	Col	1873	My	20	01	02
Phillips	Maria		Mss	1836	Ja	19	03	04	Piper	Thomas			1876	My	27	01	05
Phillips	Missouri			1879	Oc	14	01	01	Piper	Thompson	E	Col	1850	No	29	03	06
Phillips	P	M	Mr	1849	Se	27	03	05	Pipton			Mrs	1873	Mr	08	01	06
Phillips	Pleas			1878	Jl	31	01	04	Pitcher	Ben	D		1835	Jl	28	03	04
Phillips	S		Mrs	1879	Au	23	01	01	Pitcher	Charles	E	Mr	1852	Ja	23	03	07
Phillips	Sophie	M	Mrs	1837	Jn	20	03	06	Pitcher	James	Z		1837	Au	15	03	04
Phillips	Thomas		Maj	1837	Ja	17	03	04	Pitcher	Samuel	H		1843	Mr	15	03	05
Phillips	Willie			1871	Fe	16	04	05	Pitman	Matilda			1879	Se	09	01	01
Phillips	Zachariah			1873	My	18	01	02	Pits	S	D		1873	No	18	04	03
Philmot	Charles			1879	Jl	29	01	01	Pittman	Ben		Mrs	1878	Fe	13	01	06
Phipps			Rev	1871	Jl	21	01	05	Pittman	Ben		Mrs	1878	Fe	16	04	03
Phipps	Katie			1878	Fe	20	03	01	Pittman	Ben		Mrs	1878	Fe	19	02	01
Phitzgibbons	Michael			1879	Jl	29	01	03	Pittman	Jeff		Esq	1874	Ap	19	02	03
Physick	Susan		Mrs	1860	My	19	03	01	Pittman	Pheby	L	Mrs	1840	Mr	18	03	05
Piaggio	Antonio			1879	Se	27	01	01	Pitts	Charley			1876	Se	26	01	04
Piaggo	J	B		1879	Se	13	01	01	Pitts	Syoney			1878	Mr	30	01	06
Picard	Ernest			1878	Ja	09	03	02	Plamonden	Simon			1875	Mr	19	04	04
Piceita	Alfred	J		1851	Fe	07	03	06	Plant	George	P		1875	Fe	25	01	04

Last	First	MI	Ttl	Yr	Mo	Day	Pg	Col	Last	First	MI	Ttl	Yr	Mo	Day	Pg	Col
Plat	Samuel			1872	Jl	16	01	04	Porter	Benjamin	A	Cpt	1852	Fe	13	03	07
Platt	Edward		Esq	1850	Mr	01	03	06	Porter	Eli	S		1879	Ap	30	05	01
Platt	Richard		Col	1830	Ap	27	03	05	Porter	Emiline		Mrs	1849	Jn	14	03	04
Pleasanton			Mr	1855	Fe	09	04	03	Porter	J	E	Lt	1876	Jl	09	01	05
Pleasants	Dolly			1878	Se	01	01	03	Porter	James			1830	Au	18	03	05
Pleasants	Hugh	R		1870	My	07	04	01	Porter	John	C	Mr	1832	Se	12	03	04
Pleasants	Minerva	A	Mrs	1876	De	13	04	06	Porter	Leatitia		Mrs	1831	Jn	14	03	04
Pleasents	Joseph	C	Col	1863	Fe	07	01	04	Porter	Lou			1873	Au	14	01	03
Pledge	W	H	Rev	1879	De	21	03	01	Porter	Lucis			1878	Mr	03	01	03
Pledge	W	W		1878	Oc	15	01	04	Porter	W			1875	Fe	25	01	04
Pledger			Rev	1876	De	13	04	01	Porter	William			1878	Au	22	01	04
Pledger	George		Rev	1876	No	04	04	04	Porter	William	S	Jud	1873	Oc	28	01	04
Pleitz	F			1878	Se	25	01	06	Portesfield	John			1874	De	30	01	04
Plom	John	H		1879	Oc	14	01	01	Portor	Nathan		Mr	1831	No	02	03	05
Plomer				1873	Au	27	01	03	Posey	James			1879	Se	12	01	01
Plouf	S	J	Mrs	1872	Jn	29	04	06	Post	Amelia	A		1871	Se	09	01	04
Plumer	Julia	A		1837	Fe	14	03	06	Poster	D	D		1878	Se	08	01	04
Plumer	Samuel		Mr	1876	Fe	23	04	03	Postman				1876	No	04	01	04
Plummer			Mss	1878	Se	22	04	03	Postoak	John			1878	De	21	04	03
Plummer	Avery		Mr	1872	No	10	10	05	Potter			Mr	1878	Se	22	04	03
Plummer	Avery		Mrs	1872	No	10	01	05	Potter	Mary			1878	Ja	12	04	01
Plummer	B	T		1878	Se	18	01	07	Potts			Dr	1878	Se	13	01	04
Plummer	Samuel		Mrs	1845	Oc	20	03	03	Potts	John			1872	Jl	25	01	03
Plummer	Sarah			1858	Ja	02	03	03	Potts	John	G		1874	Fe	19	01	01
Plymale	Hugh			1878	Se	19	10	05	Potts	John	W		1835	Jl	21	03	06
Pocock	Edward			1877	De	09	03	01	Pound	William		Col	1877	Oc	21	01	05
Pocock	Francis			1877	De	09	03	01	Powel	George	C	Md	1849	Mr	15	03	03
Poe	Hally			1867	Au	27	03	02	Powell				1877	Oc	31	01	06
Poe	Infant			1878	Fe	20	04	02	Powell			Mr	1871	Jl	13	01	08
Pogue	J	E		1871	Jl	20	04	03	Powell	A	W	Mrs	1875	Oc	02	01	03
Pogue	Nancy		Mss	1834	Au	05	03	03	Powell	Adam			1878	Oc	15	01	03
Pohl	Thos		Mrs	1878	Se	22	04	03	Powell	Asa		Mr	1850	Se	06	03	07
Pointer	John			1874	Ap	08	04	04	Powell	Charley			1878	Se	01	01	03
Pointer	Sidney			1879	Au	24	01	01	Powell	Madison	S		1868	Ja	21	03	04
Polk	A	H		1872	Oc	30	01	03	Powell	Mary		Mrs	1877	Oc	18	04	02
Polk	Amanda			1878	Se	22	04	03	Powell	Morgan			1876	De	19	01	02
Polk	Bishop			1875	Ap	22	02	02	Powell	Morgan			1877	De	12	04	04
Polk	Bishop		Mrs	1875	Ap	22	02	02	Powell	Morgan			1878	Mr	29	07	05
Polk	Fronia	D		1867	Se	17	03	03	Powell	Nannie	E		1870	My	20	04	02
Polk	James	K	Prs	1849	Jn	21	02	02	Powell	Robert	E		1868	Ja	28	03	05
Polk	Trusten		Hon	1876	Ap	19	01	01	Powell	W	T		1878	Se	08	01	03
Pollak	William			1878	Jl	19	01	04	Powell	W	T		1878	Se	22	04	03
Pollard			Mr	1871	Mr	23	01	01	Powell	William			1876	Jn	04	01	05
Pollard	Alida			1876	De	27	01	04	Power	Richard		Maj	1870	Fe	22	04	02
Pollard	J	E		1878	Oc	08	01	03	Power	Thomas	H		1878	No	21	07	02
Pollard	J	M	Sen	1875	Oc	09	02	02	Powers	Edward			1878	Se	01	01	03
Pollard	Nancy	J	Mrs	1878	Oc	20	01	03	Powers	Hiram			1874	Ja	08	01	02
Polliests	L	E	Mr	1871	Oc	07	01	04	Powers	Joseph	M		1837	Oc	17	03	05
Pollock	Leone			1876	Jn	25	04	05	Prager	Willard			1878	Jl	06	03	01
Pomare			Qun	1877	Oc	25	01	06	Pralle	Henry		Rev	1822	Se	17	03	02
Pomeroy	Chester			1836	Au	16	03	06	Prather	George			1878	Oc	04	01	03
Pooler	Chas		Car	1877	No	25	01	04	Pratt	J	R	Mr	1871	Mr	12	03	01
Poor	William	C		1878	Ap	04	01	04	Pratt	Jack			1872	Jn	13	02	04
Pope	Ann	N		1848	Fe	24	03	04	Pratt	John			1878	Mr	15	01	06
Pope	John		Gov	1835	No	24	03	01	Pratt	Peter			1878	Au	30	01	04
Pope	John		Mrs	1879	Au	31	01	01	Pravenzale	Mike			1878	Oc	08	01	03
Pope	Juliet	L		1842	Oc	05	03	06	Prayor	Jane			1878	Se	04	01	03
Pope	Mary	G	Mrs	1846	Ja	12	02	06	Preddy			Dr	1874	Ja	27	03	02
Pope	Sophia	D		1874	Oc	17	04	08	Predigram	August			1877	De	05	01	05
Pope	William	F	Maj	1831	Jn	22	03	01	Preith	Benedict			1879	Oc	30	01	03
Poplin	George		Mr	1846	Oc	05	03	03	Prentice			Mrs	1873	Fe	13	04	03
Porter			Lt	1876	Jl	07	01	03	Prentice	George	D		1870	Ja	25	02	02
Porter			Mrs	1874	Jl	26	01	07	Prescott	O	F		1878	Oc	09	01	04
Porter	B	C		1879	Mr	21	04	02	Prescott	Walter			1878	Se	22	04	03
Porter	B	C	Mr	1879	Mr	22	04	02	Presh	Fred			1878	Se	22	04	03
Porter	B	C	Mr	1879	Mr	25	01	05									

Last	First	MI	Ttl	Yr	Mo	Day	Pg	Col
Prestidge	Claude	B		1879	Se	16	01	01
Prestidge	Gracie		Mss	1879	Au	15	01	01
Preston	Clarinda		Mrs	1838	Fe	28	03	05
Preston	John			1878	Se	22	04	03
Preston	William	H	Maj	1873	Ja	19	02	03
Prewitt	N	A	Dr	1878	Oc	13	01	04
Price			Mr	1871	Se	26	01	02
Price	Annie			1878	Ja	04	01	03
Price	Christopher	H	Maj	1832	Au	22	03	01
Price	Daniel			1877	Ja	19	01	03
Price	Edwin			1877	Oc	04	01	04
Price	George		Arm	1877	No	25	01	04
Price	Harvey			1878	Oc	21	01	03
Price	Jack			1879	Jl	01	05	01
Price	John	H		1874	Ap	05	01	03
Price	Joshua		Mr	1871	No	04	01	03
Price	Mattie			1878	Oc	16	01	03
Price	Oscar	E		1873	No	13	04	05
Price	Thomas		Ldm	1877	No	25	01	04
Price	Thomas	L	Hon	1870	Jl	27	03	01
Price	William		Dr	1874	Ap	12	04	02
Pricer	S	H	Mrs	1878	Se	12	01	03
Prichard	George			1872	No	30	01	03
Prichard	M	B	Col	1878	Se	25	04	07
Prichard	M	B	Col	1878	Se	27	04	07
Pridgeon	Anna		Mss	1874	Mr	08	01	04
Priestley	John			1873	Ja	03	01	02
Prieur	Infant			1879	My	24	08	06
Primrose	George			1878	My	31	04	06
Prince			Mr	1874	De	30	04	04
Prince	Dan			1872	Au	14	01	02
Prine			Mr	1871	De	19	04	05
Pringle			Mrs	1833	Ap	17	03	04
Pringle			Mrs	1873	Jl	27	01	05
Pringle	Christain			1820	Fe	05	03	04
Prior	G	R		1875	Oc	12	01	03
Prior	M			1878	Se	22	04	03
Pritchard	Benjamin			1879	My	29	01	02
Pritchard	Mary			1878	Au	02	04	04
Pritchett	James		Mr	1826	Au	08	03	01
Privett	James	G		1857	Mr	28	03	03
Probst	Anton			1866	My	19	03	04
Procter	John			1872	Ap	24	01	01
Procter	Reuben			1877	No	15	01	06
Proctor	W	E		1873	My	14	01	02
Proffat	John			1879	Jl	23	01	03
Prope	William		Mr	1831	Mr	30	03	05
Proras	Henry			1873	No	27	01	01
Proudfit	Phillip			1878	Ja	27	01	06
Provine	J	M		1872	Oc	12	01	03
Pruitt	Easter	P	Mrs	1859	Mr	05	03	01
Pryde	Infant			1877	De	25	01	06
Pryde	William	C	Mrs	1877	De	25	01	06
Pryor	Amanda			1876	Ap	12	04	06
Pryor	Martha	A	Mrs	1876	Jn	15	02	03
Pryor	Nathaniel		Cpt	1831	Jn	22	03	01
Puckett	William			1874	Fe	24	02	03
Pugh			Lt	1839	Se	04	01	06
Pugsley	John		Mr	1875	My	08	01	03
Pulham	Charles	H		1879	My	14	05	02
Pullen	Ben	K	Mrs	1878	Se	25	01	04
Pullen	Leonara		Mrs	1837	My	02	03	03
Pullen	Minerva			1835	Se	15	03	05
Pullett	George		Col	1872	No	23	01	04
Pulvey	N	B		1878	Se	17	01	06
Pumel	Eugene			1878	Oc	18	01	03
Purcell	Batron			1878	Oc	09	01	03
Purdom	John	W	Mr	1862	Jn	14	02	04
Purson	E	L		1873	Se	28	01	05
Putanm				1871	My	16	01	04
Putman	George	P		1872	De	24	01	04
Putnam				1871	My	26	01	03
Putnam	Fred			1875	Mr	17	01	04
Putwam	Avery	D	Mr	1873	Mr	01	01	04
Pye	Walter	A		1879	Jl	30	08	06
Pyeatt	Holly		Mrs	1837	Ap	18	03	05
Pyeatt	James		Mr	1837	My	16	03	03
Pyeatt	John		Mr	1823	Ja	28	03	02
Pyeatt	Margaret		Mrs	1822	Ja	21	02	04
Pyeatt	Patsey		Mrs	1834	Mr	25	03	04
Pyne	William	H		1872	Au	28	01	04
Pyrde	Infant			1877	De	28	01	04
Pyrde	John			1877	De	28	01	04
Pyrde	William	C	Mrs	1877	De	28	01	04

Q

Last	First	MI	Ttl	Yr	Mo	Day	Pg	Col
Qauagla	Angelo		Crd	1872	Au	29	01	02
Quad	Kerence			1879	No	05	05	02
Quail, Jr	Robert		Mr	1850	No	22	03	06
Quance	Rosa		Mrs	1873	Ja	22	01	05
Quarles				1876	Ap	22	01	04
Quarles	Sallie		Mss	1867	Ja	29	03	04
Quattlebaum	H	M	Mr	1872	Jl	02	01	01
Queen	J	W		1871	My	21	02	02
Quesenbury	William			1867	Se	03	02	07
Quiggus	Ingie			1878	Se	18	04	04
Quigley	Bernard			1875	Ap	22	01	05
Quigley	William		Mrs	1872	Au	29	01	03
Quinby				1874	Au	14	01	07
Quindley	Emma			1876	De	16	01	06
Quindley	George	W		1870	Mr	27	04	02
Quindley	John			1872	De	01	01	05
Quindley	John		Esq	1870	Fe	22	04	02
Quindley	John		Mr	1870	Fe	13	04	01
Quindley	Lucinda		Mrs	1858	De	04	03	03
Quindley	Polly	A		1834	Se	23	03	05
Quinley	John		Rev	1872	Ja	19	01	03
Quinn	E	R		1874	My	20	04	01
Quinn	James			1873	Oc	26	01	03
Quinn	L	C	Col	1852	Se	03	03	07
Quinn	Mary			1878	Ap	07	01	06
Quinn	Mary			1878	Se	22	04	03
Quinn	Mary		Mrs	1878	Fe	15	01	08
Quinn	Sallie			1874	My	20	04	01
Quinn	T	J		1878	Jn	19	04	05

R

Last	First	MI	Ttl	Yr	Mo	Day	Pg	Col
Raber	Joseph			1879	No	03	01	02
Rabes	Joseph			1879	Se	03	01	02
Rabun			Gov	1820	Ja	08	02	04
Radaway	David		Mr	1852	My	28	02	04
Radcliffe	Augustas			1875	Mr	17	01	04
Radigan	M			1879	Oc	12	01	01
Rafferty	William			1879	Ja	25	01	04
Raggio	John			1878	Se	22	04	03
Ragland	Emma		Mrs	1875	Fe	26	04	03

Last	First	MI	Ttl	Yr	Mo	Day	Pg	Col	Last	First	MI	Ttl	Yr	Mo	Day	Pg	Col
Ragsdale	Claudia			1878	Oc	20	01	04	Rawlins	Gen		Mrs	1874	No	07	01	04
Ragsdale	J			1878	Oc	20	01	04	Ray			Mrs	1878	Se	05	01	03
Raguet	John			1879	Se	07	01	01	Ray	Annie		Mrs	1855	De	28	03	06
Raines	Aria			1879	Oc	14	01	01	Ray	Eliza			1878	Jn	02	01	07
Rainey	Catharine		Mrs	1847	Oc	21	03	05	Ray	Fay			1870	Au	23	04	05
Rainey	Hiram			1837	Ja	03	03	04	Ray	Harry			1879	Jl	23	01	02
Rainey	John		Mr	1837	Ja	03	03	04	Ray	John			1876	Mr	15	01	01
Rainey	Samuel		Mr	1837	Ja	03	03	04	Ray	John			1876	Mr	15	04	06
Rainey	T	A	Esq	1853	No	11	03	05	Ray	Martin		Hon	1872	Au	06	01	05
Raino				1876	Jl	01	02	03	Ray	Mary		Mrs	1879	Jl	26	01	01
Rains	W	C		1876	Jl	08	02	03	Ray	Peter	G		1872	My	12	01	05
Raiser	M		Mr	1878	Se	17	01	04	Rayley	Jennie	R		1854	Jl	14	03	07
Raix	Jules			1874	Ap	12	01	04	Raymond	Wilbur	F		1879	Se	07	05	01
Raleigh	Richard		Mr	1872	Oc	20	01	02	Raynor	John			1871	My	30	01	03
Rall				1872	Jn	12	01	03	Read			Mrs	1878	Se	22	04	03
Rall				1872	Jn	12	01	03	Read	Charles		Mr	1837	Oc	03	03	03
Ralston	Robert			1871	De	27	01	03	Read	Clem			1878	Se	12	01	03
Rambert	Hattie			1879	Au	24	01	01	Read	George		Esq	1859	Au	06	03	02
Ramey			Mrs	1876	De	20	02	05	Read	Thomas	B		1872	My	17	02	04
Ramey	Elizabeth	B		1840	Mr	04	03	04	Reader	Tillie		Mss	1872	De	27	01	02
Rammers	Adolph			1874	Mr	12	01	04	Reading	Arrah			1876	Fe	15	04	02
Ramsay	Josiah		Maj	1835	Jn	23	03	04	Readon				1878	Fe	14	01	03
Ramsay	William		Mr	1826	Jl	18	03	02	Rear	Augusta			1878	Se	22	04	03
Ramsey	Charles	T	Rev	1836	No	22	03	05	Reardon			Mr	1871	Jn	06	04	03
Ramsey	Elizabeth	M	Mrs	1847	Ap	10	03	04	Reardon	Ann		Mrs	1860	No	10	03	01
Ramsey	George	C		1876	Oc	28	04	04	Reardon	C			1878	Se	22	04	03
Ramson	Hyatt		Col	1874	Mr	19	01	05	Reardon	Dennis			1879	De	06	05	01
Ran	John			1873	My	14	01	02	Reardon	Lambert		Esq	1849	Fe	15	03	04
Randolph	Augustus		Mr	1833	Jl	19	03	03	Reardon	Lambert	J		1854	No	03	03	06
Randolph	J			1871	Ja	14	04	02	Reaves	J			1830	Mr	09	03	03
Randolph	J			1871	My	21	02	02	Reber	Daniel			1878	Ap	07	01	04
Randolph	John		Hon	1833	Jn	19	02	05	Recher	Charles		Mr	1833	My	29	03	04
Randolph	Thomas		Maj	1872	Au	11	01	06	Reckard	Annie			1878	Se	01	01	03
Randy	D	F		1871	My	17	01	01	Reckard	Fredrick		Bts	1878	Mr	05	01	05
Raney				1877	Oc	05	04	05	Rector	Elias		Col	1822	Se	17	03	02
Ranfrau	Bettie		Mrs	1878	Oc	16	01	03	Rector	Elias		Maj	1878	No	23	01	01
Rankin	Christopher	Rep		1826	Ap	18	02	01	Rector	Elias		Maj	1878	De	01	05	03
Rankin	George		Mr	1828	Ap	09	03	01	Rector	Stephen		Mr	1826	Au	08	03	01
Rankin	John	J	Mrs	1851	My	23	03	06	Rector	Thomas		Mr	1838	Mr	28	03	01
Rankin	T	V		1873	Oc	17	04	03	Rector	Whorton		Col	1842	Fe	16	03	01
Rankin	William			1872	De	27	01	03	Rector	William		Gen	1826	Jl	04	03	01
Rankins	Washington		Mr	1832	Fe	08	03	05	Rector	William	V	Esq	1829	Se	23	03	01
Ranks	George			1871	Jl	09	01	05	Redbird	Wiley			1879	My	22	08	03
Ranter			Pvt	1876	Jl	09	01	05	Redd	Austin			1878	Se	04	01	03
Raoul	T	B		1878	Ja	26	01	04	Reddick	T	C		1875	Ap	03	04	03
Raphe			Bp	1877	Se	12	01	07	Redding	Cornelius			1870	Oc	20	01	01
Rapley	Abraham		Mr	1854	Se	29	03	05	Redding	Lizzie		Mrs	1873	Jn	17	04	05
Rapley	Ann	B	Mrs	1879	Jn	27	08	05	Reddington	Alfred		Gen	1875	My	23	01	05
Rapley	Charles		Esq	1853	Au	05	03	07	Reddy	John			1872	Ap	13	01	02
Rapley	Kittie	B		1872	Jn	20	04	05	Redford	Hiram			1873	My	17	01	03
Rarer	Martha		Mrs	1838	Ap	25	03	03	Redley				1877	Se	13	01	06
Rasoul	R	G		1878	Oc	06	01	03	Redman	A	W	Mr	1872	No	27	01	02
Ratazzi				1874	Ja	08	01	02	Redmen	John			1871	Se	09	01	04
Ratchliffe	William			1878	My	02	01	06	Redmon	John		Esq	1832	Au	29	03	02
Ratcliff	Margaret		Mss	1836	Fe	16	03	05	Redmond	Dave		Mr	1876	De	13	02	05
Ratcliffe	Mary	M	Mrs	1879	Oc	30	08	06	Redmond	Francis	P	Hon	1872	My	26	02	03
Rathage	C	F	Sea	1877	No	25	01	04	Redmond	James			1874	Ja	03	01	03
Raulstone	A	H	Maj	1868	Mr	31	03	04	Reece	Andrew	J		1871	Jl	30	01	06
Raumer	L	V		1874	Ja	08	01	02	Reed				1876	My	19	04	01
Ravenly	J			1878	Se	05	01	03	Reed			Pvt	1876	Jl	09	01	05
Rawis	Isaac		Mr	1872	Oc	26	01	02	Reed	David			1871	Se	05	01	07
Rawles	Henry		Mr	1839	Jl	31	03	04	Reed	George			1878	Se	22	04	03
Rawlings			Con	1879	Oc	15	01	01	Reed	Gus			1878	My	15	04	03
Rawlings	Charles			1879	Oc	29	08	06	Reed	Hugh		Mr	1824	Oc	26	03	01
Rawlings	Perry			1878	Se	22	04	03	Reed	James		Mr	1836	Jl	26	03	06
Rawlins			Pvt	1876	Jl	09	01	05	Reed	Jane		Mrs	1838	Jl	04	03	05

Last	First	MI	Ttl	Yr	Mo	Day	Pg	Col	Last	First	MI	Ttl	Yr	Mo	Day	Pg	Col
Reed	Jesse			1866	Oc	16	03	08	Rentz	John			1878	Se	22	04	03
Reed	John			1879	Ap	09	04	02	Ressler	Fred			1878	Se	22	04	03
Reed	John	H	Mr	1845	De	15	03	01	Restelle	Madame			1878	Ap	02	01	05
Reed	John	H	Mr	1852	Ap	16	03	06	Restemeyer				1878	Fe	07	04	04
Reed	Joseph			1871	No	03	01	05	Restinger	Fred			1878	Se	22	04	03
Reed	Margaret		Mrs	1866	Oc	23	02	07	Reugg	Aug			1878	Au	27	01	04
Reed	Orange			1879	Se	20	01	01	Reville	D		Rev	1879	Se	27	01	01
Reed	W	H	Mrs	1876	Oc	31	04	04	Rewer	Eldrige	G		1879	De	09	05	01
Reed	William			1878	Se	04	01	03	Rex	W		Mrs	1871	Au	02	01	04
Reed	William			1878	Se	22	04	03	Rexford	Hiram			1872	Se	29	01	04
Reeder	Dick			1878	Fe	19	01	05	Rexrods				1873	Au	27	01	03
Reeder	Mary	E		1840	Mr	25	03	04	Reyburn	Horace	W		1837	Se	05	03	04
Rees	Micheal			1878	Au	04	01	05	Reyburn	Jane		Mrs	1838	Au	01	03	05
Reever	David	S	Mr	1840	Se	09	03	03	Reyburn	Samuel	W	Col	1854	Jn	16	03	04
Reeves				1871	Jn	28	01	04	Reynolds			Mr	1876	Fe	03	01	05
Reeves	Albert			1874	Au	12	01	07	Reynolds	Bud			1879	De	06	08	03
Reeves	Anderson			1879	Se	23	01	01	Reynolds	Elizabeth		Mrs	1843	Jn	21	03	05
Reeves	Paul			1874	Au	08	01	06	Reynolds	J	W		1874	Ap	09	01	05
Reeves	Paul			1874	Au	12	01	07	Reynolds	John			1872	Ap	23	04	04
Reeves	William			1871	Mr	03	01	01	Reynolds	John		Mr	1871	Jl	25	01	03
Reeves	William	M		1878	No	15	02	01	Reynolds	John	W		1874	Mr	26	04	02
Regin	Cornelius			1851	Au	08	01	04	Reynolds	Mary	F		1868	Fe	04	03	05
Rehkop	Ferdinand			1879	Au	23	01	01	Reynolds	Mike			1873	Fe	04	01	04
Rehkopf	Fred			1878	Au	25	01	04	Reynolds	Terrance			1878	Ja	13	01	07
Rehlser	William			1874	Ap	27	01	03	Reynolds	Thomas	S		1844	Au	07	03	05
Reichardt	Maria	E		1876	Jn	15	04	07	Reynolds	Thomas	S	Col	1844	Jl	24	03	04
Reid	Bob			1874	Jn	06	01	04	Reynolds	William		Adm	1879	No	06	05	02
Reid	E	P		1878	Se	22	04	03	Reynolds	William		Mr	1876	Ap	12	04	07
Reid	J	S		1878	Oc	20	01	04	Reynolds	William	T		1855	Jn	15	03	06
Reid	Jacob		Mr	1873	Ja	10	01	08	Rham	H	C		1874	Ja	08	01	02
Reid	Kate		Mrs	1875	Jn	29	04	02	Rhinehart	William	H		1875	Ja	03	01	06
Reid	Kaziah		Mrs	1858	Se	11	03	04	Rhoder				1878	Ja	17	01	07
Reid	Mary	S		1860	No	24	03	01	Rhodes	A	L		1879	Au	23	01	01
Reid	Mayne			1875	Ap	28	01	05	Rhodes	Dan			1879	Au	28	01	01
Reid	Samuel	M		1868	Au	11	03	06	Rhodes	L	A	Mr	1878	Oc	16	01	03
Reider	Mary	A		1837	Jl	11	02	06	Rhodes	Sam			1879	Au	23	01	01
Reider	William			1851	Se	12	03	07	Ribble	William			1863	Jn	13	02	04
Reifel	Jacob			1878	Jn	19	04	02	Rice				1878	Ja	12	01	06
Reifel	Jacob			1878	Jn	20	04	08	Rice	Elizabeth		Mrs	1879	Oc	12	01	03
Reifel	Jacob			1878	Jn	21	04	02	Rice	Frank		Dr	1878	Mr	22	01	06
Reigler	Elouise		Mrs	1874	Jn	06	01	05	Rice	Nora		Mss	1878	Oc	20	01	04
Reiley	Willie			1878	Oc	24	01	04	Rice	Robert	R		1853	Fe	04	03	04
Reilly			Lt	1876	Jl	07	01	03	Rice	Wilbur	F	Mr	1872	De	27	01	03
Reilly	Jon	A	Rev	1878	Oc	11	01	04	Rice	Wilbur	F	Mrs	1872	De	27	01	03
Reilly	Owen			1878	Au	27	04	07	Rice	William	J		1879	Oc	12	01	03
Reilly	Thomas			1879	Se	05	01	01	Rich	Henry			1878	Se	22	04	03
Reily	George			1878	Au	02	04	04	Richads	William		Bro	1872	Oc	31	01	07
Reimers			Mrs	1875	My	12	01	04	Richard			Dsh	1874	Au	20	01	07
Reinhardt	Laura			1858	No	13	03	02	Richard	Gustave			1874	Ja	08	01	02
Reisinger	Shelley			1874	Au	08	01	06	Richards			Mrs	1873	Au	05	01	03
Reister	Ida			1879	Au	06	01	01	Richards	Andrew			1877	Se	14	01	07
Reithmiller	Conrad			1878	Jl	06	03	01	Richards	Catherine			1879	No	13	05	02
Reithmiller	Infant			1878	Jl	06	03	01	Richards	Eugene	A		1877	Ja	21	04	01
Relolski	Alex			1878	Se	05	01	04	Richards	George			1875	My	20	01	02
Reluis	Amella			1877	De	23	01	04	Richards	James		Mr	1824	Jl	06	03	01
Renchard	Robert			1879	Oc	07	01	01	Richards	James	Q	Col	1857	Ap	18	03	03
Renean	William	L	Bro	1872	Ap	17	01	03	Richards	John		Esq	1859	Fe	19	04	01
Renedethon	Alexander			1878	Ja	19	01	06	Richards	John	D		1852	De	24	03	06
Renero	J	S		1874	Ap	18	01	05	Richards	R	M		1873	Oc	14	01	04
Renforth			Mr	1871	Au	26	01	04	Richards	William			1872	Se	10	01	03
Renham	Sallie		Mss	1878	Oc	16	01	03	Richardson			Mr	1877	Ja	19	01	03
Rennell	Julia			1875	Jl	15	04	04	Richardson			Mss	1871	My	02	03	01
Renner	J	R		1878	Se	17	01	04	Richardson	Asa		Lt	1835	My	05	03	04
Reno			Gen	1878	No	24	01	01	Richardson	E	E		1873	My	06	01	02
Reno	Mattie			1879	Se	05	01	01	Richardson	Easter			1879	Jl	30	08	02
Rensfield	Joseph		Ofc	1879	Mr	13	01	03	Richardson	Edward	N		1875	Jn	10	03	01

Last	First	MI	Ttl	Yr	Mo	Day	Pg	Col	Last	First	MI	Ttl	Yr	Mo	Day	Pg	Col
Richardson	George			1874	Au	09	01	06	Rittenhouse	W	H		1872	Mr	14	01	05
Richardson	George	W		1873	De	19	04	02	Rivas			Col	1873	Se	09	01	02
Richardson	Jas			1878	Fe	01	01	06	Rivers	Byrd			1876	Mr	02	04	03
Richardson	John			1872	My	22	01	03	Rives	Alexander	L		1873	Ja	08	01	05
Richardson	Julia		Mss	1858	Oc	30	03	03	Rives	Silas	D		1839	Ja	02	01	06
Richardson	R	E	Dr	1879	Au	31	01	01	Rivola	Gustave	C	Swt	1877	No	25	01	04
Richardson	Reuben		Esq	1828	No	11	03	01	Roach	Ellen			1879	Au	22	01	01
Richardson	Samuel			1879	Se	11	01	01	Roach	Frank			1878	Se	22	04	03
Richardson	Samuel		Dr	1879	Fe	21	04	03	Roach	John	D		1878	Se	05	01	04
Richardson	W	G	Mrs	1879	Se	02	01	01	Roach	Katie			1872	Se	07	01	04
Richie	John			1872	De	27	01	02	Roach	Micheal			1878	Jn	04	04	06
Richmond			Mr	1871	Se	06	01	04	Roach	Micheal			1878	Jl	04	04	06
Richmond	J			1879	Jl	26	01	01	Roader	Phillip		Dr	1874	No	19	01	04
Richmond	John			1871	Fe	25	03	01	Roane	Andrew			1849	Jn	14	03	04
Richmond	Julia			1879	Au	03	01	01	Roane	John	S	Gov	1867	Ap	16	01	02
Richs	John			1874	Au	27	01	06	Roane	Julia		Mrs	1870	Jl	15	04	03
Ricker	Jabez		Mr	1821	Ja	20	03	04	Roane	Laura			1838	Jl	25	03	03
Rickette	Reuben		Mr	1835	Mr	24	03	06	Robards	Johnanna	P	Mrs	1875	Ap	09	01	04
Riddle	H	Y	Con	1879	Mr	30	01	03	Robbins	Ann		Mss	1878	Oc	02	01	04
Riddle	William	B		1879	Oc	08	01	02	Robbins	Horace	W		1878	Au	13	01	06
Ridenbaugh	Frank			1872	Jl	25	01	04	Robbins	J	W	Maj	1874	Se	17	01	04
Ridgeway			Mrs	1870	Oc	04	01	02	Robbins	Joseph			1875	Jn	19	01	03
Ridgeway	Robert			1870	Oc	18	01	01	Robbins	Libbie		Mss	1859	Ja	22	03	02
Ridley	J	H	Rev	1879	Au	12	01	02	Robbins	S	M	Eng	1878	Se	26	01	05
Riebold			Pvt	1876	Jl	09	01	05	Robenstein	Lena			1878	Se	05	01	03
Rieff	John		Snr	1870	Jn	09	02	04	Roberson	John	W	Cpt	1873	Mr	18	04	04
Riegler	John		Mrs	1874	Jn	06	04	02	Roberson	Sarah	J	Mrs	1867	Oc	01	03	04
Rierdon	Jerry			1870	No	26	01	02	Robert	Augustus		Mr	1836	03	22	03	05
Riggs	Marion			1878	Ja	20	03	02	Robert	Bessie			1871	Fe	15	04	05
Riggs	Reuben			1871	My	21	02	02	Robert	G	W	Mrs	1870	Se	01	04	04
Riggs	Rueben			1871	Ja	14	04	02	Robert	Madame		Mme	1820	Fe	05	03	04
Right	George			1878	Ap	20	01	05	Roberts			Mr	1875	Ap	06	01	03
Rightor	N		Mr	1874	Fe	01	03	01	Roberts	Alfred	H		1858	Oc	23	03	03
Rightor	Nicholas		Mr	1841	Se	01	03	03	Roberts	B	C	Mr	1873	Jn	27	01	04
Riley	A		Mss	1878	Oc	16	01	03	Roberts	Bud			1874	De	12	04	03
Riley	Herbert	E		1872	Oc	25	01	05	Roberts	C	W	Bkm	1878	Se	15	01	05
Riley	James			1878	Se	22	04	03	Roberts	Charles	M		1872	Ja	19	01	03
Riley	John		Cot	1872	Au	08	01	05	Roberts	David			1878	Mr	03	01	03
Riley	John	A	Rev	1878	Oc	16	01	03	Roberts	David		Mr	1852	Jl	30	03	06
Riley	Kate			1872	De	27	01	03	Roberts	Frank			1878	No	01	01	04
Riley	Mary		Mss	1878	Oc	18	01	03	Roberts	George			1878	Mr	27	01	07
Riley	Mike			1878	Se	01	01	03	Roberts	George		Ssd	1877	No	25	01	04
Riley	Ningan		Mr	1872	No	07	02	03	Roberts	Hannah			1871	Se	16	01	03
Riley	Patrick			1877	Oc	06	01	06	Roberts	Henry			1875	No	28	01	04
Riley	Sarah		Mrs	1878	Au	25	01	04	Roberts	J	F		1872	Fe	14	04	03
Rine	Richard			1879	Fe	12	01	02	Roberts	James			1871	Se	19	01	02
Ring			Mrs	1873	Jl	27	01	05	Roberts	Jesse	C	Dr	1834	Ap	29	03	05
Ring	Chester	A		1851	Jn	13	03	07	Roberts	Joseph	S		1878	Au	10	04	06
Ring	Daniel			1878	Au	29	01	04	Roberts	Josiah			1871	Se	21	01	02
Ring	Maggie			1878	Au	28	01	03	Roberts	L			1879	Au	09	01	01
Ringert	Attilla			1879	Se	05	01	01	Roberts	L			1879	Au	10	01	01
Ringgold	Elizabeth	L		1855	Au	10	03	07	Roberts	Lucy		Mrs	1868	De	20	02	04
Ringgold	Josephine			1848	Fe	24	03	04	Roberts	M		Mrs	1870	Oc	28	01	02
Ringo	Daniel		Jud	1873	Se	04	01	01	Roberts	Mary	A	Mrs	1870	My	12	02	03
Ringo	Frank			1878	Jn	04	04	02	Roberts	Powhatan		Com	1870	My	04	03	01
Ringo	Mary	F	Mss	1856	Oc	04	03	04	Roberts	Sam			1872	My	31	01	01
Ringo	Waldo		Mr	1854	Fe	17	03	06	Roberts	Sidney	R	Col	1862	Se	13	02	04
Ringo	William	A		1856	Jn	28	03	06	Roberts	Stephen		Mr	1821	Mr	31	03	04
Ringwald	S			1878	Se	22	04	03	Roberts	Susie			1879	Oc	12	01	01
Riobst	S	M	Rev	1876	De	24	01	04	Roberts	Van			1871	Jl	20	01	05
Ripley	Mat			1871	Se	20	01	04	Roberts	Van			1871	No	04	01	05
Rison	Adelia		Mrs	1872	No	30	01	03	Roberts	William	L		1878	Jl	09	04	02
Rison	G	W		1872	No	30	01	03	Roberts	Wilson	L	Mr	1874	Se	06	04	01
Risson	J	W	Mr	1871	Jl	18	01	06	Robertson	Adaline		Mrs	1835	Jn	09	03	05
Ritchie	James		Mr	1821	No	03	03	01	Robertson	F			1879	No	14	01	02
Ritchie	James		Mrs	1821	No	03	03	01	Robertson	J	H		1871	Mr	15	03	01

Last	First	MI	Ttl	Yr	Mo	Day	Pg	Col	Last	First	MI	Ttl	Yr	Mo	Day	Pg	Col
Robertson	J	J	Sea	1877	No	25	01	04	Rockett	F	Y		1872	Au	23	02	03
Robertson	John		Rev	1870	My	04	03	01	Rockfellow	John			1871	Jl	11	01	06
Robertson	John	P	Jot	1877	No	25	01	04	Rockwell	Sherman	S		1875	Ap	06	04	02
Robertson	P		Bro	1869	De	25	02	03	Rockwell	William	S	Bro	1870	Fe	27	02	03
Robertson	Stephen			1870	Se	08	02	03	Rockwood	William			1878	Se	27	01	04
Robideaux	Thomas			1874	Ap	15	04	03	Rodgers			Dlm	1878	My	21	02	04
Robinett	Thomas	I		1820	Se	23	03	04	Rodgers			Mr	1872	Se	18	02	05
Robins	Anna	C	Mrs	1866	De	03	02	07	Rodgers	Emily			1878	Se	22	04	03
Robins	Clara			1850	Mr	22	03	06	Rodgers	Henry	J		1879	Au	22	05	02
Robins	E	C	Mrs	1866	No	13	03	03	Rodjeski			Mr	1872	De	25	01	02
Robins	Elijah		Mr	1850	My	24	03	06	Rodman	Thomas	J	Lcl	1871	Jl	18	01	05
Robins	John		Esq	1869	Au	07	02	02	Rodman	Willie	F		1859	Ja	29	03	01
Robins	Julius			1873	Se	26	03	01	Rodney	George	C	Lt	1839	De	18	03	03
Robins	Maria	S		1852	Jn	25	03	06	Rodt	M			1878	Se	05	01	03
Robins	Nancy		Mrs	1831	My	18	03	05	Roe	Frank			1871	Jl	18	01	05
Robins	Urana	A		1838	Se	12	03	06	Roe	Jesse		Sea	1877	No	25	01	04
Robinson			Dr	1871	De	23	01	02	Roe	Maud			1879	Au	15	01	01
Robinson	Aaron		Mr	1873	My	13	04	04	Roeberg	Joe			1872	Ap	23	01	04
Robinson	Abel		Mr	1876	Oc	26	04	04	Roesch	Christian			1878	Oc	04	04	07
Robinson	Alex		Mr	1878	Se	04	04	03	Roesch	Mary	S	Mss	1868	Jn	02	03	05
Robinson	Alex		Mrs	1878	Se	04	04	03	Roesh	Henry	A		1878	My	22	04	07
Robinson	Alexander			1872	Ap	25	01	03	Rogan	J	W	Col	1873	Jn	22	02	02
Robinson	Annie			1879	Se	04	01	01	Roger	Dolly			1879	Se	30	01	01
Robinson	Clayton	T		1876	Ap	09	03	01	Roger	James	W	Col	1873	My	18	01	02
Robinson	D	H	Mr	1872	Mr	06	04	03	Roger	Lewis		Dr	1875	Jn	15	01	04
Robinson	Dick			1879	Jl	29	01	01	Rogers	Benard		Ldm	1877	No	25	01	04
Robinson	Eliza			1878	Se	22	04	03	Rogers	Carrie		Mss	1872	De	31	01	03
Robinson	Elizabeth		Mrs	1879	Au	13	01	01	Rogers	E	W	Maj	1874	Mr	17	02	03
Robinson	Emily		Mss	1871	Jn	28	01	04	Rogers	Emily		Mrs	1872	Au	25	04	02
Robinson	F	M		1871	Ja	14	04	02	Rogers	Henry			1872	De	07	01	06
Robinson	F	M		1871	My	21	02	02	Rogers	Henry			1878	Ja	09	03	02
Robinson	Fannie			1879	Se	14	01	01	Rogers	Hester		Mss	1873	Se	28	01	05
Robinson	Frances	L	Mrs	1842	Ja	05	03	03	Rogers	J	W		1872	Au	25	04	02
Robinson	Francis			1877	Oc	27	04	06	Rogers	James		Mr	1830	De	22	03	05
Robinson	Francis	H		1846	Ja	05	02	06	Rogers	John	C	Dr	1878	Au	25	01	04
Robinson	George			1878	Se	22	04	03	Rogers	John	N		1873	Mr	25	01	03
Robinson	George		Mr	1835	Oc	13	03	02	Rogers	L	F		1871	My	19	01	03
Robinson	H	B		1878	Au	15	03	02	Rogers	Mary	J		1836	Se	27	03	05
Robinson	Hamilton			1852	Au	06	03	06	Rogers	Peter			1879	Ap	22	01	02
Robinson	Hardy		Gen	1853	Ap	22	03	06	Rogers	Reuben			1875	Jl	18	03	01
Robinson	J	T		1879	Se	07	08	06	Rogers	T	R	Dr	1875	Jn	15	03	01
Robinson	J	T	Mrs	1879	Se	07	08	02	Rogers	Timothy		Cpt	1873	Mr	09	01	05
Robinson	James			1874	Ap	29	01	02	Rogers	W	J	Hon	1869	Oc	02	04	01
Robinson	James	M		1855	Jn	29	03	07	Rogers	William	H	Cpt	1847	Ja	10	03	04
Robinson	John			1878	Mr	31	01	06	Rohback	John			1878	Ap	07	01	04
Robinson	John		Mr	1839	Oc	09	03	05	Roland	Daniel	C		1859	Fe	19	03	02
Robinson	John		Mr	1850	Ap	19	05	07	Roland	Elizabeth			1846	Ap	27	03	05
Robinson	John		Mr	1878	Ja	20	04	01	Roland	John			1878	Au	22	04	02
Robinson	John	B	Dr	1852	De	17	03	07	Roland	John	F	Maj	1852	Oc	15	03	06
Robinson	Littlebe	M	Mr	1851	De	05	03	07	Roland	William	T		1846	Ap	27	03	05
Robinson	Maria	L		1833	Au	21	03	03	Rolland				1871	Mr	24	03	01
Robinson	Mary			1878	Se	22	04	03	Rollin	Ledre			1875	Ja	03	01	06
Robinson	Minerva		Mrs	1857	Au	01	03	03	Rollins	Sam		Mrs	1877	De	20	03	01
Robinson	Nancy	F		1857	Se	19	03	04	Roman	Avilia	B		1873	Oc	22	02	02
Robinson	P			1878	Se	22	04	03	Romango	John			1878	Se	22	04	03
Robinson	Perry			1878	Se	01	01	03	Romani			Maj	1873	Jn	26	01	03
Robinson	S	C		1874	De	03	01	05	Romar	Henry			1871	Oc	06	01	04
Robinson	Samuel		Mr	1842	De	28	03	05	Romey			Mss	1872	De	27	01	02
Robinson	Theodore			1878	Fe	19	02	02	Ronan	M	R	Cpt	1874	Ja	22	04	02
Robinson	Thomas			1874	Ap	24	01	03	Roody	John		Jud	1847	Au	05	03	03
Robinson	Thomas			1874	Ja	08	01	02	Rooks	Ellen			1878	Au	27	01	04
Robinson	William			1879	Oc	16	01	01	Roone	James		Dr	1833	Mr	27	03	04
Robinson	William	H		1869	Jl	31	02	03	Rooney	Pat			1871	Se	07	01	04
Robinson	William	H		1878	Jn	02	01	07	Roosa	James			1879	Au	28	01	01
Roche	W	A	Dr	1878	Oc	19	01	03	Roosevelt	Lydia	M	Mrs	1878	Mr	09	01	04
Rochefort	Henry		Mrs	1874	Ap	19	01	03	Roosevelt	Theodore			1878	Fe	12	04	05

Last	First	MI	Ttl	Yr	Mo	Day	Pg	Col	Last	First	MI	Ttl	Yr	Mo	Day	Pg	Col
Roosevelt	Theodore			1878	Fe	17	01	04	Rover	J	W		1878	Ap	14	04	06
Root	Charley			1874	Jn	03	01	05	Roverall	Alfred			1878	Se	05	01	03
Root	Edward	W		1870	No	16	01	02	Rowes	Billy			1872	Jn	14	01	04
Rooth	Adam			1872	Mr	19	01	04	Rowland	John			1878	Au	20	04	02
Roper				1877	No	28	01	06	Rowland	John		Mr	1858	Oc	23	03	04
Roper	William	G	Mr	1841	Ap	21	03	06	Rowland	Maria			1876	Ja	28	04	04
Rorie	Absalom			1874	Jn	16	04	04	Rowland	S	T	Mss	1878	No	13	04	06
Rosarguest	J	H		1873	Au	29	01	04	Roxe	Samuel	D	Mr	1836	My	10	03	06
Rosas	Ryos		Snr	1873	No	05	01	03	Roy	James	P	Lcl	1875	Ap	30	02	03
Rosch	Henry		Mr	1871	Ap	06	01	01	Royal	John	F		1878	Oc	27	01	04
Rosch	Mary		Mrs	1868	My	12	03	03	Royster	F	W	Jr	1878	Se	12	01	03
Rose			Maj	1841	Fe	03	03	02	Royster	Frank			1878	Se	22	04	03
Rose	Ezra		Dr	1879	My	08	01	03	Royster	John	R		1836	Jn	07	03	05
Rose	H	B	Mr	1841	Fe	10	03	02	Rozell	Mary	G		1879	Au	30	08	06
Rose	J	S		1876	Se	20	01	04	Ruan	Gracie	M		1873	Jn	01	04	05
Rose	James			1871	Jl	23	01	05	Rubnels	Albert			1878	Mr	24	01	06
Rose	John			1878	Mr	10	01	04	Rucks	D	J	Mrs	1876	Ap	05	03	01
Rose	Patrick			1859	Mr	12	03	01	Rudd	Julia	A	Mrs	1856	Se	20	03	06
Rose	W	W		1873	No	18	05	03	Rudd	William	A		1878	Se	22	04	03
Rosebourough	Nick			1876	De	12	01	01	Ruddell	Abraham		Mr	1841	Mr	17	03	05
Rosebury	D	K	Rev	1878	Se	22	04	03	Ruddell	Minerva			1839	Jl	24	03	04
Rosebury	K		Rev	1878	Se	10	01	03	Rudolph			Mr	1873	Ja	30	01	05
Rosecranz	Adrian	L	Rev	1876	My	12	01	05	Rue	Vincent			1878	Se	01	01	03
Rosenbrough	John			1871	Jn	10	01	02	Ruff	A		Mr	1878	Mr	15	03	01
Rosenfeld	Joseph		Pol	1879	My	31	05	02	Ruffin	Isaac			1874	De	06	04	02
Rosenstein	Lewis			1874	Fe	04	01	05	Ruffin	Mollie			1878	Oc	16	01	03
Rosin	Adolph	J		1878	No	06	01	06	Ruffner	Johnnie		Mrs	1868	Se	08	03	06
Rosinold	Felix			1874	De	31	01	04	Ruhn	Edward			1872	Fe	24	01	05
Rosique	Francise	T	Mr	1835	Jl	21	03	06	Ruloff				1871	My	26	04	02
Rospoil				1878	Ja	12	01	05	Ruloff	Edward	H		1871	My	19	01	03
Rospoil	Francois	V		1878	Ja	09	01	04	Rulofson	W	H		1878	No	03	01	04
Ross	Agnes		Mss	1873	Ja	14	01	04	Rumbaugh	Coline			1878	Mr	16	04	05
Ross	Clark			1874	Mr	01	01	05	Rumery	J	M		1877	Se	16	01	04
Ross	Cook		Rev	1874	Oc	31	02	02	Rummell	A			1878	Au	30	01	04
Ross	D	W		1877	De	27	01	05	Rundell	John	T		1878	Oc	09	01	04
Ross	Henry		Col	1873	Au	01	03	02	Runyan	Frank			1874	Au	09	04	05
Ross	Infant			1877	De	29	03	01	Rupe	David			1873	Jn	03	01	01
Ross	John	M		1854	Se	08	03	06	Ruprecht	R		Mr	1873	Fe	19	01	04
Ross	John	M	Mr	1852	No	19	03	06	Rushing	Sarah			1874	My	31	04	03
Ross	John	W		1852	Oc	01	03	05	Rushing	Sarah			1874	Jn	03	04	03
Ross	L	W	Mr	1857	Fe	14	03	03	Rushing	Sarah			1874	Jn	04	04	02
Ross	Margaret	A		1853	Ja	21	03	04	Rusk	Chas			1878	Se	22	04	03
Ross	Mary	J		1852	De	31	03	06	Russel			Cmr	1878	Se	25	01	06
Ross	Melissa	A		1853	Ja	14	03	06	Russel			Erl	1878	Jn	02	01	06
Ross	Nancy	P	Mrs	1847	Fe	20	03	01	Russel	James			1878	Se	01	01	03
Ross	Paul			1879	Au	19	01	01	Russel	Mary			1871	Se	06	01	03
Ross	Susan			1873	Se	28	01	05	Russel	Win		Mr	1826	No	28	03	01
Ross	T			1879	Se	25	01	01	Russell				1873	Au	31	01	04
Ross	Tom			1878	Jl	31	01	04	Russell			Pvt	1876	Jl	09	01	05
Ross	W	H		1878	Se	10	01	03	Russell	Harry			1877	No	18	01	05
Ross	William			1873	Jn	14	01	03	Russell	Joe			1878	Se	01	01	03
Ross	William	H		1853	Mr	11	03	06	Russell	Jonathan		Mr	1832	Ap	04	03	03
Roth	G	T		1878	Se	25	01	04	Russell	Julia			1879	Au	24	01	01
Rothschild	Alex			1878	Jl	18	01	06	Russell	Thomas			1879	No	25	09	01
Rothschild	Mayer		Bar	1874	Fe	06	01	05	Russell	William			1878	Se	22	04	03
Roulack	George			1878	Oc	04	01	03	Russell	Willis			1875	Jl	04	01	03
Roundtree	Jesse		Mr	1829	Ap	22	03	01	Russell	Willis			1875	Jl	08	03	01
Rouns	B	B		1878	Au	21	01	04	Rust	Albert		Gen	1870	Ap	06	04	01
Rounsaville	F	M	Dr	1869	Ja	26	03	02	Ruth			Mr	1872	Se	18	02	03
Rounsaville	Mary		Mrs	1859	Jn	18	02	08	Ruth	Isaac	M		1871	My	06	01	03
Rounsaville	Mary	E	Mrs	1866	Oc	23	02	07	Ruth	Isaac	M		1871	My	07	01	05
Rous	Alfred		Mr	1825	Jl	26	03	01	Ruth	Isaac	M		1871	Oc	14	01	02
Rousaville	Asoph	H		1859	My	21	02	08	Ruth	Sister			1878	Se	19	01	04
Rouse			Mr	1873	Mr	11	01	07	Rutherford	E	M	Mrs	1867	Se	17	03	03
Rouse	Lewis		Mr	1821	Se	22	03	01	Rutherford	Joseph		Mr	1834	De	09	03	02
Rovenos	A	R		1878	Se	05	01	03	Rutherford	Mary	A	Mrs	1854	De	01	03	07

Last	First	MI	Ttl	Yr	Mo	Day	Pg	Col
Rutherford	Nancy		Mrs	1858	De	04	03	03
Rutherford	Samuel	M	Col	1867	Ap	16	01	02
Ryan				1873	No	23	01	05
Ryan			Com	1877	De	02	01	07
Ryan			Cor	1876	Jl	09	01	05
Ryan	George	P	Com	1877	De	07	04	05
Ryan	Herman			1872	De	27	01	03
Ryan	James			1860	De	01	03	01
Ryan	James		Mrs	1876	Oc	14	01	03
Ryan	Jas	F		1878	Se	22	04	03
Ryan	Jerry			1875	My	27	01	04
Ryan	Jimmy			1878	Se	22	04	03
Ryan	Joanna			1878	De	10	01	01
Ryan	John			1872	Jn	15	02	04
Ryan	Loius		Mrs	1871	Jn	07	01	02
Ryan	Maggie		Mss	1870	Mr	23	04	02
Ryan	Phillip	J		1879	Au	23	01	01
Ryan	R	J		1879	Se	09	01	03
Ryan	William	F		1879	Oc	30	08	06
Ryan	William	J		1879	Se	23	01	01
Ryburn	Montgomery		Mr	1848	My	25	03	04
Ryordan	Father			1878	Se	18	01	07

S

Last	First	MI	Ttl	Yr	Mo	Day	Pg	Col
Sabine	Lorenzo			1878	Ja	09	03	02
Sack	Solyne			1878	Jl	18	01	06
Sackett			Mr	1872	No	22	01	03
Sackett	Charles	H		1873	My	06	01	02
Saddler	James	T		1855	Jl	20	03	06
Saddler	Margaret		Mrs	1869	Fe	07	02	04
Sadler	Alonzo	C	Mr	1839	De	04	03	02
Sadler	G	C	Rev	1862	De	20	02	02
Sadler	Laudicia	M	Mrs	1838	Fe	14	03	05
Sadler	William	A	Bro	1873	Fe	23	04	08
Saffarans	Jas			1878	Se	22	04	04
Saffirans	A			1878	Se	22	04	03
Sage	B	H	Col	1875	Jn	24	01	03
Sage	Jacob	C		1879	No	04	05	01
Sailor	Albert		Yeo	1877	No	25	01	04
Sailor	Bettie		Mss	1858	Au	07	03	03
Saint	J	C		1879	Oc	02	01	01
Saising	Balthazar			1878	Jl	21	01	04
Sale	John	F	Gen	1872	No	19	01	03
Sale	R	D		1873	No	18	04	03
Sallis	Lorentz			1879	Au	19	01	01
Sallitts	Letie			1874	Au	18	01	03
Sallor			Mrs	1878	Se	22	04	03
Salseiger	H	S		1878	Au	30	01	04
Saltamachia	F			1878	Se	22	04	03
Saltsbury	W	S		1878	My	08	01	07
Salveta	Griffo			1879	Au	19	01	01
Sammons	Harriet			1878	Se	01	01	03
Sample	J	F		1878	Oc	08	01	03
Sample	W	A	Mr	1875	Fe	27	04	03
Samples	Claibourne			1876	No	12	02	03
Sampson	Magdalen	M	Mrs	1841	Mr	17	03	05
Sampson	Robert		Ldm	1877	No	25	01	04
Samuel	Henry	F	Mr	1849	My	17	03	04
Samuel	Linch			1830	Fe	02	03	04
Samuels	Infant			1879	Jl	01	08	02
Samuels	Richard		Rev	1878	Au	06	01	03
Samuelson	Alfred			1871	My	21	01	06
Sanders			Mss	1871	Au	23	01	02

Last	First	MI	Ttl	Yr	Mo	Day	Pg	Col
Sanders	Britton	B	Bro	1872	My	03	04	05
Sanders	Caroline	M	Mrs	1836	Ap	19	03	05
Sanders	Francis			1834	Se	02	03	03
Sanders	G	W	Maj	1852	Jn	11	03	07
Sanders	Hiram			1873	Oc	10	01	02
Sanders	Infant			1876	Ap	12	04	06
Sanders	J	C		1876	My	18	01	02
Sanders	Mary			1834	Au	19	03	03
Sanders	Osea			1876	Ap	21	01	03
Sanders	Osea			1876	Ap	22	01	03
Sanders	Sarah			1876	My	11	02	03
Sanders	T	H	Rev	1868	Mr	03	03	05
Sanders	William			1874	Fe	14	02	03
Sanders	Willie			1874	Jn	09	04	02
Sanderson	William		Mr	1878	Au	17	01	06
Sanderson	William		Mrs	1878	Au	17	01	06
Sandford	Howe			1878	Fe	27	04	05
Sandherr	Elizabeth	J	Mrs	1858	Ja	09	03	02
Sandlin	Matilda	J	Mrs	1858	Oc	30	03	03
Sandman	J	H		1872	De	31	01	03
Sands	George			1873	Jl	11	01	03
Sandusky	E			1871	Oc	31	04	02
Sanebez	Henry			1873	No	01	01	03
Sanford	Cornelia	F		1845	Oc	06	03	04
Sanford	Patsy	M	Mrs	1834	Mr	11	03	05
Sanford	Samuella			1867	De	31	02	06
Sanger	Mary	A	Mrs	1855	No	09	03	06
Sangster	James			1871	Jl	18	04	01
Sanguinet	Charles			1874	Ap	11	01	02
Sanliend	William	W		1874	Jn	02	03	01
Sanside	James			1871	Jl	28	01	04
Santra	William			1878	Se	22	04	03
Sarasin	Jacob			1843	Ja	25	03	03
Sarasin	Johanna	L		1868	Oc	27	03	06
Sarasin	Martha	A		1868	Oc	27	03	06
Sarasin	Martha	A	Mrs	1869	Jl	11	02	03
Sargent			Mr	1877	Se	18	01	05
Saro			Mr	1871	Au	11	01	02
Sartles	J	B		1878	Se	22	04	03
Sartoris	F	W	Mrs	1879	Au	19	01	03
Sartoris	Nellie	G	Mrs	1879	Au	17	01	03
Sartorius	Otto			1879	Se	04	01	01
Sasowsky	Louis			1867	No	05	07	02
Satterfield	Joseph	E		1860	Au	25	03	01
Saul	Jacob			1878	Oc	29	01	04
Saunders			Mrs	1871	Jl	02	01	05
Saunders	Carney	N	Pap	1877	No	25	01	04
Saunders	James	P		1874	Jl	02	01	04
Saunders	John	H		1871	De	21	01	02
Saunders	John	J		1871	De	21	01	04
Saunders	Neal			1879	Oc	18	08	05
Saunders	Pink			1879	No	08	01	03
Saunders	W	O		1878	Se	22	04	04
Saupe	Susanna			1878	Oc	18	01	03
Sauter	Chas			1878	Au	25	01	04
Savage	Henrietta		Mrs	1879	Fe	08	04	06
Savage	Lula			1878	Au	27	04	02
Savage	Mary	B		1852	Jn	11	03	07
Savage	S			1875	Mr	04	04	03
Savnders	Carney		Pap	1877	De	02	01	07
Savory			Cpt	1878	Mr	24	01	04
Sawball	Mary			1852	De	17	03	07
Sawers	Columbus		Mr	1839	Mr	20	03	03
Saxer	Infant			1877	Se	21	04	04
Saxton	John		Mr	1871	Ap	28	02	02
Sayers	Alex	B	Mrs	1878	Jl	14	01	05

Last	First	MI	Ttl	Yr	Mo	Day	Pg	Col	Last	First	MI	Ttl	Yr	Mo	Day	Pg	Col
Sayle	W	A	Dr	1874	Ja	29	04	02	Schonfeldt			Mr	1871	Jn	06	04	04
Saylor	Butler			1878	Au	30	01	04	Schooles	James			1879	Au	14	01	01
Saylor	John	W		1831	Au	31	03	01	Schrader	Bernardo			1878	Se	08	04	06
Saylor	Jos			1878	Se	22	04	03	Schrcer	Cales		Mrs	1872	Se	08	01	04
Saylor	Mary	A		1831	My	11	03	04	Schroberg	Mark		May	1870	No	11	01	02
Sayward	R	S		1871	No	18	04	02	Schroder	Sue		Mrs	1867	My	21	03	03
Scaffer	John			1873	Fe	09	01	07	Schroeder	Andrew			1872	Se	06	01	04
Scales	Henry			1876	Oc	26	01	01	Schuelder			Mrs	1878	Se	22	04	03
Scales	J	R		1877	Se	13	01	06	Schuerer	Charles			1879	No	15	01	02
Scales	Mariah			1879	Se	16	01	01	Schuler	Mollie			1878	Se	22	04	03
Scallions	Joseph			1875	Fe	17	02	03	Schulthers	Wilhelmina			1879	Se	09	01	03
Scanland	J	E	Dr	1871	Ap	09	01	05	Schultz	A	A		1878	Se	08	01	03
Scannel	Father			1878	Se	20	01	04	Schultz	A	P	Mrs	1878	Se	22	04	03
Scannell	Alderman	F		1870	Se	27	02	03	Schultz	Fredrick		Mr	1873	Jl	25	01	04
Scarborough	Myra			1870	Au	07	04	05	Schultz	G			1878	Se	22	04	03
Scarlet	William	P		1871	My	25	02	03	Schultz	Henry			1878	Au	23	01	03
Schaad	Richard			1876	Mr	04	04	04	Schultz	John	A		1865	My	20	03	02
Schaaf			Mrs	1878	Se	22	04	03	Schultz	John	D	Mr	1858	Jn	26	03	03
Schader	Albert	L	Mrs	1879	Ja	18	04	08	Schultz	William	H		1855	Ap	20	03	06
Schaefer	Herman			1878	Au	29	01	04	Schulz	August			1871	Se	27	01	03
Schaeffer	Louis			1871	No	05	01	04	Schumme				1877	De	16	01	08
Schaer	Adam			1868	Oc	06	03	06	Schup	Peer		Dr	1876	Ap	21	01	01
Schaer	Elizabeth		Mrs	1876	Oc	18	04	05	Schup	Peer		Mrs	1876	Ap	21	01	01
Schaer	Elizabeth		Mrs	1876	Oc	19	04	07	Schurmeyer	Carl	A		1879	Se	28	01	01
Schafer	Adam			1872	Jl	14	01	05	Schurz	Carl		Mrs	1876	Mr	17	01	04
Schafer	F	S		1878	Se	22	04	03	Schuyler	L	B	Rev	1878	Se	19	01	04
Schafer	Jacob			1872	Jl	14	01	05	Schwab	Anthony			1878	Au	23	01	03
Schaffer			Gov	1870	No	03	01	01	Schwab	Jacob			1879	Se	10	05	02
Scharff				1873	Oc	16	01	01	Schwartz	George			1879	Se	05	04	02
Schaum	George			1873	My	04	01	05	Schwartz	Lizzie			1879	Se	05	01	01
Scheider	Charles			1879	Se	26	01	01	Schwartz	N			1878	Au	22	01	05
Schell	Pink			1878	De	25	01	01	Scipio	Ring			1877	Ja	11	04	02
Schell	Richard			1879	No	11	01	03	Scogin	Heather		Mss	1834	Ap	08	03	04
Schercer	Cales		Mr	1872	Se	08	01	04	Scott				1871	My	17	01	03
Scherfing	Jacob		Mrs	1873	Jl	17	01	03	Scott				1871	Jn	02	04	03
Schermeyer	E	P		1878	Oc	08	01	03	Scott				1873	Se	04	01	03
Schieff	Louis		Mr	1871	Ap	11	01	03	Scott				1873	No	18	04	03
Schilling	Herman			1874	No	14	03	01	Scott				1876	Jn	16	04	01
Schilling	Herman			1875	Jn	10	03	01	Scott			Mr	1871	Jl	12	04	02
Schilling	L			1878	Se	26	01	04	Scott			Mr	1874	Fe	19	03	01
Schindler	E			1878	Au	23	01	03	Scott			Pvt	1876	Jl	09	01	05
Schiner	John			1875	Ja	12	03	01	Scott	Abram	M	Gov	1833	Jl	03	03	03
Schleimmer	Chas	H		1878	Au	25	01	04	Scott	Alexander			1879	Ap	22	01	02
Schlelmerer	Henry			1878	Au	22	01	04	Scott	Augustus	W	Mr	1839	Ja	30	03	02
Schley	William		Hon	1872	Mr	21	01	05	Scott	Charles	G	Jr	1866	Se	25	03	03
Schmidt			Pvt	1876	Jl	09	01	05	Scott	Christofer	C	Jud	1859	Ja	22	02	01
Schmidt	Carl			1875	My	12	01	04	Scott	Conway			1866	De	11	02	07
Schmidt	L			1873	No	18	04	03	Scott	Conway			1875	My	01	04	02
Schmidt	Lizzie			1875	Jl	07	01	02	Scott	Conway			1875	My	02	04	02
Schmidt	Lizzie			1875	Jl	09	01	04	Scott	Daniel	S	Dr	1857	Jn	06	03	02
Schmuck	Peter	S		1878	Se	05	01	03	Scott	Eleanor		Mrs	1838	Ap	25	03	03
Schneider	Chas			1878	Se	12	01	06	Scott	Elenor	B		1835	Se	22	03	05
Schneider	Chas		Cag	1877	No	25	01	04	Scott	Eliza		Mrs	1835	Mr	17	03	06
Schneider	H			1875	Jn	06	03	02	Scott	Emma			1878	Se	22	04	03
Schneider	W	F	Rev	1879	Au	24	01	02	Scott	F	P	Jud	1873	Oc	14	01	04
Schnoelman	Sophia			1878	Jl	06	03	01	Scott	Frances	L		1852	De	17	03	07
Schoeffer	Phillip			1879	Se	26	01	01	Scott	Frank			1875	Oc	08	01	04
Schoenberg	Mary			1878	Oc	23	01	03	Scott	Frank			1876	Ja	04	01	02
Schofield				1871	Jl	07	01	06	Scott	Frank			1876	Ja	07	01	05
Schofield	E	M		1870	My	04	03	01	Scott	G	R		1878	Se	20	02	05
Schofield	Edward			1879	Fe	27	04	06	Scott	George			1876	Ja	29	04	03
Schofield	James			1877	Se	16	01	04	Scott	George			1878	Au	30	01	04
Schofield	William	S	Dr	1852	Ja	02	03	06	Scott	George	W	Mr	1851	Se	05	03	07
Scholastic			Sis	1875	Mr	26	04	05	Scott	Helen	S		1839	Au	21	03	05
Schonchin			Mr	1874	Ap	22	01	03	Scott	Henry	A	Mr	1826	No	14	03	01
Schonchin	Jack		Cpt	1873	Oc	04	01	03	Scott	Infant			1874	Mr	18	03	01

Last	First	MI	Ttl	Yr	Mo	Day	Pg	Col	Last	First	MI	Ttl	Yr	Mo	Day	Pg	Col
Scott	Joseph			1878	No	10	01	01	Seiger	Adolph			1877	Se	28	01	05
Scott	Joseph	N		1867	My	21	03	03	Seigter	Frank			1876	De	23	01	04
Scott	Lizzie			1875	De	08	04	03	Seiler	Infant			1878	My	04	01	06
Scott	Martha		Mrs	1852	My	21	03	06	Seitz	Abraham			1876	No	22	03	01
Scott	Mary			1836	No	15	03	02	Selby	Thomas	H		1875	Jn	11	03	02
Scott	Nathaniel			1868	Jl	21	03	05	Selby	Walter	B	Mr	1874	Ap	29	04	02
Scott	Oliver	C		1871	Au	02	01	04	Selden	David			1878	Se	22	04	03
Scott	Robert	H		1878	Se	24	01	05	Selden	Harriet		Mss	1825	Mr	01	03	01
Scott	Sophia		Mrs	1841	Jl	21	03	05	Sellars	John		Mr	1873	Jn	25	03	01
Scott	Thomas			1878	Au	10	04	02	Sellars	Samuel		Mr	1873	Jn	22	04	06
Scott	Thomas			1878	Au	11	04	06	Selleck	James		Mrs	1873	No	20	01	04
Scott	Tommie			1878	Au	09	04	02	Sellers	John			1873	My	03	02	04
Scott	Walter		Sir	1872	Jl	19	01	04	Selling	Sarah		Mrs	1876	De	24	01	04
Scott	William			1845	My	12	03	04	Selvage	George			1872	Ap	26	01	02
Scott	William			1878	Se	22	04	04	Selvidge	George			1872	Ap	24	01	01
Scott	William		Mr	1838	Se	26	03	04	Selvin	John			1878	Se	22	04	03
Scranton	Joseph			1872	Jl	14	01	05	Semmes	William			1873	Fe	23	01	05
Scribner	Charles			1871	Au	29	01	03	Semon	Flora			1873	Oc	15	01	02
Scroggins	N	G		1873	Mr	11	04	05	Semos	Alex			1878	Se	01	01	03
Scruggs	Edward	E		1875	Jl	06	04	03	Sempke			Cpt	1878	Mr	05	01	05
Scruggs	Eletha	S	Mrs	1835	Mr	10	03	05	Senter	R	W	Dr	1872	De	10	01	03
Scruggs	Thomas			1876	Ap	12	04	06	Sergues			Pri	1877	Oc	26	04	05
Scudder	Matthew		Mr	1852	De	24	03	06	Session	John	R		1876	Ap	12	04	06
Scull	Benjamin	M	Mr	1829	Fe	13	03	03	Sesson	Edward			1878	De	15	01	01
Scull	Elizabeth	M	Mrs	1850	Au	30	03	07	Settles	Cosandra			1879	Oc	14	01	01
Scull	Hewes			1833	Jn	05	03	02	Seull	John			1878	Au	24	04	07
Scull	Hewes		Esq	1852	No	05	03	03	Severe				1871	Mr	15	03	02
Scull	Hewes		Mrs	1830	Ja	06	03	01	Sevier	Elizabeth	B		1840	Oc	28	03	05
Scull	J	K		1873	My	18	01	03	Sevier	Infant			1879	Jn	12	08	03
Scull	Joseph		Esq	1838	Jl	11	03	04	Sevier	Juliet		Mrs	1845	Mr	17	03	05
Scull	Joseph	P	Mr	1852	Ja	23	03	07	Sevier	Matilda			1840	Oc	28	03	05
Scull	Louisa		Mrs	1845	Se	08	03	04	Sevier	Richard	C	Esq	1835	Oc	13	03	02
Scull	Mary	H	Mss	1839	No	27	03	05	Sevier	Robert		Maj	1879	My	20	04	04
Scull	Mary	J		1869	Jl	17	02	03	Sevier	Valentine		Gen	1854	Ja	20	03	07
Scull	Nicholas	P	Mr	1852	Ap	23	03	07	Seville	Millie			1877	Oc	27	04	06
Scully	Mike			1879	Se	05	01	01	Sewall				1878	Fe	16	01	08
Scultz	Martha	R		1857	Au	01	03	03	Sewall	D	W		1879	Ja	03	04	06
Scwansen			Pvt	1876	Jl	09	01	05	Seward	Jas	R	Jud	1879	Ap	05	01	04
Sea	Joseph			1879	Oc	26	01	01	Seward	William	H		1872	Oc	12	01	03
Seales	Elvira			1878	Mr	27	04	04	Seward	William	H		1872	Oc	12	02	03
Sealey	Isham			1876	Ap	21	01	03	Seward	William	H		1872	Oc	13	01	04
Sealey	Isham			1876	Ap	22	01	03	Seward	William	H		1872	Oc	15	01	03
Seamon	Grace			1872	De	27	01	02	Seward	William	H		1872	Oc	17	01	03
Searcy	James		Esq	1837	Fe	28	03	05	Seward	William	H		1873	Ja	30	01	05
Searcy	Martha	A	Mrs	1837	Se	19	03	05	Seward	William	H		1873	Mr	29	01	02
Searcy	Mary	L	Mrs	1863	Fe	07	01	04	Sewell				1877	De	09	01	06
Searcy	Richard		Esq	1833	Ja	09	03	04	Sewell	Hannah		Mss	1878	Fe	14	04	05
Searcy	Robert	C		1859	Au	06	03	02	Sewell	John	W		1878	Fe	15	04	05
Seat	Harrison		Mr	1833	Oc	23	03	05	Sexton			Mr	1871	Ja	13	01	01
Seaton	Augustus	F	Lt	1835	De	22	03	04	Seymour	John			1873	Mr	30	04	04
Seavey	Valorcous	A		1879	Se	14	01	03	Seymour	Joseph			1878	Au	30	01	04
Seavry			Mss	1873	Au	24	01	04	Shackelford	Thomas		Jud	1877	De	20	01	05
Seawell	Martha		Mrs	1839	De	25	03	01	Shadford			Mr	1871	Se	21	01	03
Seawell	Washington		Lt	1836	Ap	12	03	04	Shaeffer	Hezekiah		Mrs	1878	Jl	11	01	05
Seay	Will			1878	Mr	31	01	06	Shafer			Gov	1870	No	01	01	01
Sebastian	Edward	L		1877	No	06	01	04	Shafer	Kite		Mrs	1878	My	15	04	03
Seckendorff	Ernestine	V	Mrs	1870	Ap	12	02	03	Shafler	Hezekiah			1879	Ap	18	01	01
Secreat	Samson	G		1835	De	29	03	02	Shafner	W	E		1878	No	14	01	03
Secrest	Abraham		Mr	1836	Fe	16	03	05	Shailer	Hezekiah			1878	Jl	11	01	05
Sedgwick	Adam		Rev	1873	Ja	29	01	06	Shale	D	F	Maj	1874	Ap	22	04	05
Sedgwick	Adam		Rev	1874	Ja	08	01	02	Shaler	S	H		1877	Ja	12	01	05
Seeden	Jas			1878	Se	01	01	03	Shall	David	F	Maj	1874	Ap	24	04	02
Seeley	Bradford			1874	Jl	19	01	03	Shall	Mary			1871	Au	10	04	03
Seemental	John			1879	De	17	08	03	Shall	Mary			1871	Se	13	04	04
Seibert	Jacob			1878	Mr	03	01	03	Shall	Mary		Mss	1871	Jl	21	04	03
Seidel	William	R		1879	Se	20	01	01	Shall	Mary	E	Mrs	1854	Oc	13	03	05

Last	First	MI	Ttl	Yr	Mo	Day	Pg	Col	Last	First	MI	Ttl	Yr	Mo	Day	Pg	Col
Shaltington	John			1878	Ap	14	04	06	Shepard	W	B	Mrs	1878	Se	18	01	07
Shane	Pat		Frm	1878	Au	16	04	05	Shepherd			Ofc	1872	Oc	09	01	06
Shank				1871	Au	19	01	05	Shepherd	Laura			1878	Au	28	01	03
Shann	Ferdinand		Mr	1874	Ap	13	01	02	Shepherd	R	R		1871	No	06	01	03
Shann	Ferdinand		Mrs	1874	Ap	13	01	02	Shepherd	William			1878	Oc	08	01	03
Shannon			Mr	1832	Se	12	02	03	Shepley	Ether		Cj	1878	Ja	09	03	02
Shannon	Granville	B	Mr	1873	Fe	02	02	02	Sheppard	B	E		1878	Se	22	04	03
Shannon	Patrick			1878	De	14	04	05	Sheppard	Daisy			1878	Oc	01	01	04
Shannon	Samuel			1871	My	19	01	01	Sheppard	Elinor		Mrs	1879	Ja	29	04	07
Shaper	Fred	S		1878	Se	11	01	05	Sheppard	George	M	Sea	1877	No	25	01	04
Sharleville	John		Mr	1829	Jl	15	03	01	Sheppard	Josephine			1877	De	22	01	06
Sharp	Aurelia		Mss	1877	De	15	03	01	Sheppard	Seias	E	Rev	1877	Oc	13	01	04
Sharp	Aurella		Mss	1877	De	04	03	04	Sheppard	William	J		1873	Ja	08	01	05
Sharp	James		Mr	1871	Jn	04	01	05	Shepperd	Socrates			1843	Au	02	03	05
Sharp	James	M		1871	My	31	01	04	Sherams	Lew			1879	Jn	15	01	02
Sharp	John	F	Mrs	1879	Se	09	05	01	Sheran	Robert			1879	Mr	28	01	02
Sharp	Joseph			1879	Se	17	01	01	Shercer	Cales		Mr	1872	Se	08	01	04
Sharp	Richard			1879	Se	17	01	01	Sheridan	F	W		1874	Fe	12	01	05
Sharp	Sadie			1878	Ja	08	01	06	Sherlock	John			1872	Mr	13	01	04
Sharp	Sam		Cpt	1873	Ja	10	02	02	Sherman				1871	Jl	02	01	04
Sharpe	Ellen			1850	Au	23	03	06	Sherman				1871	Jl	02	01	04
Sharpe	Thos	B		1878	Se	21	01	05	Sherman	C	T	Jud	1879	Ja	05	01	06
Sharron	W	H	Maj	1876	Jl	09	01	05	Sherman	Charles	B		1876	Mr	02	04	03
Shattucr	Benjarmin		Cpt	1831	Jn	01	03	04	Sherman	Horatio	F		1873	Ja	19	01	06
Shaughnahan	John			1874	Ap	26	01	03	Sherman	Isiah			1872	No	03	01	04
Shaw	A			1878	Se	22	04	03	Sherman	James			1872	No	03	01	04
Shaw	Charles	G		1875	My	15	01	03	Sherman	John	L		1870	Se	27	02	03
Shaw	Charles	H		1879	Se	12	01	01	Sherman	Mary		Mrs	1850	Ap	19	03	07
Shaw	Delilah	R	Mrs	1857	Mr	14	03	04	Sherman	N	H		1871	Jl	02	01	04
Shaw	Frank			1878	Se	14	01	06	Sherman	Sidney		Gen	1873	Au	03	01	06
Shaw	Henry	F	Esq	1853	Jn	03	03	07	Sherman	William			1872	De	27	01	02
Shaw	J	M		1879	Oc	14	01	01	Shermon			Gen	1879	Mr	23	01	02
Shaw	J	M	Mss	1878	Oc	06	01	03	Shernell	William			1877	No	17	01	06
Shaw	John		Com	1823	No	11	03	03	Sherwood			Lt	1874	Ap	17	01	02
Shaw	John	E		1874	Ap	10	01	04	Sherwood			Lt	1873	My	08	01	04
Shaw	Knowles		Rev	1878	Jn	08	04	07	Shettley	John			1878	Au	22	01	04
Shaw	Mike			1878	Jl	13	01	06	Shickar			Mr	1874	Oc	29	04	04
Shaw	Mike		Mrs	1878	Jl	13	01	06	Shield	Henry			1877	Oc	04	01	04
Shaw	Robert	W	Frm	1877	No	25	01	04	Shields			Gen	1879	Jn	11	07	01
Shay			Mr	1875	Oc	02	01	03	Shields	James		Gen	1879	Jn	03	01	03
Shay	Ed			1878	Se	22	04	03	Shields	James		Gen	1879	Jn	05	04	01
Shay	Husting			1877	Oc	03	01	06	Shilee	Leonard			1878	Se	24	01	07
Shcumar	Louis			1871	Au	27	01	04	Shillenit	Emsley	C		1858	Se	11	03	04
Shea			Mr	1875	Mr	30	01	05	Shillinger	Nicholas		Eng	1879	Ap	01	01	03
Shea			Pvt	1876	Jl	09	01	05	Shipley	George	W	Mr	1839	De	18	03	03
Shea	Patrick			1876	No	07	04	03	Shippe	Rufus		Eng	1873	Jl	22	01	03
Shea	Thomas			1878	Se	01	01	03	Shire				1874	Ap	14	03	01
Shea	William			1873	Au	31	01	04	Shire			Mr	1874	Mr	31	01	04
Sheehan			Con	1879	Au	20	01	01	Shirkley	Amelia		Mss	1873	Mr	09	01	06
Sheehan	Dennis			1878	Oc	13	01	06	Shirley	John	T	Cpt	1873	Se	10	01	04
Sheets	George			1873	Mr	21	01	04	Shirley	Z	M	Cpt	1879	Fe	19	01	03
Sheholm	Fred			1871	No	14	01	02	Shives	Lizzie			1870	Se	16	03	01
Shelby	George			1878	Se	22	04	03	Shoaff	James			1874	Ap	14	01	05
Shelby	Isaac		Mr	1826	Au	15	03	01	Shode			Pvt	1876	Jl	09	01	05
Shelby	Jacob			1876	De	29	04	01	Shodied			Pvt	1876	Jl	09	01	05
Shelby	R	H		1878	Au	22	01	04	Shoemaker	William			1878	Ap	07	01	04
Sheldon	Infant			1821	Jn	16	03	01	Shon	John			1875	Fe	21	01	05
Sheldon	Joshua			1874	Jl	10	01	05	Shonberger	John	H		1869	De	28	04	03
Shell	Elizabeth	H		1852	De	24	03	06	Shook	Suan		Mrs	1833	Se	11	03	05
Shell	Jane	J	Mss	1841	Jl	28	03	03	Shopel	Alice	O		1878	Se	01	01	03
Shelton	Andrew			1879	Au	17	01	01	Shoptau	Alfred		Mr	1872	Jn	22	01	03
Shelton	C		Mrs	1878	Oc	29	01	04	Shordan	James			1876	Fe	16	01	05
Shelton	R	W		1878	Oc	03	01	03	Short			Pvt	1876	Jl	09	01	05
Shepard			Ofc	1872	Oc	09	01	06	Shoup	J	T	Bro	1869	De	25	02	03
Shepard	Francis	E	Mrs	1878	Au	28	01	03	Shrewsberry			May	1872	Ap	24	01	03
Shepard	W	B		1878	Se	19	01	04	Shroyer	W	P		1878	Oc	16	01	03

Last	First	MI	Ttl	Yr	Mo	Day	Pg	Col	Last	First	MI	Ttl	Yr	Mo	Day	Pg	Col
Shtrox	Bettie			1878	Se	22	04	03	Sissel	Elvira	C		1862	De	13	02	02
Shubrick			Adm	1874	My	28	01	06	Sizemore			Mr	1872	Jl	21	01	06
Shultis	Charles			1878	No	12	01	03	Sizer	David	T		1859	Se	03	03	03
Shultz	Von		Col	1839	Fe	13	01	06	Skaggs	John	H		1870	Se	04	02	03
Shultz	Von		Col	1839	Fe	13	03	02	Skeflington	John	S		1879	Se	05	01	01
Shultz	Wick			1871	Jn	08	03	01	Skela	Huldah		Mrs	1851	Jl	04	03	06
Shumaker	J	H	Cpt	1878	Au	04	01	05	Skidmore	David	W	Mr	1876	Fe	01	01	06
Shurlds	Rachel		Mrs	1831	My	11	03	04	Skidmore	Robert			1874	Au	08	04	04
Shuttleworth	A			1878	Se	22	04	03	Skinner	Frank			1867	No	19	03	02
Shwartz	Adam			1871	Mr	11	01	02	Skinner	O	J		1878	Oc	21	01	03
Sibley	A	H	Maj	1878	Jl	11	01	05	Skipper	M			1878	Se	22	04	03
Sibley	Amelia		Mrs	1873	Jn	17	04	05	Skipwith	Mattie	S	Mrs	1870	Fe	08	02	02
Sibley	Walter	S		1870	Se	08	04	04	Skron				1874	Mr	25	01	05
Sides	William			1874	De	27	01	04	Skruggs	Martha		Mss	1879	Mr	09	04	02
Siedel	Fritz	J		1878	Oc	06	01	06	Slack	Chester			1859	Jn	04	03	01
Sietz	Oswald			1878	Oc	17	01	03	Slack	Infant			1878	Mr	06	04	06
Signaigo	Gus		Mr	1878	Ja	23	04	01	Slack	Lizzie			1878	Se	22	04	03
Signiago	J	A		1876	Oc	06	01	05	Slagie	Nellie	M		1879	Mr	04	04	05
Silk	Sam			1872	Jn	19	01	03	Slagle	Frederick	H		1869	Jl	02	02	03
Sill	George			1876	Oc	08	01	02	Slagle	Harriet	H		1870	Au	16	04	02
Sillman	Henry		Mrs	1873	My	10	02	03	Slantger	William			1878	Au	28	01	03
Sillwell	Fanny	F		1856	Ap	19	03	05	Slater				1871	Ap	22	01	03
Silver	Antony			1878	Jl	13	04	02	Slater	C		Mrs	1878	Oc	13	01	03
Simmons			Mrs	1878	Se	22	04	03	Slater	E	C	Mrs	1878	Oc	13	01	03
Simmons	A		Hon	1875	Ap	29	01	03	Slater	Helen		Mrs	1878	Au	30	01	04
Simmons	I			1878	Se	22	04	03	Slater	R	E		1878	Se	22	04	03
Simmons	J	A		1878	Se	22	04	03	Slater	Sallie			1878	Se	28	01	04
Simmons	Jennie			1868	Mr	31	03	04	Slatham	John	H		1878	Jn	29	01	06
Simmons	S	O	Lt	1877	No	25	01	04	Slatter	Mollie			1878	Oc	16	01	03
Simmons	Sarah		Mrs	1843	Mr	08	03	05	Slatterly	N	J		1871	Jl	13	01	03
Simms	Emily		Mrs	1821	Mr	17	03	01	Slaughter	J	A	Mrs	1870	Oc	16	04	05
Simms	Gilmore	W		1879	Au	28	01	01	Slaughter	J	E		1873	Ja	07	01	03
Simms	John		Mr	1840	Au	12	03	05	Slaughter	J	K		1871	Ja	14	04	02
Simms	William	G		1870	Jn	18	02	02	Slaughter	J	R		1871	My	21	02	02
Simon	Sol			1873	No	18	04	03	Slaughter	Richard	B		1844	Ap	10	03	04
Simonds	William	E		1866	Oc	16	03	08	Slayton			Mr	1871	Jn	24	01	02
Simons			Lt	1877	De	07	04	05	Slesher	Isiah			1871	Jl	26	01	02
Simons	Charles	F		1873	De	24	01	03	Sleyman	Morris			1878	Se	01	01	03
Simons	J	A		1878	Se	14	01	04	Slinger	Thomas			1878	Jn	13	03	02
Simonson	Josephine		Mrs	1851	Ap	11	03	05	Slinger	Thomas			1878	Jl	25	03	01
Simpson	Bird	M	Col	1838	Jl	11	03	04	Sloan	Anna		Mrs	1834	Oc	07	03	03
Simpson	D	C		1877	De	06	01	05	Sloan	Henry			1872	Oc	22	01	06
Simpson	Elizabeth		Mrs	1840	Se	09	03	03	Sloan	Jennie			1879	Au	29	01	01
Simpson	Frances		Mrs	1837	Au	22	03	03	Sloan	Mathew		Bro	1869	De	25	02	03
Simpson	G	W	Mrs	1878	Oc	20	01	03	Sloan	Racheal			1879	Au	29	01	01
Simpson	George			1874	Jl	21	01	06	Sloan	Wiley			1871	Mr	11	03	01
Simpson	James			1820	Jl	08	03	04	Slocum			Mr	1873	Fe	01	01	05
Simpson	John			1874	Se	09	03	03	Smart	E	K	Hon	1872	Oc	01	01	04
Simpson	John	A		1871	Oc	04	01	04	Smead	Ezra			1820	Se	16	03	03
Simpson	Robert			1874	Mr	24	03	01	Smedly	Joshua		Mrs	1835	Jl	28	03	04
Simpson	Thompson		Esq	1834	Mr	11	03	05	Smelser	J	W	Dr	1874	Ap	08	01	01
Simpson	William			1834	Ap	22	03	04	Smelser	Marshall	E		1875	My	09	01	08
Simpson	William			1871	Oc	04	01	04	Smith			Lt	1876	Jl	07	01	03
Sims	John			1879	Au	16	08	02	Smith			Mr	1875	Jl	01	03	01
Sims	Louella		Mss	1866	Oc	30	02	07	Smith			Mr	1877	Ja	03	02	04
Sims	Mary	J	Mrs	1846	Au	31	03	05	Smith			Mrs	1875	My	20	01	05
Sims	T	W	Col	1875	My	27	01	06	Smith			Pm	1872	Ja	16	01	03
Simson			Mr	1876	No	05	01	02	Smith			Ram	1878	Ja	09	03	02
Sinclair	James	D	Cpt	1877	De	23	03	02	Smith			Sup	1877	De	30	01	06
Sinclear	Robert		Esq	1833	No	20	03	05	Smith	A	C		1871	Au	13	01	06
Singleton	Harry			1878	Oc	10	01	03	Smith	A	E	Cpt	1876	Jl	09	01	05
Sinnot	Martin			1879	Jn	27	08	02	Smith	A	M		1877	De	19	01	05
Sinnott	Nicholas	C		1872	Au	07	01	04	Smith	Abe			1878	Se	24	01	06
Sins	Elias			1878	Oc	01	04	05	Smith	Abraham			1878	Fe	07	01	08
Sinsor	W		Dr	1878	Oc	19	01	03	Smith	Agnes		Mrs	1873	My	16	04	07
Sisk	James	M	Mr	1830	Ja	13	03	01	Smith	Albert			1878	No	23	01	02

Last	First	MI	Ttl	Yr	Mo	Day	Pg	Col	Last	First	MI	Ttl	Yr	Mo	Day	Pg	Col
Smith	Albert		Pro	1878	Fe	24	01	05	Smith	John			1872	Au	17	01	04
Smith	Alma			1871	Jn	11	01	04	Smith	John			1872	No	13	01	05
Smith	Amanda	F	Mss	1833	Se	18	03	03	Smith	John			1878	Au	30	01	04
Smith	Ann		Mrs	1875	Mr	09	01	03	Smith	John			1878	Se	01	01	03
Smith	Anne		Mrs	1833	Se	25	03	02	Smith	John			1878	Se	05	01	03
Smith	Archibald			1857	Oc	03	03	05	Smith	John			1878	Oc	23	01	03
Smith	Asa	D	Upr	1878	Ja	09	03	02	Smith	John		Mr	1820	Oc	14	03	02
Smith	Barbra	E		1842	Oc	12	03	05	Smith	John		Mr	1844	Jn	19	03	01
Smith	Benjamin			1877	Ja	23	04	04	Smith	John	C	Hon	1867	De	31	02	06
Smith	Bernard			1876	Jl	02	01	04	Smith	John	C	Rev	1878	Ja	25	01	06
Smith	Bernard		Col	1835	Jl	14	03	05	Smith	John	R		1874	No	17	04	02
Smith	C	M		1878	Se	22	04	03	Smith	John	J		1837	Oc	17	03	05
Smith	Canning	C		1873	Oc	15	02	03	Smith	Joseph			1871	Jn	10	01	01
Smith	Charles			1869	Se	08	03	01	Smith	Joseph	C	Mr	1839	Jl	10	03	04
Smith	Charles			1876	My	20	01	03	Smith	Kettie	T		1878	Mr	01	04	02
Smith	Charles		Mr	1871	Ap	06	04	02	Smith	Kucy			1876	Ap	12	04	06
Smith	Charlotte	N	Mss	1877	Ja	04	01	07	Smith	L		Sea	1877	No	25	01	04
Smith	Chas	M		1878	Se	11	01	05	Smith	Lizzie			1871	Au	01	01	05
Smith	Christopher	B		1879	Oc	12	01	03	Smith	Lizzie		Mrs	1871	Au	29	01	03
Smith	Cynthia		Mrs	1855	Se	14	03	06	Smith	Luther		Rev	1879	Jl	22	06	01
Smith	Cyrus	T		1845	Jn	09	03	03	Smith	Madison		Mr	1832	Se	26	03	03
Smith	D	E	Mrs	1879	No	07	07	01	Smith	Marhta	N	Mss	1877	Ja	04	01	07
Smith	D	S	Mrs	1821	No	03	03	01	Smith	Mark			1874	Se	27	01	07
Smith	Dave			1878	Oc	15	01	03	Smith	Martha	A	Mrs	1839	Jn	26	03	05
Smith	David			1879	Mr	12	04	06	Smith	Martin			1876	Ap	12	04	06
Smith	David			1879	Se	13	01	01	Smith	Mary	C	Mrs	1835	Mr	31	03	05
Smith	E			1871	Ja	14	04	02	Smith	Mary	E		1837	Oc	17	03	05
Smith	E			1871	My	21	02	02	Smith	Mary	E	Mrs	1839	Fe	13	03	02
Smith	E		Mrs	1841	Jl	21	03	05	Smith	Mathew	H		1879	No	09	01	02
Smith	E	S		1877	Oc	27	04	06	Smith	Maurice		Col	1871	My	25	01	04
Smith	Ed			1878	Se	04	01	03	Smith	Minnie	M		1878	Se	22	04	03
Smith	Edmund			1874	Mr	14	01	04	Smith	Otis	B		1878	Fe	15	04	05
Smith	Edward			1874	Ja	04	01	03	Smith	P	H	Mrs	1839	Au	07	03	04
Smith	Emma			1878	Se	22	04	03	Smith	Pennie	A	Mrs	1877	De	30	04	05
Smith	Ezra	P	Mrs	1877	Oc	26	02	03	Smith	Peyton			1878	Au	30	01	04
Smith	Floyd		Mr	1878	No	13	01	06	Smith	Philip		Esq	1870	Se	08	02	03
Smith	Floyd		Mrs	1878	No	13	01	06	Smith	Preston	S		1873	Mr	02	01	04
Smith	Frank			1876	Mr	02	04	03	Smith	R		Mrs	1878	Se	22	04	03
Smith	Frederick		Lt	1828	Jl	09	03	01	Smith	Rees		Hon	1871	Jn	25	01	05
Smith	G	E		1874	Jl	21	01	03	Smith	Richard		Pro	1877	Ja	26	01	06
Smith	George			1871	Oc	05	01	08	Smith	Richard	H		1878	Au	03	01	03
Smith	George			1873	Au	12	01	03	Smith	Ruth		Mss	1873	Jn	19	01	03
Smith	George			1873	Oc	07	03	01	Smith	Sally		Mss	1874	Jn	13	01	06
Smith	George	K		1878	Ap	21	04	05	Smith	Samuel			1873	My	11	01	03
Smith	George	S		1859	Mr	12	03	01	Smith	Samuel	M		1874	De	01	01	03
Smith	Gerritt			1874	De	31	01	05	Smith	Samuel	O	Gen	1835	Se	22	03	05
Smith	Gerritt			1875	Mr	09	01	03	Smith	Samuel	S	Mr	1835	Oc	20	03	05
Smith	H			1878	Se	22	04	04	Smith	Sarah		Mrs	1852	De	03	03	05
Smith	H	A	Bro	1871	Ap	30	01	07	Smith	Sevenup			1878	Au	02	04	05
Smith	H	M	Mr	1878	Au	06	01	06	Smith	Stephen			1870	No	12	01	02
Smith	Harry			1879	My	29	08	06	Smith	Susan			1876	My	13	04	02
Smith	Henry	B		1851	No	14	03	07	Smith	Susan	B		1853	Se	16	03	06
Smith	Henry	G		1879	Ja	03	04	06	Smith	Thomas		Mr	1870	Se	21	03	01
Smith	Henry	M		1877	No	13	03	01	Smith	Thomas	H		1858	Oc	30	03	02
Smith	Henry	N	Pro	1878	Ja	09	03	02	Smith	Thomas	L		1878	Oc	20	01	04
Smith	Hester			1878	Se	22	04	03	Smith	Thomas	R	Jud	1872	Mr	08	01	05
Smith	J			1878	Se	22	04	03	Smith	Turner		Mrs	1876	Fe	25	04	02
Smith	J	F		1878	Mr	30	03	01	Smith	V		Mrs	1878	Se	12	01	06
Smith	J	W		1877	Ja	04	01	07	Smith	Victor	A		1876	Mr	02	01	06
Smith	J	W	Maj	1873	Au	19	01	02	Smith	W	A	Cdr	1873	My	02	01	04
Smith	James			1877	Ja	13	04	02	Smith	W	J		1870	No	13	01	01
Smith	James		Col	1858	De	11	03	02	Smith	W	J	Mrs	1878	Se	01	01	03
Smith	James		Col	1879	Mr	30	04	04	Smith	W	R		1879	Oc	15	01	01
Smith	James		Mrs	1836	De	20	03	05	Smith	Washington		Mr	1852	Ja	09	03	06
Smith	James	D		1833	Se	25	03	02	Smith	Willam		Mr	1832	Fe	15	03	05
Smith	James	S	Col	1874	Ap	30	01	01	Smith	William			1872	Jl	06	01	03

Last	First	MI	Ttl	Yr	Mo	Day	Pg	Col	Last	First	MI	Ttl	Yr	Mo	Day	Pg	Col
Smith	William			1875	Jn	25	04	02	South	John			1878	Au	29	01	04
Smith	William			1878	Jn	05	01	06	Southall	J	T	Mr	1871	No	03	04	05
Smith	William	C	Hon	1858	Oc	02	03	03	Southall	Madison			1879	Oc	19	01	01
Smith	William	H		1872	Ja	20	01	03	Southerland	Alexander		Bro	1868	Fe	11	03	04
Smith	William	H		1874	Ap	18	01	04	Sowders	Jos	S		1872	Ap	21	04	01
Smith	William	H	Mr	1839	Jl	31	03	04	Spade	Lizzie			1878	Mr	06	04	06
Smith	William	J		1841	Ja	06	02	04	Spague	Hattie			1879	Se	27	01	01
Smith	William	R	Mr	1852	Ja	30	03	07	Spain	Lucy			1878	Se	22	04	03
Smith	William	W		1842	Oc	12	03	05	Spain	Thomas			1878	Oc	09	01	04
Smithee	Mary			1875	Jn	12	04	05	Spalding	John	R		1872	Oc	12	01	04
Smithee	Samuel	H		1876	Se	22	04	04	Spark	Henry			1872	Oc	18	01	05
Smithee	Samuel	P		1867	Oc	08	03	03	Sparks	Henderson			1879	Se	02	08	04
Smithson	Bryon	H	Gen	1858	De	11	02	01	Sparks	Henderson			1879	Se	06	08	03
Smithson	Franklin		Mr	1850	No	22	03	06	Sparks	Henderson			1879	Se	09	08	03
Smoot	G	P		1875	Mr	04	04	03	Sparks	J	H	Maj	1879	Fe	01	02	03
Smoot	William			1873	Mr	20	04	05	Sparks	Levi		Gen	1875	Mr	27	01	05
Smoot	William			1873	Mr	21	04	04	Sparks	Thomas	B		1867	Ja	15	02	08
Snake	Jack		Mr	1820	De	23	03	02	Sparrew	William		Rev	1874	Ja	18	01	03
Snapp	Julia	I		1857	Mr	07	03	04	Spartling	Catherine			1879	Oc	12	01	03
Snedicker	Fred			1879	Fe	08	01	03	Spartling	Edith			1879	Oc	12	01	03
Sneed	Laura			1878	Se	05	01	03	Spartling	Marian			1879	Oc	12	01	03
Sneethe	J	W		1875	Ap	16	01	02	Spaulding			Son	1876	Mr	01	04	02
Snell	William	H	Bro	1860	No	10	03	01	Spaulding	Martin	J	Abp	1872	Fe	15	02	02
Snelling	Josiah		Col	1828	Se	23	03	02	Spaulding	W	W		1876	Mr	04	04	04
Snider	Maria		Mrs	1875	My	16	03	01	Speadling	Leonard			1858	No	06	03	02
Snigg	Ed			1878	Oc	02	01	04	Speague	Alden		Dr	1847	My	01	03	04
Snow			Pvt	1876	Jl	09	01	05	Spear	Alfred			1875	My	16	01	03
Snow	John		Mrs	1878	Ja	22	04	05	Spear	Anna		Mss	1876	Oc	27	01	04
Snow	Walter			1873	Au	31	01	04	Spears			Mr	1872	Oc	19	02	06
Snowden	Andrew		Hon	1872	Jl	18	01	03	Spears	Mary		Mrs	1873	No	11	04	05
Snuggs	William	R	Mr	1842	Au	10	03	05	Speckernagle	William			1878	Au	28	01	03
Snyder			Mss	1872	Au	28	01	03	Speed	James			1873	Fe	01	01	05
Snyder	Harriet			1873	Au	13	01	04	Speed	Jimmy			1872	No	20	01	04
Snyder	Heary			1873	Au	13	01	04	Speer	Andrew		Mr	1837	Fe	21	03	05
Snyder	Katie			1878	Se	22	04	03	Speers	Allen	K		1879	Au	23	01	01
Snyder	Simon			1820	Ja	22	03	01	Speke	Charles	L		1874	Au	02	01	06
Snyder	Simon			1820	Ja	22	03	01	Spellman	P			1878	Se	07	01	03
Snyder	William			1871	Ap	20	04	03	Spelmore	John		Mrs	1873	Fe	11	01	06
Soberton	Willaim			1874	Jn	26	01	06	Spence	Alex			1879	Ap	22	01	02
Sohms	Louis	F		1879	Se	20	01	01	Spence	Jane		Mss	1839	Au	21	03	05
Solly	William			1878	Oc	16	04	02	Spence	Patrick		Mr	1832	Au	29	03	02
Solmore	Samuel		Mrs	1878	Se	28	01	06	Spence	Solomon		Col	1872	Se	25	01	02
Soloman	A			1879	Se	25	01	01	Spence	Solomon		Mr	1872	Se	21	02	06
Soloman	Daniel			1874	Fe	06	04	02	Spencer			Cpt	1871	Jl	13	01	06
Soloman	W	M		1879	Ja	03	04	06	Spencer	Chas			1877	Se	15	01	07
Solomon	Dan		Col	1873	Oc	19	04	04	Spencer	Nora			1878	Au	30	01	04
Solomon	W	M		1879	Ja	03	04	06	Spencer	Robert			1879	Oc	22	08	02
Soloy	P			1878	Oc	02	04	04	Spencer	W	H		1876	Oc	20	01	01
Somers	John			1879	No	13	05	02	Speren	Ann		Mrs	1878	Se	22	01	05
Somers	Lizzie			1879	Au	15	01	01	Spicer			Cdr	1878	No	30	01	01
Somers	Louis			1872	No	01	01	03	Spinlow	Jasper			1877	Oc	21	01	06
Somerville	Alexander	H	Maj	1839	Fe	20	03	03	Spinx	Burrel			1876	My	27	01	05
Somerville	Joseph			1876	Mr	04	04	04	Spivey	Joseph	W	Mr	1870	Ap	17	03	01
Somerville	Richard			1872	Jl	13	01	04	Spooner	George	H		1877	Ja	06	01	03
Sommers	William	B	Mr	1837	Ja	03	03	04	Spooner	William	B	Dcn	1877	No	13	04	03
Songster	James			1871	Jl	15	01	01	Spradlin	Ambrose	B	Mr	1840	Se	16	03	04
Sonill	Pierre			1878	Oc	06	01	03	Sprague			Cj	1872	Fe	25	02	02
Sonts	F	W		1878	Se	01	01	03	Sprague			Cj	1872	Fe	29	01	03
Sord	Allen	M		1878	Fe	02	02	03	Sprague	A	H	Mr	1853	Se	30	03	07
Sorrell	M	D		1877	Oc	07	01	05	Sprague	Sophroni	S	Mrs	1853	De	30	03	06
Sorrels	Samuel	J		1868	Mr	93	03	05	Spratt	W	D	Dr	1878	Oc	02	01	05
Soule	Pierre		Sen	1870	Ap	05	02	02	Spring	Gardner			1874	Ja	08	01	02
Soules	Levi			1873	My	29	01	04	Spring	Harry		Mrs	1872	De	01	04	03
Sour	Margret		Mrs	1878	Oc	08	01	03	Spring	Jessie	M		1858	Fe	27	03	04
Sousorie	Joseph			1874	Ja	07	01	02	Spring	Katie	M		1866	Oc	16	03	08
South			Pvt	1876	Jl	09	01	05	Sproat	Fredrick			1878	Se	21	01	05

Last	First	MI	Ttl	Yr	Mo	Day	Pg	Col	Last	First	MI	Ttl	Yr	Mo	Day	Pg	Col
Sproule	Samuel		Mr	1839	Ap	10	03	03	Steele	Agnus		Mrs	1879	Oc	14	01	01
Spruill			Mrs	1867	Ja	08	01	02	Steele	C	L		1878	Se	22	04	03
Spurzhein	Gaspard		Dr	1832	De	12	02	03	Steele	E		Mr	1834	Jn	24	03	04
Stabbs	Louis			1873	Se	02	01	03	Steele	George		Gen	1879	My	09	02	01
Stackpole	Clara		Mss	1873	My	10	02	03	Steele	George	C		1878	Se	25	01	06
Stackpole	Rosa		Mss	1873	My	10	02	03	Steele	John			1877	Oc	05	04	05
Stafford	Edward		Mr	1879	No	05	08	02	Steele	Mary		Mrs	1834	Au	12	03	03
Stafford	Edward		Mr	1879	No	07	08	05	Steele	Sam	B	Mr	1871	Mr	26	04	05
Staley				1873	Oc	04	01	03	Steele	Timothy		Mrs	1875	Jn	29	04	03
Stanard	Mary			1878	Oc	19	01	05	Steigerwaid	Julia			1878	Fe	02	01	06
Stanberg	Ed	A		1878	Au	27	01	04	Stein	Willie			1879	Au	24	01	01
Stanberry	Ernest			1878	Au	25	01	04	Steinecke			Ms	1872	Au	29	01	02
Stancell	John	H		1873	Mr	18	04	04	Steinman	Jacob			1877	Se	16	01	04
Standing	Joseph			1879	Jl	22	01	03	Steiwecke			Mss	1872	Au	29	01	02
Standish	Miles			1872	Oc	08	01	04	Stelfox	Harriet		Mrs	1854	Ja	13	03	04
Standlee	Nancy		Mrs	1826	Fe	28	03	01	Stemler	Anna	M		1867	De	03	03	02
Standley	P	U	Mrs	1878	Oc	25	01	04	Stenette	John			1878	Se	01	01	03
Standridge	James		Mr	1853	My	20	03	07	Stephans	L	M		1877	De	16	02	03
Stanellan			Pvt	1876	Jl	09	01	05	Stephanson	Joe			1877	De	20	03	01
Staner	Harriet		Mrs	1877	Oc	24	04	04	Stephens			Mr	1872	My	19	01	02
Staner	Harriet		Mrs	1877	No	03	04	02	Stephens	Atherton	H	Col	1872	No	15	01	04
Staner	Tom			1877	No	03	04	02	Stephens	B	C		1876	De	21	01	03
Stanfield	Precilla			1876	Mr	02	04	03	Stephens	E	B		1875	My	02	01	04
Stanfield	Walker		Mr	1873	No	23	04	02	Stephens	James			1872	Se	21	02	06
Stanfill	M	M	Mrs	1878	Oc	13	01	03	Stephens	Linton		Jud	1872	Jl	16	01	04
Stanislaus			Sis	1878	Se	22	04	03	Stephens	Linton		Jud	1872	Jl	26	02	05
Stanislaus	Mary			1874	Se	01	04	05	Stephens	Nicholas			1878	Jl	19	01	04
Stanislaus	Sister			1878	Se	13	01	04	Stephens	R	R		1872	Jl	27	01	05
Stanley			Gov	1872	Jl	14	01	02	Stephenson	Charles		Sgt	1841	Mr	03	03	05
Stanley	Infant			1878	Ap	13	01	06	Stephenson	H	M		1878	Se	14	01	04
Stanley	Obediah		Mr	1835	Jn	09	03	05	Stephenson	S	S	Col	1851	Ja	10	03	07
Stansbury	Dixon			1835	No	24	03	03	Stephenson	William		Mrs	1824	De	14	03	01
Stansbury	Stanley	J		1870	Mr	25	02	03	Stephenton	W	G		1878	Se	22	04	03
Stanton	Edward			1873	My	30	01	03	Stephney	Ellen			1871	Jl	27	01	05
Stanton	Edwin	M	Sec	1874	No	20	02	03	Stephney	Rolla	G		1871	Jl	27	01	05
Stanton	John			1873	Jl	01	01	04	Sterling	Fanny			1873	Jn	12	01	03
Stanton	Louis		Mrs	1877	Se	28	01	05	Sterling	Katy			1873	My	10	02	03
Stanton	M			1879	Fe	22	01	05	Stetson			Mrs	1872	Au	02	04	02
Stanton	S		Pm	1878	Mr	15	03	01	Stetson	Adelia			1878	Se	04	01	03
Stanton	William		Frm	1877	No	25	01	04	Stetson	Charles			1873	De	28	01	03
Stanwood	Frank		Cpt	1872	De	22	01	04	Stetson	James	P		1874	Ap	19	01	04
Staples			Cor	1876	Jl	09	01	05	Steuart	Charles	A		1857	Se	05	03	03
Staples	Harrison		Mrs	1872	Se	10	01	03	Steuz			Cgm	1877	De	06	01	06
Starbuck	Alexander			1839	My	29	03	02	Stevens			Mr	1871	Jl	07	04	02
Starbuck	Calvin	W		1870	No	16	01	02	Stevens			Mr	1871	Au	24	01	02
Starbuck	Calvin	W		1870	No	18	01	02	Stevens	Ellen		Mss	1873	Au	07	01	03
Starbuck	David	C	Mr	1852	Se	17	03	05	Stevens	Horatio		Gen	1873	Jn	20	01	03
Starbuck	Olive	S	Mrs	1840	Ap	22	03	02	Stevens	James		Mrs	1879	Au	14	01	03
Starffer	James	H		1871	Jl	07	01	06	Stevens	Justus	P	Mr	1843	My	24	03	05
Stark	Charles			1873	Au	20	01	01	Stevens	Manley			1879	Jn	15	01	02
Stark	Charles			1873	Au	20	01	05	Stevens	Manley		Mrs	1879	Jn	15	01	02
Stark	Wa	C	Qug	1877	No	25	01	04	Stevens	Martin			1870	Oc	19	01	03
Starke	Miles	K	Dr	1874	Ap	09	04	06	Stevens	Mr			1871	Au	29	01	02
Starke	Miles	K	Dr	1874	Ap	10	04	06	Stevens	William	B		1873	De	31	01	03
Starke	Miles	K	Dr	1874	Ap	13	04	05	Stevenson			Mr	1873	Jn	19	01	03
Starks	Calvin			1849	Jn	14	03	04	Stevenson	John	C		1852	Ja	02	03	06
Starretgrant	Fannie	E		1878	Se	05	01	03	Stevenson	Joseph			1879	My	29	01	02
Starring	Fred	A	Gen	1870	Fe	27	02	02	Stevenson	Maria			1874	Mr	22	04	02
Startsman	O	P		1865	Se	16	03	03	Stevenson	Maria		Mrs	1874	Mr	22	01	01
Staunton	Howard			1874	Jn	27	01	04	Stevenson	Maria	J		1836	Jn	28	03	04
St Charles	Alfred			1878	De	24	04	07	Stevenson	Marie			1859	Au	06	03	02
St Clair	Edward		Pvt	1876	Jl	09	01	05	Stevenson	Samuel		Rev	1878	Ap	09	04	02
St Clair	J	C	Dr	1878	Oc	09	01	04	Stevenson	William	W	Rev	1834	Ja	01	03	05
Stearns			Gov	1878	De	29	01	02	Stewart				1874	Mr	12	03	01
Stedge	John			1879	My	30	08	03	Stewart				1877	Se	25	01	05
Steel	Laura	M		1857	Ja	03	03	04	Stewart				1877	De	02	01	07

Last	First	MI	Ttl	Yr	Mo	Day	Pg	Col	Last	First	MI	Ttl	Yr	Mo	Day	Pg	Col
Stewart			Mr	1871	Fe	21	01	01	Sting	Adam		Mrs	1875	My	30	01	04
Stewart	A	T		1876	Ap	11	01	04	Stinson			Mr	1870	No	05	01	01
Stewart	A	T		1876	Ap	12	01	02	Stinson	Jack			1876	Ja	01	01	03
Stewart	A	T		1876	Ap	13	02	02	Stirman	James	H		1879	No	21	08	02
Stewart	A	T		1876	Ap	15	01	02	Stirrelle	Eddie			1879	Se	19	01	01
Stewart	A	T		1878	No	08	01	04	Stix	Charles			1878	Se	20	01	07
Stewart	A	T	Mr	1878	No	10	01	05	St John			Pvt	1876	Jl	09	01	05
Stewart	A	T	Mr	1878	No	10	02	01	St Mais			Mr	1876	De	19	01	04
Stewart	Albert			1878	Se	22	04	03	Stock	James			1871	Jl	27	01	05
Stewart	Alphonso			1878	Mr	06	04	06	Stockton	J	W		1877	Ja	28	01	02
Stewart	Andrew		Hon	1872	Jl	18	01	03	Stockton	James	M	Mr	1875	Fe	26	04	07
Stewart	Anthony			1871	Oc	10	02	03	Stockton	Jesse			1878	Mr	09	01	06
Stewart	Burrell			1872	Fe	17	04	02	Stockton	Richard	C		1837	De	05	03	05
Stewart	Caroline			1878	Se	22	04	03	Stockwell	William			1830	Mr	09	03	03
Stewart	Dennis			1879	Fe	05	04	05	Stokes	John	C		1878	Au	24	01	03
Stewart	Eliza		Mss	1867	Ja	29	03	04	Stokes	Montford		Hon	1842	No	23	03	03
Stewart	Elizabeth		Mrs	1878	Oc	08	01	04	Stokes	Montfort		Gov	1842	De	07	03	03
Stewart	Henri			1879	Au	30	05	01	Stolz			Mrs	1877	Oc	13	01	04
Stewart	Hugh			1873	Oc	11	01	03	Stone			Mr	1877	No	01	02	03
Stewart	Hugh		Mr	1872	Jl	19	02	05	Stone	Alva	C		1872	Ap	12	01	03
Stewart	J			1878	No	15	01	04	Stone	Caroline			1853	Fe	04	03	04
Stewart	J			1878	No	16	01	05	Stone	Cornkliu		Mr	1854	Se	15	03	06
Stewart	J	B		1872	Ap	13	01	02	Stone	Infant			1877	No	01	02	03
Stewart	J	D		1879	Au	27	01	01	Stone	Perry			1878	Oc	13	01	04
Stewart	J	W		1873	Oc	10	01	02	Stone	Thomas			1849	Au	09	03	04
Stewart	James		Mr	1827	No	13	03	04	Stone	William		Mr	1871	Jl	25	01	03
Stewart	James	E	Jud	1875	Ap	08	01	04	Stone	Willie			1867	Oc	08	03	03
Stewart	John			1874	Au	30	01	07	Stoo	To		Cpt	1870	Oc	11	04	02
Stewart	John	M	Dr	1874	No	13	04	07	Storrett	Essex		Mr	1835	Jl	14	03	02
Stewart	Maggie			1878	Au	30	01	04	Storrs	R	S		1874	Ja	08	01	02
Stewart	Margaret	E	Mrs	1879	Oc	03	01	01	Story	B	F		1873	De	12	01	03
Stewart	P	B		1878	Se	22	04	03	Story	Hellen			1878	Se	22	04	03
Stewart	Polly		Mss	1868	Jn	02	03	05	Stott	Dan			1878	Ap	05	02	04
Stewart	Samuel			1873	Ja	17	04	04	Stoughman	John			1878	Mr	30	01	06
Stewart	Sip			1876	De	12	01	01	Stovall	Mollie			1878	Se	22	04	03
Stewart	Thomas			1878	Oc	08	01	03	Stover			Mr	1875	Jn	10	04	03
Stewart	W	D		1876	No	03	01	04	Stover			Mrs	1875	De	07	04	03
Stickey	James			1878	Se	22	04	03	Stow	Thomas	A		1877	No	29	01	06
Stickley	Nellie			1878	Jl	25	01	06	Straine	Mary			1875	Jl	15	04	02
Stidham	George			1858	Oc	02	03	03	Strange	John	P	Maj	1875	My	19	01	05
Stidham	Maxmelia			1840	Oc	14	03	05	Strathers	John			1876	No	01	01	03
Stidham	William		Mr	1876	My	24	04	01	Stratman	John		Mrs	1872	Se	07	01	04
Stiegall	Bob			1875	Ap	02	04	02	Strattman	A			1878	Oc	06	01	03
Stiegall	Bob			1875	Ap	06	04	03	Stratton	James			1872	Mr	02	01	04
Stiegall	Bob			1876	Fe	13	04	04	Straub	Jacob			1872	My	14	01	02
Stienburg	Sam			1878	Ap	20	01	06	Straub	Nicholas		Mrs	1868	Fe	25	02	08
Stienhardt	Ephraim			1873	Au	12	01	02	Strauss	Joshua			1874	My	03	01	07
Stienkup	Margret		Mrs	1878	Se	19	01	04	Streek	Herschel	P		1867	De	03	03	02
Stiers	William			1871	Mr	05	03	01	Strehl	J	A	Mrs	1878	Oc	08	01	03
Stiles	Charles			1871	No	12	01	05	Strehl	Mollie			1878	Se	04	01	03
Stiles	Kate		Mrs	1879	Au	08	05	01	Strehl	Sarah	A		1878	Se	22	04	03
Still	Betsey	A		1869	Se	01	04	01	Strickland				1873	Se	10	04	02
Stillman	Henry			1878	Se	04	01	03	Strickland	S	A	Mr	1871	My	02	01	03
Stillwell	Caroline	M	Mrs	1857	No	14	03	03	Strickland	W	W		1874	No	29	01	05
Stillwell	Harold		Mr	1850	My	17	03	07	Stringer	David		Eye	1877	No	25	01	04
Stillwell	John		Mr	1832	Ja	18	03	05	Stringer	Louisa	F	Mrs	1872	Mr	17	04	05
Stillwell	Joseph		Esq	1822	Se	24	03	01	Stringfellow	William			1873	No	18	05	03
Stillwell	Mary	A		1858	Jn	12	03	03	Strodel	Mathias			1878	Ja	22	04	05
Stillwell	Thomas	N	Col	1874	Ja	15	01	04	Strong				1878	Se	05	01	03
Stillwell	William		Mr	1828	Jl	30	03	01	Strong	Caleb			1820	Ja	22	03	01
Stillzenreit				1874	Mr	22	01	03	Strong	Caleb			1820	Ja	22	03	01
Stillzenreit	Fritz			1874	Mr	24	01	02	Strong	Frank			1874	My	19	04	02
Stilwell	Benjamin			1876	No	17	01	04	Strong	J	E	Cpt	1876	Jl	01	02	03
Stilwell	Benjamin			1876	No	18	01	04	Strong	J	E	Cpt	1876	Jl	08	02	03
Stinette	James			1879	Oc	14	01	01	Strong	Ruth			1874	Oc	24	04	07
Sting	Adam			1875	My	30	01	04	Strong	Theron	R	Jud	1873	My	15	01	01

Last	First	MI	Ttl	Yr	Mo	Day	Pg	Col	Last	First	MI	Ttl	Yr	Mo	Day	Pg	Col
Strothers	George			1878	Oc	09	01	04	Sumner			Sen	1874	Mr	15	01	05
Stroud	Leonard		Mr	1878	Ap	20	01	05	Sumner	Albert			1874	Ap	05	01	03
Stroud	Leonard		Mrs	1878	Ap	20	01	05	Sumner	Charles			1874	Mr	14	01	02
Stroud	Mary	L		1844	Oc	16	03	04	Sumner	Charles			1874	Jn	04	01	06
Stroup	Margaret	I	Mrs	1869	Jn	08	02	04	Sumner	Charles		Mr	1874	Mr	13	02	02
Strout	Fred	H	Col	1878	Au	22	01	06	Sumner	Charles		Sen	1874	Mr	13	01	02
Struve	F	G		1874	Jl	02	01	04	Sumner	Charles		Sen	1874	Mr	13	01	03
Stuart			Col	1822	Mr	12	03	01	Sumner	Charles		Sen	1874	Mr	13	01	04
Stuart			Mr	1871	Fe	25	03	01	Sumner	Charles		Sen	1874	Mr	14	01	01
Stuart			Mr	1872	Jl	19	02	04	Sumner	Charles		Sen	1874	Mr	17	01	03
Stuart			Pvt	1876	Jl	09	01	05	Sumner	Duke			1879	Se	13	08	04
Stuart	Abraham		Col	1836	Se	13	03	04	Sumner	Lenora		Mss	1854	Fe	17	03	06
Stuart	Abram		Mrs	1833	Au	21	03	03	Suple	Henry			1878	Jn	15	01	06
Stuart	Ada		Mrs	1872	Ja	19	01	04	Surratt			Mrs	1871	Oc	14	04	05
Stuart	Asenath		Mss	1824	Fe	17	03	01	Sust	Clara			1875	My	12	01	04
Stuart	Eddie			1875	Ap	10	01	04	Sutherland				1873	No	18	04	03
Stuart	Evelyn			1877	No	13	04	03	Suttlers	D	C		1878	De	01	01	01
Stuart	James	M	Maj	1825	Mr	08	03	01	Sutton			Mr	1871	Oc	04	01	04
Stuart	John		Cpt	1839	Ja	02	03	04	Sutton	Carlton			1872	Ap	28	01	01
Stuart	John	W		1873	Oc	17	02	02	Sutton	James		Mr	1858	Oc	09	03	03
Stuart	Susannah		Mrs	1869	Au	01	02	03	Sutton	John			1831	Oc	12	03	05
Stuart	T	F	Mr	1876	Oc	04	04	06	Sutton	M			1878	Se	22	04	03
Stuart	Virginia	S		1867	Oc	01	03	04	Sutton	Noah			1873	My	29	01	04
Stubblefield	Feilding			1866	Oc	30	02	07	Sutton	Robert	B	Mr	1842	Mr	09	03	02
Stump	Harrison			1872	Ap	19	01	03	Sutton	Rufus			1879	Se	11	01	01
Sturges	J	B		1878	Oc	27	01	04	Sutton	Thos			1878	Se	22	04	03
Sturges	Johnathan			1874	De	01	01	03	Sutton	W	H	Jud	1878	De	22	02	01
Sturgis			Lt	1876	Jl	07	01	03	Sutton	Willie			1878	Se	22	04	03
Sturgis			Lt	1876	Jl	09	01	05	Swain	Mary	A	Mrs	1872	Ja	19	01	04
Sturman			Dr	1879	Se	17	01	01	Swain	R	B		1872	Jn	16	01	03
Sturteuant	Bradley			1872	No	26	01	02	Swain	William		Mr	1851	No	21	03	06
Sturtevant	William	E		1875	My	08	01	04	Swan	Robert			1878	Jn	02	04	03
Sturvevant			Mrs	1878	Se	04	01	03	Swan	Samuel			1872	No	30	01	03
Sullivan			Mrs	1878	Se	05	01	03	Swan	Sarah			1872	No	30	01	03
Sullivan			Pvt	1876	Jl	09	01	05	Swan	Walter			1879	My	27	05	01
Sullivan	Andy			1876	Oc	13	01	03	Swanander	John			1879	Au	13	01	01
Sullivan	C	L	Mr	1854	Jn	23	03	07	Swartz	George	M		1879	Au	22	08	06
Sullivan	Con			1875	Mr	10	01	05	Swatkins	Jesse			1878	Au	13	01	05
Sullivan	Daniel	E		1879	Se	17	01	01	Swavel	Michael			1873	Jl	16	01	02
Sullivan	Dennis			1878	Se	26	04	02	Swayne	J	T	Jud	1873	Oc	15	02	03
Sullivan	Hal			1871	Oc	15	01	02	Sweeney	Alexander	W	Cpt	1834	Se	09	03	05
Sullivan	Henrietta	S		1878	Au	28	01	03	Sweeney	James			1872	Ap	26	01	04
Sullivan	Ida			1859	Jn	18	02	08	Sweeney	James	M	Mr	1836	De	20	03	05
Sullivan	J	J		1878	Se	11	01	05	Sweeney	Jerry			1870	Oc	12	01	02
Sullivan	J	J		1878	Se	22	04	03	Sweeny	J	H		1878	Se	22	04	03
Sullivan	J	W	Cph	1877	No	25	01	04	Sweeny	John			1878	Fe	03	01	06
Sullivan	John	J		1878	Oc	20	01	04	Sweet			Dcm	1874	Ja	03	01	03
Sullivan	Julia	A	Mrs	1869	Oc	23	04	03	Sweet			Mrs	1871	Ja	29	03	01
Sullivan	Lewis			1876	Oc	08	01	02	Sweet	Annie		Mss	1878	Jl	09	01	05
Sullivan	Maggie			1879	Se	09	01	01	Sweet	B	J	Mrs	1878	Au	15	01	06
Sullivan	Mary			1878	Se	04	01	03	Sweifel	Gust			1879	Oc	16	01	01
Sullivan	Mary		Mrs	1873	My	10	02	03	Swetser	Lelia			1873	Oc	10	01	02
Sullivan	Michael			1875	Ap	10	01	03	Swett	Dan			1879	Fe	12	01	02
Sullivan	Nelson		Mr	1837	Ja	03	03	04	Swift	Harvey			1872	De	28	01	04
Sullivan	Thos			1878	Se	22	04	03	Swift	Katharine	T	Mrs	1836	Ja	12	03	04
Sullivan	William	E	Mr	1837	Jn	06	02	06	Swigaert	Henry			1872	Au	01	01	08
Sullman	David			1877	De	01	01	07	Swigert	Henry			1872	Au	01	01	08
Sullman	David	F	Mrs	1877	De	01	01	07	Swing	Thomas			1878	Jn	03	04	06
Summer	Charles			1871	Oc	22	04	02	Swint	Valentine			1877	Se	14	01	07
Summer	Duke			1878	Ja	20	03	02	Swisshelm	S	M	Mr	1840	Jn	03	03	05
Summers	Abbie		Mss	1872	Mr	17	01	05	Switzer			Pvt	1876	Jl	09	01	05
Summers	C	H		1878	Se	22	04	03	Switzer	Henry		Mr	1871	Ap	05	01	03
Summers	James			1879	Jl	09	01	03	Swobold	Joseph			1872	Ap	19	01	03
Summers	M		Mrs	1878	Oc	25	01	04	Swope	Hugh			1875	Mr	16	01	03
Sumner			Mr	1874	Mr	15	01	01	Swope	Lee			1871	Se	09	01	04
Sumner			Sen	1874	Mr	12	01	03	Swotzkey	Mary			1878	Se	05	01	03

Last	First	MI	Ttl	Yr	Mo	Day	Pg	Col	Last	First	MI	Ttl	Yr	Mo	Day	Pg	Col
Sylvester	James			1874	Mr	26	02	02	Taylor	James			1875	Mr	19	01	04
Symmes	John	C	Cpt	1829	Jl	08	03	01	Taylor	James			1879	Mr	22	01	04
Synder	Charlie			1879	Se	30	08	03	Taylor	James		Mr	1836	Ap	12	03	04
Sypher	Alex			1878	Se	12	01	06	Taylor	Jane		Mrs	1838	Jl	04	03	05
Sypho	Albert	S		1876	Mr	02	04	03	Taylor	Jennie			1878	Se	04	01	03
									Taylor	John		Mrs	1879	Mr	13	04	03
									Taylor	John	B		1872	Mr	16	01	04
			T						Taylor	John	L	Mr	1834	Oc	21	03	03
									Taylor	Joseph		Maj	1823	Oc	07	03	02
Tafree	H			1875	Mr	10	01	05	Taylor	Louise		Mss	1878	No	14	01	03
Taglioni			Mr	1874	Ap	22	01	04	Taylor	Madison		Mr	1834	Ap	29	03	05
Tainor	William			1877	De	08	01	07	Taylor	Mary	A		1879	Au	13	01	01
Talbot	S		Prs	1874	Ja	08	01	02	Taylor	Mary	E		1831	Jn	29	03	05
Taliafero	Nicholas			1871	Jl	04	01	01	Taylor	Mary	F		1837	No	28	03	05
Tall	H		Cpt	1873	My	11	01	01	Taylor	Michael			1879	Au	26	01	01
Talley	Minnie			1879	Au	21	01	01	Taylor	Moses			1873	Au	21	01	04
Talmadge	Daniel			1875	Ap	10	01	03	Taylor	Nora			1878	Se	22	04	03
Tammeny	J	M	Mrs	1878	Oc	06	01	03	Taylor	P		Mrs	1877	No	03	04	02
Tanti	Sesa		Mrs	1859	Ja	29	03	01	Taylor	Parke			1878	Oc	08	01	03
Tapman	William		Mr	1840	Jl	15	03	04	Taylor	Pat			1871	De	09	04	03
Tappan	Lewis			1874	Ja	08	01	02	Taylor	Racheal			1878	Oc	04	01	03
Tappan	Lewis	D	Mr	1873	Jn	24	01	04	Taylor	Richard		Gen	1879	Ap	13	01	01
Tappen	C	W		1878	Mr	17	04	04	Taylor	Richard		Gen	1879	Ap	29	07	01
Tapscott	William	H	Mr	1834	Mr	11	03	05	Taylor	Richard	C		1837	No	21	03	05
Tarbox			Pvt	1876	Jl	09	01	05	Taylor	Samuel			1871	Jl	11	01	06
Tarkington			Mr	1876	Fe	20	04	03	Taylor	Samuel			1877	Ja	19	01	03
Tarlton	Lucretia			1878	Se	25	01	06	Taylor	Stratton		Mrs	1872	Ap	19	01	03
Tastit	Jane	T	Maj	1840	Oc	28	03	05	Taylor	Susan		Mss	1875	Mr	13	01	03
Tate	Abner	C		1871	Au	24	01	04	Taylor	Thomas		Cpt	1878	Se	24	01	04
Tate	Ezra	M	Bro	1872	Oc	02	04	06	Taylor	Tom			1872	Mr	26	01	05
Tate	Jesse	M		1878	Oc	01	01	04	Taylor	William		Dr	1872	My	08	01	05
Tate	R		Dr	1878	Se	22	01	04	Taylor	Willie			1879	Jl	25	01	01
Tatum			Mr	1872	Ja	09	01	01	Taylor	Zachary		Prs	1875	De	02	02	02
Taylor				1870	Se	27	02	03	Tea	Charles			1873	Fe	04	01	04
Taylor			Cpt	1876	Jn	07	01	06	Teal	A		Mrs	1839	Fe	27	03	03
Taylor			Mrs	1832	Fe	08	03	05	Teal	Nancy		Mrs	1822	Jl	16	03	01
Taylor			Mrs	1877	Ja	25	01	02	Teal	Peter			1875	Jl	13	03	01
Taylor			Mrs	1877	Oc	24	04	04	Teale			Mr	1871	Ap	30	01	06
Taylor	A	W	Mr	1836	Se	27	03	05	Tedro	J	H		1878	Se	18	04	04
Taylor	Andrew			1878	Ap	03	04	03	Teely	James			1871	Oc	18	01	03
Taylor	Andrew			1878	Jn	07	04	07	Teets	William			1879	Jl	10	01	03
Taylor	Annie		Mrs	1878	Se	07	01	03	Telfair	Mary		Mss	1875	Jn	08	03	01
Taylor	Arthur	K	Mrs	1872	Jn	19	01	06	Temple	Belle			1878	Ja	17	01	07
Taylor	Bayard			1878	De	22	02	03	Temple	Flora			1877	De	23	01	07
Taylor	Bayard			1879	Mr	15	01	05	Temple	Isaac	B	Mr	1866	Au	18	03	04
Taylor	Bayard			1879	Mr	16	01	04	Temple	Lucien		Col	1878	Jl	16	01	04
Taylor	Bayord			1878	De	20	04	04	Temple	Maria	J		1858	Se	18	03	03
Taylor	Bayord			1879	Mr	09	01	03	Temple	Rebecca			1873	Fe	23	04	08
Taylor	Bert			1878	Se	22	01	07	Temple	Willie	W		1870	Oc	05	04	04
Taylor	C			1873	Oc	30	04	02	Templeton	Mellie		Mrs	1879	Se	25	08	02
Taylor	Creed		Mrs	1879	Jl	18	04	02	Templeton	Thomas		Mr	1876	Ap	04	04	03
Taylor	E	T		1878	Oc	02	04	04	Teneyck	John	C	Sen	1879	Au	26	05	01
Taylor	Eulalia		Mrs	1827	Au	07	03	01	Tennant	Christian		Mrs	1840	Oc	28	03	05
Taylor	Frank			1872	De	27	01	03	Tense				1877	De	02	01	07
Taylor	George		Mrs	1878	Se	22	01	05	Termoth	Beral			1878	Se	22	04	03
Taylor	George	E		1879	Au	29	01	01	Terrel	Ed			1878	Oc	01	01	04
Taylor	George	W		1878	Ap	05	04	05	Terrell	E			1879	Oc	16	01	01
Taylor	Henrietta			1879	Jl	25	01	01	Terrence	Hugh			1878	Se	22	04	03
Taylor	Irene			1870	Au	21	04	02	Terrill	James		Mr	1871	Mr	11	04	04
Taylor	Irene	M		1878	Au	04	04	07	Terrill	Johnny			1877	De	27	01	05
Taylor	Irene	M	Mrs	1878	Jl	31	04	01	Terrill	Lillie	N		1871	De	05	04	04
Taylor	J	B		1872	Au	20	01	06	Terrill	Thomas		Mrs	1877	De	27	01	05
Taylor	J	L		1872	Jn	19	01	06	Terrill	Willian	J		1877	De	27	01	05
Taylor	J	S		1873	Se	28	01	05	Terry	Joseph	H		1867	Oc	01	03	04
Taylor	James			1836	Se	06	03	05	Tessier			Pvt	1876	Jl	09	01	05
									Tessier	William			1879	No	04	05	01

Last	First	MI	Ttl	Yr	Mo	Day	Pg	Col	Last	First	MI	Ttl	Yr	Mo	Day	Pg	Col
Thackery	John			1875	Mr	16	01	03	Thomied				1870	No	15	01	01
Thalberg			Mr	1871	Ap	30	01	06	Thomkin	R	W		1878	No	21	01	01
Thatcher	Samuel		Mr	1845	Mr	21	04	05	Thompson			Cpt	1870	Oc	18	01	01
Thatcher	Sarah	E		1846	Ap	20	03	05	Thompson			Mr	1873	Au	31	03	01
Thayer			Mrs	1876	Oc	15	01	02	Thompson			Mrs	1828	Se	23	03	02
Thayer	Alfred			1874	Ja	09	04	02	Thompson			Pm	1878	Se	05	01	03
Thayer	Infant			1876	Oc	15	01	02	Thompson	A	T		1878	Se	22	04	03
Thebaud	Julius	S	Dr	1876	Oc	21	01	03	Thompson	B	F		1879	Jn	12	08	02
Thecia			Sis	1878	Se	22	04	03	Thompson	B	F		1879	Oc	02	08	03
Thecia	Sister			1878	Se	14	01	04	Thompson	B	F		1879	Oc	16	08	02
Theo			Jud	1878	Se	22	04	03	Thompson	B	T		1879	Au	17	08	02
Thetford	William	T		1855	Au	10	03	07	Thompson	Catherine			1879	Jn	22	05	02
Theummler	Thomas	E		1878	Jn	25	04	06	Thompson	David		Mr	1839	Se	18	03	04
Thibault	F	J	Mr	1874	No	07	04	03	Thompson	F	B	Cpt	1877	Ja	27	04	06
Thierkauf	John	B		1879	Au	26	01	01	Thompson	Francis			1876	No	04	01	02
Thierry	Amadee			1874	Ja	08	01	02	Thompson	Frank			1874	Au	09	04	05
Thiers	L	A		1878	Ja	09	03	02	Thompson	G	V		1878	Oc	20	01	03
Thoburn	Stephen	B	Lt	1871	Jl	18	01	05	Thompson	George			1872	Mr	19	01	04
Thomas			Com	1874	Ap	17	01	02	Thompson	Harriet	E	Mrs	1866	No	13	03	03
Thomas			Dr	1874	Ap	26	02	03	Thompson	J			1871	Au	16	01	04
Thomas			Dsh	1878	Oc	13	01	05	Thompson	J	W	Mr	1878	Se	19	04	07
Thomas			Mr	1871	Jl	29	01	04	Thompson	Jerry			1879	Ap	04	04	03
Thomas			Rev	1874	Ap	25	02	02	Thompson	John			1872	Oc	29	01	04
Thomas	A		Rev	1878	Se	05	01	03	Thompson	John		Mr	1836	No	01	03	04
Thomas	A	J	Cpt	1875	Mr	30	01	03	Thompson	John	B	Sen	1874	Ja	11	03	01
Thomas	Albert			1871	Ap	14	03	01	Thompson	John	C		1872	Oc	08	01	05
Thomas	Angenot			1875	My	14	01	04	Thompson	John	L	Mr	1871	Ap	09	01	05
Thomas	Annie			1871	Ja	17	01	01	Thompson	Julius			1871	Mr	21	04	02
Thomas	Belle		Mrs	1878	Mr	13	04	02	Thompson	Lauretta	C	Mrs	1837	Fe	07	03	04
Thomas	Charles		Gen	1878	Fe	05	01	05	Thompson	Lavana			1878	Ap	14	04	06
Thomas	David			1872	Au	06	01	05	Thompson	Lewis			1878	Se	17	01	05
Thomas	Edward			1876	Jn	22	01	04	Thompson	Lewis	C		1872	No	15	01	03
Thomas	Elizabeth			1875	Ap	30	01	04	Thompson	Lizzie	A	Mrs	1868	Se	15	03	06
Thomas	Elizabeth			1875	My	02	01	04	Thompson	Mattle			1878	Se	22	04	03
Thomas	G	H	Gen	1870	Ap	09	03	01	Thompson	Mortimer			1875	Jn	30	02	02
Thomas	G	H	Gen	1870	My	06	03	01	Thompson	R	A		1878	Se	05	01	03
Thomas	George	E	Gen	1879	No	20	01	01	Thompson	Rob			1879	Jl	23	01	02
Thomas	George	H	Gen	1872	Fe	25	01	04	Thompson	Sallie	E	Mrs	1866	Oc	02	03	01
Thomas	H	P		1878	Jl	09	04	02	Thompson	T	L	Pro	1875	Fe	18	04	02
Thomas	Heath			1878	Se	22	04	03	Thompson	Thomas	J		1866	Se	25	03	03
Thomas	Henry			1875	Ja	16	04	03	Thompson	W	A		1878	Oc	02	01	07
Thomas	Henry			1879	Ja	11	01	04	Thompson	William			1877	Se	13	01	06
Thomas	J	C	Dr	1876	De	07	01	06	Thompson	William			1878	Se	22	04	03
Thomas	James	M	Bro	1871	Jl	19	01	05	Thompson	William	M		1836	Oc	25	03	05
Thomas	John			1877	Se	13	01	06	Thompson	William	P	Esq	1836	De	06	03	05
Thomas	John		Ldm	1877	No	25	01	04	Thompson	Willie			1878	Se	22	04	03
Thomas	Joseph	V	Cpt	1877	Ja	20	04	01	Thomson	Harry	W		1867	Se	17	03	03
Thomas	Joseph	V	Cpt	1877	Ja	20	04	06	Thorn	Charles	E		1839	Au	14	03	05
Thomas	Joseph	V	Cpt	1877	Ja	26	04	05	Thorn	George	E		1839	Au	21	03	05
Thomas	Lucy	C		1877	Ja	03	01	04	Thorn	Malinda		Mss	1852	Oc	08	03	06
Thomas	Martha			1872	Jn	04	04	02	Thorn	Maria	E	Mss	1839	Ja	02	03	04
Thomas	Mary		Mrs	1828	Oc	28	03	01	Thorn	William	B	Dr	1850	Oc	18	03	06
Thomas	Mary		Mrs	1837	Mr	28	03	05	Thorn	William	E		1838	Jn	06	03	05
Thomas	Oliver	H	Cpt	1822	De	10	03	01	Thornhill	Joseph		Mr	1825	No	01	03	06
Thomas	Robert		Mr	1877	De	29	03	01	Thornsburg	Mary	J	Mss	1859	Au	20	03	02
Thomas	Samuel	H	Esq	1872	De	01	01	02	Thornton	Isaac			1876	Se	23	01	03
Thomas	Thad			1878	Oc	04	01	03	Thornton	Jim			1871	Se	20	01	04
Thomas	Thomas	E		1872	Oc	18	01	06	Thornton	Maria	P		1845	My	19	03	03
Thomas	W	A	Mrs	1878	Se	07	01	04	Thornton	Richard			1853	Jl	29	03	06
Thomas	Washington			1878	No	07	01	06	Thorp	John			1875	Ap	03	04	03
Thomas	William			1872	Oc	29	01	03	Thorps	Christine			1872	Jn	25	01	05
Thomas	William			1879	Au	24	01	01	Thorton	Alice			1879	Jn	15	08	04
Thomas	William		Mr	1878	Ap	07	01	06	Thrall	C	C	Jud	1878	Se	10	01	03
Thomas	William		Mrs	1878	Ap	07	01	06	Thrasher			Mrs	1873	Fe	27	04	06
Thomas	Wyatt	C	Col	1874	Fe	28	03	01	Thrasher	J	B	Jud	1878	Oc	02	01	04
Thomason	E		Mr	1872	Mr	08	01	01	Thrasher	Samuel	P		1871	Jn	10	01	02

Last	First	MI	Ttl	Yr	Mo	Day	Pg	Col	Last	First	MI	Ttl	Yr	Mo	Day	Pg	Col
Thredgill	John	B	Esq	1851	No	28	03	07	Titumphs	Quit			1879	Ja	12	01	03
Thrower	William			1868	Ja	07	03	01	Titus			Mr	1876	Fe	01	01	06
Thrwater	Helen		Mrs	1838	Jl	04	03	05	Titus			Mrs	1876	Fe	01	01	06
Thuemmler	Emilie			1879	Au	20	08	06	Titus			Mss	1872	Ja	21	01	03
Thuemmler	Thomas	E		1878	Jn	25	04	06	Titus	Tracy			1877	Se	13	01	06
Thurman			Mr	1875	Jl	07	03	01	Tivoli	John			1871	Jl	04	01	04
Thurmel	Adolph			1878	Se	04	01	04	Tneveuth	Robert			1878	Se	22	04	03
Thurmond			Mr	1871	De	28	01	03	Tobin	George			1879	Se	20	01	03
Thurmond	Judith		Mrs	1833	Oc	23	03	05	Tobin	J	P	Cpt	1879	Se	20	01	03
Thurston	Lemuel		Mr	1841	Oc	20	03	06	Tobin	J	P	Mrs	1879	Se	20	01	03
Thweatte	P	B	Mr	1875	Fe	24	04	02	Tobler	Edward			1879	Au	10	01	01
Tibbs	Giles			1879	Oc	15	01	01	Todd			Maj	1878	My	14	04	05
Ticer			Mr	1869	Ja	30	02	04	Todd			Rev	1879	Ap	25	04	05
Ticer	William			1869	Jl	27	02	03	Todd	Burtis	R		1867	Oc	29	05	06
Tickner	Samuel	F	Mrs	1879	No	26	04	04	Todd	David	H	Cpt	1871	Au	01	01	03
Tidwell	Rowland		Hon	1837	Se	12	03	04	Todd	G	R		1873	No	18	05	03
Tidwell	S	A	Mrs	1874	Fe	05	04	05	Todd	James		Cdt	1878	Au	22	04	07
Tiernay	Maggie			1878	Au	28	01	03	Todd	Lillie			1879	Au	14	01	01
Tierney			Mr	1873	Fe	01	01	04	Todd	W	M	Rev	1879	Jn	18	04	02
Tierney	John		Ldm	1877	No	25	01	04	Todd	William		Rev	1879	Ap	25	04	03
Tierney	William		Mr	1874	Ap	03	04	06	Tolin	John			1877	De	05	01	05
Tiffany	Charles	F		1879	Oc	02	05	02	Toll	David			1878	Au	30	01	04
Tiffert	Otis	A	Mrs	1878	Au	13	01	04	Tolleson			Mrs	1872	Jl	23	02	05
Tighe	Catherine			1874	Se	01	01	08	Tolleson	Margaret	B	Mrs	1839	De	25	03	01
Tighe	Frank		Mrs	1878	Mr	02	03	01	Tolleson	Mary	A	Esq	1836	No	15	03	02
Tighe	J	M		1879	Au	15	01	01	Tolover	C	H	Ldm	1877	No	25	01	04
Tighe	Peter			1878	Au	21	01	04	Tomeney	Tom			1878	Oc	01	01	04
Tighe	Samuel			1878	Se	08	01	03	Tomeny	J	M		1878	Oc	09	01	03
Tilcomp	Herman			1879	Se	26	01	01	Tompkins	Daniel	D	Esq	1825	Jl	19	03	02
Tilden			Mr	1872	My	11	01	03	Toncray	Daniel	C	Mr	1829	Se	23	03	01
Tillar			Mr	1875	Mr	14	04	05	Toncray	Daniel	E		1834	Ap	29	03	05
Tillar			Mr	1875	Mr	16	04	04	Toncray	Elizabeth		Mrs	1834	Ja	15	03	04
Tiller			Mr	1875	Mr	21	01	03	Toncray	Isaac	A		1830	Fe	23	03	05
Tiller	T	B	Mr	1852	Oc	22	02	07	Tond	John		Rev	1874	Ja	08	01	02
Tillery	L	B	Mr	1872	Au	02	04	03	Toney	James			1877	De	19	01	07
Tilley	Child			1851	Se	12	03	07	Toney	Patrick			1873	Fe	15	04	01
Tillinghast	Wilbur	R	Rev	1879	Au	21	01	03	Tonison	Chas			1878	Se	22	04	03
Tillman			Mrs	1871	Oc	20	01	04	Tonnickson	Henry	H		1876	De	24	01	04
Tillman			Mss	1871	Oc	20	01	04	Toomey	John	J	Cag	1877	No	25	01	04
Tillman	Asa			1857	Se	26	03	04	Tootbaker	Lucretia			1878	Fe	22	04	04
Tillman	W	G		1870	Ja	04	02	03	Topp	Robertson		Col	1876	Jn	14	01	02
Tilton			Mrs	1871	Au	03	01	05	Torbett	Granville	C		1872	Fe	16	01	04
Tilton	Virginia		Mrs	1835	Ja	13	03	05	Torpey	James			1876	No	24	01	06
Timberlake	George		Mr	1871	Ap	09	01	05	Torrence	Hugh			1878	Se	11	01	05
Timberlake	J	R		1879	Ap	11	04	04	Torruga	Henry			1872	Mr	17	01	05
Timms	Elisha		Cpt	1867	My	14	03	04	Tottell	Alexander			1870	Oc	08	01	01
Timms	Frank			1874	My	09	01	01	Totten	B	C	Hon	1869	Oc	02	04	01
Timms	Frank			1874	My	09	04	03	Totten	Benjamin	C	Bro	1869	Au	28	03	01
Timms	Frank			1874	Jn	16	04	05	Totten	James		Gen	1871	Oc	04	01	02
Timms	Frank	H		1875	My	09	04	03	Totten	James		Gen	1871	Oc	29	01	01
Timms	Frank	H		1875	My	11	04	02	Totten	William			1872	Ja	10	01	03
Timms	James		Bro	1869	Oc	23	04	03	Totten	William		Dr	1856	Oc	04	03	04
Tindall	Thomas	H	Mrs	1831	Ja	26	03	01	Tottle	J	W	Cpt	1878	Mr	07	01	06
Tingey	Thomas		Com	1829	Mr	25	03	03	Totton	Silas		Min	1874	Ja	08	01	02
Tingley	Gardener		Mr	1879	Ja	05	01	03	Town	Ernest			1878	Se	22	04	03
Tingley	Gardener		Mrs	1879	Ja	05	01	03	Townley	Sam			1878	Se	22	04	03
Tinnin	Hugh		Col	1838	My	23	03	03	Townsend	James			1871	De	10	04	04
Tipton	John		Gen	1839	My	01	03	04	Townsend	Willie			1878	Se	05	01	03
Tisdale	William			1879	Se	07	01	01	Townsley	George			1879	Oc	04	08	02
Titens	Mille			1877	Oc	25	04	04	Toyler	Anthony			1876	Fe	12	04	04
Titiens	Teresa		Mme	1877	Oc	04	01	03	Tracey	Dave			1874	Ap	05	01	04
Titiens	Therese			1878	Ja	09	03	02	Tracey	Thomas		Rev	1872	Au	13	01	05
Titler	Frances		Mss	1872	Mr	26	01	05	Tracey	Willie			1872	Se	24	01	04
Titsworth	Isaac		Col	1832	Fe	01	03	04	Tracy	George			1871	Jn	28	01	04
Tittsworth	Newton			1879	Au	16	08	04	Tracy	John		Hon	1875	Jl	13	01	02
Tittsworth	Newton	J		1879	Au	23	08	05	Trainer	E	P	Sea	1877	No	25	01	04

Last	First	MI	Ttl	Yr	Mo	Day	Pg	Col	Last	First	MI	Ttl	Yr	Mo	Day	Pg	Col
Trainer	Micheal		Woc	1877	No	25	01	04	Tucker	Sarah		Mrs	1832	Jl	04	03	05
Trammel	Elizabeth		Mrs	1858	De	18	03	04	Tucker	Wood			1836	Se	13	03	04
Trash	G	H	Md	1873	Se	30	03	01	Tuerke	P		Dr	1878	Oc	01	01	04
Travers	John			1878	My	03	04	05	Tuetford	Milo	L		1858	My	22	03	04
Travis	Jane	E	Mrs	1839	Se	11	03	02	Tufel	B		Mss	1878	Se	22	04	03
Traviss	John			1872	Fe	23	01	04	Tufts	Peter		Dpi	1878	Se	28	01	04
Tray	Charity			1872	Oc	15	01	03	Tulley	Micheal			1878	Se	04	01	03
Treadwell	Thomas	J	Col	1879	Au	03	05	02	Tullis	A	M		1879	Ja	12	01	04
Trebring	Samuel		Rev	1872	Oc	11	01	07	Tullis	Jerry			1878	Mr	12	01	06
Tremain	Lyman		Con	1878	De	01	01	01	Tunnah	Robert	B		1873	Au	24	04	06
Trent	Selah	B	Rev	1878	Ja	09	03	02	Tunnard	J	C		1877	Se	23	01	04
Tress	Herman		Blm	1877	No	25	01	04	Tunstall	James	M	Bro	1860	Ap	21	03	01
Trevalyan				1873	Au	09	01	03	Tunstall	William	W	Cpt	1858	Ap	17	03	03
Trezavant	May	H	Mrs	1879	Jn	28	08	06	Tupper	Carnie			1877	De	16	04	01
Trezevant	I	C	Mr	1871	Jn	07	01	04	Turax	Theodore		Mr	1871	Mr	10	04	03
Trezevant	John	P	Maj	1878	Se	26	01	04	Turball	Thomas			1873	My	24	01	03
Trezevant	William	H	Rev	1873	De	16	01	06	Turbeton	Barnhart		Mr	1866	Oc	23	02	07
Trezvant	L	C		1871	Jn	08	04	02	Turnbow	Andrew			1844	No	06	03	03
Trezvant	Louis	C		1871	Jn	11	04	04	Turnbull	R		Rev	1878	Ja	09	03	02
Triest	Leska		Rev	1878	Oc	17	01	03	Turnee	Sallie			1878	Se	22	04	04
Trigg	Frances	B	Mrs	1852	My	07	03	07	Turner			Mr	1826	Au	22	05	01
Trigg	Jackson			1879	No	01	10	03	Turner	Abner			1874	De	18	01	03
Trigg	Julia	A	Mrs	1868	Fe	25	02	08	Turner	Betsey ann			1833	Se	25	03	02
Trim				1876	Oc	15	01	02	Turner	Dick			1877	No	01	04	02
Trimble	David		Col	1833	Jl	24	02	03	Turner	Dolph			1872	Ap	25	04	04
Trimble	Elizabeth		Mrs	1836	My	17	03	06	Turner	Hiram		Jud	1871	Jn	06	01	02
Trimble	Henry	S		1848	Jn	22	03	02	Turner	James		Mr	1874	Oc	04	01	06
Trimble	Mary	E	Mrs	1859	Se	24	03	02	Turner	James	D	Mrs	1857	De	05	03	03
Trimble	Robert		Hon	1828	Se	23	03	02	Turner	Jesse	D	Mr	1873	De	09	04	03
Trimble	Sarah	E		1837	Oc	24	03	04	Turner	John	B	Esq	1834	Au	19	03	03
Trimble	W	W	Mr	1840	Oc	21	03	06	Turner	Pheobe		Mrs	1874	Ap	11	04	03
Trimble	William	A	Sen	1822	Fe	09	03	03	Turner	Thomas	J	Jud	1874	Ap	15	03	01
Trimble	Willis			1871	De	12	01	02	Turner	Wesley			1878	Ap	23	01	06
Trimble	Willis			1871	De	14	04	02	Turner	William			1871	Ja	20	01	01
Trimble	Willis			1871	De	19	04	05	Turner	William			1871	Jn	30	01	04
Triplett	Hedgeman		Maj	1840	De	23	03	04	Turtelot	A	C	Dr	1838	Ja	17	03	05
Triplett	William	H		1877	Ja	11	04	06	Tustin	Isaae			1877	Oc	06	01	06
Trippit			Mr	1874	Ja	01	03	01	Tustin	Jonas			1877	Oc	06	01	06
Trist	Nicholas	P		1874	Fe	28	02	02	Tutewiler	Jacob		Dr	1854	Jn	02	03	06
Trotter	Benjamin		Mr	1833	Oc	02	03	04	Tutewiler	Josephine	V	Mss	1853	Se	30	03	07
Trotter	W	D	Maj	1874	Ja	11	04	02	Tuttle			Mr	1874	Au	06	01	05
Trousdale	James	A		1873	Se	30	03	01	Tuttle	H	B		1878	Ap	10	01	07
Trout	Jacob			1878	No	19	01	02	Twebon	John		Dr	1871	Se	19	01	03
Trovick	William		Mr	1878	Oc	10	01	03	Tweed			Pvt	1876	Jl	09	01	05
Trovick	William		Mrs	1878	Oc	10	01	03	Tweed	William			1878	Ap	13	01	04
Truit				1874	Ap	18	01	04	Tweed	William			1878	Ap	18	04	03
Truitt	Charles			1879	De	12	08	04	Tweedy	Lewis	S	Mr	1835	De	08	03	02
Truly	Adriana	A	Mrs	1852	Au	27	03	06	Tweedy	Thomas			1878	Au	30	01	04
Trundle	Christina		Mrs	1873	Au	05	04	05	Twitchell				1876	My	17	02	05
Trundle	Ellen	L		1873	My	27	04	06	Twomey	Bridgett			1879	Jl	30	01	01
Trundle	Sarah	A	Mrs	1870	Ap	06	04	03	Twomey	John			1879	Jl	30	01	01
Tsuwahahnosk	John	G		1874	Fe	28	03	01	Tyer	Lewis		Mr	1832	De	12	03	05
Tucka	Rabbie			1871	Ja	05	01	01	Tyler				1871	Mr	07	01	01
Tucker			Com	1833	Ap	17	02	03	Tyler				1873	No	15	03	01
Tucker			Mr	1872	Ap	17	01	01	Tyler				1873	No	22	04	04
Tucker			Mr	1873	Mr	20	01	01	Tyler	Charles			1878	Au	27	01	06
Tucker	Andrew		Mr	1850	Se	27	03	01	Tyler	Edward		Cpt	1870	Oc	19	01	03
Tucker	Chas			1878	Se	22	04	04	Tyler	Finley	A		1871	Mr	08	01	01
Tucker	Faytie			1875	Jl	17	04	03	Tyler	H	R	Mas	1877	No	25	01	04
Tucker	Faytie			1875	Jl	18	04	04	Tyler	John			1878	Jl	13	01	06
Tucker	Jacob			1875	Jl	07	01	02	Tyree	W	B		1871	Jl	23	01	02
Tucker	James	W	Cpt	1872	Ap	16	01	01	Tyrons				1873	De	31	01	03
Tucker	Jimmy			1869	Mr	05	02	04									
Tucker	Joe			1872	Jl	10	04	02									
Tucker	Joseph	W	Mr	1852	Oc	01	03	05									
Tucker	Sallie		Mrs	1878	No	03	01	03									

Last	First	MI	Ttl	Yr	Mo	Day	Pg	Col
			U					
Uhlric	Lillie		Mss	1871	Au	02	01	04
Ullison	George	T	Eng	1873	Jn	28	01	02
Ullman	Henry	J		1871	Oc	14	01	01
Ullman	Karl			1878	Au	30	01	04
Ulmer	John			1875	Ja	15	04	02
Underhill	Alice			1874	Ap	16	01	03
Underhill	Henry	W		1848	De	14	03	03
Underhill	W	D		1878	Oc	19	01	03
Underwood			Mr	1871	Jn	06	01	04
Underwood			Mr	1871	Au	29	01	03
Underwood	Albert	P		1856	Au	30	03	06
Underwood	J	B		1874	Jn	27	01	05
Underwood	John	C	Jud	1873	De	12	02	02
Underwood	Q	K	Jud	1876	Mr	18	01	01
Underwood	Washington	L	Mr	1851	Au	29	03	07
Unvarzogt	William			1878	Au	25	01	04
Upchruch	Charles	H		1878	Au	29	01	04
Upchurch	C	H		1878	Au	28	01	03
Upfold			Bp	1872	Au	27	01	04
Upfold			Bp	1872	Au	30	01	04
Upper	H		Mrs	1878	Se	22	04	03
Upton	George		Mr	1876	No	25	03	01
Urban	Julius			1872	Jl	24	01	03
Urtera	Egard			1871	Ap	22	01	03
Ury	Ashbury		Lt	1838	My	30	03	03
Utley	S	A		1872	Ap	19	04	06
			V					
Vaccarro	Alonzo			1878	Oc	09	01	03
Vacelef	John	D		1878	Oc	25	01	06
Vaden	Catherine	B	Mrs	1852	De	24	03	06
Vail	G	L	Bro	1873	Mr	12	04	04
Vail	George		Hon	1875	My	26	01	04
Vail	Victoria	W		1873	Oc	07	01	03
Valandro	Carl			1879	Se	13	01	01
Valentine	Jim			1874	De	22	01	03
Valentine	R	M		1879	Fe	18	03	02
Vales	William			1878	No	23	01	02
Vallandigham	C L		Mr	1871	Jn	25	01	05
Vallandigham	Clement	L	Mr	1871	Jn	22	01	01
Vallandighan	C	L	Mrs	1871	Au	15	01	04
Van der heyd		Bar		1874	Jn	14	01	06
Van dyke			Mr	1877	De	22	01	04
Van dyke			Mrs	1877	De	22	01	04
Van hook			Mrs	1871	Mr	02	01	01
Van liew	Frederick		Lt	1840	Mr	04	03	04
Van molt	John	A	Fgs	1877	De	16	01	07
Van ness			Mr	1871	Jl	18	02	02
Van noorhees				1877	No	22	01	07
Van noorhees			Mrs	1877	No	22	01	07
Van zant	James		Mr	1834	Mr	04	03	04
Vanalstine	James	H		1878	No	21	04	05
Vanalstine	James	R		1878	No	21	04	05
Vanbethma	Meritz			1877	De	06	01	06
Vanbrynck	George			1879	Au	21	01	01
Vance	Frank	R	Cap	1874	Au	02	04	05
Vance	John	R	Mr	1838	Jl	04	03	05
Vance	Maggie		Mrs	1878	Jl	12	04	06
Vanderberg	Roger		Cpt	1873	Au	20	01	03
Vanderbilt				1877	Ja	05	01	03
Vanderbilt				1877	Ja	06	01	01
Vanderbilt				1877	Ja	07	01	02
Vanderbilt	Cornelius			1878	Ja	09	03	02
Vandercenter	Christopher		Col	1838	My	30	03	03
Vanderhoof	George			1871	Oc	17	01	04
Vanhook	Jim			1878	Au	30	01	04
Vanhorn			Mr	1874	Mr	15	01	06
Vanhuesen	Jacob			1879	Ja	05	01	02
Vann	Ida		Mss	1873	My	10	02	03
Vann	Jesse		Esq	1828	Oc	21	03	02
Vannese			Mr	1874	Ja	31	04	03
Vanordstrand	Jerome			1879	Se	30	01	01
Vantrostenbe	Father			1878	Se	20	01	04
Varden			Sgt	1876	Jl	09	01	05
Varden	Dolly		Mss	1872	Jn	25	04	05
Varney	Mary	N		1862	No	01	02	03
Varona			Cpt	1872	Jn	22	01	04
Varsier	Etheldre		Mr	1840	No	11	03	02
Varsisur	Francis		Mr	1836	Ja	12	03	04
Vashon	George		Cpt	1836	Ja	19	03	04
Vaughan	James	L		1869	Se	09	02	03
Vaughan	John	W	Esq	1872	Mr	26	01	02
Vaughan	Martha	E		1866	Oc	23	02	07
Vaughan	Mattie		Mrs	1857	Mr	28	03	03
Vaughan	Tod	R		1859	Ja	08	03	02
Vaughan	William	B		1866	Oc	09	03	02
Vaughn	Frank		Cpt	1879	De	19	08	03
Vaughn	J	F		1879	De	14	08	04
Vaughn	J	F	Mr	1879	De	13	08	02
Vaugine	Francis	N		1846	Mr	02	03	03
Vaugint	Francois		Maj	1831	Ap	27	03	05
Veazey	Mary	D	Mrs	1852	Jl	30	03	06
Veight	Fraz		Pro	1878	Oc	20	01	03
Veil	Cerf			1867	Oc	08	03	03
Vellbar	John			1878	Au	30	01	04
Venable			Dr	1878	Se	11	01	05
Venable	Thomas	W		1870	Au	10	03	01
Vennoy			Mss	1875	Ap	25	01	04
Vennuille	Count			1874	Ja	08	01	02
Ventable	Joseph			1878	Se	22	04	03
Ventars	James			1872	De	29	01	05
Verdin	Bill			1878	Mr	10	01	04
Verend	John	A		1874	My	20	01	07
Vermilye	Robert	J	Rev	1875	Jl	07	03	01
Vermilye	William	R		1876	De	24	01	04
Verona				1873	No	23	01	05
Verona	Bernabe			1873	No	08	01	03
Verplanke	Isaac	A		1874	Ap	17	01	03
Verse	Hanry			1876	Jl	09	01	05
Vess	Frank	H		1878	Jn	21	01	06
Vietory	Frank			1879	Au	06	01	02
Villiers	Clementina			1859	Ja	15	03	01
Villinger	Jack		Mrs	1878	Jn	14	04	06
Vincent	Charles			1876	Jl	09	01	05
Vincent	J	B		1878	Oc	27	01	04
Vincent	Rose			1878	Ap	11	01	07
Vincentia	Sister			1878	Se	13	01	04
Vines	Little	H		1850	Ap	19	03	07
Vinet	Jules			1871	My	02	01	03
Vinetntia			Sis	1878	Se	22	04	03
Vinford	Henry			1878	Se	22	04	03
Vinson	Solomon			1878	Se	04	01	03
Vinsten	Wesley			1878	Se	01	01	03
Vintngdor	Mollie	E		1877	De	04	03	04

Last	First	MI	Ttl	Yr	Mo	Day	Pg	Col	Last	First	MI	Ttl	Yr	Mo	Day	Pg	Col
Voah	James			1873	Oc	16	01	01	Walker			Mr	1871	Jl	15	04	04
Volkmar	Frederick			1879	Se	18	01	01	Walker			Mrs	1871	Mr	07	01	02
Volkmer	Edward			1879	Oc	08	01	01	Walker	Alexander	S	Col	1837	Jl	18	03	03
Volmann	Charles			1872	Ap	02	01	04	Walker	Anna			1854	Au	18	03	07
Vondonhoff	F	A		1878	Se	22	04	03	Walker	Charles			1872	My	19	01	05
Von phul	W			1876	Oc	12	01	02	Walker	Charles			1876	No	18	01	04
Vonwangel	Fredrick		Bar	1877	No	03	01	06	Walker	Chas			1879	Oc	25	01	01
Vonwrangel			Fmr	1878	Ja	09	03	02	Walker	David			1820	My	13	03	04
Voorhies	Lizzie		Mss	1872	Jl	03	01	03	Walker	David			1879	No	25	05	01
Voss	Henry	F		1879	Ap	01	01	02	Walker	David		Esq	1834	Ap	22	03	04
Voss	Willie			1879	Oc	22	01	01	Walker	David		Mrs	1833	Jl	10	03	03
Vougine	Lafayette			1879	Oc	28	08	06	Walker	G	W	Mr	1874	Oc	17	01	04
Vowels			Mr	1873	Jl	03	01	03	Walker	George			1878	Se	05	01	03
Vrooman			Fat	1876	My	30	01	02	Walker	Hattie		Mrs	1879	Se	09	01	01
Vrooman			Son	1876	My	30	01	02	Walker	Henry			1879	My	08	01	03
									Walker	J	J	Pro	1872	No	21	01	05
									Walker	J	P	Hon	1872	Mr	31	01	04
		W							Walker	Jacob	W		1839	Ja	02	03	04
									Walker	Jacob	W	Mr	1838	De	19	03	05
									Walker	James			1874	De	25	01	03
Waddell	W	S		1878	Se	20	01	07	Walker	James			1878	Oc	06	01	06
Waddill	James	F	Esq	1852	Ap	23	03	07	Walker	James		Cpt	1852	Fe	13	03	07
Waddill	James	J	Esq	1852	My	07	03	06	Walker	James		Mr	1871	Jn	28	01	03
Waddle			Mr	1872	Mr	12	01	01	Walker	James	H	Mrs	1838	Fe	07	03	05
Wade				1873	No	07	01	03	Walker	James	P	Mr	1838	De	19	03	05
Wade			Mr	1871	Au	24	01	02	Walker	John		Esq	1838	Jl	04	03	05
Wade			Sen	1878	Mr	08	04	04	Walker	Joseph			1873	Ja	14	01	07
Wade	B	F	Hon	1878	Mr	03	01	03	Walker	Lavinia			1877	De	21	04	06
Wade	Thomas		Mr	1876	Ap	15	02	04	Walker	Levi		Hon	1874	Ap	27	01	04
Wade	Thomas		Mrs	1873	My	10	02	03	Walker	Lording			1878	Se	17	01	05
Wadleigh	Issac	H		1877	No	13	04	03	Walker	Lording			1878	Se	17	01	05
Wadley	Minerva		Mrs	1866	Se	25	03	03	Walker	Lulu			1872	Mr	02	04	05
Wadsworth	Clara		Mss	1878	Se	22	01	05	Walker	Martha			1878	Se	04	01	03
Waggoner	Parmelia	W	Mrs	1870	My	29	02	04	Walker	Mary			1831	De	28	03	05
Waggoner	Permelia	W	Mrs	1870	My	12	04	01	Walker	Mary			1850	Oc	11	03	07
Wagner			Mr	1875	Jn	26	01	03	Walker	Quaco			1876	Mr	21	04	06
Wagner			Mrs	1875	My	12	01	04	Walker	Richard	W		1874	Jn	18	01	07
Wagner	Ike			1876	Se	20	03	01	Walker	Robert	D		1859	Ap	02	03	01
Wagner	Mike			1879	Jn	15	01	02	Walker	S	R	Rev	1859	Jl	02	03	02
Wagner	Nicholaus			1871	No	08	01	02	Walker	Sam	P	Col	1870	No	08	01	01
Wagner	Tom			1874	No	18	01	04	Walker	Samuel	W	Mr	1840	Ja	01	03	04
Wagner	William		Mr	1874	Oc	04	04	07	Walker	Sarah	A		1835	Ap	21	03	05
Wagoner				1878	Se	22	04	03	Walker	Sarah	A	Mrs	1876	Ap	15	01	02
Wagoner	David			1878	Jl	06	03	03	Walker	Thomas	B	Mr	1850	Oc	25	03	07
Wagonhurst			Mr	1875	Jn	06	03	01	Walker	William	R	Dr	1872	Jn	30	01	02
Wahler	Henry			1878	Fe	24	01	05	Wall	Ann			1879	Ja	18	04	07
Wahlookee			Mr	1874	Fe	14	02	03	Wall	Joseph	E	Mrs	1878	Fe	19	01	05
Waife	Frank			1877	No	25	01	07	Wall	Lizzie			1879	Ja	18	04	07
Wait	Lambert	R		1851	Oc	31	03	07	Wall	Richard		Dr	1873	No	19	04	05
Waite	Julia		Mss	1878	Se	10	01	03	Wall	William		Mr	1855	Fe	16	03	06
Waite	S	D		1877	Ja	03	01	04	Wallace			Mr	1872	Se	08	01	04
Waite	Seth			1872	Au	23	01	03	Wallace			Mrs	1854	Jn	09	03	06
Wakefield	Cyrus			1874	Ja	08	01	02	Wallace			Mrs	1872	Se	08	01	04
Wakefield	John	A		1869	Jl	01	03	01	Wallace	Annie			1878	Se	05	01	03
Waldridge	Hiram		Mrs	1874	Ja	30	01	04	Wallace	Charles			1874	Jl	19	02	03
Waldrip	William	P	Bro	1869	Oc	09	03	01	Wallace	E		Mrs	1873	My	10	02	03
Waldron	James			1878	Se	05	01	03	Wallace	Elias			1872	Jl	12	01	04
Waldron	Victer		Col	1848	Mr	09	03	04	Wallace	Etta		Mrs	1878	No	05	01	01
Walford	Riley		Mr	1878	Au	08	04	03	Wallace	George			1869	Ja	30	02	04
Walker				1857	Au	22	03	04	Wallace	George			1873	Fe	02	04	04
Walker				1873	No	18	04	03	Wallace	George		Mrs	1878	Mr	22	01	06
Walker				1876	No	01	01	01	Wallace	Infant			1878	Mr	22	01	06
Walker				1876	No	04	01	02	Wallace	J	C		1873	Se	24	01	03
Walker			Jud	1879	Oc	03	08	02	Wallace	John	W	Col	1870	Ap	10	02	03
Walker			Mr	1840	Jn	17	03	01	Wallace	Joseph			1872	No	13	01	07
Walker			Mr	1871	Mr	07	01	02	Wallace	Joseph	F		1870	Mr	22	04	02

Last	First	MI	Ttl	Yr	Mo	Day	Pg	Col	Last	First	MI	Ttl	Yr	Mo	Day	Pg	Col
Wallace	Los			1872	No	27	01	02	Ward	Samuel			1839	De	25	03	01
Wallace	Sid			1874	Mr	14	04	03	Ward	T	F		1878	Se	22	04	03
Wallace	Sid			1874	Mr	15	01	03	Ward	Thomas			1879	Se	13	01	01
Wallace	W	R		1874	Jl	28	04	08	Ward	W	W		1879	Se	13	01	01
Waller	Jenny	H	Mrs	1876	Ja	29	03	01	Ward	William			1879	Jl	26	01	01
Waller	Leonard		Mr	1825	Fe	15	03	02	Ward	William	D	Mr	1840	Se	23	03	06
Wallin	Betty			1878	Se	22	04	03	Ward	William	W		1863	Fe	14	02	02
Wallis	Ann	B		1836	Fe	09	03	06	Warden	Charles			1879	Se	25	01	01
Walls	D			1873	Se	28	01	05	Warden	John	L	Lt	1873	My	06	01	02
Walls	Frank		Frm	1877	No	25	01	04	Warden	John	L	Mrs	1873	My	06	01	02
Walls	Gertrude			1879	Au	16	01	01	Warden	Simon			1878	Se	22	01	04
Walls	Hannah			1878	Se	04	01	03	Wardlaw	D	A		1878	Se	14	01	04
Walpole	M		Mr	1873	My	17	04	03	Wardlaw	D	A		1878	Se	22	04	03
Walsh	Bridget			1878	Se	22	04	03	Ware			Mr	1875	Mr	27	04	04
Walsh	Clare		Sis	1871	Ja	07	04	05	Ware	Bella			1866	Oc	16	03	08
Walsh	John			1878	Se	22	04	03	Ware	Dad			1874	Ap	05	01	04
Walsh	Lizzie			1879	Au	24	01	01	Ware	George	E		1879	Se	17	01	01
Walsh	Martin		Rev	1878	Au	30	01	04	Ware	Isaac			1879	Au	30	01	01
Walsh	Michael		Rev	1870	Se	29	01	02	Ware	John			1871	De	16	01	04
Walsh	Micheal			1877	De	30	01	07	Ware	Milton		Mr	1830	Ja	19	03	05
Walsh	Richard		Cpt	1825	De	06	03	01	Warfield			Mrs	1878	Ja	09	03	02
Walsh	Thos			1878	Se	22	04	03	Warford	A	B	Gen	1873	Au	19	01	03
Walsh	William			1877	No	08	03	02	Waring	Alonzo	M		1840	Se	16	03	04
Walsh	William		Fat	1878	Se	11	01	05	Waring	H	L		1878	Se	22	04	03
Walshe	Lizzie			1878	Au	28	01	03	Waring	H	S		1878	Se	15	01	04
Walt	Frank			1877	No	13	01	06	Waring	Jane	E	Mss	1867	No	26	02	08
Walter			Mrs	1878	Se	04	01	03	Warneke	Caroline			1878	Se	22	04	03
Walter	Sarah			1878	Au	08	04	06	Warner	Angelane		Mrs	1857	Se	19	03	04
Walters	Morris			1870	Au	10	03	01	Warner	Daniel			1878	Ap	21	04	05
Walton	Billy			1879	Jn	14	03	01	Warner	David			1873	De	24	01	03
Walton	C			1878	Au	28	01	03	Warner	David	E		1878	Oc	02	01	04
Walton	George			1877	De	12	02	02	Warner	Howard	E		1878	Ja	17	04	05
Walton	John			1871	Se	02	04	03	Warner	J	S		1872	Ap	12	01	04
Walton	John	L		1852	My	21	03	06	Warner	James		Cpt	1878	Ja	09	03	02
Walton	Taylor			1874	Ap	03	02	04	Warner	Lorena		Mrs	1877	Ja	10	04	04
Waltz				1874	My	03	01	07	Warner	Tom			1878	Au	27	01	04
Waltz	Ludewig			1878	Jl	06	03	01	Warner	Truman			1876	No	21	04	04
Walworth			Mr	1873	Jn	11	02	03	Warner	William	M		1867	My	21	03	03
Walworth			Mr	1873	Jn	13	01	03	Warnick	Alexander		Mr	1878	Jl	14	04	04
Walworth	Chancellor	Mrs		1874	Jl	16	01	07	Warnock	James			1872	Jl	03	01	03
Walworth	Mansfield	T		1874	Ja	08	01	02	Warnock	William			1871	My	07	01	05
Wamsey	George			1879	No	27	01	02	Warren			Pvt	1876	Jl	09	01	05
Wand	James		Esq	1833	Oc	02	03	04	Warren			Pvt	1876	Jl	09	01	05
Wandanua	Signor			1875	My	11	01	02	Warren	E	A	Col	1875	Jl	04	04	02
Want	James			1872	Ap	16	01	01	Warren	Edward	A	Col	1875	Jl	06	02	02
Warburton	E	T	Cae	1877	No	25	01	04	Warren	Kate			1878	Se	28	01	05
Ward	Albert			1878	Au	27	01	04	Warren	Mamie			1870	Jn	30	04	03
Ward	Augustus	M		1872	Oc	16	01	04	Warren	Mason			1879	My	14	02	01
Ward	Augustus	M	Bro	1872	Oc	31	01	07	Warren	N	J	Mrs	1869	Se	14	02	03
Ward	Dan			1873	No	18	04	03	Warren	O	R		1868	Se	08	03	06
Ward	Ed			1870	My	04	03	01	Warren	Palmer			1820	Ap	01	03	03
Ward	Helen	J	Mrs	1879	De	30	01	03	Warwick	Alex		Mr	1878	Jl	16	04	02
Ward	Isaac		Esq	1835	My	05	03	04	Warwick	Kate	F		1871	Au	25	04	02
Ward	J	C		1878	Se	22	04	03	Wash			Pvt	1876	Jl	09	01	05
Ward	James			1872	Ap	24	01	01	Washbourne	Cephas		Rev	1860	Mr	24	02	08
Ward	James			1872	Ap	26	01	02	Washbourne	J	W		1872	Ja	10	02	03
Ward	John		Maj	1852	De	31	03	06	Washbourne	J	W	Mr	1872	Ja	05	01	02
Ward	John	H	Mr	1870	Au	18	04	03	Washbourne	Susan	C	Mrs	1871	Se	10	04	04
Ward	John	H	Mr	1870	Au	24	03	03	Washburn	A	H	Dr	1877	Ja	03	01	04
Ward	Lilly			1878	Se	22	04	03	Washburn	Abbie		Mrs	1879	My	14	02	01
Ward	Maria			1879	Se	18	01	01	Washburn	Emery		Gov	1878	Ja	09	03	02
Ward	Mary		Mrs	1834	Jl	15	03	04	Washington	B	F	Col	1872	Mr	05	02	03
Ward	Mary	E		1858	Oc	09	03	03	Washington	George			1871	My	16	01	02
Ward	Nancy		Mrs	1835	Oc	20	03	05	Washington	George			1873	No	02	04	04
Ward	P	E		1873	No	18	04	03	Washington	George			1874	Oc	28	04	02
Ward	Pryor			1879	Se	24	01	02	Washington	George			1879	Fe	22	01	04

Last	First	MI	Ttl	Yr	Mo	Day	Pg	Col	Last	First	MI	Ttl	Yr	Mo	Day	Pg	Col
Washington	Henry			1874	De	22	01	03	Watterson	Frederick	L		1872	Jn	05	04	05
Washington	Infant			1873	Jn	22	04	02	Watts	Charles		Hon	1851	Ja	31	03	06
Washington	J	D		1879	Ap	01	04	02	Watts	Thomas	E	Mr	1866	No	27	03	02
Washington	Lou		Mrs	1859	Jl	23	03	02	Watts	Williams	M	Sen	1870	No	19	01	02
Washington	Stark		Maj	1839	Ja	16	03	03	Wavery	Henry		Frm	1877	No	25	01	04
Washington	T	J	Mrs	1878	Oc	06	01	03	Way			Mr	1874	Au	21	01	07
Wassell				1878	Au	30	01	04	Waymoth	Charles		Mr	1877	De	07	04	04
Wassell	Sarah	E		1840	Oc	07	03	04	Waynesburg	John	W		1878	Oc	06	01	03
Wassell	Willie			1857	Se	12	03	04	Weatherly			Mr	1871	Jn	24	01	02
Waterman	Guy	C	Mr	1840	Ap	08	03	04	Weatherly	Ephraim			1872	Jl	20	02	05
Waterman	Stephen			1871	No	04	01	06	Weatherly	William			1878	Oc	27	01	04
Waters			Dr	1871	Se	05	01	06	Weathers	Gertrude			1878	Au	23	01	04
Waters	Henry		Frm	1877	No	25	01	04	Weaver	J	B		1878	Oc	02	01	04
Waters	John			1879	Au	06	01	01	Weaver	John			1877	No	24	03	02
Waters	M	T	Col	1879	Au	31	08	06	Weaver	Mary	W	Mrs	1867	My	28	03	04
Waters	M	T	Cpt	1879	Au	31	08	02	Weaver	Omer	C		1870	Jl	14	04	03
Waters	Margaret			1870	Oc	12	01	02	Weaver	Thomas	J	Bro	1875	My	04	04	05
Waters	Robert	S	S	1871	No	15	04	05	Weaver	W	H		1878	No	23	01	01
Watie	Saledin		Cpt	1868	Mr	03	03	05	Webb	Alexander		Mr	1870	No	04	04	04
Watie	Stand		Gen	1871	Se	29	01	03	Webb	Elizabeth		Mrs	1849	Mr	01	03	05
Watkins	Alfred	B		1879	Se	30	01	01	Webb	Elizabeth	M	Mrs	1846	Fe	09	03	05
Watkins	Anderson		Dr	1828	Oc	14	03	02	Webb	Frank			1875	My	21	01	04
Watkins	Anna			1873	Au	21	04	05	Webb	James	R		1874	De	01	01	06
Watkins	Belle			1878	Se	05	01	03	Webb	Joseph			1871	Jl	11	01	03
Watkins	Catharine			1828	Se	23	03	02	Webb	Kendall		Bro	1873	Fe	25	01	06
Watkins	Ed			1878	Se	05	01	03	Webb	Nannie			1878	Se	22	04	04
Watkins	Eliza			1878	Se	04	01	03	Webb	Robert	E		1879	Au	09	09	01
Watkins	G	G		1876	Mr	04	04	04	Webb	Sam	H		1879	Oc	16	04	02
Watkins	George	C	Hon	1872	De	08	02	02	Webb	Sarah	H	Mrs	1853	Jn	03	03	07
Watkins	George	C	Hon	1872	De	10	01	06	Webb	Townsend		Maj	1826	Ap	11	02	03
Watkins	George	C	Hon	1872	De	11	04	04	Webber	Charles		Mr	1868	Mr	03	03	05
Watkins	George	C	Hon	1872	De	12	01	06	Webber	George		Rev	1875	My	12	01	04
Watkins	George	C	Hon	1872	De	12	04	03	Webber	George	F		1877	De	08	01	07
Watkins	George	C	Hon	1872	De	12	04	04	Webber	P	J		1878	Se	18	04	04
Watkins	George	C	Hon	1872	De	15	04	03	Weber	James			1875	Jn	22	01	04
Watkins	George	C	Hon	1872	De	19	02	04	Weber	Theodore	B		1879	My	03	01	02
Watkins	George	C	Hon	1873	Fe	15	04	02	Webster			Gen	1876	Mr	17	01	04
Watkins	George	P		1835	My	19	03	04	Webster	A	E	Mrs	1868	Mr	31	03	04
Watkins	Henry			1876	Ap	21	01	03	Wedrig	C	M		1879	Jl	29	01	01
Watkins	Henry	C		1823	Oc	23	03	01	Weed	J	J	Mr	1872	Ja	09	04	02
Watkins	Isaac			1846	Au	31	03	05	Weeden				1876	Oc	25	01	02
Watkins	Isaac		Mr	1827	De	18	03	05	Weeks	Fleet			1876	Fe	01	01	06
Watkins	J	B		1873	Oc	31	01	03	Weeks	Marion			1872	Au	21	01	04
Watkins	James	D		1857	Oc	24	03	03	Weems	J		Mrs	1873	Ja	16	02	02
Watkins	Mary			1835	Jl	14	03	02	Weems	Nancy		Mss	1833	Au	14	03	03
Watkins	Mary		Mss	1878	Oc	03	04	02	Wegner	Amanda	M		1871	Jn	27	01	04
Watkins	N	W	Gen	1876	Mr	24	01	01	Wehr	Albert			1878	Oc	18	04	06
Watkins	William			1874	Ap	29	01	01	Wehrum	Fritz			1879	Au	05	01	01
Watkins	William			1878	Fe	16	01	06	Wehrum	H	C		1879	Jl	26	01	01
Waton	S			1876	No	15	04	03	Wehrumer	L	H		1879	Jl	29	01	01
Watson	Francis	B		1879	Se	06	01	01	Weidan	Frank			1878	Se	04	01	03
Watson	Frank			1871	Au	31	01	04	Weigart	George		Mr	1834	Jl	29	03	03
Watson	George			1874	Jl	01	01	01	Weiker	Pierre			1877	Oc	21	02	03
Watson	George		Mrs	1877	Ja	03	01	04	Weinbecker	Frank			1878	Oc	31	01	05
Watson	J			1870	My	04	03	01	Weir	John		Mr	1830	Au	11	03	01
Watson	K	P	Dr	1878	Au	30	01	04	Weir	William	B	Lt	1879	No	05	05	02
Watson	Margaret			1872	Fe	23	01	04	Weisiger	J	H		1871	De	08	01	02
Watson	Michael			1879	Au	26	01	01	Weiss	Camillus		Mr	1874	Ja	20	04	02
Watson	N	W	Rev	1878	Se	08	01	04	Weisse	Anna			1879	Au	20	01	01
Watson	Phillip		Mr	1878	Fe	02	04	06	Welborn	Archer	T		1829	De	09	03	01
Watson	Phillip		Mrs	1877	Se	12	01	05	Welborn	Archer	T		1829	De	16	03	01
Watson	Phillip		Mrs	1878	Fe	02	04	06	Welborn	Archer	T		1829	De	23	03	01
Watson	R	L		1878	Se	18	04	04	Welch			Mr	1871	Oc	04	01	04
Watson	Walter			1879	Ap	04	01	05	Welch	David			1874	Ap	25	01	01
Watt	Henry			1879	Ap	08	03	01	Welch	Frank		Con	1878	Se	06	01	06
Watterson	Elizabeth		Mrs	1873	Oc	30	04	05	Welch	Martha		Mrs	1867	Oc	15	02	08

Last	First	MI	Ttl	Yr	Mo	Day	Pg	Col	Last	First	MI	Ttl	Yr	Mo	Day	Pg	Col
Weldon	John		Mr	1835	Ap	21	03	05	Wetzell	J	W		1873	Se	06	01	01
Weldt	Charlotte			1878	Au	25	01	04	Wheat	Thomas	I	Mr	1855	No	02	03	06
Well	A			1878	Oc	03	01	03	Wheatley	Hugh			1878	Oc	31	01	04
Well	Nellie			1878	Se	28	04	07	Wheeler	A	J		1878	Se	08	01	03
Weller	Cyrus	W	Esq	1844	De	30	03	04	Wheeler	Amos		Cpt	1822	Jl	09	03	02
Wellington	Henry	M	Mr	1873	Jn	25	01	05	Wheeler	Ed		Frm	1878	Se	15	01	05
Wells	Donald			1870	No	19	01	02	Wheeler	Lilie			1878	Au	27	01	04
Wells	Donald			1870	No	22	02	03	Wheeler	Nancy		Mrs	1852	Mr	05	03	06
Wells	Edward		Mrs	1871	Jn	10	01	02	Wheelock	A	D	Dr	1873	Jn	19	01	03
Wells	Eligah		Cpt	1877	Oc	14	01	05	Wheelock	F	B	Lt	1836	Au	02	03	05
Wells	George			1873	Mr	22	01	01	Whelan	John			1879	Jl	26	01	01
Wells	George			1874	Ap	03	02	03	Wheldon				1876	Se	20	01	02
Wells	Gideon			1878	Fe	13	01	06	Wheller	Sophronia			1871	My	23	01	01
Wells	Gideon			1878	Fe	15	01	08	Wheyland	Walter	R		1872	Ja	11	01	03
Wells	Gideon		Hon	1878	Fe	12	01	05	Whipple	Charlotte			1858	Mr	06	03	04
Wells	James			1872	Fe	08	01	03	Whitaker	William	B	Bro	1870	Jl	15	03	01
Wells	James			1878	Se	24	01	05	Whitby			Mr	1870	No	26	04	04
Wells	Jimmy			1872	Fe	14	01	02	White				1878	Se	22	04	03
Wells	John			1878	Se	22	04	03	White			Mrs	1875	My	02	01	04
Wells	John	B	Dr	1853	Au	26	03	06	White	A			1873	Oc	28	01	04
Wells	L	A		1878	Ja	08	02	02	White	A	L		1878	Oc	02	04	04
Wells	M	C	Cpt	1875	Ap	13	04	02	White	Alexander			1872	Mr	20	01	04
Wells	Madera		Mrs	1878	Jn	14	04	01	White	Allen	A	Mr	1837	Fe	28	03	05
Wells	Martin		Rev	1835	Mr	24	03	06	White	Alvin			1878	Oc	20	01	04
Wells	Samuel			1871	Oc	18	01	04	White	Ambrose			1874	Ja	08	01	02
Wells	Thomas	H	Cpt	1876	My	11	02	03	White	Ambrose	H		1875	Jl	11	01	03
Wells	W	W	Cpt	1877	No	01	01	06	White	Arthur	T		1879	Au	19	01	01
Wells	William	H	Jud	1871	Oc	31	04	02	White	Benjamin		Col	1873	My	14	01	02
Welsh	Henry			1875	Mr	11	01	03	White	Bertie			1878	Se	05	01	03
Welsh	James		Mr	1838	Oc	17	03	05	White	Charles	E		1870	De	04	04	04
Welsh	William			1878	Fe	14	04	05	White	Charlotte			1879	Oc	03	01	01
Welton			Mr	1871	Se	09	03	01	White	Dan			1875	Ap	29	01	03
Welty	H		Maj	1859	No	12	04	01	White	Daniel			1871	Jl	09	01	05
Wendel	Leonora	B		1876	Jn	27	04	01	White	Daniel			1871	Jl	11	01	06
Wenderman	Lewis			1879	Jl	10	05	01	White	David		Cap	1874	Au	04	01	05
Wendler	John			1878	Se	04	01	03	White	Dudley			1874	Ja	14	01	05
Wentworth	Henry	B		1872	Jn	19	01	03	White	Edward			1878	Jl	11	04	05
Wescher			Mrs	1878	Se	22	04	03	White	Eliza		Mrs	1824	Jn	15	03	01
Wesehe	A			1878	Se	22	04	03	White	Emeline	K	Mrs	1841	Se	22	03	04
Wesley	John			1876	Se	21	01	02	White	Emiline	K	Mrs	1841	Se	01	03	03
Wesley	Silas			1872	Ap	16	04	03	White	Garland			1874	De	06	04	02
Wesley	Silas			1872	Ap	18	04	03	White	George			1879	Au	06	01	01
Wesleyan	Everitt	A		1879	No	09	01	02	White	Henderson		Dr	1835	Se	22	03	05
West			Shr	1878	Oc	09	01	04	White	Henry			1879	Jl	02	05	02
West	Benjamin		Esq	1820	Jl	15	03	04	White	Herbert	C		1876	Oc	21	01	04
West	Daniel	W		1874	My	17	04	02	White	Hugh	L	Hon	1840	Ap	29	03	03
West	Daniel	W		1874	My	20	05	02	White	Isaac	M		1878	De	13	04	04
West	Daniel	W		1874	My	26	01	06	White	Issac			1877	De	28	01	05
West	J	M	Cap	1874	Se	20	02	02	White	James		Mr	1829	Mr	11	03	01
West	James			1873	Au	23	01	03	White	James	D		1873	Oc	17	04	07
West	James		Lt	1834	Oc	14	03	03	White	Jefferson			1872	Au	22	01	03
West	Jennett			1878	Se	01	01	03	White	Jeremiah		Hon	1874	No	06	01	05
West	Jennie			1874	De	18	04	06	White	John			1872	De	27	01	03
West	John	I		1879	My	17	01	03	White	John	H		1858	De	18	03	04
West	Tom			1878	Ja	12	01	06	White	John	T	Mr	1835	Jl	21	03	06
West	William	H		1879	Se	02	01	01	White	Joseph			1875	Ap	18	01	05
Weste			Mrs	1875	My	12	01	04	White	Joseph		Mr	1830	My	18	02	05
Westerfield	Charles			1872	De	13	01	04	White	Julia		Mrs	1879	Oc	22	01	01
Western	Henry			1877	De	05	01	04	White	L	C	Mrs	1872	Se	14	01	02
Westervelt			May	1879	Fe	22	01	05	White	Lewis			1874	Ja	27	03	02
Westfield	A	G		1878	Se	22	04	03	White	Lizzie	E	Mrs	1870	Ja	27	04	02
Westland	Mark		Mr	1825	Fe	03	01	01	White	Louis			1878	Se	22	04	03
Westmoreland	Shade			1874	No	21	01	02	White	Martha		Mrs	1841	Jl	14	03	04
Weston	Silas			1872	No	01	01	03	White	Mary		Mrs	1851	No	28	03	07
Weston	Silas			1872	No	08	02	05	White	Mary	E	Mrs	1870	Mr	15	01	02
Wetmore	W	B	Pro	1876	Mr	17	01	04	White	Mary	S		1878	Se	22	04	03

Last	First	MI	Ttl	Yr	Mo	Day	Pg	Col
White	McKimey	W	Mr	1837	Ja	31	03	05
White	Mike			1878	Ap	18	01	06
White	Mollie		Mss	1868	Mr	10	03	04
White	Rugehe	D		1878	Se	22	04	03
White	Thomas		Cpt	1830	Fe	23	03	05
White	Thomas		Mr	1827	Ap	10	03	01
White	W	S		1879	Se	23	01	01
White	Weston			1878	Se	22	04	03
White	William			1871	Mr	12	03	01
White	William		Lt	1836	Oc	11	03	04
Whitehead	Eliza			1879	Au	30	01	01
Whitehead	P	J	Dr	1878	Se	06	01	05
Whitehead	Pauline			1879	Se	09	01	01
Whitehouse	Harriet	B	Mss	1871	Jn	28	01	04
Whitehouse	Henry	J	Rev	1874	Au	16	01	07
Whitfield	Arthur		Esq	1849	Ja	25	03	04
Whitfield	E	H		1877	Oc	07	SP	02
Whitfield	E	H		1877	Oc	09	SP	01
Whitfield	James		Gov	1875	Jl	01	02	02
Whitfield	Mary		Mrs	1844	Jn	19	03	01
Whitfield	Thos			1878	Se	22	04	03
Whitham	Thomas		Ldm	1877	No	25	01	04
Whiting	George	W	Mr	1832	Au	22	03	01
Whitley			Mss	1875	My	21	01	04
Whitlock			Mr	1871	Ap	12	01	03
Whitlock	Obediah			1875	Oc	16	04	02
Whitney	Asa			1872	Se	26	02	02
Whitney	James	R		1872	Mr	20	01	04
Whittaker	Mary	G		1879	Jl	15	05	03
Whittington	H	A	Hon	1857	De	12	03	02
Whittington	Mary		Mrs	1851	Ap	18	03	06
Whittington	Mary	E		1841	De	15	03	05
Whittington	Thomas		Mr	1825	No	15	03	01
Whyte	James	E	Mr	1875	Jn	09	02	02
Wichol	Sophia	T	Mrs	1872	My	14	04	02
Wickliffe	D	C	Esq	1870	My	12	02	02
Wicks	George			1870	Oc	04	01	02
Wide			Cor	1876	Jl	09	01	05
Widen	Joseph			1873	Se	02	01	03
Widgery	John		May	1873	Au	17	02	02
Widrig	Eva			1879	Jl	29	01	01
Wieners	William			1878	Fe	02	04	06
Wiggin	Charles			1873	Fe	02	01	04
Wiggins				1871	My	21	02	02
Wiggins			Mr	1872	Ap	13	01	02
Wiggins	Richard	M		1877	Se	14	01	07
Wiggs	Mary		Mrs	1875	Mr	07	04	04
Wiggs	Mary	B	Mrs	1875	Mr	02	04	07
Wiggs	William	B	Dr	1876	Jn	07	04	05
Wilamowicz	Ignatius			1871	My	16	01	05
Wilamowicz	Ignatius		Mr	1871	My	16	04	02
Wilberforce	Samuel		Bp	1874	Ja	08	01	02
Wilbey			Mrs	1877	No	07	01	05
Wilbey	Infant			1877	No	07	01	05
Wilbur			Pro	1871	Oc	07	01	02
Wilburn			Mr	1826	Jl	18	03	02
Wilburn	R	L	Mrs	1878	Ap	03	04	04
Wilcox	Cyrus		Mr	1840	Au	19	03	05
Wilcox	Thomas	W	Gen	1870	My	04	03	01
Wilcox	William			1874	Jl	07	01	07
Wild	John	H		1879	Au	06	05	01
Wildberger	Jas			1878	Se	01	01	03
Wildberger	Stella			1878	Se	05	01	03
Wildes			Ram	1878	Ja	09	03	02
Wilds	John			1874	Mr	20	03	01
Wilds	Morgan			1833	Ja	02	03	02

Last	First	MI	Ttl	Yr	Mo	Day	Pg	Col
Wiley	Edward		Mr	1846	De	12	03	01
Wiley	William			1878	Se	04	01	03
Wilford	Patsy			1879	Se	06	01	01
Wilhaf	Leonard		Mr	1867	Ja	01	01	05
Wilhelm	Melissa		Mss	1873	My	10	02	03
Wilhelmina			Sis	1878	Se	22	04	03
Wilhelst	F			1878	Se	22	04	03
Wilkerson	David			1874	Jl	26	01	05
Wilkerson	Louis			1878	Se	12	04	05
Wilkerson	P	M	Mss	1871	Jl	07	01	05
Wilkie	B	O		1879	Au	29	01	01
Wilkie	Minnie			1879	Au	27	01	01
Wilkie	Minnie		Mrs	1879	Au	26	01	02
Wilkins			Dr	1878	Au	22	01	04
Wilkins	J	S		1878	Se	14	01	04
Wilkinson			Dml	1873	No	08	04	04
Wilkinson	Robert			1878	Jl	28	04	02
Wilkinson	Robert		Eng	1878	Jl	27	04	03
Wilkinson	Robert		Eng	1878	Jl	27	04	06
Wilkinson	Thomas		Mr	1878	Jn	18	01	06
Wilkinson	Thomas		Mrs	1878	Jn	18	01	06
Wilkinson	William		Cpt	1845	Ja	06	03	04
Wilkson	Wallace			1879	My	17	01	03
Will	John	F		1879	Oc	02	01	03
Willach	August		Gen	1878	Ja	25	01	06
Willaims				1876	My	05	04	02
Willaims	Fred			1876	De	12	01	01
Willaims	Mary	E	Mrs	1874	Ap	26	04	04
Willers	Daniel			1871	Jl	09	01	06
Willeth			Mrs	1878	Se	22	04	03
Willett			Mrs	1878	Se	22	04	03
Willett	Marinus		Col	1830	Se	29	03	05
Willetts	Fernando	C		1875	Jl	08	01	04
Willey			Cpt	1873	Ja	21	01	05
Willey	Martha	A		1853	Oc	21	03	06
Willey	Mary	J		1852	Oc	01	03	05
William	Benjamin		Mrs	1835	Jl	21	03	06
William	Charles			1873	Au	02	04	02
William	George			1878	Se	22	04	04
Williams				1873	Au	19	01	03
Williams				1876	Jn	25	01	04
Williams				1877	Se	14	01	07
Williams				1877	No	18	01	04
Williams				1878	Se	22	04	03
Williams			Dr	1878	Se	08	01	03
Williams			Gen	1878	De	22	04	05
Williams			Mr	1872	Ja	23	01	03
Williams			Mr	1872	Mr	22	01	02
Williams			Mr	1875	Se	28	01	03
Williams			Mrs	1833	Jl	10	03	03
Williams			Mrs	1879	Se	27	04	04
Williams			Rev	1872	My	25	04	02
Williams	Alexander		Mr	1871	My	23	01	01
Williams	Ambrose		Mr	1838	Au	22	03	04
Williams	Ambrose		Rev	1876	No	04	04	04
Williams	Antonio		Sea	1877	No	25	01	04
Williams	Arthur			1878	Ap	07	01	04
Williams	Barney			1870	Mr	12	02	02
Williams	Barney			1876	Ap	26	01	05
Williams	Biddy			1878	Au	30	01	04
Williams	Bill			1871	Oc	04	01	02
Williams	Bill			1876	Ja	04	01	02
Williams	Bill			1876	Ja	07	01	05
Williams	Billy			1876	Se	20	04	02
Williams	Caleb			1879	Se	23	01	01
Williams	Charles			1874	Oc	21	01	06

Last	First	MI	Ttl	Yr	Mo	Day	Pg	Col	Last	First	MI	Ttl	Yr	Mo	Day	Pg	Col
Williams	Charles			1879	Mr	18	01	06	Williams	W	T		1878	Oc	11	01	03
Williams	Charles		Mrs	1871	My	18	01	03	Williams	Wash			1875	Jn	05	04	02
Williams	Charles	M		1875	Jl	09	04	02	Williams	Washington			1875	Jn	06	04	03
Williams	Clark			1879	Oc	12	01	01	Williams	William		Mr	1831	No	30	03	04
Williams	Cornelia	A		1859	Mr	05	03	01	Williams	William		Mr	1874	Ja	20	02	03
Williams	Dan			1877	De	15	04	02	Williams	William		Mr	1876	Oc	31	04	03
Williams	Daniel	E	Cpt	1858	Ap	03	03	03	Williams	William	L		1860	Mr	10	03	01
Williams	E	D		1872	Oc	31	01	06	Williamson				1877	Se	30	01	05
Williams	Ed			1878	Se	05	01	03	Williamson				1878	Se	22	04	03
Williams	Edwin	M		1858	Se	25	03	04	Williamson	Billy			1879	Se	25	01	01
Williams	Elijah			1871	Jl	20	01	05	Williamson	Buena	V	Mrs	1868	Mr	31	03	04
Williams	Eugene			1879	Se	03	01	01	Williamson	Ed			1878	Se	04	01	03
Williams	Eva			1879	My	31	05	02	Williamson	John			1874	Ja	01	03	01
Williams	Francis	S	Mrs	1870	Oc	18	04	05	Williamson	William			1872	De	31	01	03
Williams	Frank			1870	Oc	04	01	02	Williford	W	L	Esq	1871	Mr	02	03	01
Williams	Fred	S		1872	Jn	18	04	06	Willingham	J	T		1878	Jl	07	04	08
Williams	George			1873	My	06	01	02	Willis				1873	Au	30	04	05
Williams	George			1878	Ja	20	01	06	Willis			Mr	1871	My	21	02	03
Williams	George			1878	No	22	01	02	Willis	Charlie			1870	No	08	01	01
Williams	Gilbert	M		1872	Ap	27	04	05	Willis	Francis			1878	Se	01	01	03
Williams	H	C		1874	De	13	04	03	Willis	Paulina		Mrs	1840	Mr	11	03	05
Williams	Harry			1870	No	23	01	01	Willis	Robert		Mr	1876	Jn	17	04	02
Williams	Hellen		Mss	1851	Se	12	03	07	Willis	Van		Mss	1879	Se	05	01	01
Williams	Henry			1871	Oc	18	01	04	Willis	William		Maj	1878	Se	17	01	04
Williams	Henry			1878	Fe	24	01	05	Wills	Ben		Cpt	1876	Oc	21	04	01
Williams	Isaae			1878	Se	05	01	04	Wills	E	R		1878	Oc	24	01	04
Williams	J	D	Mr	1871	Au	08	01	02	Wills	Nettie			1870	Au	11	04	02
Williams	Joe			1872	Se	12	04	06	Wills	Nettie			1870	Au	24	03	04
Williams	John			1871	De	03	01	01	Wills	Robert			1871	Jn	25	01	05
Williams	John			1879	My	20	08	03	Wills	Talbot			1878	Oc	11	01	04
Williams	John		Mr	1871	Au	17	01	03	Willson	John	E		1836	De	20	03	05
Williams	John		Mrs	1877	Se	23	04	05	Wilopolsky	Marquis			1878	Ja	06	01	05
Williams	John	C		1872	Au	01	04	04	Wilson			Mar	1872	Ap	21	01	05
Williams	John	E		1877	Se	21	04	04	Wilson			Mr	1871	No	03	02	02
Williams	John	G		1872	Ap	06	01	02	Wilson			Mr	1872	Jl	26	02	05
Williams	John	S		1876	No	16	01	04	Wilson			Mrs	1878	Se	22	04	03
Williams	John	W	Sen	1875	Fe	11	04	02	Wilson			Son	1876	No	02	01	02
Williams	Johnathan			1876	Ja	15	01	06	Wilson			Vpr	1875	No	27	01	03
Williams	Johnnie	M		1869	My	18	02	05	Wilson			Vpr	1875	No	30	01	03
Williams	Joseph			1879	De	11	08	02	Wilson			Vpr	1875	De	02	01	03
Williams	Leroy			1844	Ja	31	03	05	Wilson	A		Mrs	1866	No	13	03	03
Williams	Lewis		Hon	1877	Oc	27	04	01	Wilson	A	G	Con	1874	Ja	08	01	02
Williams	Lewis	P	Mr	1859	Mr	26	03	02	Wilson	Aaron			1876	Ap	21	01	03
Williams	Lucy	A	Mrs	1872	Ja	25	01	03	Wilson	Aaron			1876	Ap	22	01	03
Williams	M	J		1872	Au	30	01	05	Wilson	Abraham	L	Bro	1872	Mr	20	01	04
Williams	Martha			1878	Mr	23	04	02	Wilson	Alfred			1840	Au	05	03	05
Williams	Mary	A	Mrs	1879	No	08	05	01	Wilson	Andrew			1871	No	03	01	04
Williams	Mol			1878	Se	04	01	03	Wilson	Brooks			1879	Au	01	01	01
Williams	N	H	Mrs	1878	Se	22	04	03	Wilson	Charles			1874	Mr	26	03	01
Williams	Nancy			1878	Se	01	01	03	Wilson	Charles			1877	Se	28	01	05
Williams	R	N	Dr	1871	De	12	01	02	Wilson	Cyrus	W	Hon	1849	Se	27	03	05
Williams	Rhoda	A	Mrs	1852	De	03	03	05	Wilson	Daniel	E	Mr	1837	Ja	31	03	05
Williams	Robert			1872	Au	21	01	04	Wilson	David			1872	Jn	30	01	02
Williams	Rueben		Rev	1872	My	02	04	04	Wilson	David	C		1871	Oc	29	04	06
Williams	Ruth		Mrs	1852	Oc	29	03	05	Wilson	David	J		1852	Oc	15	03	06
Williams	Sib			1870	Oc	25	04	03	Wilson	Dickson		Mr	1851	Oc	10	03	07
Williams	Thomas			1877	Oc	03	01	06	Wilson	E	D		1874	Jl	11	01	06
Williams	Thomas			1878	Mr	28	01	07	Wilson	Fred			1876	Oc	15	01	02
Williams	Thomas	J		1877	Oc	12	01	04	Wilson	Fred	W	Mr	1871	Jn	06	01	04
Williams	Thomas	J		1877	Oc	13	01	04	Wilson	G	G	Mr	1874	Jn	02	03	01
Williams	Thomas	W		1833	Ap	24	03	05	Wilson	George	W		1872	Ap	17	01	02
Williams	Thos	J	Mr	1878	Jl	25	03	01	Wilson	Goss			1873	Jl	25	01	04
Williams	Tom			1878	My	29	04	04	Wilson	Genie			1875	Jl	15	04	04
Williams	W			1871	Ja	14	04	02	Wilson	Harry			1877	No	04	01	06
Williams	W			1871	My	21	02	02	Wilson	Henry			1879	Oc	22	01	02
Williams	W	L		1876	Jl	08	02	04	Wilson	Henry		Vpr	1875	De	02	02	02

Last	First	MI	Ttl	Yr	Mo	Day	Pg	Col	Last	First	MI	Ttl	Yr	Mo	Day	Pg	Col
Wilson	Isabelle		Mrs	1857	Oc	03	03	05	Wison			Mr	1872	Ap	19	01	03
Wilson	Isaiah			1871	My	23	01	02	Withall	Carrie			1878	Jl	17	04	06
Wilson	J	T	Shr	1879	Ja	25	04	05	Withall	Infant			1876	Oc	06	04	02
Wilson	James		Col	1845	Oc	20	03	03	Witherspoon	Laura	A		1856	No	22	03	02
Wilson	James	H		1838	Ap	11	03	03	Within	Theo			1878	Mr	08	04	02
Wilson	Joel Jr			1867	Au	27	03	02	Witkowsky	Joseph			1873	Oc	19	04	03
Wilson	John	H		1879	Ja	18	04	08	Witson	William		Mr	1820	Oc	14	03	02
Wilson	John	R	Mr	1873	Au	12	03	01	Witt	Stillman		Mr	1875	My	04	01	03
Wilson	Joseph	G	Hon	1873	Jl	03	01	04	Wittenberg	Julia	M		1871	No	15	04	05
Wilson	Joseph	S		1874	Jl	03	01	01	Wittenberg	Walter			1873	Oc	03	04	07
Wilson	Lewis			1874	Fe	01	01	04	Witter	L	J	Mrs	1871	Ja	19	03	01
Wilson	Louis			1873	Jl	29	01	05	Wittle	Dan			1874	Mr	27	01	02
Wilson	Martin	V		1843	Ja	04	03	02	Wiuf	Eliza			1867	Oc	29	05	06
Wilson	Marv			1878	Mr	27	04	04	Woerne	Charles			1879	Au	26	08	06
Wilson	Mary	A	Mrs	1840	Jn	10	03	05	Wolbrecht	Adolph			1879	Oc	09	01	01
Wilson	Mary	J		1845	Ja	20	03	04	Wolch	Isaac		Sen	1875	De	01	01	02
Wilson	N	H		1878	Se	22	04	03	Wolcott	Oliver		Hon	1833	Jl	03	03	03
Wilson	Perry			1849	Jn	14	03	04	Wolez	Lewis			1873	Se	28	01	05
Wilson	Precilla		Mrs	1835	Se	01	03	06	Wolf	Martin		Mr	1833	My	01	03	04
Wilson	Row			1878	Oc	10	01	03	Wolf	Robert	L	Bro	1870	Jn	19	02	04
Wilson	Sophia		Mrs	1866	No	06	03	01	Wolfe	Amanda			1854	My	26	03	06
Wilson	Thomas	H	Esq	1844	Au	21	03	05	Wolfe	Ann		Mrs	1832	Se	26	03	03
Wilson	Thos	P		1878	No	23	01	02	Wolfe	Harry	J		1872	No	24	01	04
Wilson	W	J		1871	Au	03	01	02	Wolff				1873	Se	28	01	05
Wilson	William			1877	Ja	06	01	03	Wolff	Charles			1873	No	18	04	03
Wilson	William			1878	Se	22	04	03	Wollage			Mrs	1871	Mr	10	03	01
Wilson	William			1879	Se	13	01	01	Wolvemon	Baron			1874	Ja	08	01	02
Wilsonjohn	A			1872	Jl	02	01	04	Wolverton	F	M	Bro	1875	Jn	09	04	04
Wims			Mrs	1872	De	14	02	03	Wood			Mr	1873	Mr	11	01	07
Winams	Ross		Eng	1878	Ja	09	03	02	Wood	Ann		Mrs	1879	My	13	08	04
Winaus	Thos			1878	Jn	15	01	06	Wood	Freddie	M		1878	Au	13	01	04
Windegger	Jeanette		Mrs	1877	De	06	04	06	Wood	George		Mrs	1872	Ja	16	01	03
Winder	Edward	S	Esq	1840	Ap	08	03	03	Wood	H	T		1875	De	02	01	03
Windsor	M	H	Mrs	1879	Jl	03	08	02	Wood	Homer	F		1871	My	17	01	03
Windsor	Tazewell			1876	De	05	01	06	Wood	Homer	F	Mr	1871	My	09	01	04
Winedex	A			1878	Se	22	04	03	Wood	Homer	F	Mr	1871	My	09	04	02
Winfield	James		Col	1874	Ap	04	01	06	Wood	Homer	F	Mr	1871	My	10	04	03
Winfield	Minnie			1879	Fe	04	04	06	Wood	J			1874	Mr	06	01	04
Winfield	W	F		1879	Oc	02	08	03	Wood	James	A	Bro	1867	Mr	19	03	05
Winfrey	Henry		Cpt	1850	Mr	01	03	06	Wood	Lillie			1878	Se	04	01	03
Wing	George			1878	Se	10	01	03	Wood	Samuel			1878	Mr	22	01	06
Wing	William			1878	Fe	14	01	07	Wood	Thomas	D	Hon	1850	My	31	03	06
Winn			Mr	1875	My	09	04	02	Wood	W	D		1879	Oc	14	01	01
Winn	G	W		1871	De	16	04	02	Wood	W	T	Mrs	1875	Fe	19	04	04
Winnry			Sgt	1876	Jl	09	01	05	Wood	William			1870	Mr	05	04	02
Winsfield	W	H	Mr	1879	Oc	03	08	03	Wood	William			1872	Fe	18	01	04
Winslow			Adm	1873	Oc	01	01	04	Wood	William			1877	Oc	25	01	06
Winslow	Charles			1874	Mr	05	01	04	Wood	William	C		1875	Jl	17	01	04
Winstead	Frank			1873	Au	23	01	03	Woodall	Ann		Mrs	1868	Ap	07	03	04
Winster	Precilla	S		1876	Mr	02	04	03	Woodard	J			1878	Au	20	03	02
Winston	Charles			1878	Au	28	01	03	Woodard	William	S		1859	Jl	02	03	02
Winston	Lucy			1879	Oc	01	01	01	Woodbury			Mr	1874	My	23	04	06
Wintergill	Ralph		Mrs	1877	Oc	31	01	05	Woodfort	Christian			1873	Se	07	01	03
Wintermute	Peter			1877	Ja	30	01	07	Woodfuff	Henry			1877	De	21	01	06
Winters	Lem			1878	Au	28	01	03	Woodrooth	Chas	G		1879	Jl	08	01	03
Winters	Wesley			1879	Au	23	01	03	Woodruff	Al			1872	Jl	16	01	04
Winzenried	Fred	F		1872	Jl	09	01	06	Woodruff	Amanda	E		1837	Oc	31	03	05
Wirt	William		Esq	1834	Mr	18	03	05	Woodruff	E			1873	My	20	01	04
Wise	Henry			1878	Jl	14	01	05	Woodruff	Elias		Mr	1874	Ap	26	04	08
Wiseley	Julia			1878	Se	22	04	03	Woodruff	Eliza		Mrs	1862	No	22	02	03
Wiseman	Robert			1878	Se	24	01	06	Woodruff	George			1871	Jn	29	01	04
Wiseman	Robert		Cop	1878	Se	24	01	06	Woodruff	George	W		1830	Au	04	03	02
Wishard	R	W		1876	My	21	01	03	Woodruff	Hannah		Mrs	1852	De	17	03	07
Wishard	R	W	Cpt	1875	Jn	05	04	02	Woodruff	John	W		1858	Mr	27	03	02
Wishart			Col	1872	Jl	31	02	04	Woodruff	Lizzie	A		1854	No	03	03	06
Wishart	Absalom		Bro	1872	Jl	31	02	04	Woodruff	Maria	J		1834	Jl	15	03	04

Last	First	MI	Ttl	Yr	Mo	Day	Pg	Col	Last	First	MI	Ttl	Yr	Mo	Day	Pg	Col
Woodruff	Nathaniel	M	Mr	1860	Mr	17	02	08	Worthington	A	L		1872	Fe	06	01	02
Woodruff	William			1862	No	29	02	02	Worthington	James		Dr	1871	Mr	19	03	01
Woodruff	William	E		1842	Oc	05	03	06	Wortield	Thomas	W		1877	De	28	01	05
Woodruff	William	E	Mr	1840	Au	05	03	05	Wray	Benjamin			1872	Jl	02	01	04
Woods			Mrs	1878	Se	22	04	03	Wren				1876	My	12	01	05
Woods	Amanda	C		1845	Oc	13	03	04	Wrenn	Micheal			1871	Se	09	01	04
Woods	Carl			1874	Se	16	01	05	Wrestler			Mr	1871	No	04	01	05
Woods	Chas	J		1871	Ap	01	01	02	Wreu				1877	No	01	01	05
Woods	Edward	R		1849	Jn	07	03	02	Wright			Con	1873	Au	07	01	03
Woods	Frank			1876	Oc	13	01	02	Wright			Mr	1871	Jl	06	01	04
Woods	Joseph			1878	Fe	02	04	06	Wright			Pvt	1876	Jl	09	01	05
Woods	Leonard		Rev	1878	De	27	01	02	Wright	Abigail			1879	Se	03	05	02
Woods	Martha			1879	Au	12	01	01	Wright	Ambrose	R	Gen	1872	De	22	01	04
Woods	Riley			1872	Ap	24	01	01	Wright	Casper			1878	Se	28	01	04
Woods	Riley			1872	Ap	26	01	02	Wright	Clayborn		Esq	1829	De	16	03	02
Woods	Robert			1875	Mr	04	04	03	Wright	Crocker		Mrs	1878	Se	04	01	03
Woods	Samuel			1875	My	30	04	02	Wright	David			1871	Jl	20	01	05
Woods	Stephan			1878	Fe	02	04	06	Wright	George	W	Bro	1873	Ja	03	01	03
Woods	William	S	Att	1836	Se	13	03	04	Wright	Harry			1878	Se	22	04	03
Woodson	Charles			1875	Mr	16	01	05	Wright	Harvey			1843	Au	02	03	05
Woodson	Renester			1879	My	08	08	02	Wright	Isaac			1866	No	06	03	01
Woodson	Renester			1879	My	10	08	02	Wright	Issac			1877	De	30	01	06
Woodson	Renester			1879	My	27	08	02	Wright	J	A	Mr	1872	No	22	01	03
Woodson	W	O	Maj	1878	Jl	06	03	02	Wright	J	J	Dr	1872	No	30	01	03
Woodward			Cj	1875	My	11	01	04	Wright	J	J	Dr	1872	De	01	04	02
Woodward			Cj	1875	Jl	11	01	04	Wright	J	J	Dr	1872	De	03	04	04
Woodward	A	F	Jud	1876	De	08	04	03	Wright	J	J	Md	1872	De	01	01	05
Woodward	Alex			1878	Se	04	01	03	Wright	Jacob	F		1873	Jl	10	01	02
Woodward	Augustus	F	Jud	1876	De	10	01	06	Wright	James			1845	Ja	27	03	05
Woodward	Elvira			1871	Oc	05	01	07	Wright	John	C		1873	Au	05	01	04
Woodward	J	D		1878	Se	22	04	03	Wright	John	W	Cpt	1869	Se	05	02	02
Woodward	J	S	Dr	1878	Se	14	01	04	Wright	John	W	Cpt	1869	Oc	09	04	03
Woodward	Jane		Mrs	1829	Fe	10	03	02	Wright	Lulu			1868	Ja	28	03	05
Woodward	Oliver			1873	De	07	01	04	Wright	Mary			1844	No	06	03	03
Woodward	Sarah	C	Mrs	1870	Ja	08	02	02	Wright	Morris	M		1874	Ap	24	03	01
Woodward	William		Esq	1824	De	07	03	04	Wright	Morris	M		1874	My	03	02	03
Woodworth			Mrs	1878	Se	01	01	03	Wright	Nat			1873	Oc	10	01	02
Woolep	Will	C		1878	Se	12	01	06	Wright	Nelson			1873	My	11	02	02
Wooley	James			1878	Fe	15	01	05	Wright	Owen			1877	No	03	01	06
Wooley	James		Mrs	1878	Fe	15	01	05	Wright	P			1871	Ja	14	04	02
Woolfolk	Pichegrew		Col	1870	My	04	03	01	Wright	P			1871	My	21	02	02
Woolford	Anna		Mrs	1871	Au	05	04	04	Wright	P	M		1873	Se	28	01	05
Woolford	Israel		Mr	1841	De	29	03	03	Wright	R	A		1872	No	24	01	04
Woolford	John	J		1859	Se	24	03	02	Wright	R	J		1872	Oc	09	01	06
Woolsey	Charles	E		1871	No	06	01	03	Wright	Richard			1859	Fe	05	03	02
Woolsey	Melaneth	T	Com	1838	Jn	06	03	05	Wright	Robert			1878	Au	22	01	04
Wooten	Abe			1879	Mr	06	01	05	Wright	Siias			1878	Mr	03	01	03
Worcester	Samuel		Rev	1821	Se	08	03	02	Wright	Tom			1873	Jn	07	01	01
Word	David			1873	Jn	01	01	04	Wright	Travis	J	Hon	1875	Se	26	02	02
Word	Drusilla	J	Mrs	1839	De	25	03	01	Wright	W	N	Dsh	1872	Oc	09	01	06
Word	George	B		1859	Ap	23	03	01	Wright	William		Mr	1836	No	01	02	02
Work	Mollie			1873	Se	28	01	05	Wright	William	F		1879	Jn	12	08	05
Workman	Adeline			1873	Oc	10	01	02	Wright	Zack			1879	Se	06	01	01
Wormley	James		Mr	1878	Fe	16	01	08	Wurtenberg			Mrs	1873	Se	07	01	04
Wormley	James		Mrs	1878	Fe	16	01	08	Wyatt	Alnarada	M		1851	No	21	03	07
Worsham	Charles			1872	Ap	13	01	02	Wyatt	Charles			1874	Fe	06	01	05
Worsham	J	J		1871	Au	02	01	02	Wyatt	Edward	M	Mr	1850	My	24	03	06
Worsham	Precilla		Mrs	1866	Oc	09	03	02	Wyche	James	E	Jud	1873	Au	31	01	02
Worsham	R	T		1878	Se	17	01	04	Wyckoff	Win	H	Rev	1877	No	04	01	04
Worsham	Robert	C		1873	Mr	22	01	01	Wyekoff	Florence			1878	De	15	01	01
Worshaw	J	J	Col	1873	Mr	23	01	01	Wyeth	Charles	J		1874	Ap	13	01	02
Worthen	Elizabeth	B	Mrs	1848	Ap	20	03	03	Wykoff	H		Dr	1878	Jl	19	01	04
Worthen	George	A	Mr	1879	No	06	08	04	Wylds	David			1868	My	19	02	07
Worthen	John	R	Mr	1844	Ap	03	03	04	Wylie			Mr	1870	Oc	26	04	02
Worthen	Paul			1868	No	17	03	03	Wyndam			Pvt	1876	Jl	09	01	05
Worthen	Thomas	J	Mr	1855	De	14	03	06	Wynn			Mr	1871	De	21	01	02

Last	First	MI	Ttl	Yr	Mo	Day	Pg	Col
Wynn			Mr	1872	Ja	30	01	01
Wynne	V	P		1872	Fe	21	01	03
Wyrick	John	B		1872	Ap	26	01	02
Wywer	P			1872	Oc	18	01	05

Y

Last	First	MI	Ttl	Yr	Mo	Day	Pg	Col
Yager	Jeremiah		Ldm	1877	No	25	01	04
Yandell	Lunsard	P	Dr	1878	Fe	05	04	04
Yarborough			Esq	1875	Jn	23	01	04
Yarborough			Esq	1875	Jn	26	01	04
Yarborough	Brad		Jp	1875	Jn	22	01	04
Yates			Col	1876	Jl	07	01	03
Yates	Amanda			1879	Au	22	01	01
Yates	L	W	Mrs	1874	Ja	06	04	05
Yates	Richard		Gov	1874	Ja	08	01	02
Yeadon	Richard		Hon	1870	My	07	04	01
Yeager	Catherine		Mrs	1873	Au	22	01	03
Yeamans	Peter			1871	Se	29	01	05
Yearby	A	N		1878	Oc	29	01	04
Yearger	Mary			1846	My	11	03	04
Yearion				1871	Ja	05	01	02
Yeates	Richard	H		1852	De	24	03	06
Yeatman	Thomas			1833	Jl	03	03	03
Yeatman	William	T	Mrs	1871	Jl	06	01	04
Yell	Archibald			1874	Jl	22	03	01
Yell	Martha		Mrs	1849	Ap	26	03	04
Yell	Nancy	J	Mrs	1835	Oc	20	03	05
Yeomans	Martha	A	Mrs	1850	My	24	03	06
Yerger	Edwin	M	Hon	1871	Mr	10	04	03
Yerger	William		Jud	1872	Jn	12	02	02
Yerkes	Harry	C		1879	Au	29	05	04
Yerzley	Sallie	J		1871	Se	20	04	04
York			Mrs	1873	Jn	17	01	03
York	Thompas			1879	Se	21	01	01
York	William	H	Dr	1873	My	18	02	03
Yost				1876	Se	21	01	04
Yost	Edward			1875	Mr	07	01	04
Young			Mr	1871	Jn	06	04	04
Young			Mr	1871	Au	18	01	05
Young	Annie			1878	Se	22	04	03
Young	Brigham			1877	Oc	13	02	02
Young	Brigham			1878	Ja	09	03	02
Young	Christian			1872	Mr	28	04	05
Young	Henry			1873	No	29	01	02
Young	Irene			1858	De	18	03	04
Young	Jacob		Mr	1878	Jn	04	04	06
Young	Jacob		Mr	1878	Jl	04	04	06
Young	Jacob		Mrs	1878	Jn	04	04	06
Young	Jacob		Mrs	1878	Jl	04	04	06
Young	Jake			1873	Fe	09	04	02
Young	James		Ltg	1878	Fe	13	01	06
Young	Jno			1878	Oc	16	01	03
Young	Joseph			1872	Au	27	04	06
Young	Lewis			1830	Mr	09	03	03
Young	Lewis	M	Mr	1832	Au	15	03	05
Young	Luejen		Ens	1877	No	25	01	04
Young	Mabel			1875	Jn	10	01	03
Young	Mabel			1876	My	27	01	05
Young	Mary		Mrs	1832	Au	08	03	05
Young	R	H	Col	1859	My	07	03	01
Young	Robert		Mr	1830	Fe	09	03	05
Young	Thomas		Dr	1878	Oc	09	01	04
Young	Thomas	I	Mr	1834	My	13	03	05
Young	William			1871	Jn	23	01	03
Young	William			1878	Oc	20	01	04
Young	William	R	Mr	1840	Oc	14	03	05
Younger	Jim			1874	Mr	27	01	03
Younger	John			1874	Mr	24	03	02
Younger	Thomas			1873	De	18	01	03
Younghouse	John			1871	Jl	28	01	04
Yount	A	R		1876	Oc	18	01	02
Younts	Mary			1873	Oc	26	04	04
Yucton			Gen	1872	Jn	22	01	04

Z

Last	First	MI	Ttl	Yr	Mo	Day	Pg	Col
Zacher	Frank	A		1876	No	01	01	04
Zahn	Maggie			1879	Jl	26	01	01
Zeak	F	A		1878	Se	08	01	05
Zeigler	F			1873	No	18	04	03
Zeisler	Infant			1878	Jl	11	04	01
Zeke	John			1872	Fe	28	01	03
Zeph	Mary			1878	Au	30	01	04
Zetland	Earl			1874	Ja	08	01	02
Ziegenhein	Jacob		Mr	1871	Jl	26	01	02
Zimmeramn	Andrew			1871	Au	29	01	03
Zimmerman				1878	Ja	26	01	04
Zimmerman	Elbert	R		1868	No	03	03	06
Zimmerman	Emma			1879	Se	09	01	01
Zinckeisen	Annie			1875	My	12	01	04
Zirchblaur			Mrs	1875	My	12	01	04
Zoeller	Christian	E	Mr	1822	Oc	08	03	04